GEGE AKUTAMI

What're you lookin' at?

GEGE AKUTAMI published a few short
works before starting *Jujutsu Kaisen*, which began
serialization in *Weekly Shonen Jump* in 2018.

JUJUTSU KAISEN

VOLUME 13
SHONEN JUMP MANGA EDITION

BY GEGE AKUTAMI

TRANSLATION **Stefan Koza**
TOUCH-UP ART & LETTERING **Snir Aharon**
DESIGN **Joy Zhang**
EDITOR **John Bae**
CONSULTING EDITOR **Erika Onabe**

JUJUTSU KAISEN © 2018 by Gege Akutami
All rights reserved.
First published in Japan in 2018 by SHUEISHA Inc., Tokyo.
English translation rights arranged by SHUEISHA Inc.

The stories, characters, and incidents mentioned
in this publication are entirely fictional.

Printed in the U.S.A.

Published by VIZ Media, LLC
P.O. Box 77010
San Francisco, CA 94107

10 9 8 7 6 5 4 3 2 1
First printing, December 2021

VIZ MEDIA
viz.com

JUJUTSU KAISEN

13

THE SHIBUYA
INCIDENT
—THUNDERCLAP—

STORY AND ART BY GEGE AKUTAMI

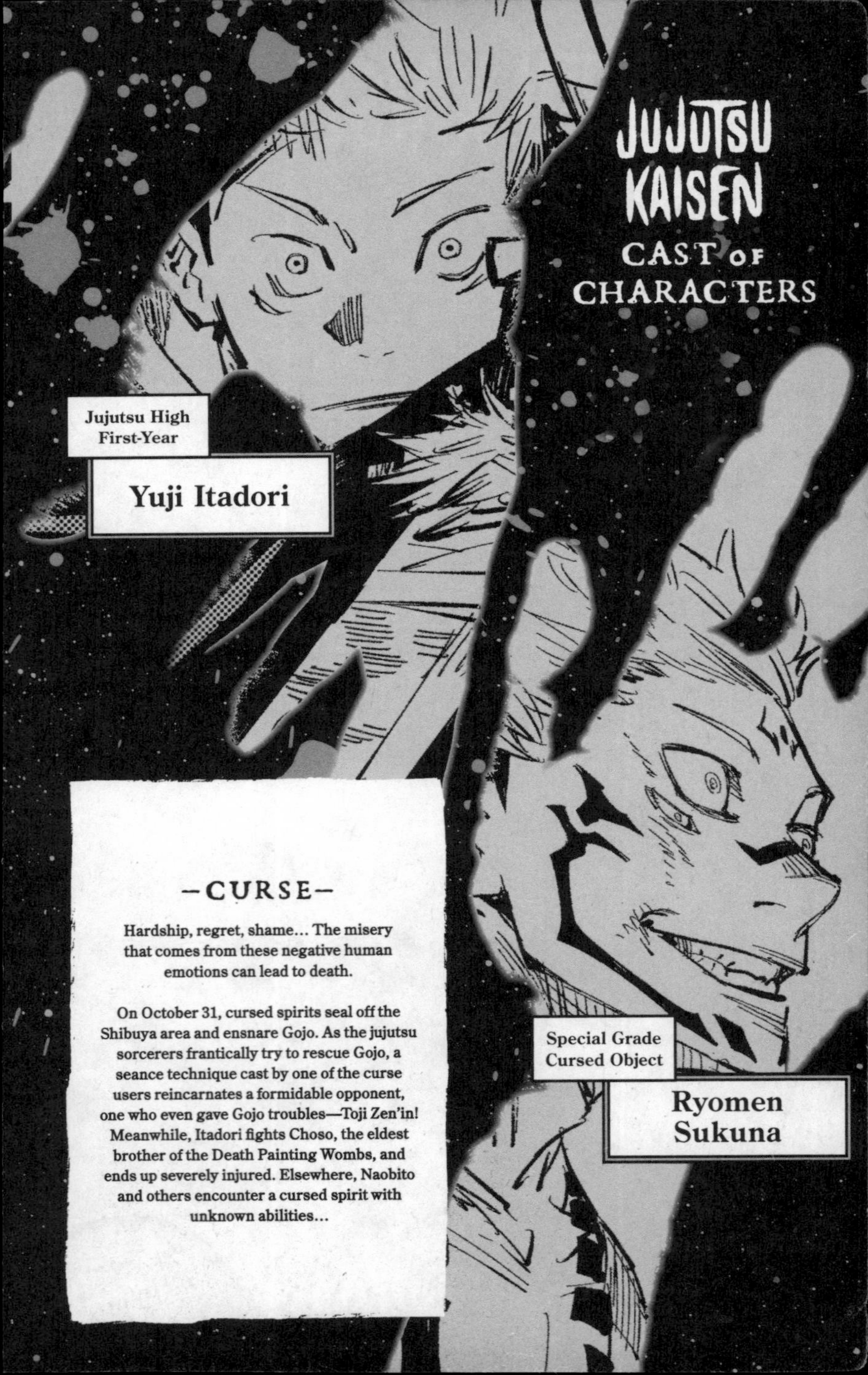
JUJUTSU KAISEN
CAST OF CHARACTERS
Jujutsu High
First-Year
Yuji Itadori
Special Grade
Cursed Object
Ryomen
Sukuna

—CURSE—

Hardship, regret, shame... The misery that comes from these negative human emotions can lead to death.

On October 31, cursed spirits seal off the Shibuya area and ensnare Gojo. As the jujutsu sorcerers frantically try to rescue Gojo, a seance technique cast by one of the curse users reincarnates a formidable opponent, one who even gave Gojo troubles—Toji Zen'in! Meanwhile, Itadori fights Choso, the eldest brother of the Death Painting Wombs, and ends up severely injured. Elsewhere, Naobito and others encounter a cursed spirit with unknown abilities...

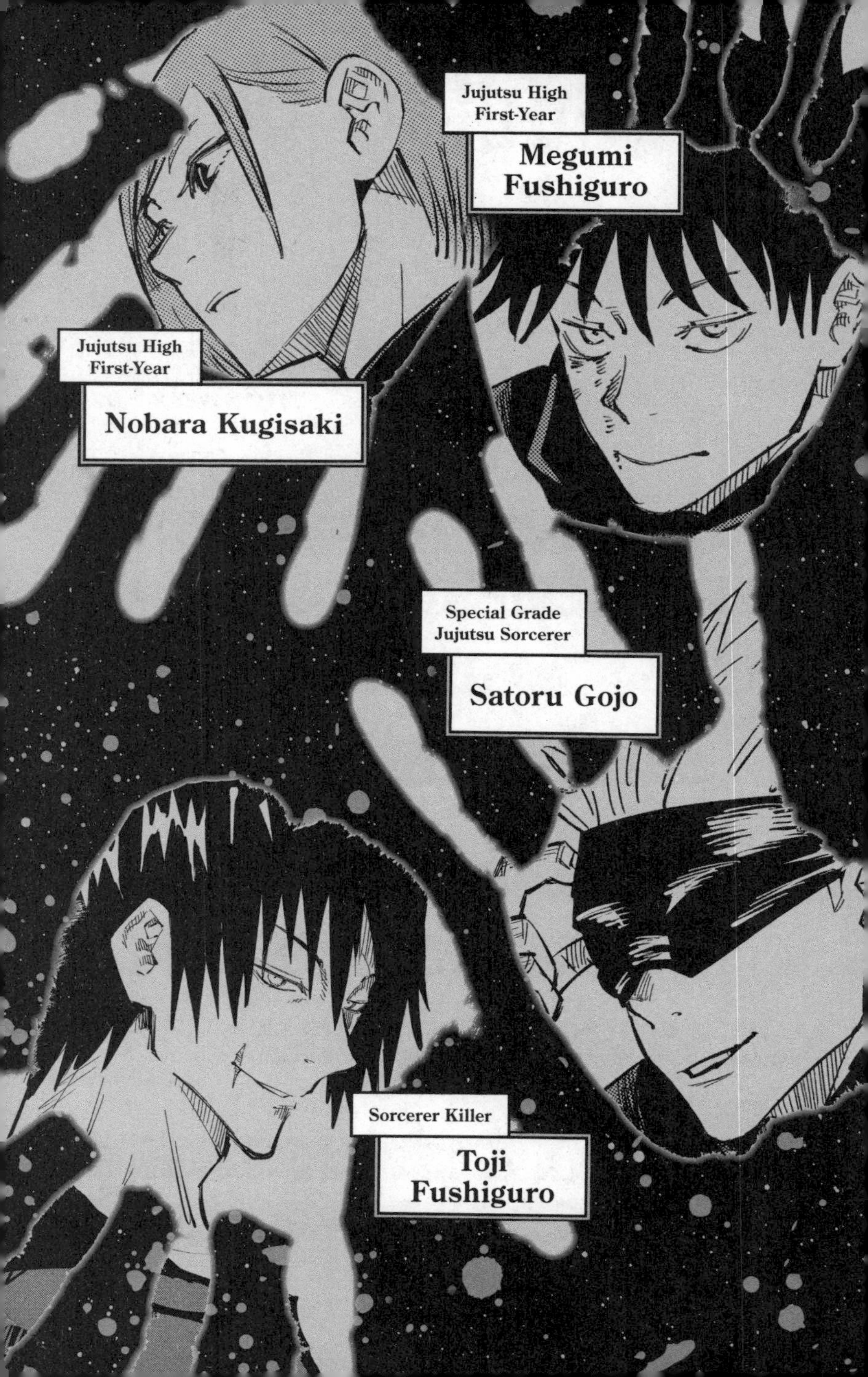
Jujutsu High
First-Year
Megumi
Fushiguro
Jujutsu High
First-Year
Nobara Kugisaki
Special Grade
Jujutsu Sorcerer
Satoru Gojo
Sorcerer Killer
Toji
Fushiguro

JUJUTSU KAISEN

13

THE SHIBUYA INCIDENT
—THUNDERCLAP—

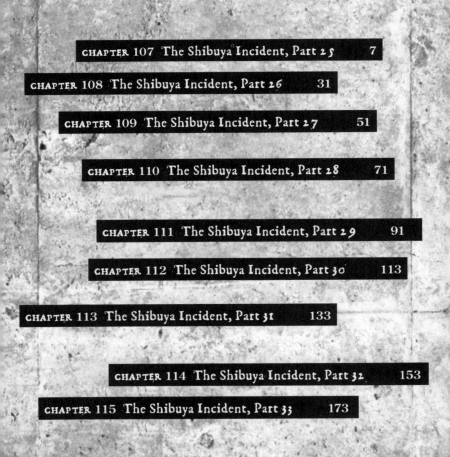

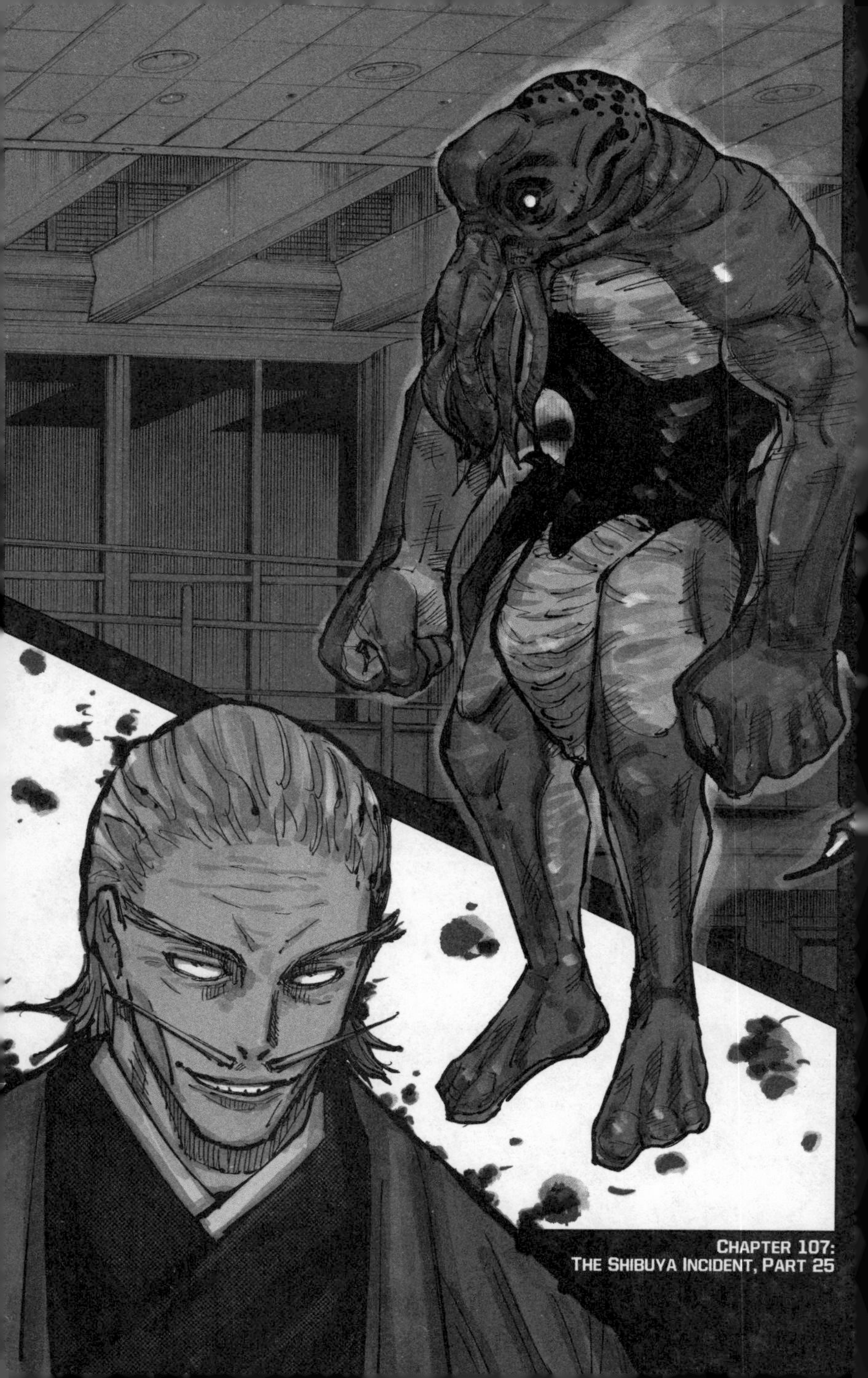
CHAPTER 107:
THE SHIBUYA INCIDENT, PART 25

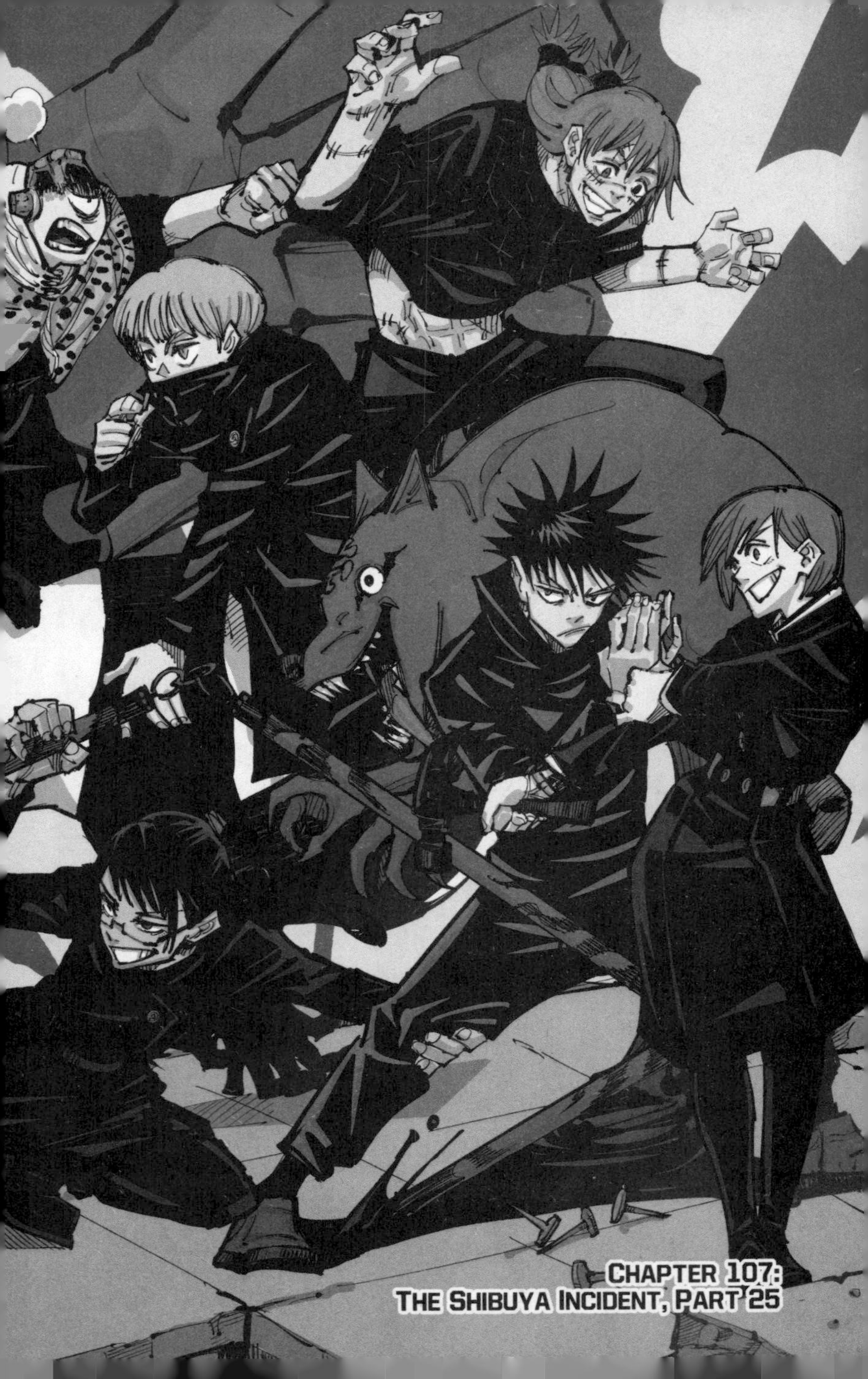

CHAPTER 107:
THE SHIBUYA INCIDENT, PART 25

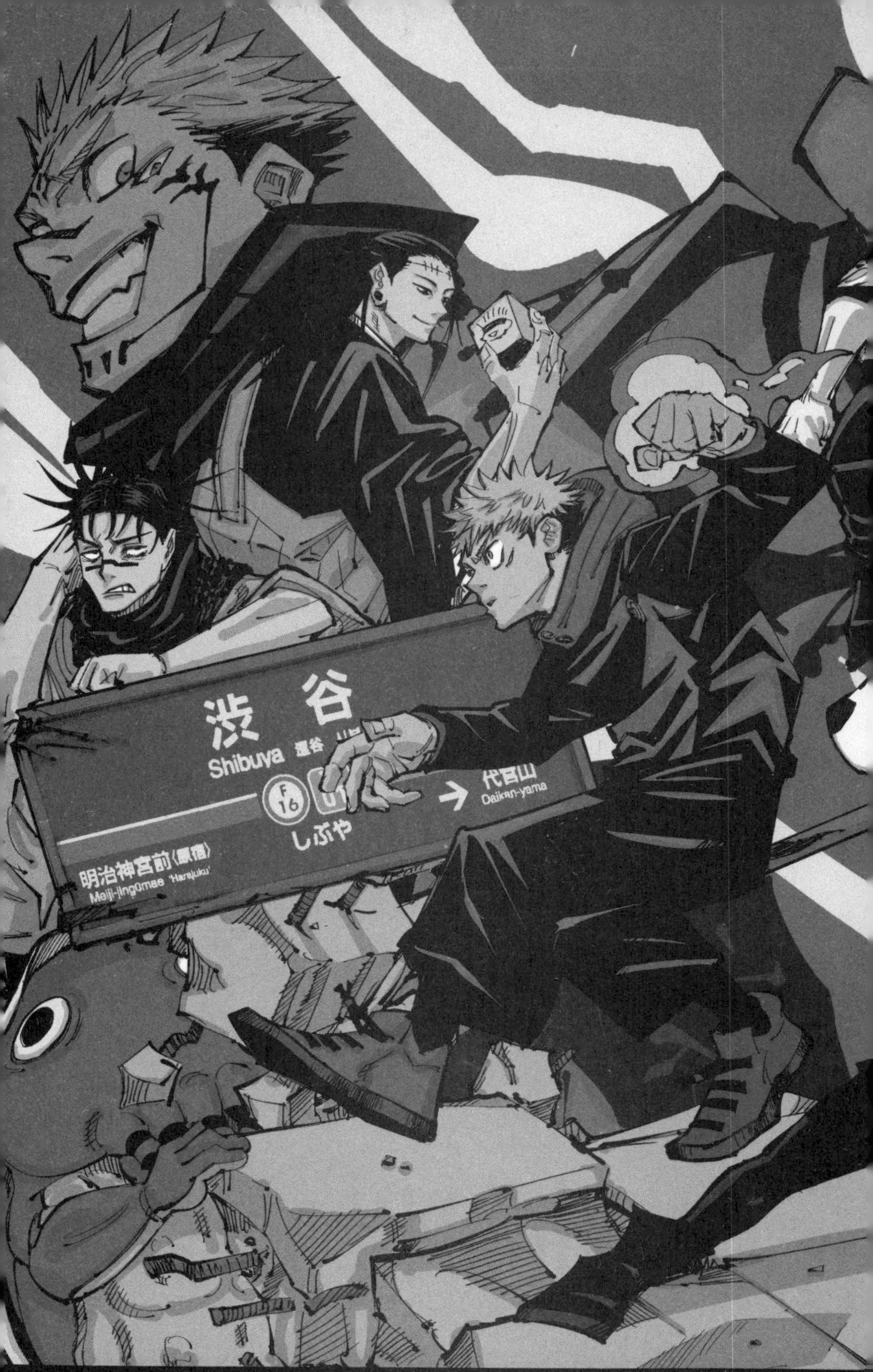
渋谷
Shibuya
F 16
しぶや
代官山
Daikan-yama
明治神宮前
Meiji-jing0mae

JUJUTSU KAISEN

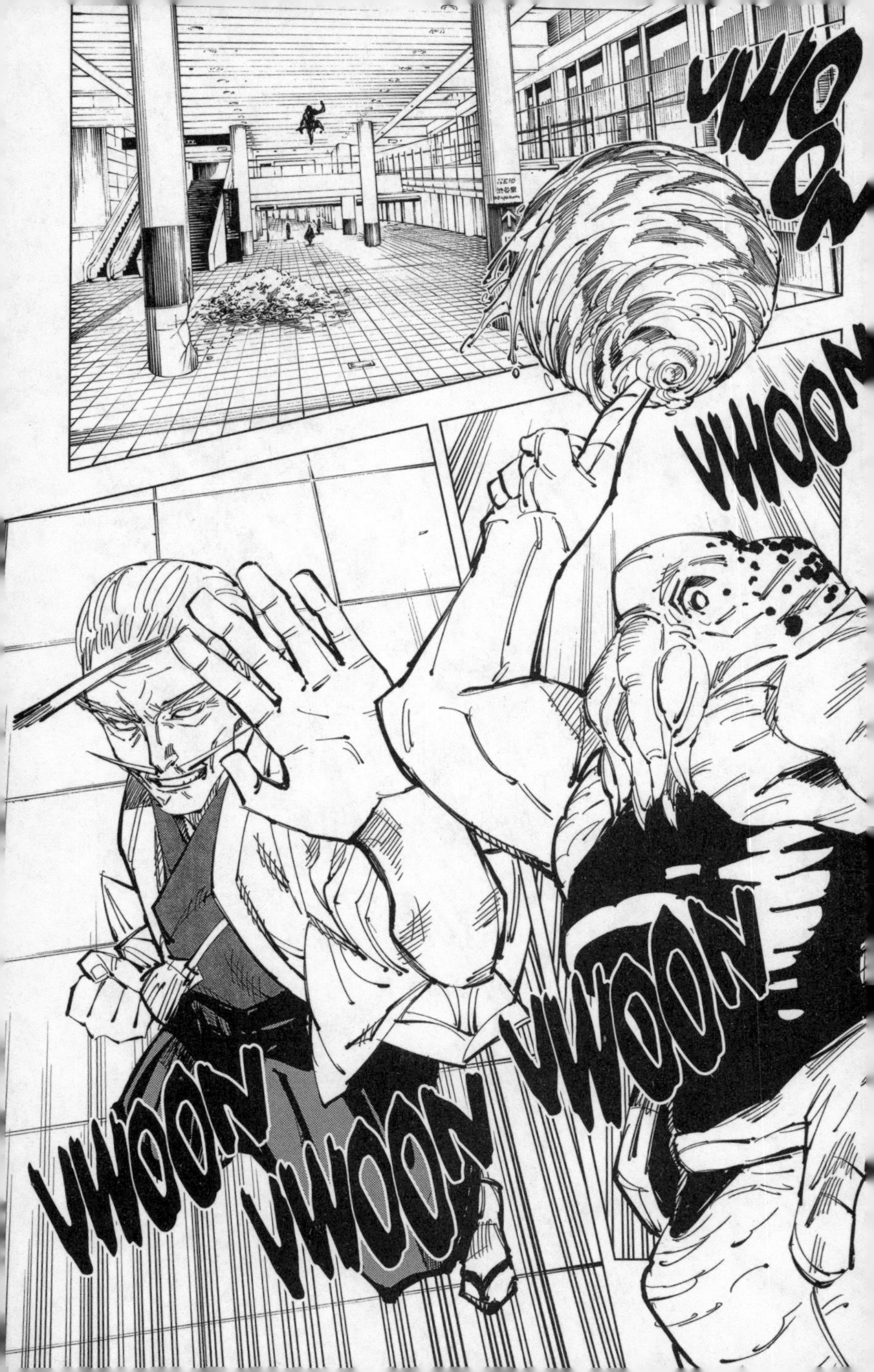
VWOON
VWOON
VWOON
VWOON
VWOON
VWOON

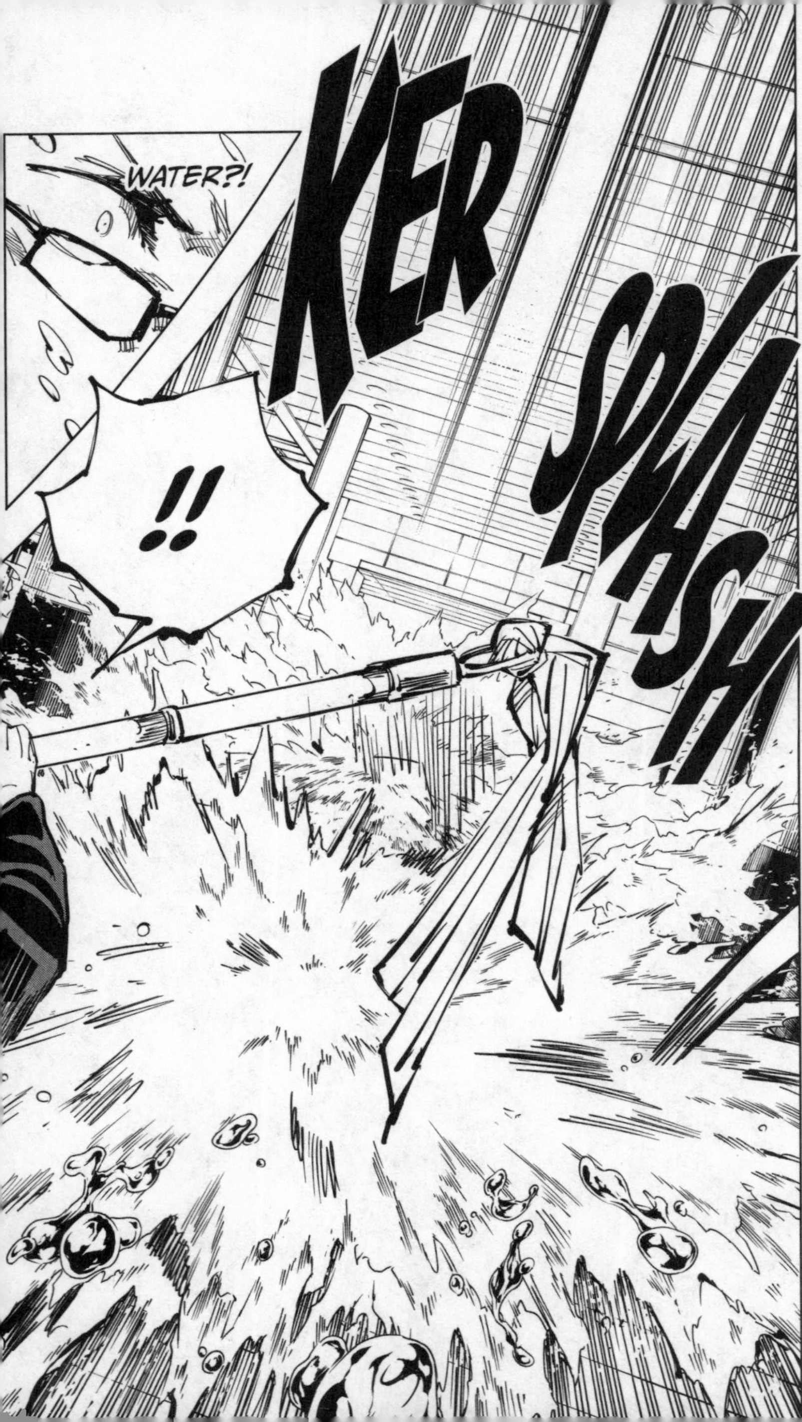
KER
SPLASH
WATER?!
!!

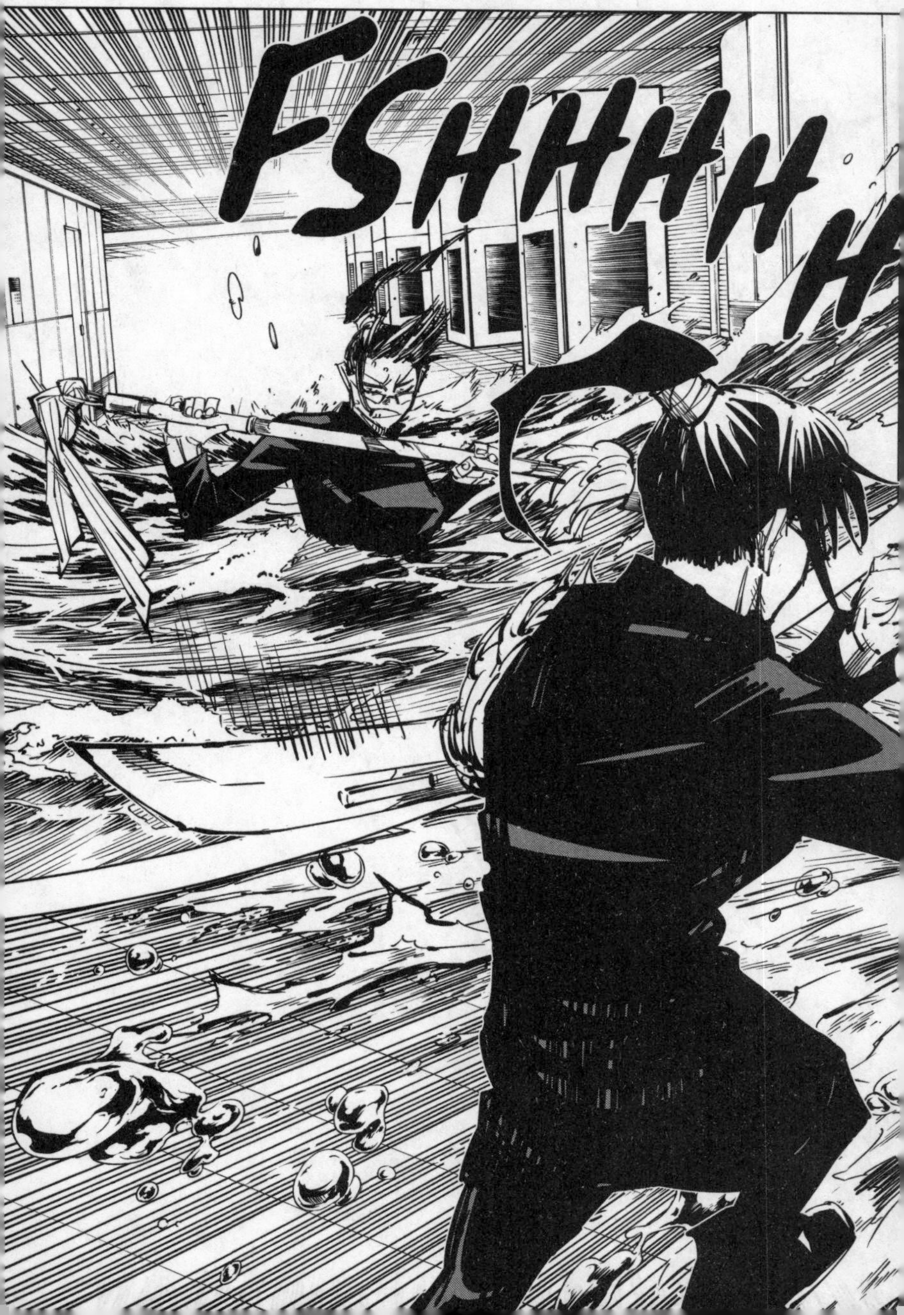
FSHHHHH

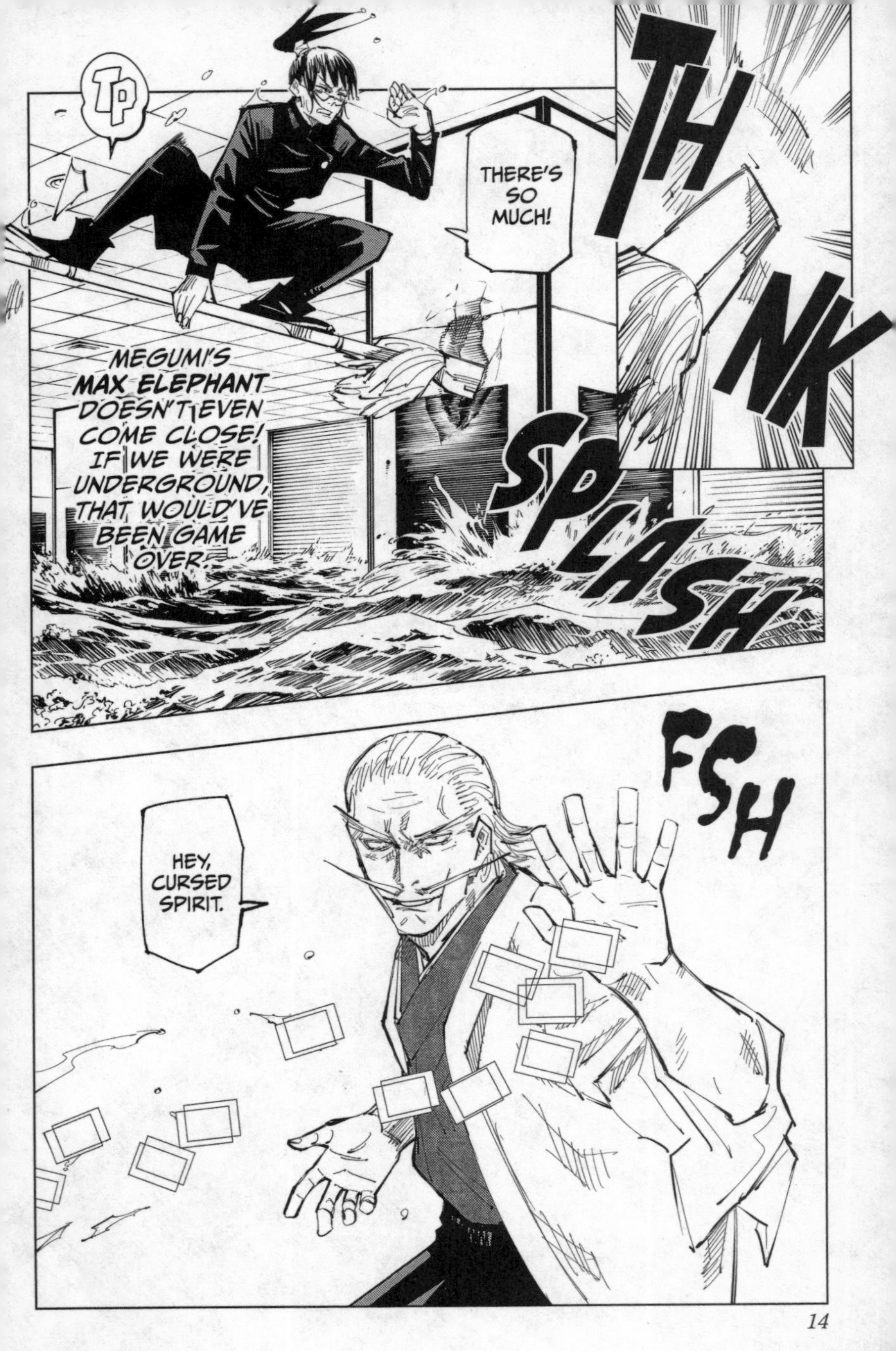
THNK
THERE'S SO MUCH!
TP
MEGUMI'S MAX ELEPHANT DOESN'T EVEN COME CLOSE! IF WE WERE UNDERGROUND, THAT WOULD'VE BEEN GAME OVER.
SPLASH
FSH
HEY, CURSED SPIRIT.

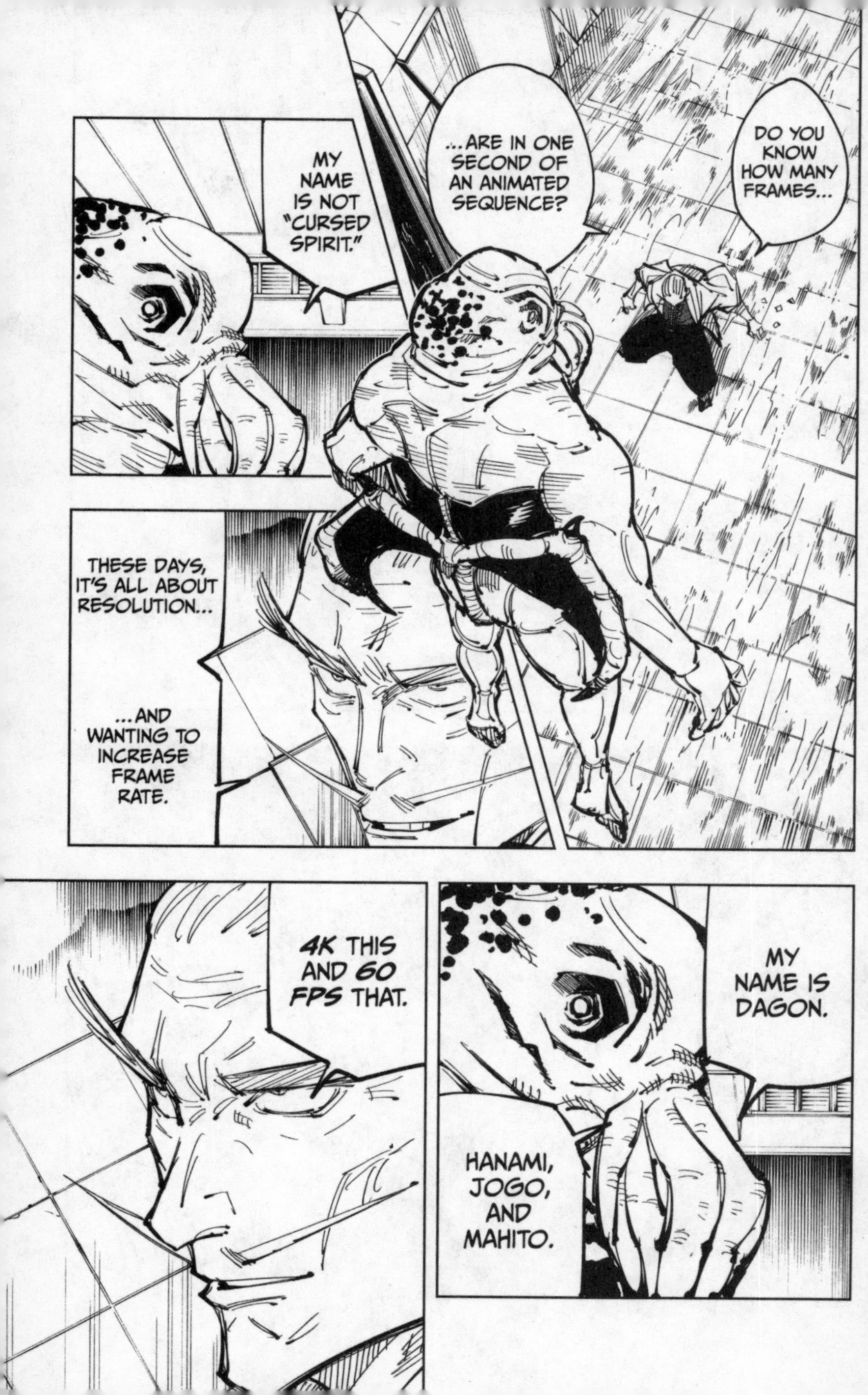
DO YOU KNOW HOW MANY FRAMES...
...ARE IN ONE SECOND OF AN ANIMATED SEQUENCE?
MY NAME IS NOT "CURSED SPIRIT."
THESE DAYS, IT'S ALL ABOUT RESOLUTION...
...AND WANTING TO INCREASE FRAME RATE.
MY NAME IS DAGON.
HANAMI, JOGO, AND MAHITO.
4K THIS AND 60 FPS THAT.

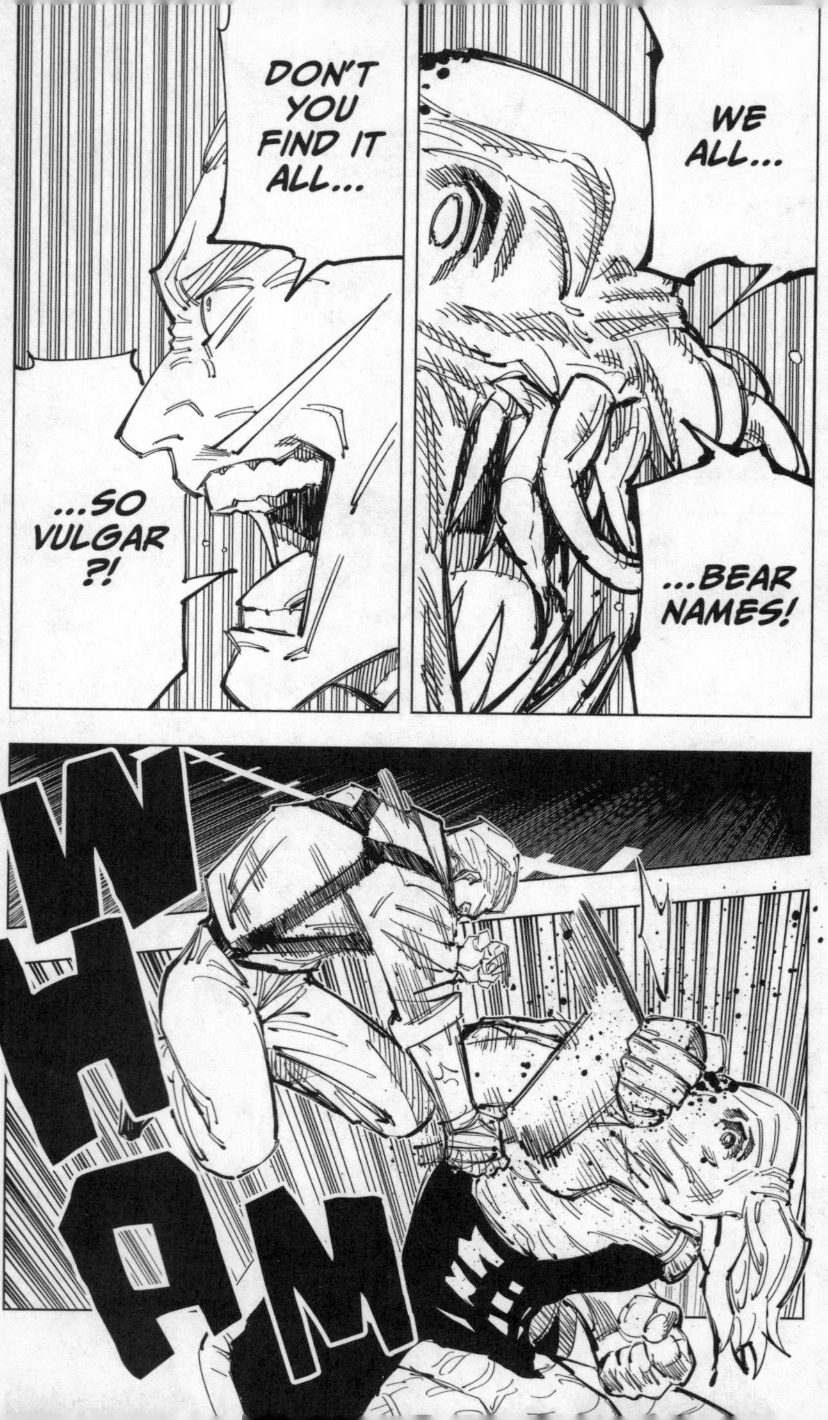
WE ALL...
...BEAR NAMES!
DON'T YOU FIND IT ALL...
...SO VULGAR?!
WHAM

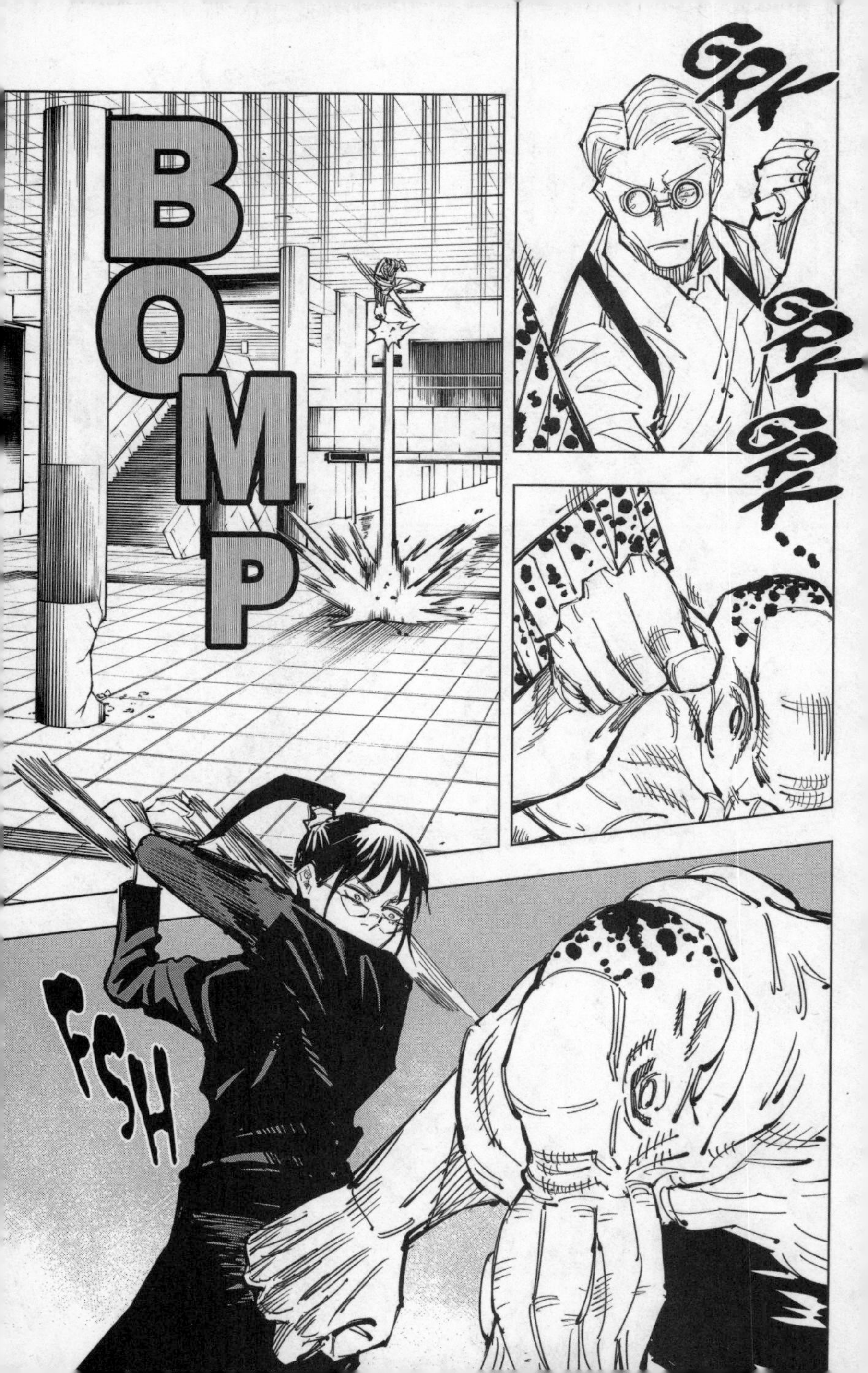
GRK
GRK
GRK
GRK...
BOMP
FSH

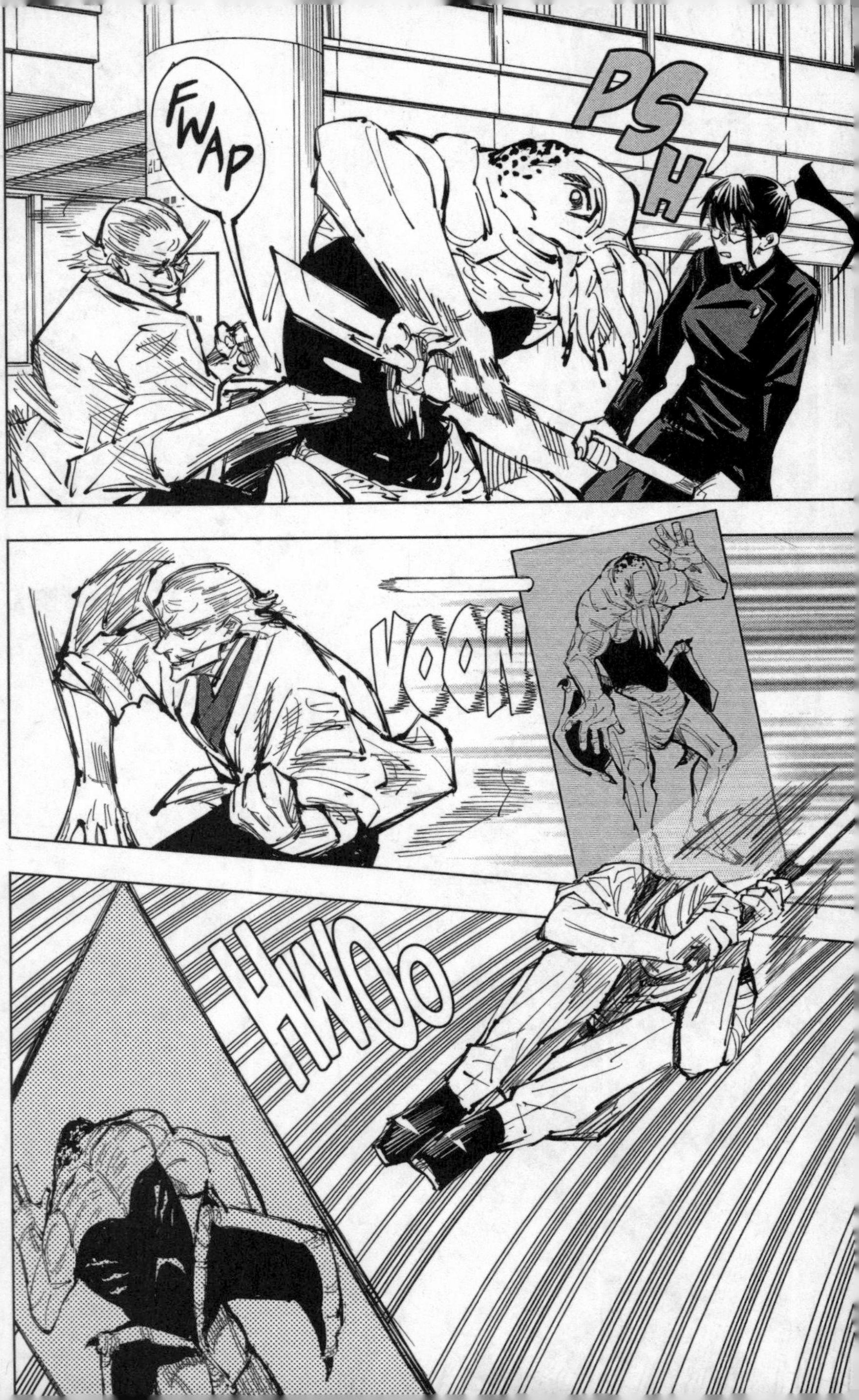
PSH
FWAP
VOOM
HWOO

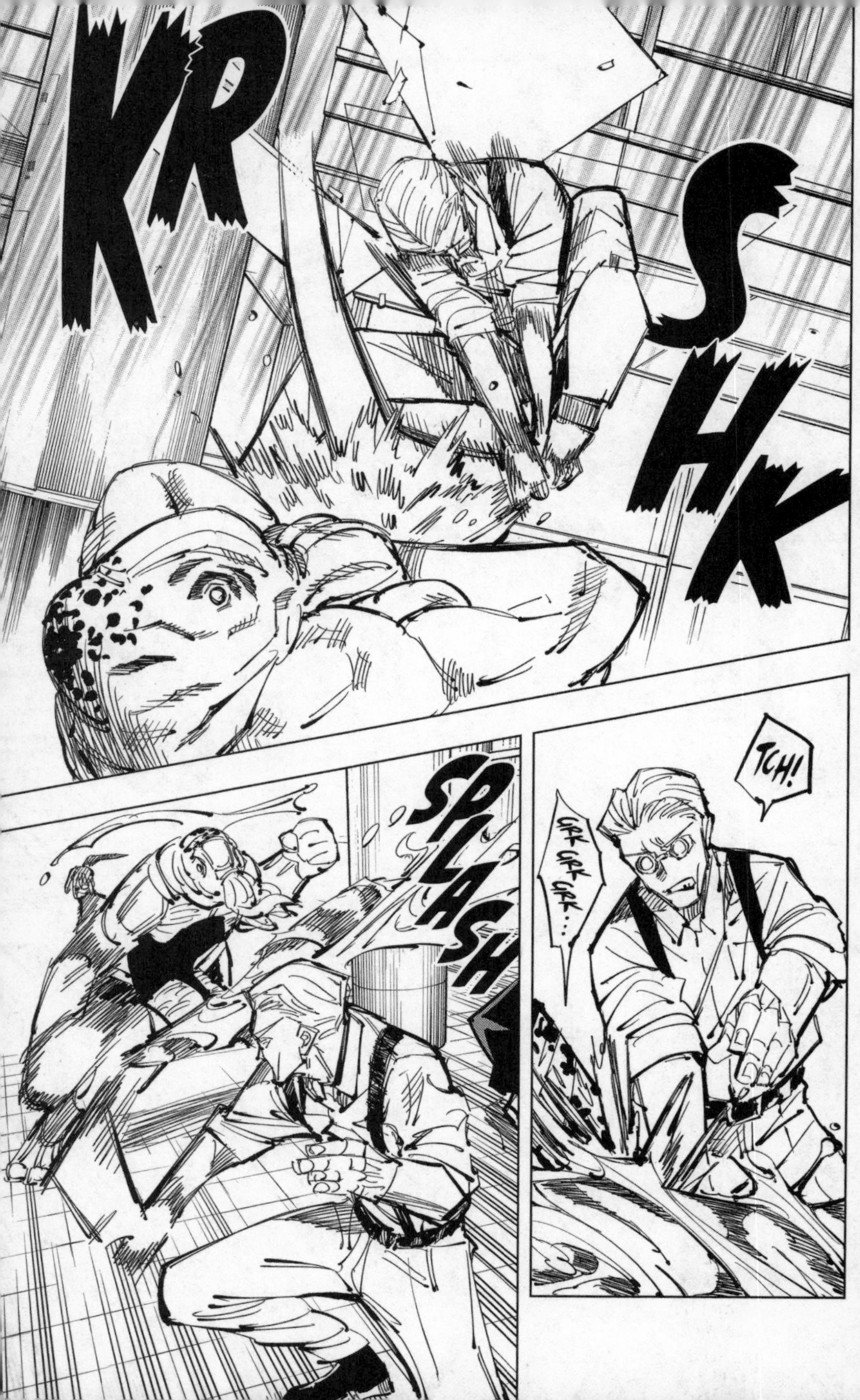
KRSHK
TCH!
GRK GRK GRK...
SPLASH

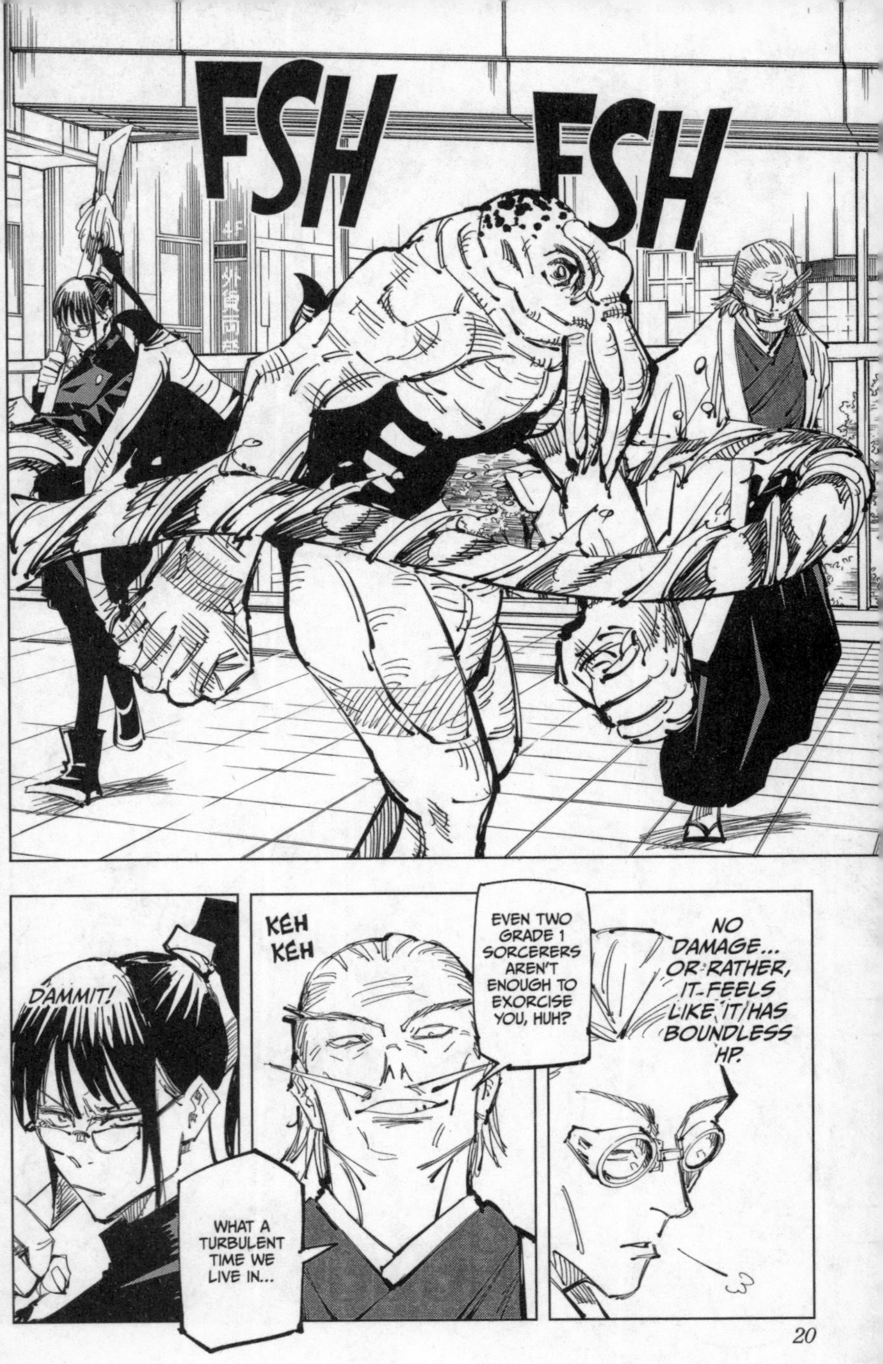
FSH FSH
NO DAMAGE... OR RATHER, IT FEELS LIKE IT HAS BOUNDLESS HP.
KEH KEH
EVEN TWO GRADE 1 SORCERERS AREN'T ENOUGH TO EXORCISE YOU, HUH?
WHAT A TURBULENT TIME WE LIVE IN...
DAMMIT!

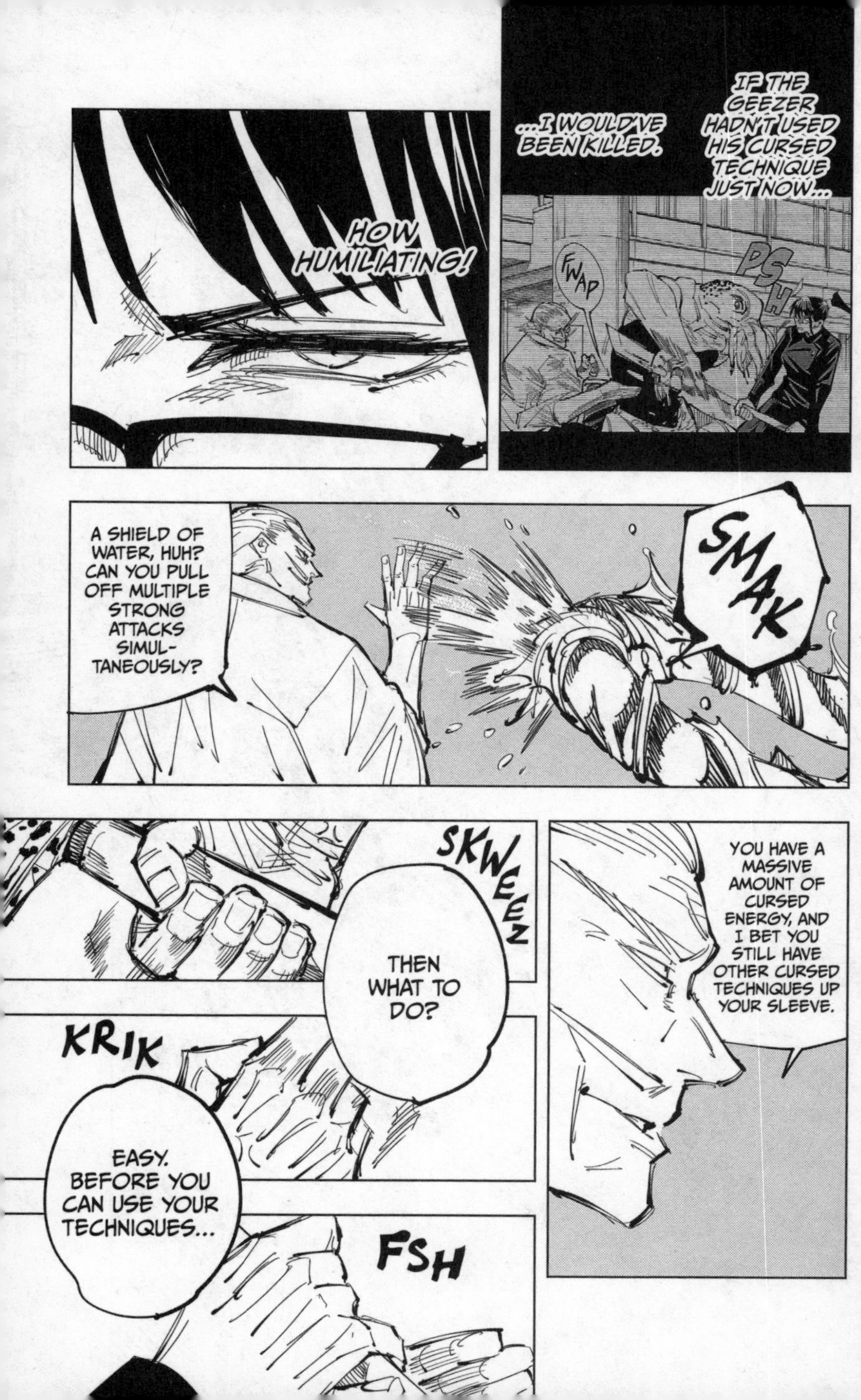
IF THE GEEZER HADN'T USED HIS CURSED TECHNIQUE JUST NOW...
...I WOULD'VE BEEN KILLED.
PSH
FWAP
HOW HUMILIATING!
SMAK
A SHIELD OF WATER, HUH? CAN YOU PULL OFF MULTIPLE STRONG ATTACKS SIMUL-TANEOUSLY?
YOU HAVE A MASSIVE AMOUNT OF CURSED ENERGY, AND I BET YOU STILL HAVE OTHER CURSED TECHNIQUES UP YOUR SLEEVE.
SKWEEZ
THEN WHAT TO DO?
KRIK
EASY. BEFORE YOU CAN USE YOUR TECHNIQUES...
FSH

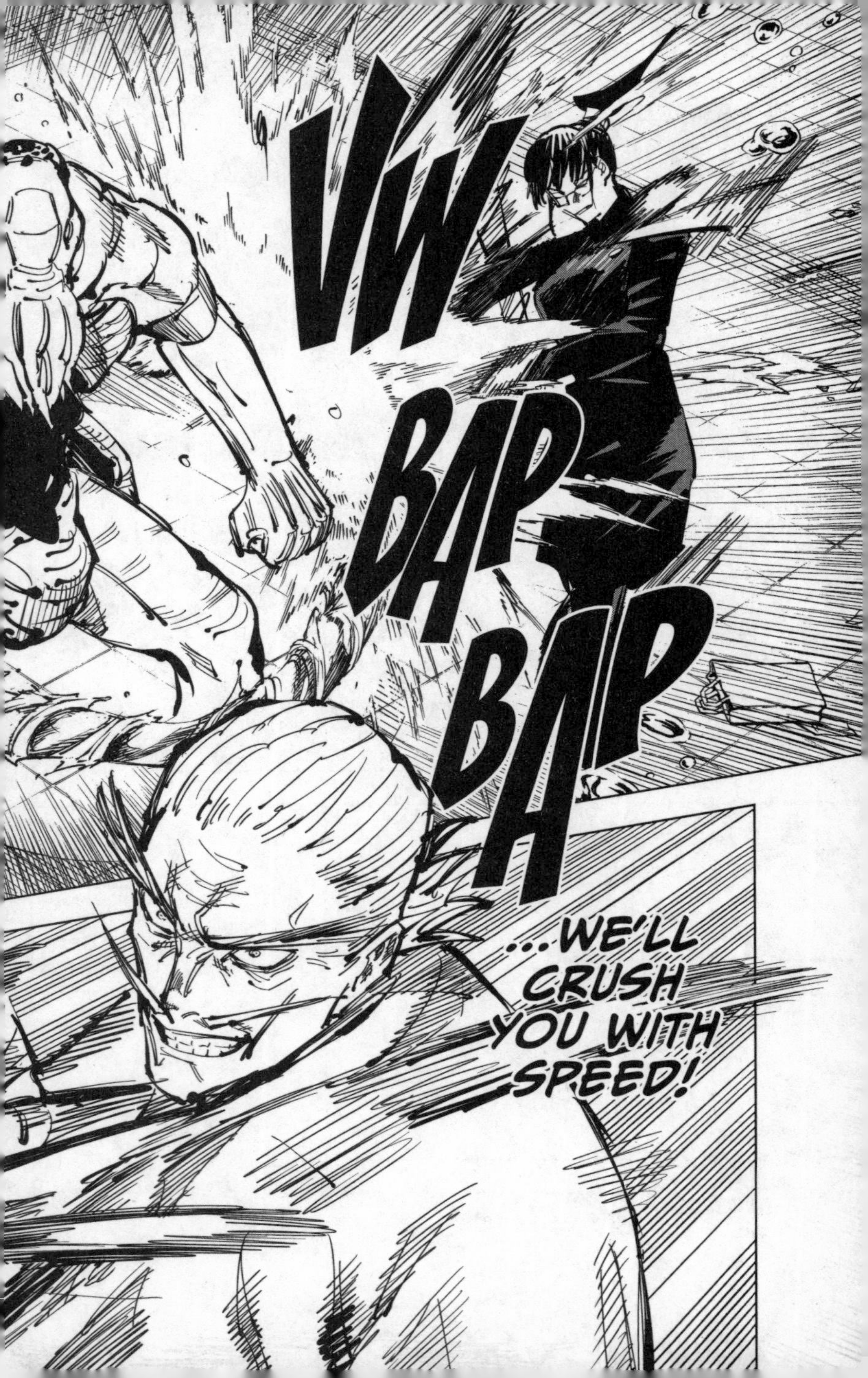
VW
BAP BAP
...WE'LL CRUSH YOU WITH SPEED!

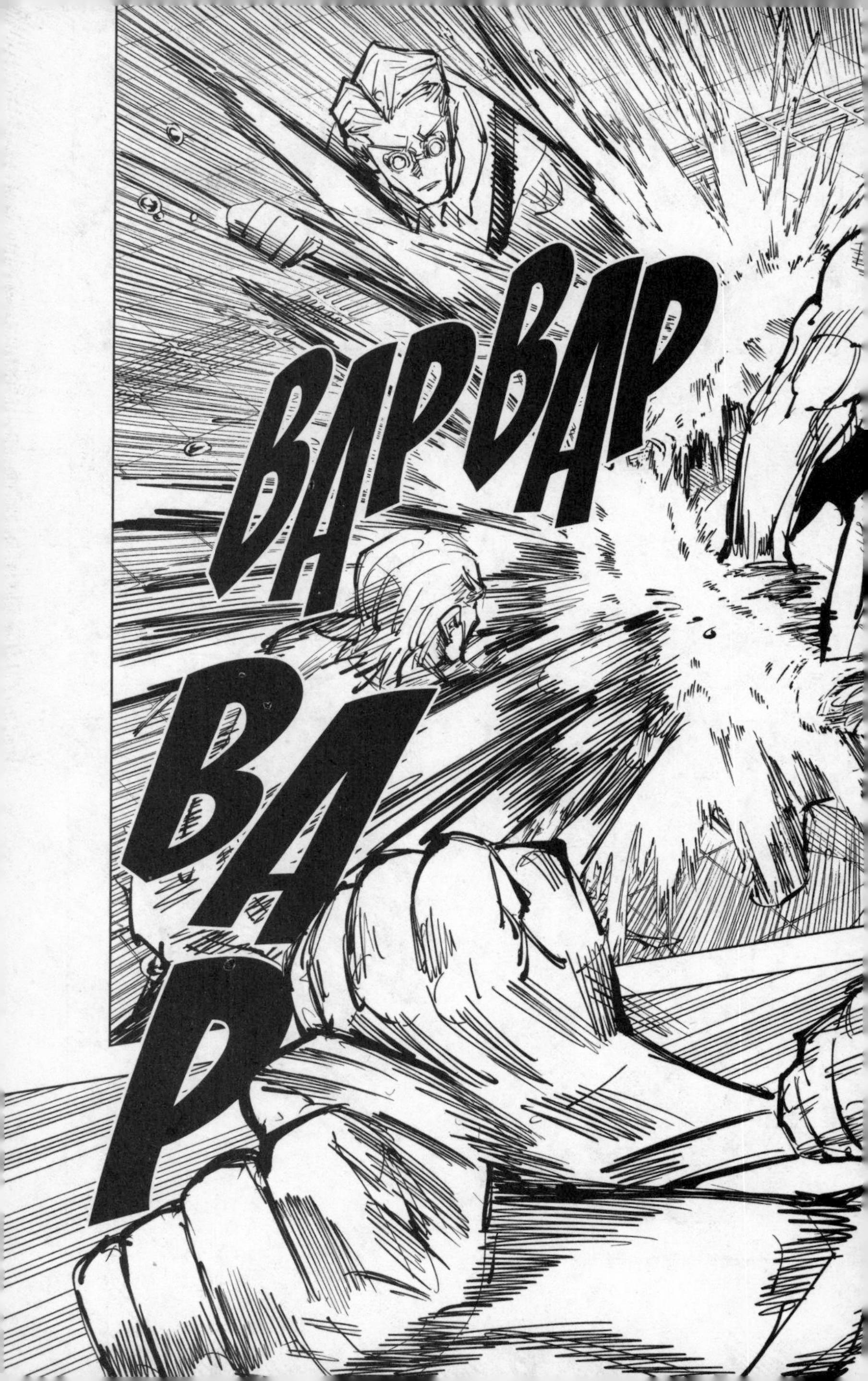
BAP BAP
BAP
BAP

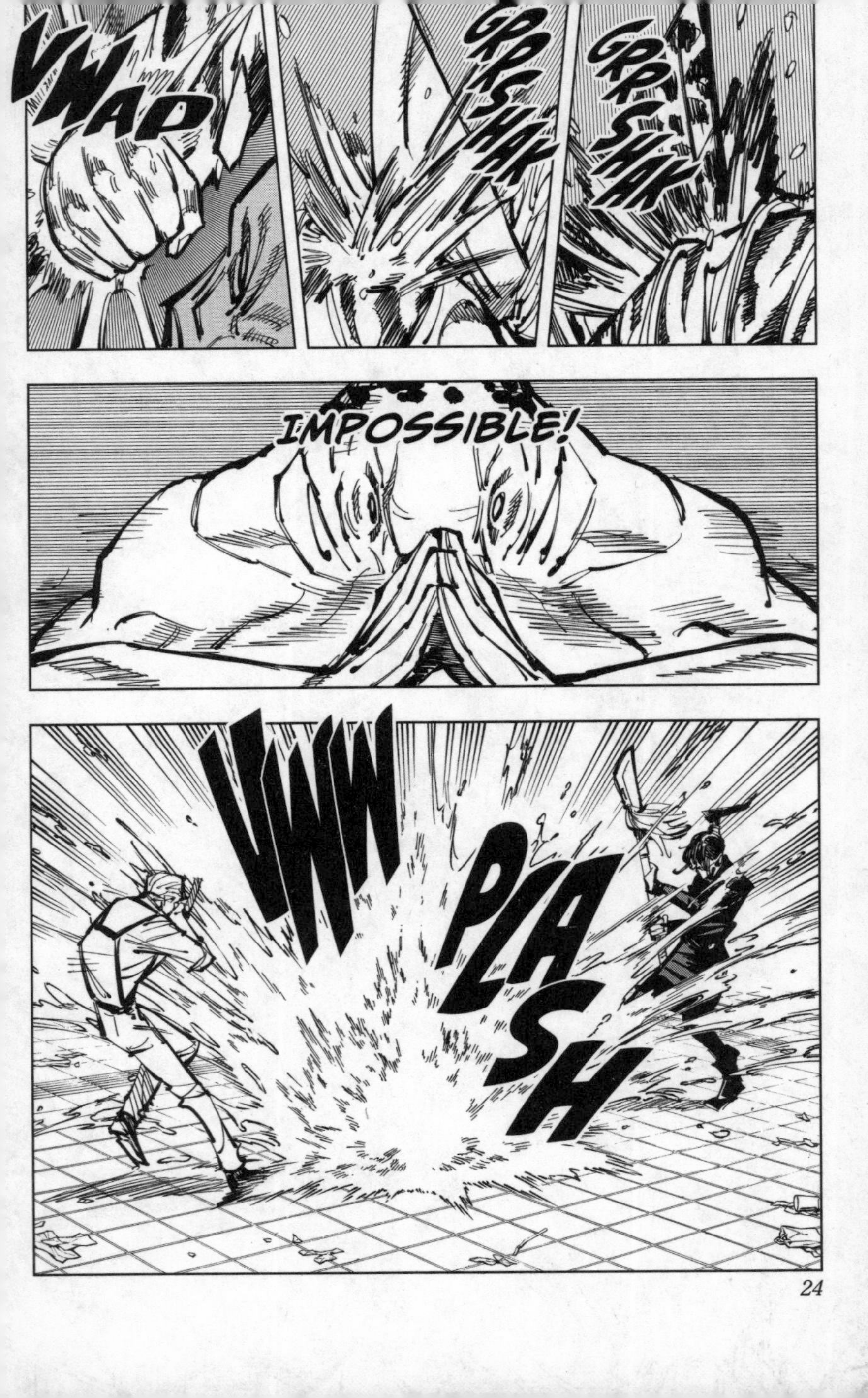
GRR SHAK
GRR SHAK
VWAP
IMPOSSIBLE!
VWWN
PLASH

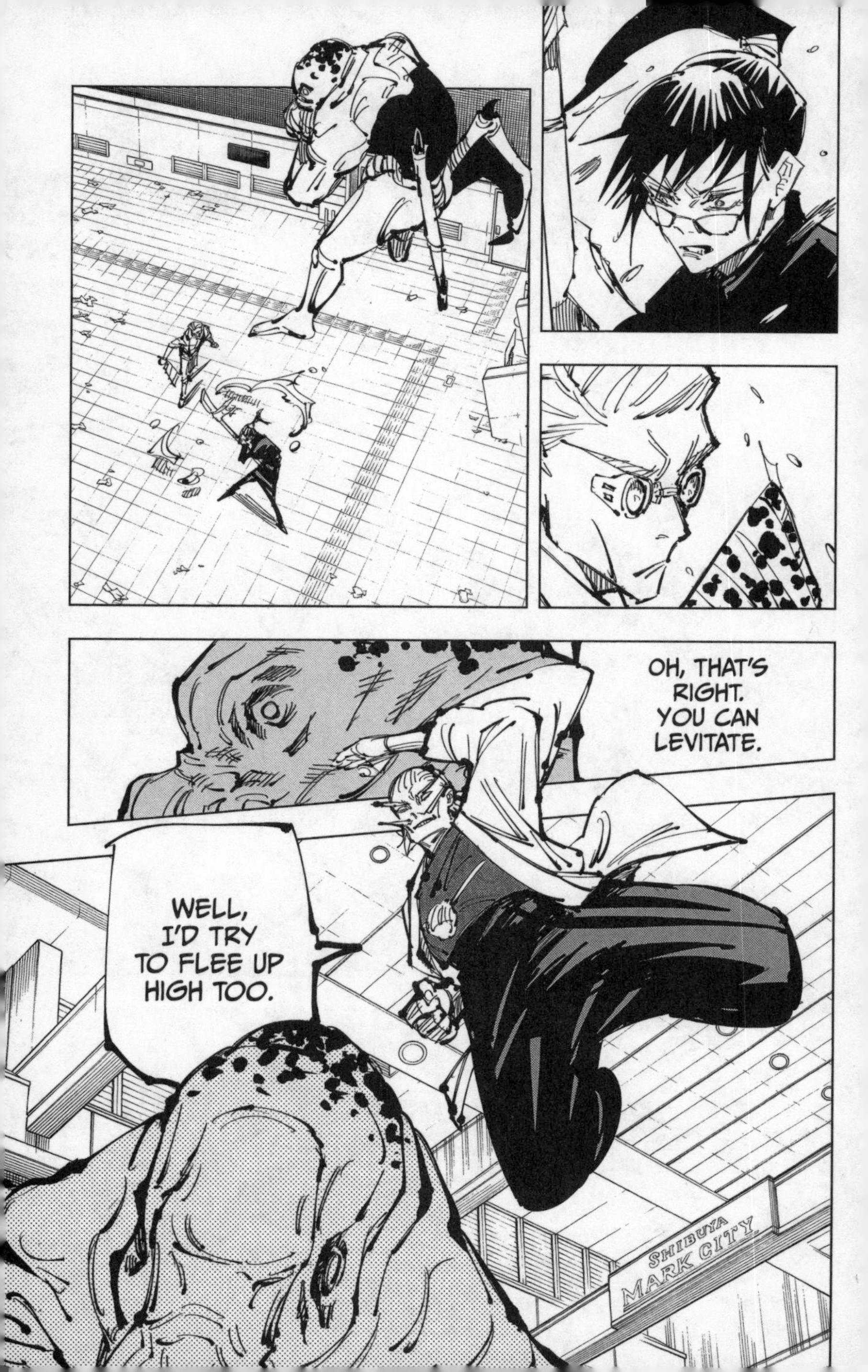
OH, THAT'S RIGHT. YOU CAN LEVITATE.
WELL, I'D TRY TO FLEE UP HIGH TOO.
SHIBUYA
MARK CITY

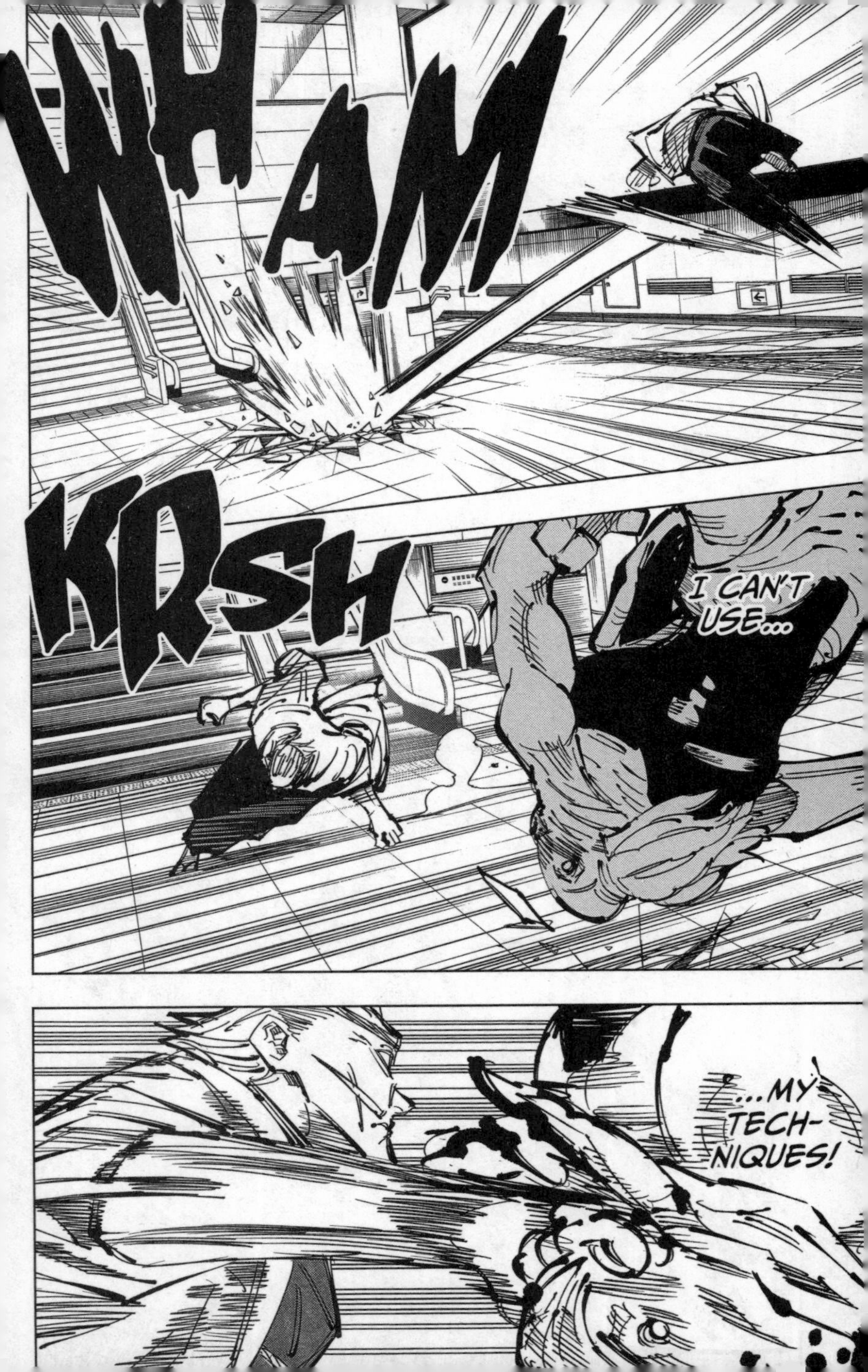
WHAM
KRSH
I CAN'T USE...
...MY TECH-NIQUES!

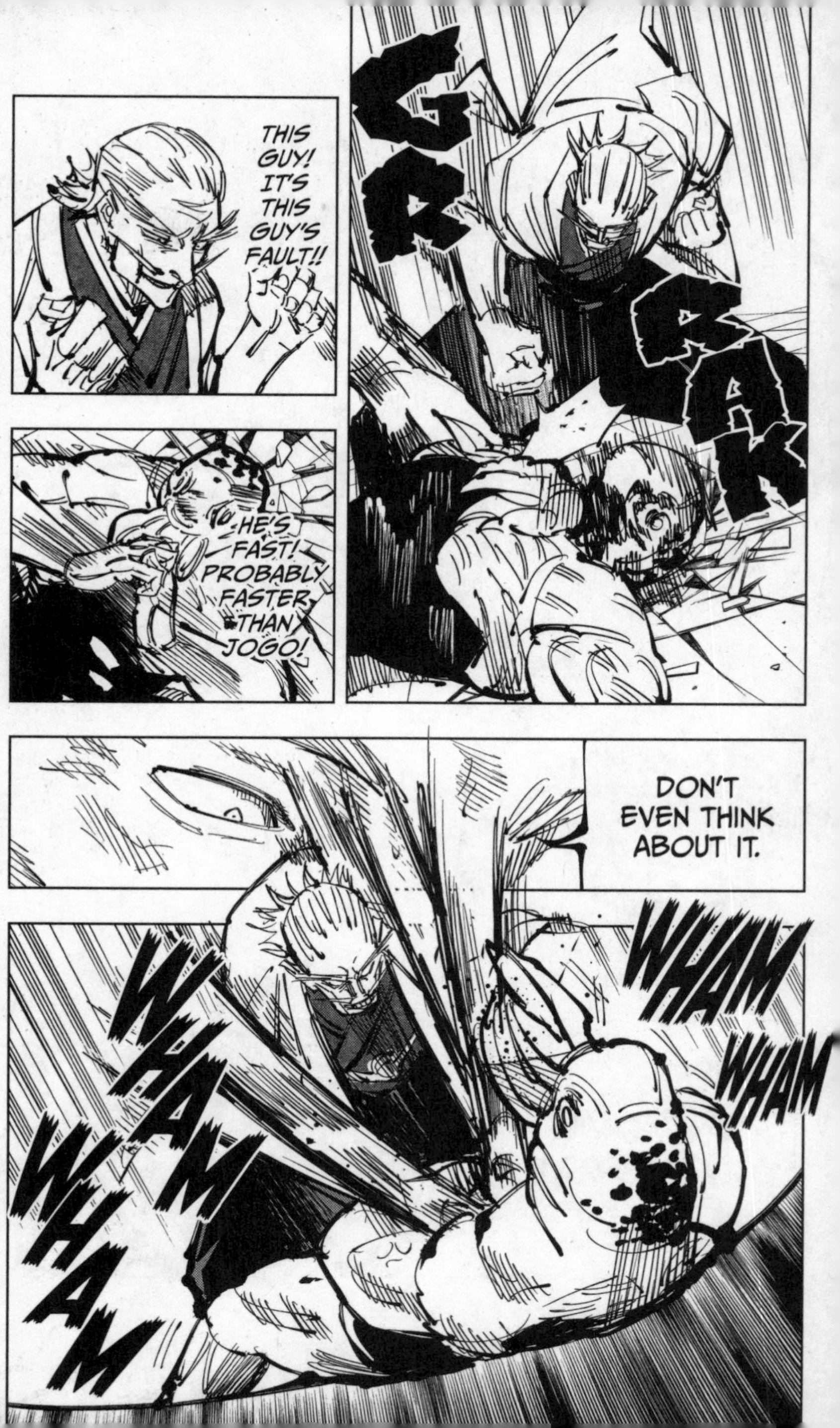
GRAK
THIS GUY! IT'S THIS GUY'S FAULT!!
HE'S FAST! PROBABLY FASTER THAN JOGO!
DON'T EVEN THINK ABOUT IT.
WHAM WHAM
WHAM WHAM WHAM

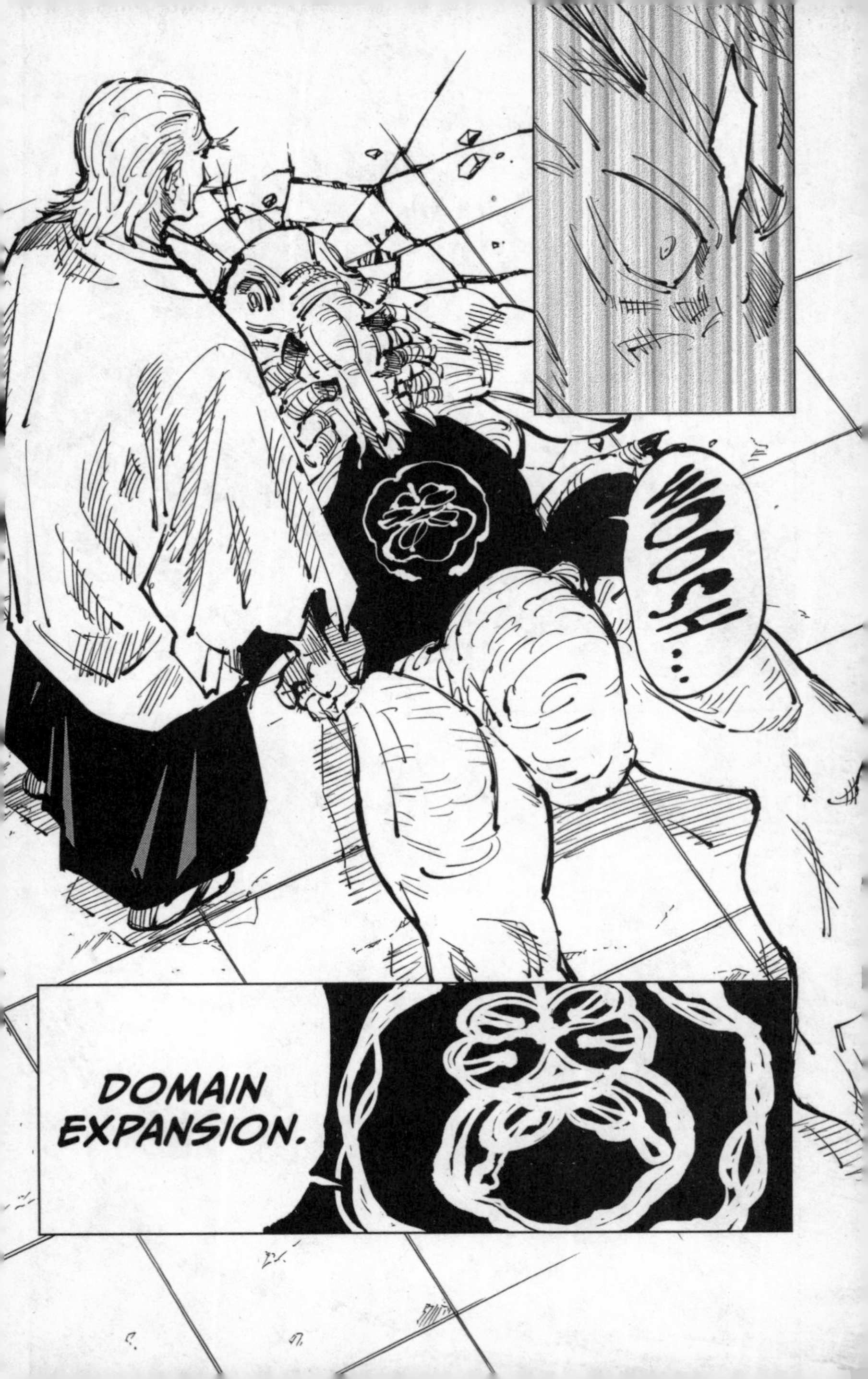
WOOSH...
DOMAIN EXPANSION.

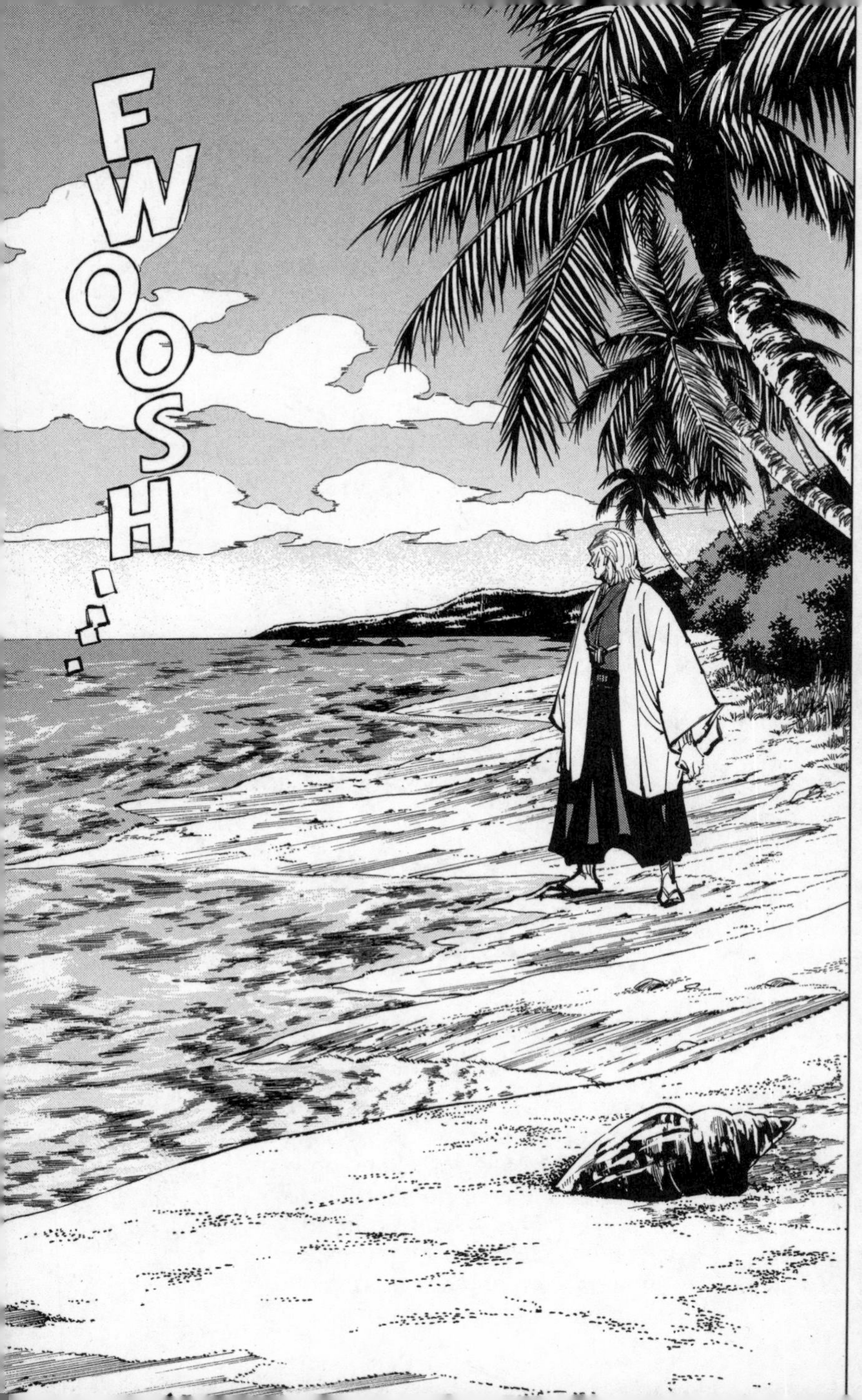
FWOOSH

Scenes I was planning to address but forgot about until now, part 1

• Dagon's cursed seal

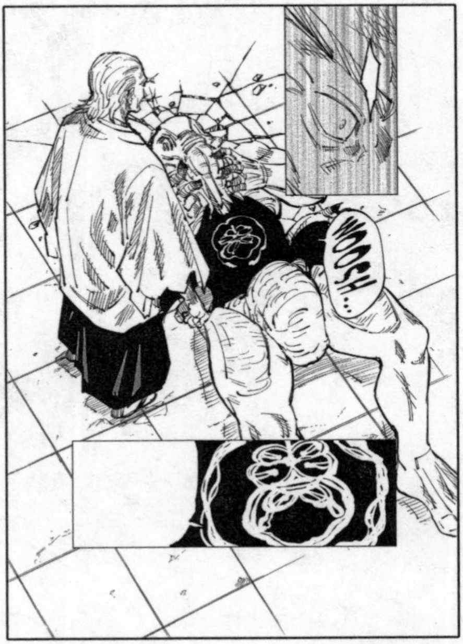
WOOSH...

For domain expansion, Dagon tried to complete the seal with his hands, but Naobito interfered, so he drew a cursed seal on his stomach. The design is that of a *houtai* (purse), which can also be used for male kimonos worn at *miyamairi* (shinto rite of passage for newborns).

Chapter 108:
The Shibuya Incident, Part 26

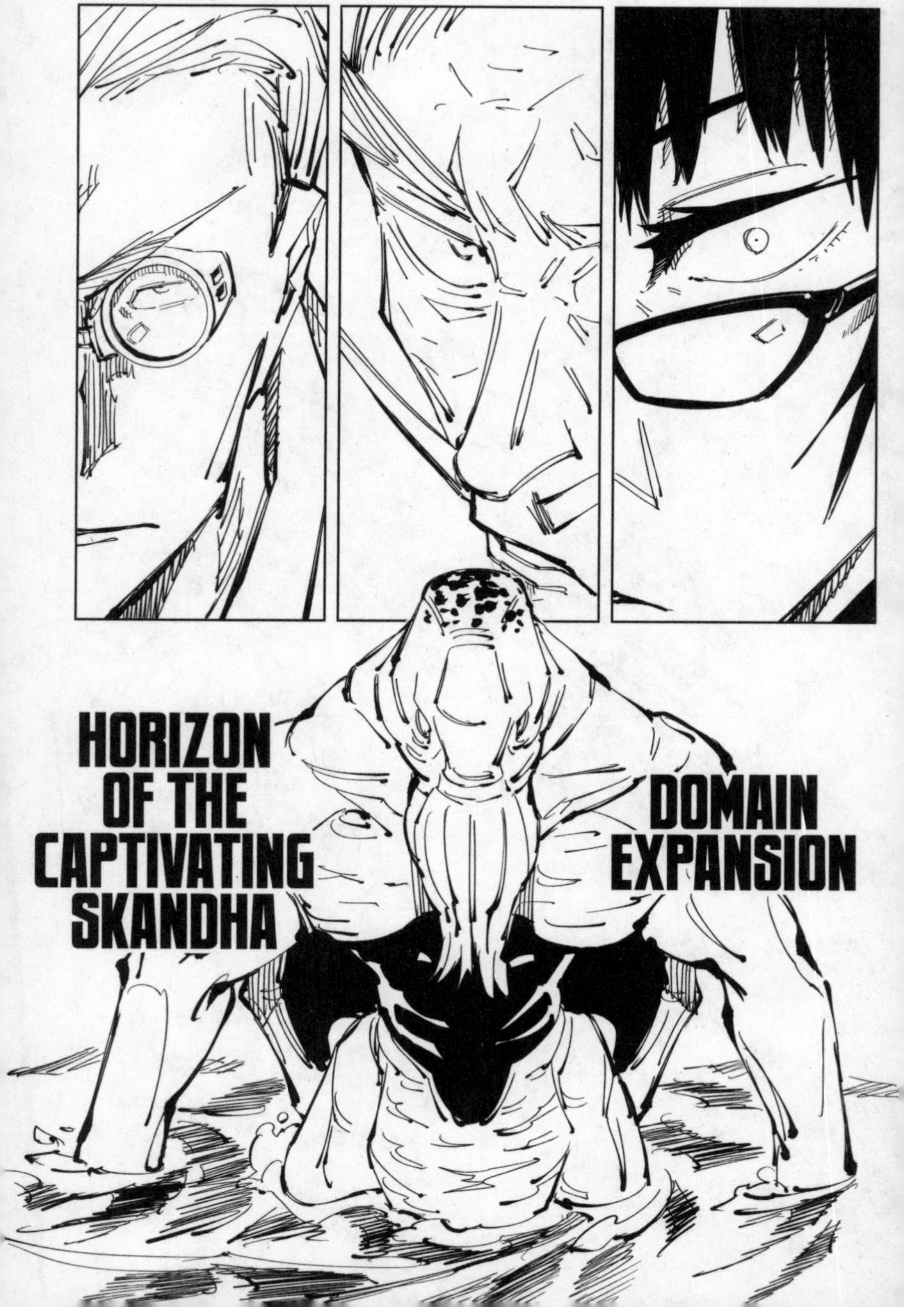
DOMAIN EXPANSION
HORIZON OF THE CAPTIVATING SKANDHA

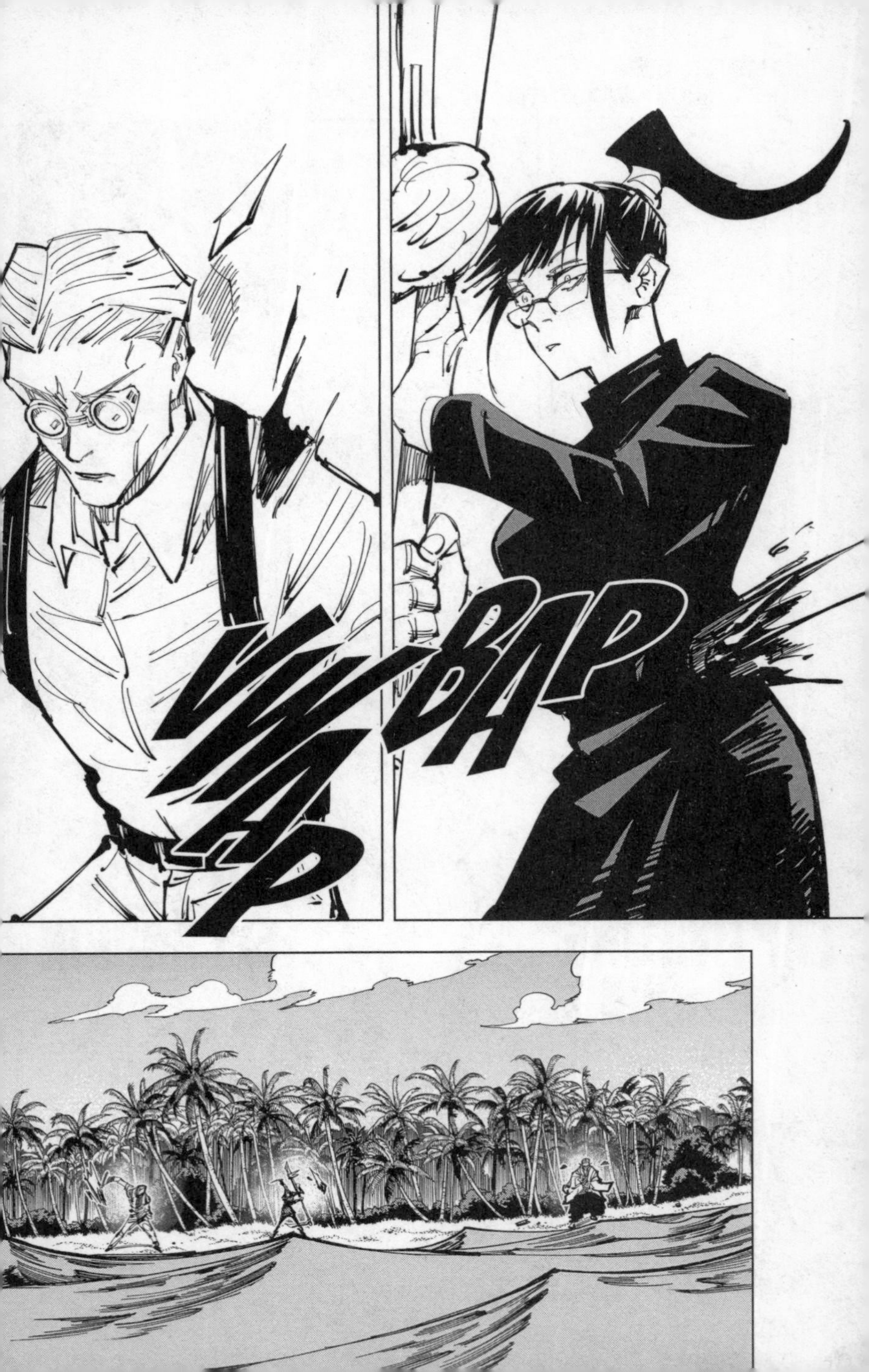
BAP
WHAP

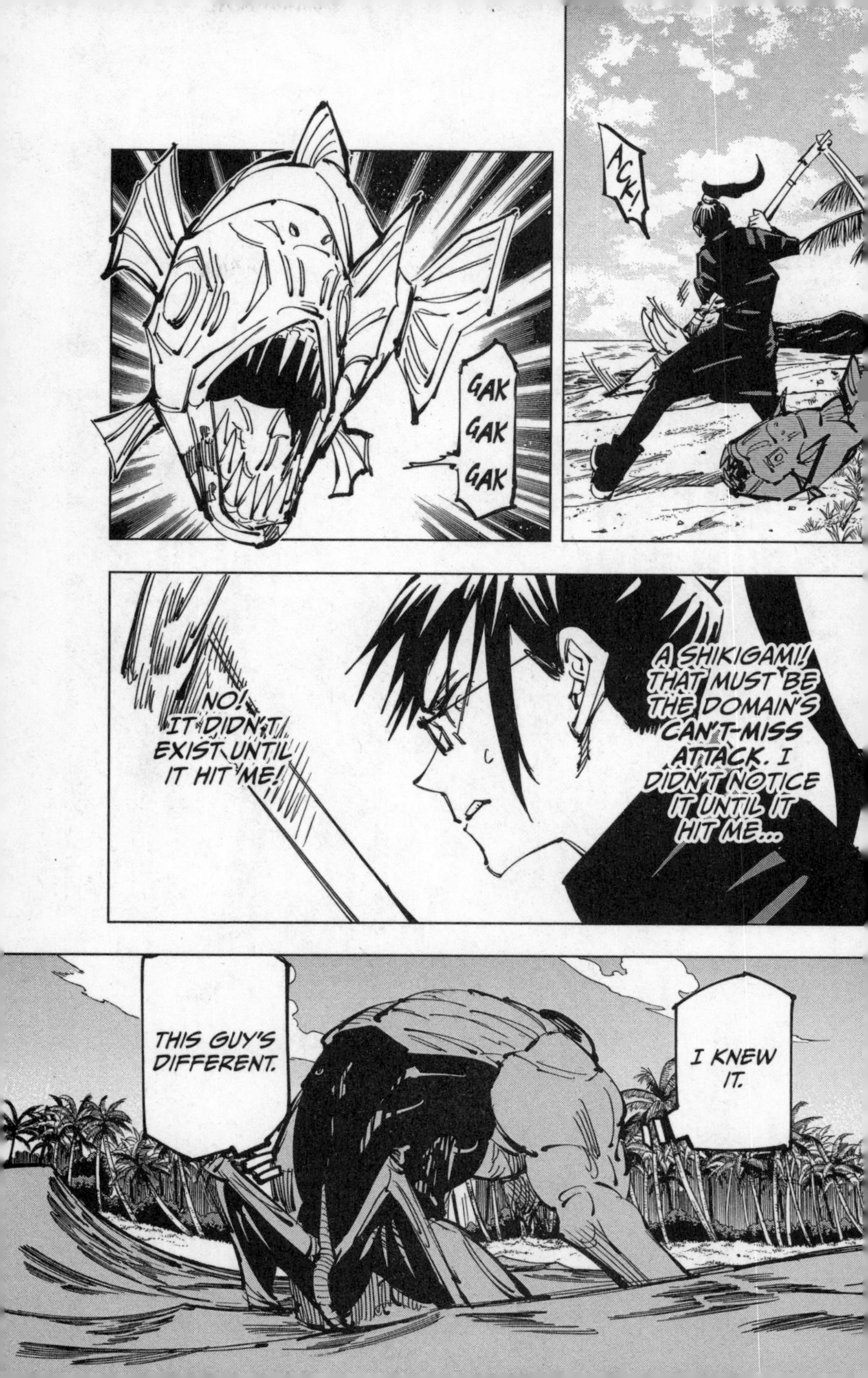
ACK!
GAK GAK GAK
A SHIKIGAMI! THAT MUST BE THE DOMAIN'S CAN'T-MISS ATTACK. I DIDN'T NOTICE IT UNTIL IT HIT ME...
NO! IT DIDN'T EXIST UNTIL IT HIT ME!
I KNEW IT.
THIS GUY'S DIFFERENT.

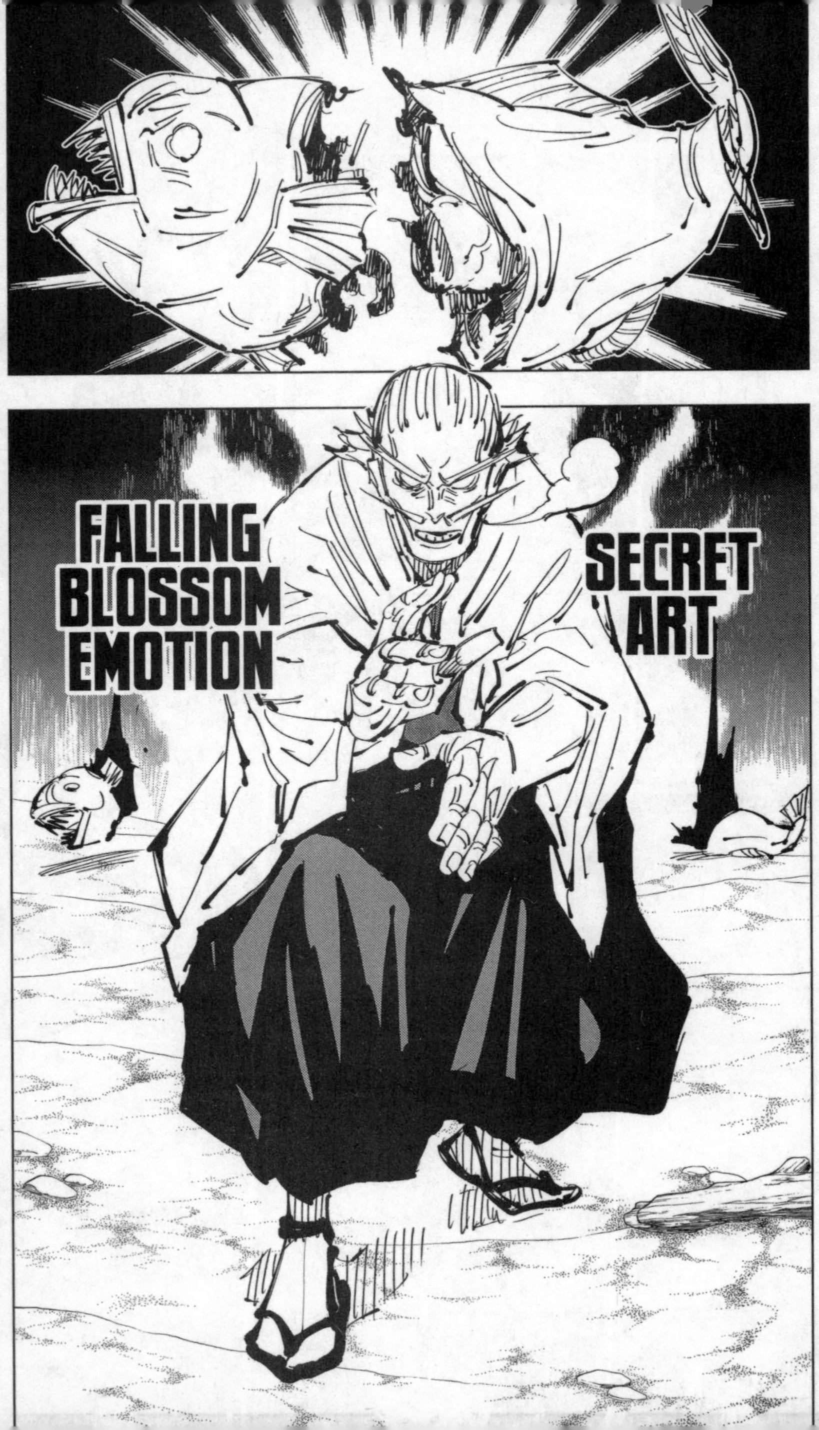
SECRET ART
FALLING BLOSSOM EMOTION

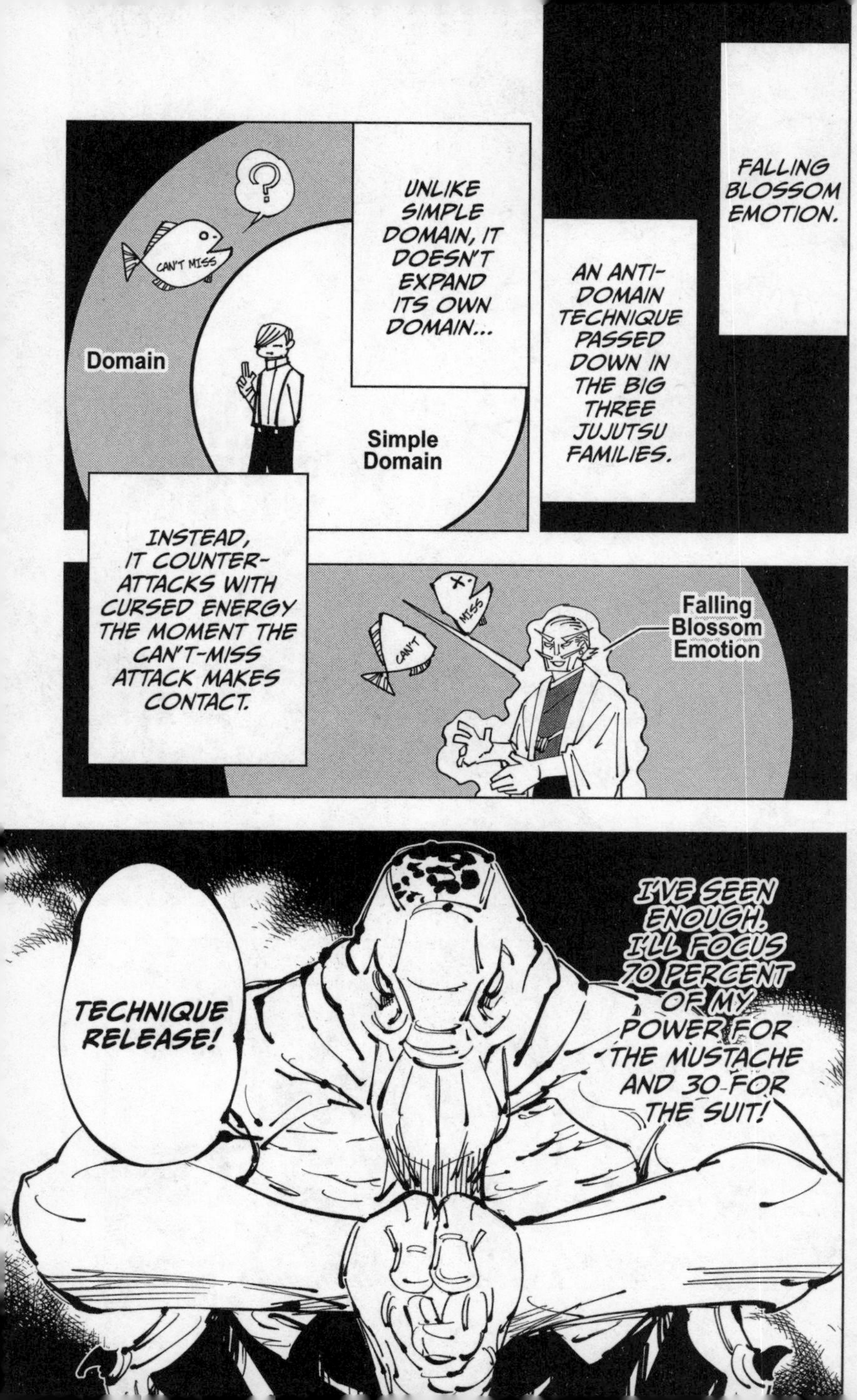

FALLING BLOSSOM EMOTION.
AN ANTI-DOMAIN TECHNIQUE PASSED DOWN IN THE BIG THREE JUJUTSU FAMILIES.
UNLIKE SIMPLE DOMAIN, IT DOESN'T EXPAND ITS OWN DOMAIN...
?
CAN'T MISS
Domain
Simple Domain
INSTEAD, IT COUNTER-ATTACKS WITH CURSED ENERGY THE MOMENT THE CAN'T-MISS ATTACK MAKES CONTACT.
Falling Blossom Emotion
MISS
CAN'T
I'VE SEEN ENOUGH. I'LL FOCUS 70 PERCENT OF MY POWER FOR THE MUSTACHE AND 30 FOR THE SUIT!
TECHNIQUE RELEASE!

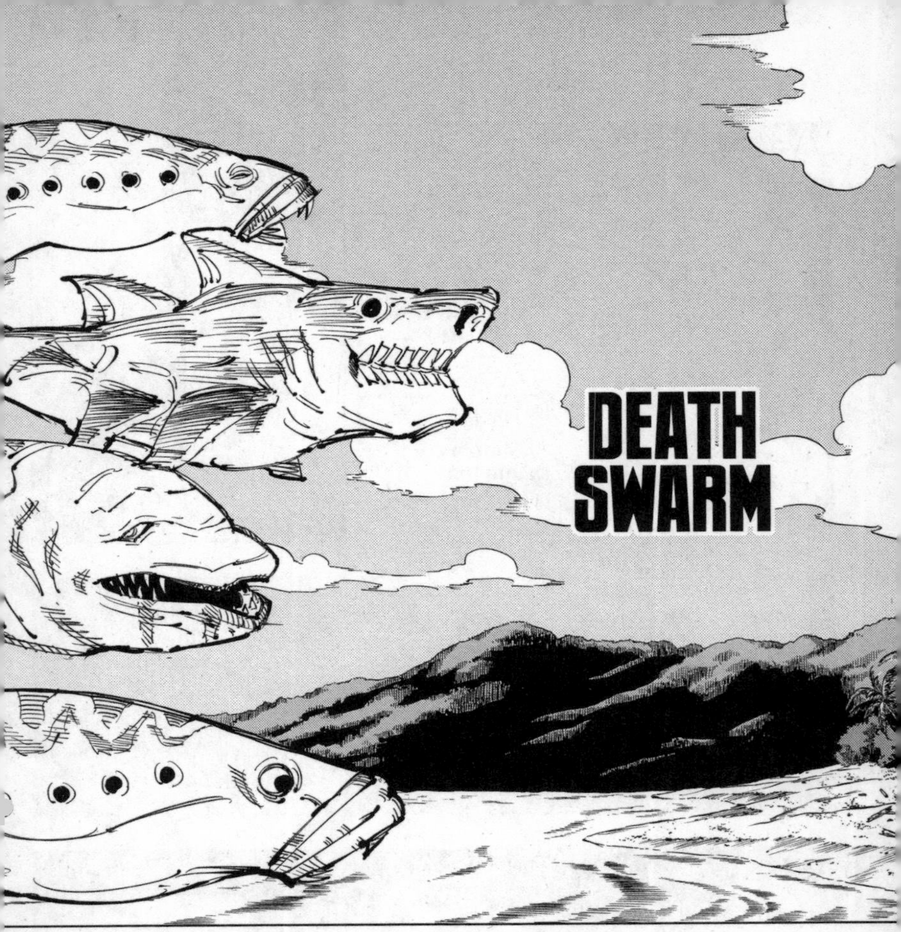
DEATH SWARM

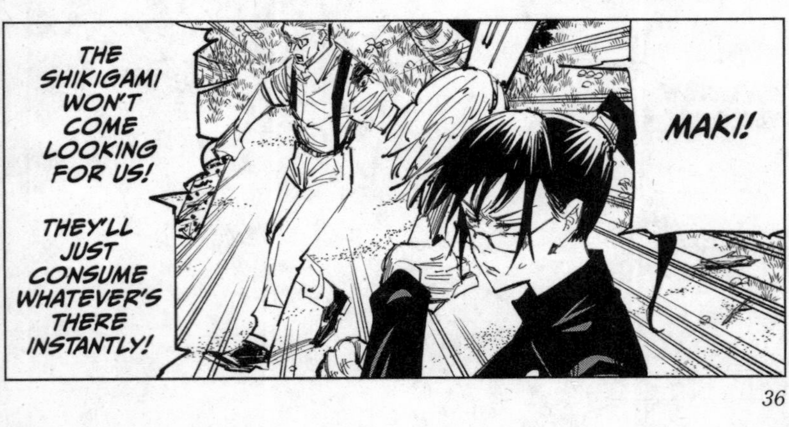
MAKI!
THE SHIKIGAMI WON'T COME LOOKING FOR US!
THEY'LL JUST CONSUME WHATEVER'S THERE INSTANTLY!

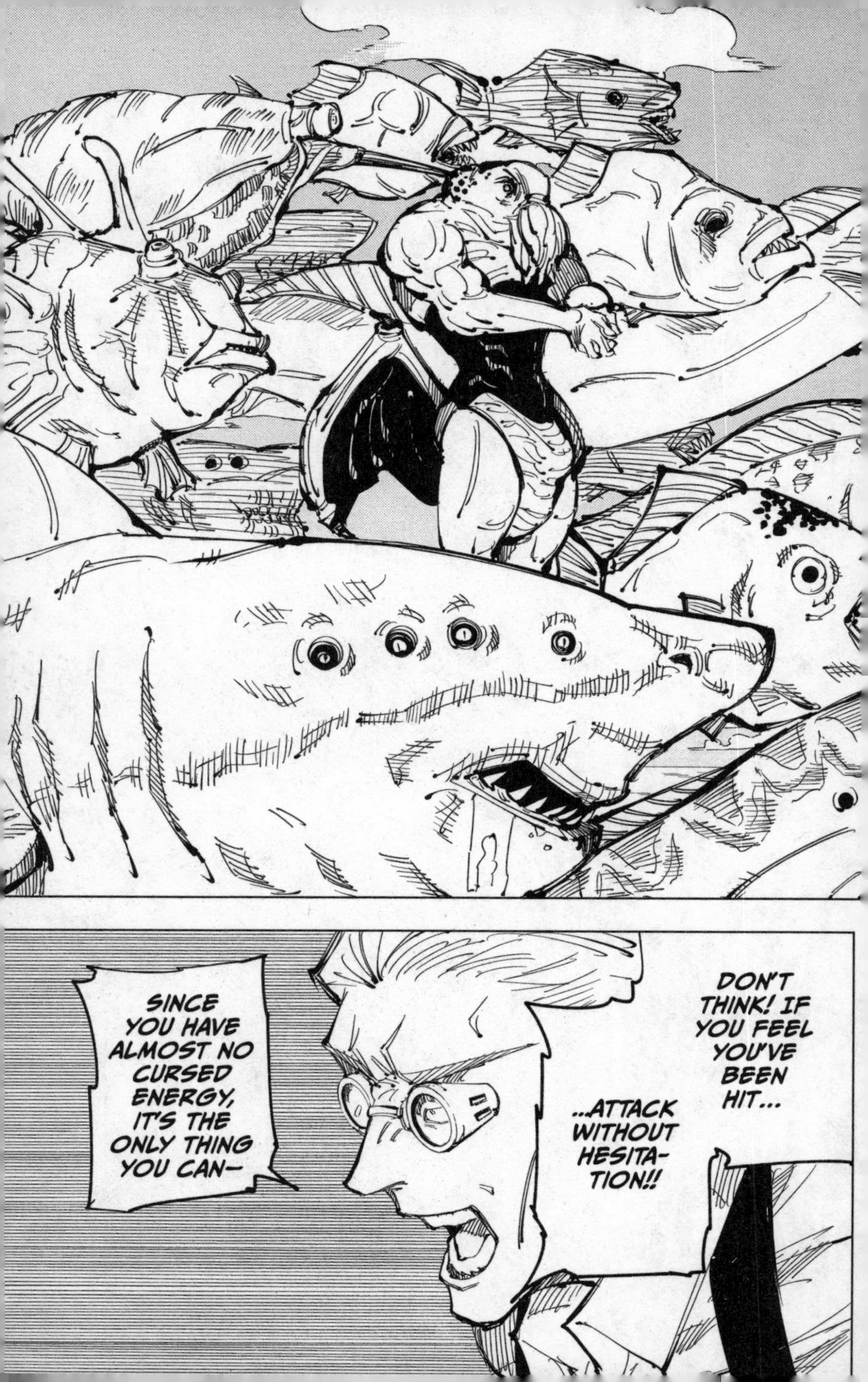
DON'T THINK! IF YOU FEEL YOU'VE BEEN HIT...
...ATTACK WITHOUT HESITA-TION!!
SINCE YOU HAVE ALMOST NO CURSED ENERGY, IT'S THE ONLY THING YOU CAN—

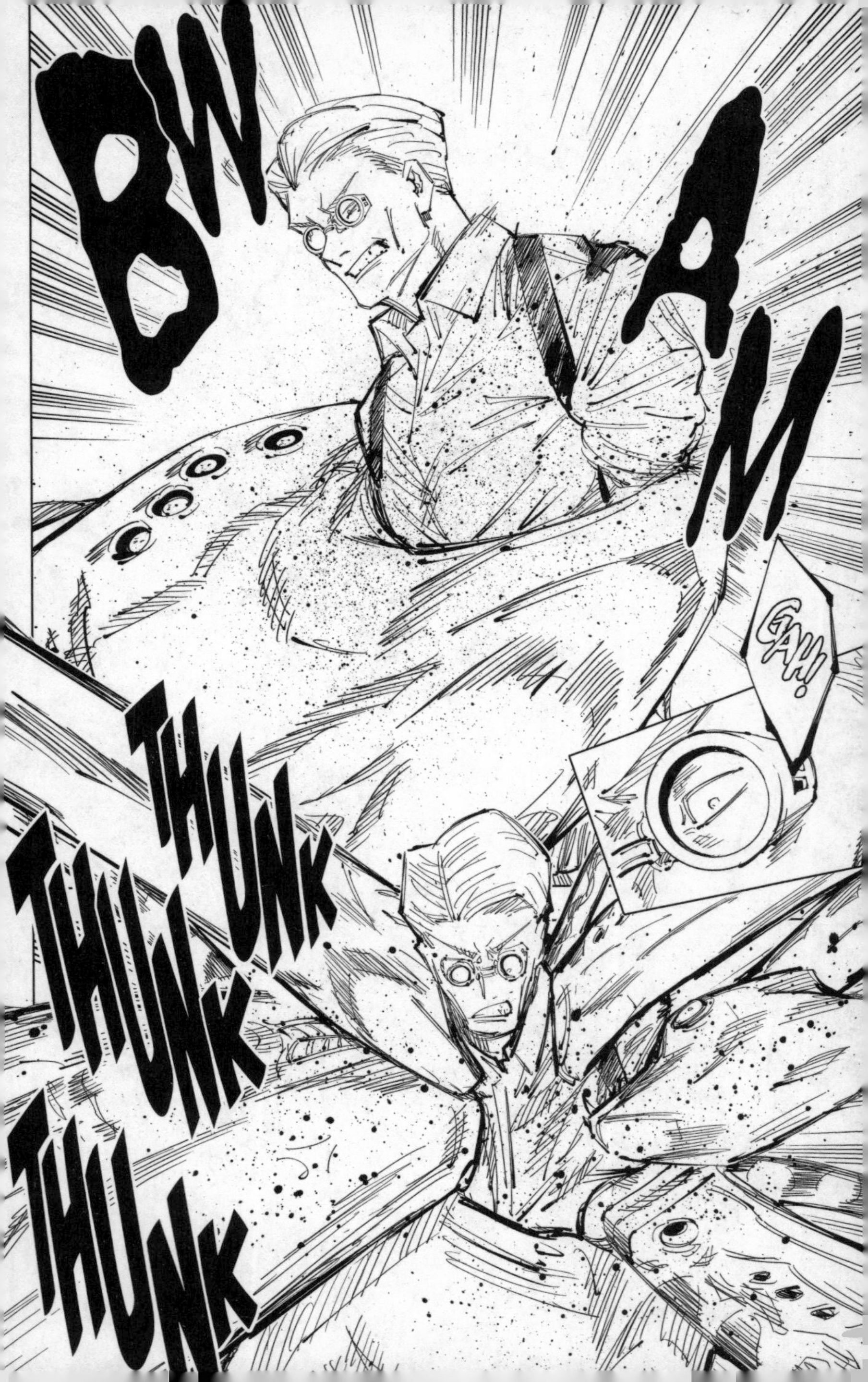
BAM
GAH!
THUNK
THUNK
THUNK

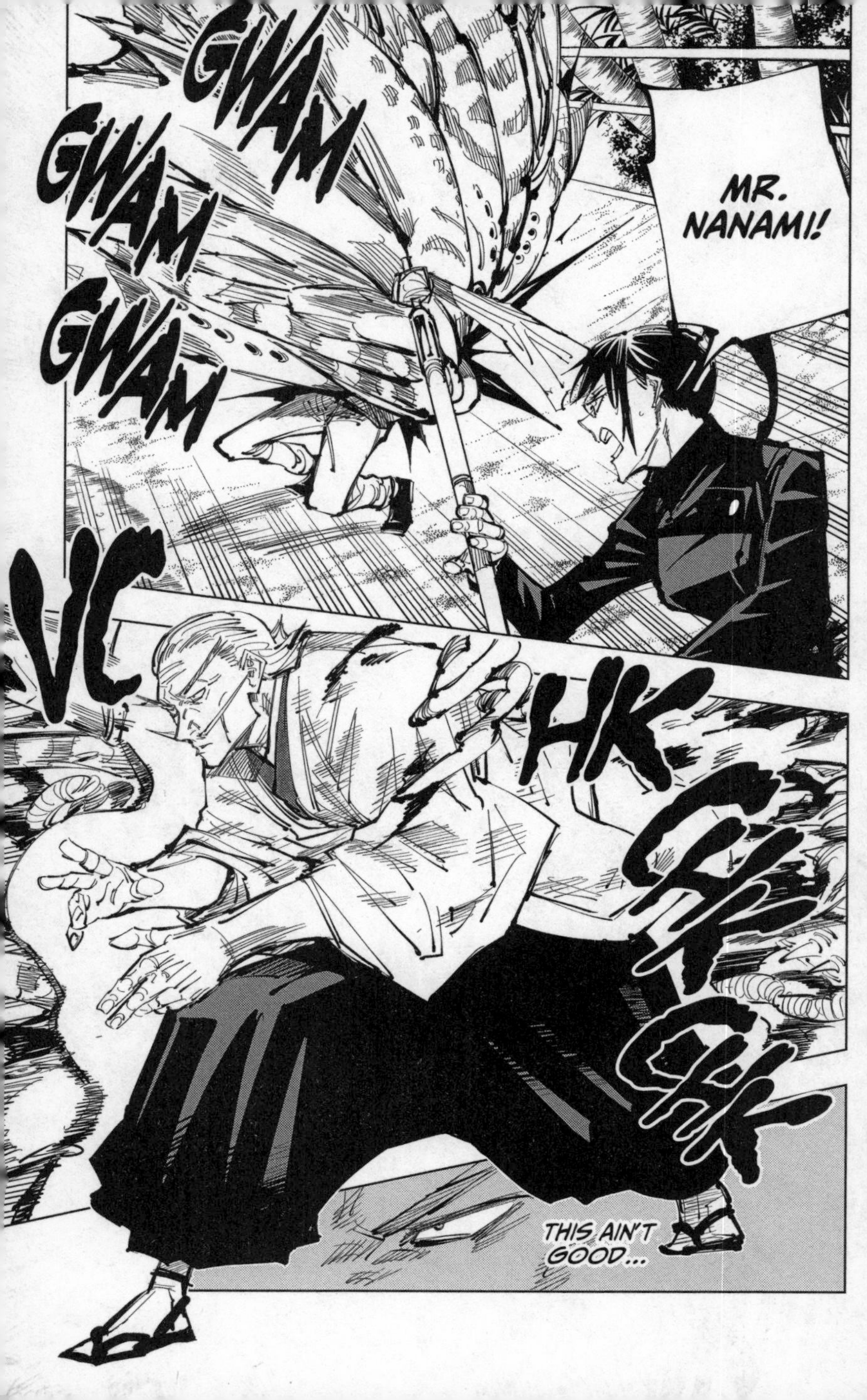
MR. NANAMI!
GWAM GWAM GWAM GWAM
HK CHK CHK CHK
THIS AIN'T GOOD...
VC

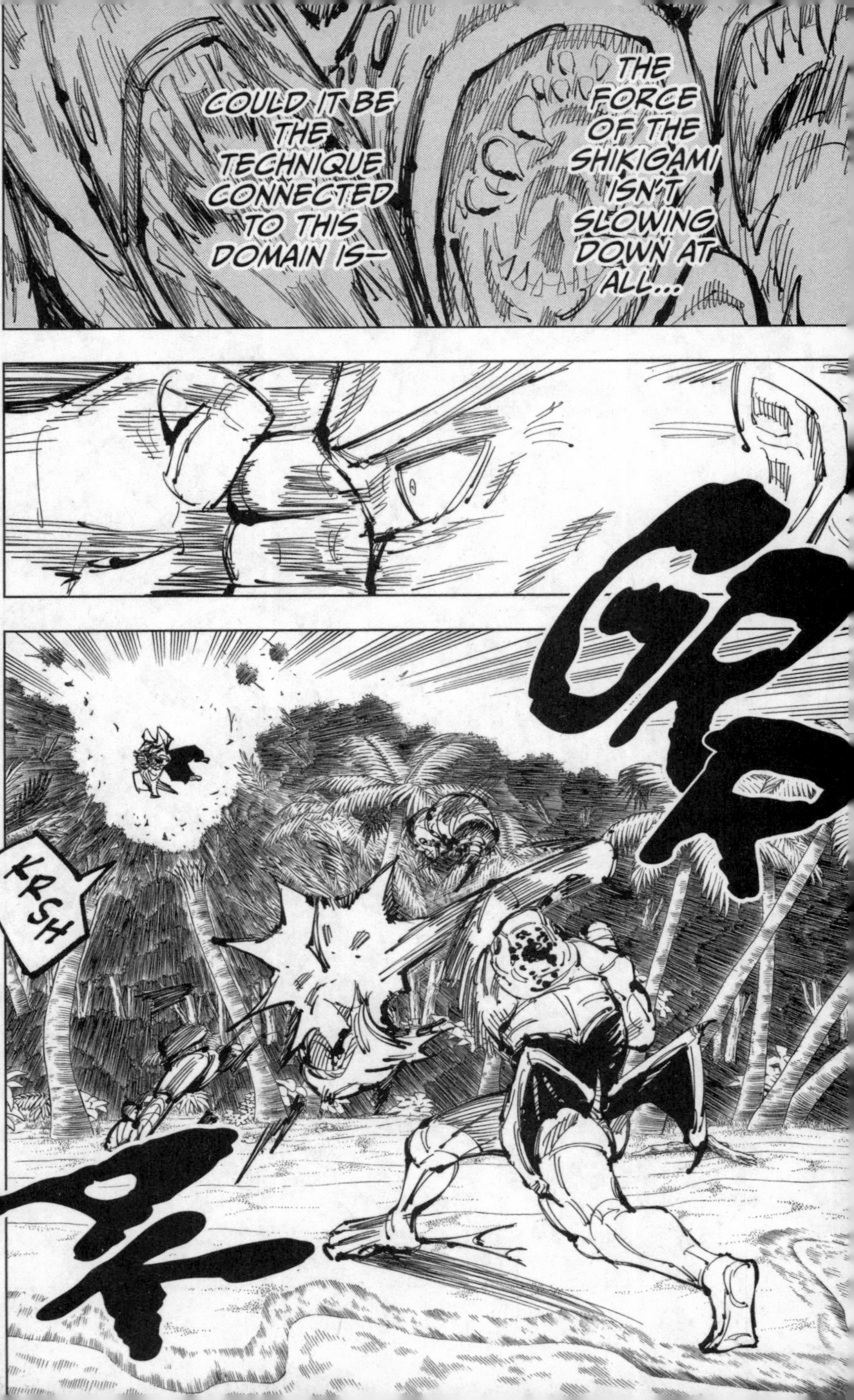
THE FORCE OF THE SHIKIGAMI ISN'T SLOWING DOWN AT ALL...
COULD IT BE THE TECHNIQUE CONNECTED TO THIS DOMAIN IS—
CRAK
KRSH

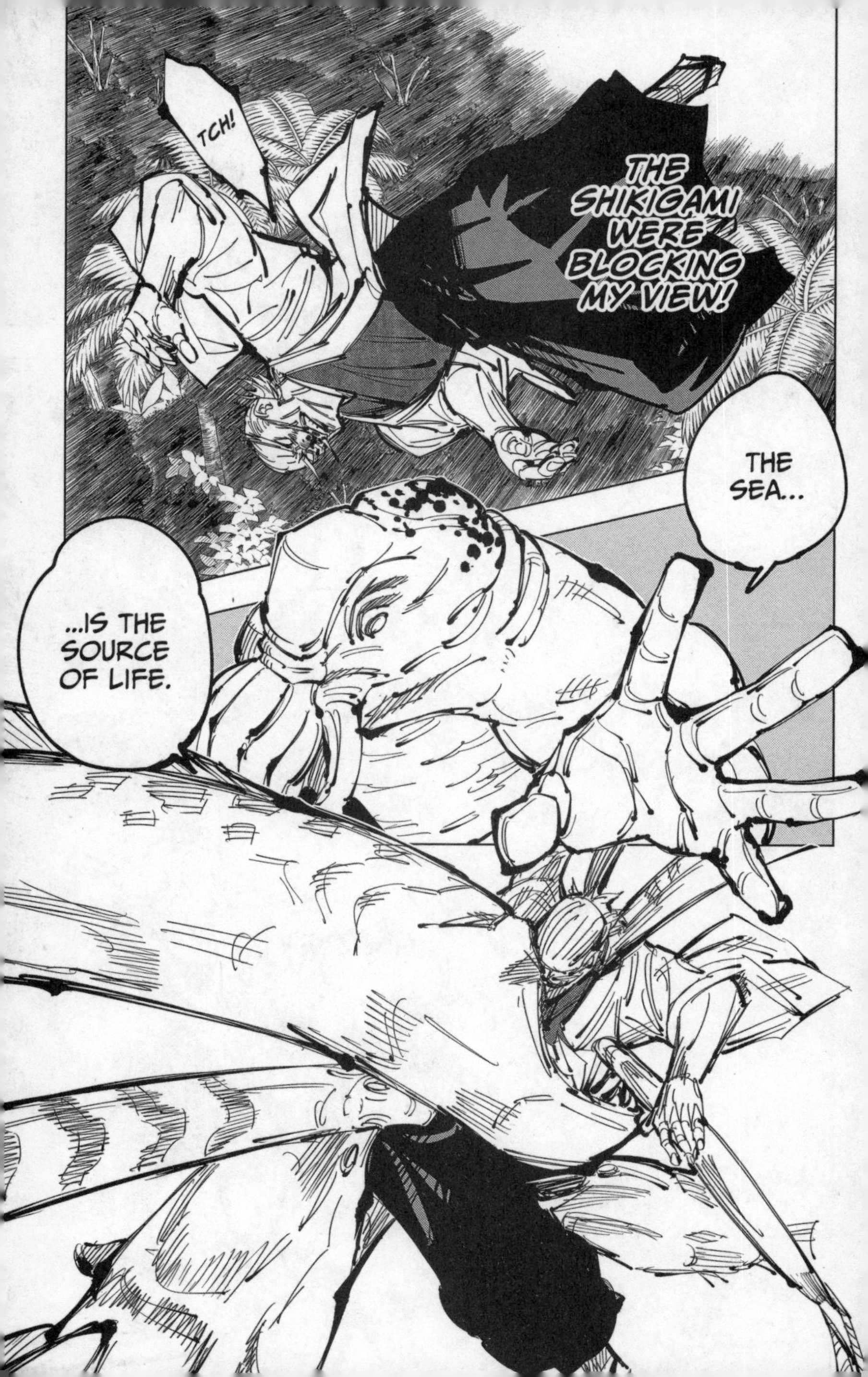
TCH!
THE SHIKIGAMI WERE BLOCKING MY VIEW!
THE SEA...
...IS THE SOURCE OF LIFE.

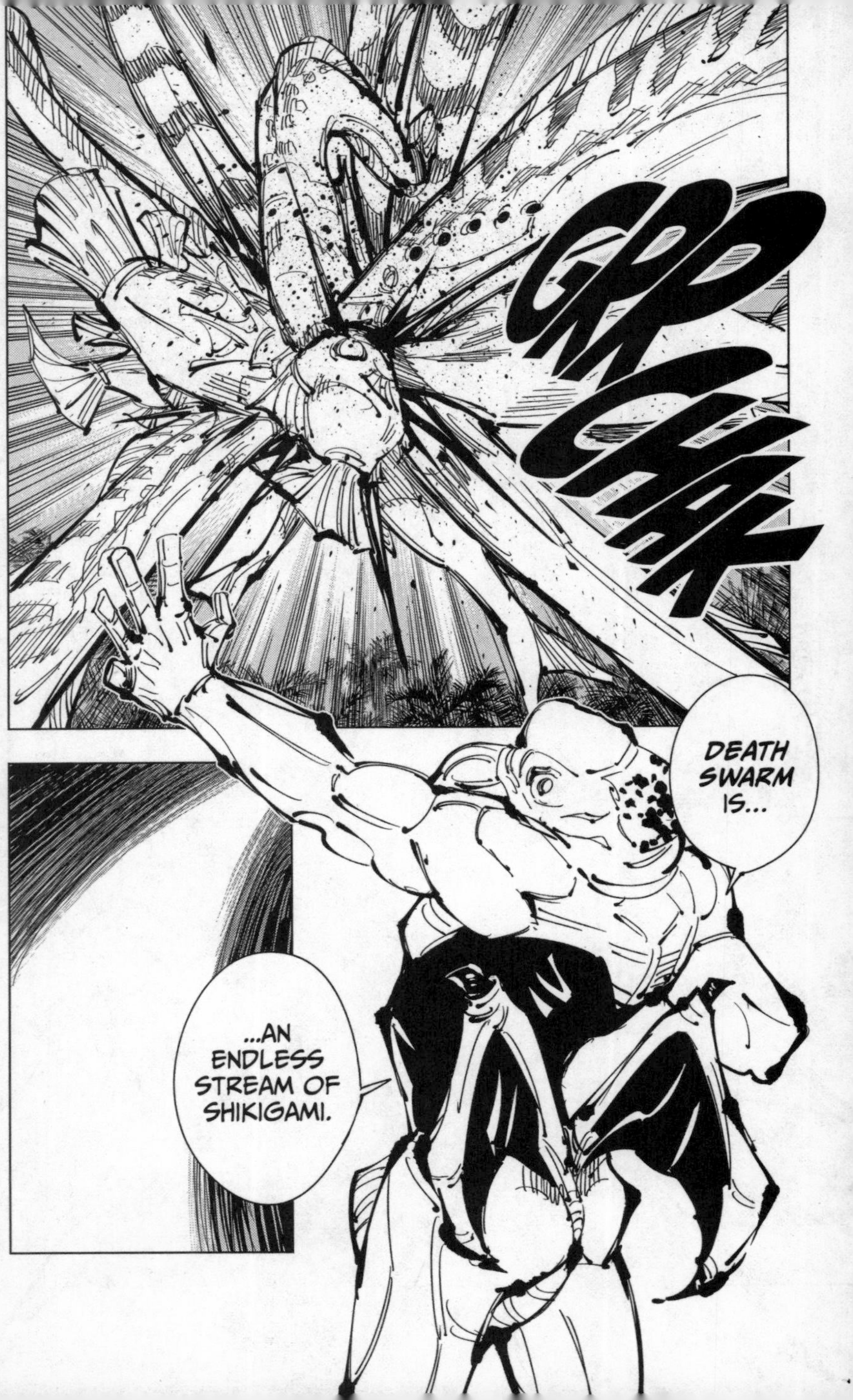
GRR GHAK
DEATH SWARM IS...
...AN ENDLESS STREAM OF SHIKIGAMI.

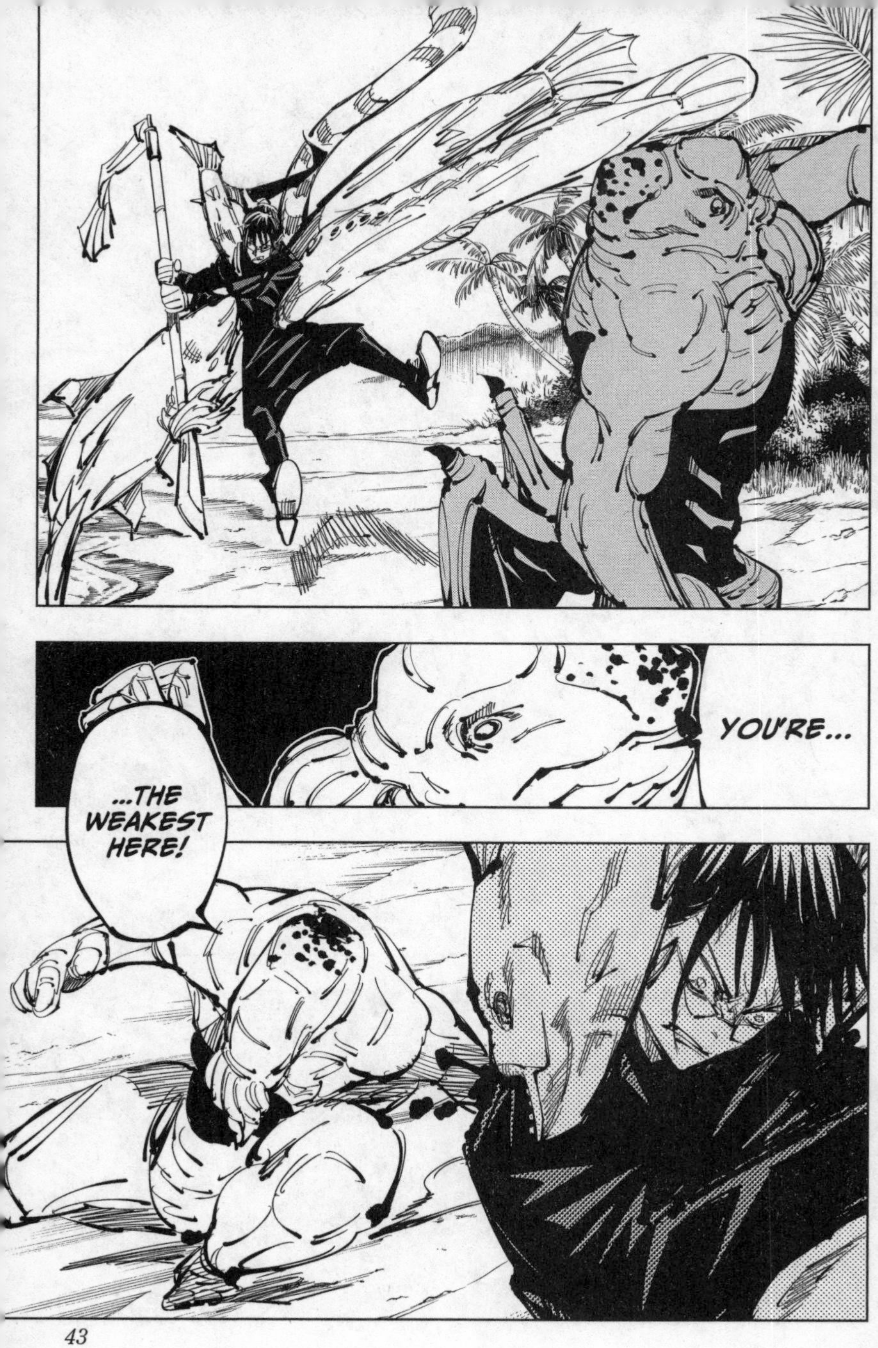
YOU'RE...
...THE WEAKEST HERE!

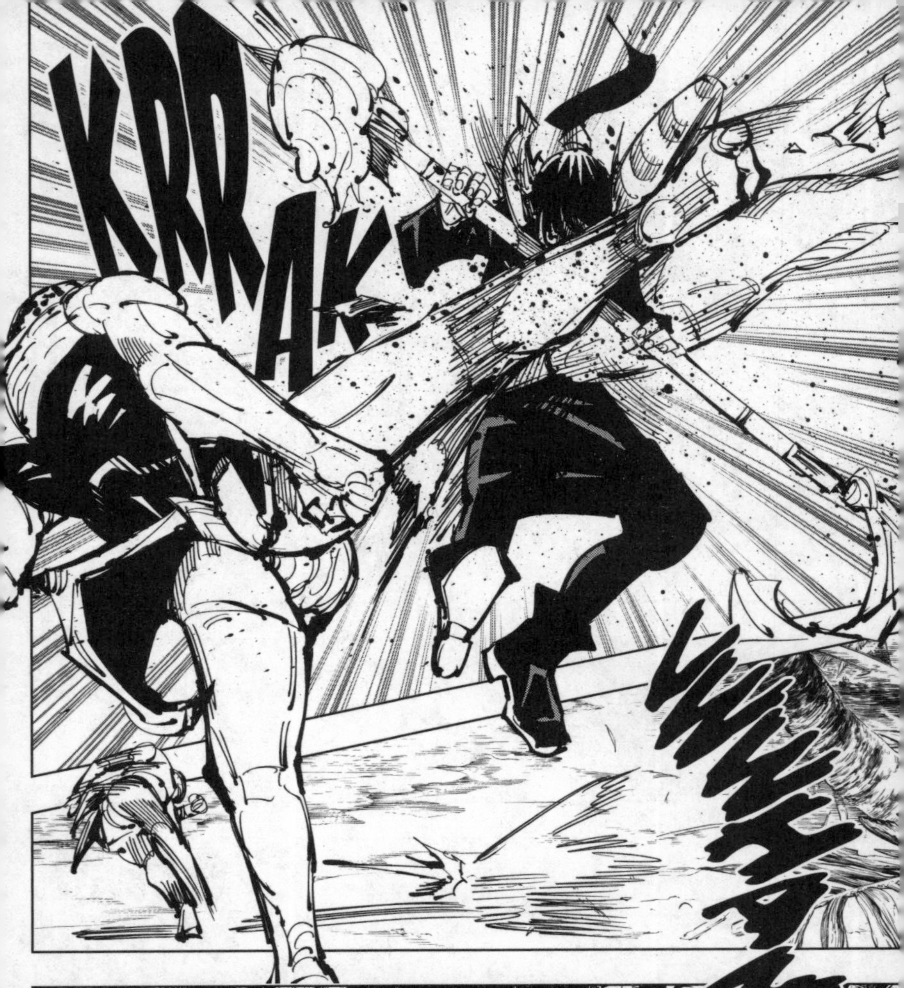
KRRAK
VWWWHAM...
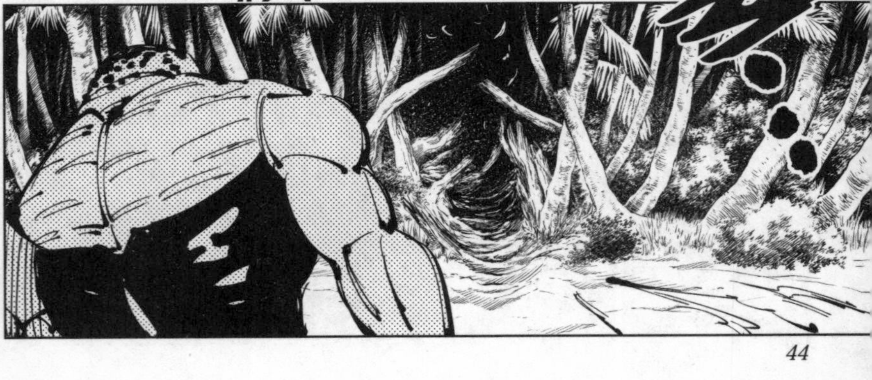

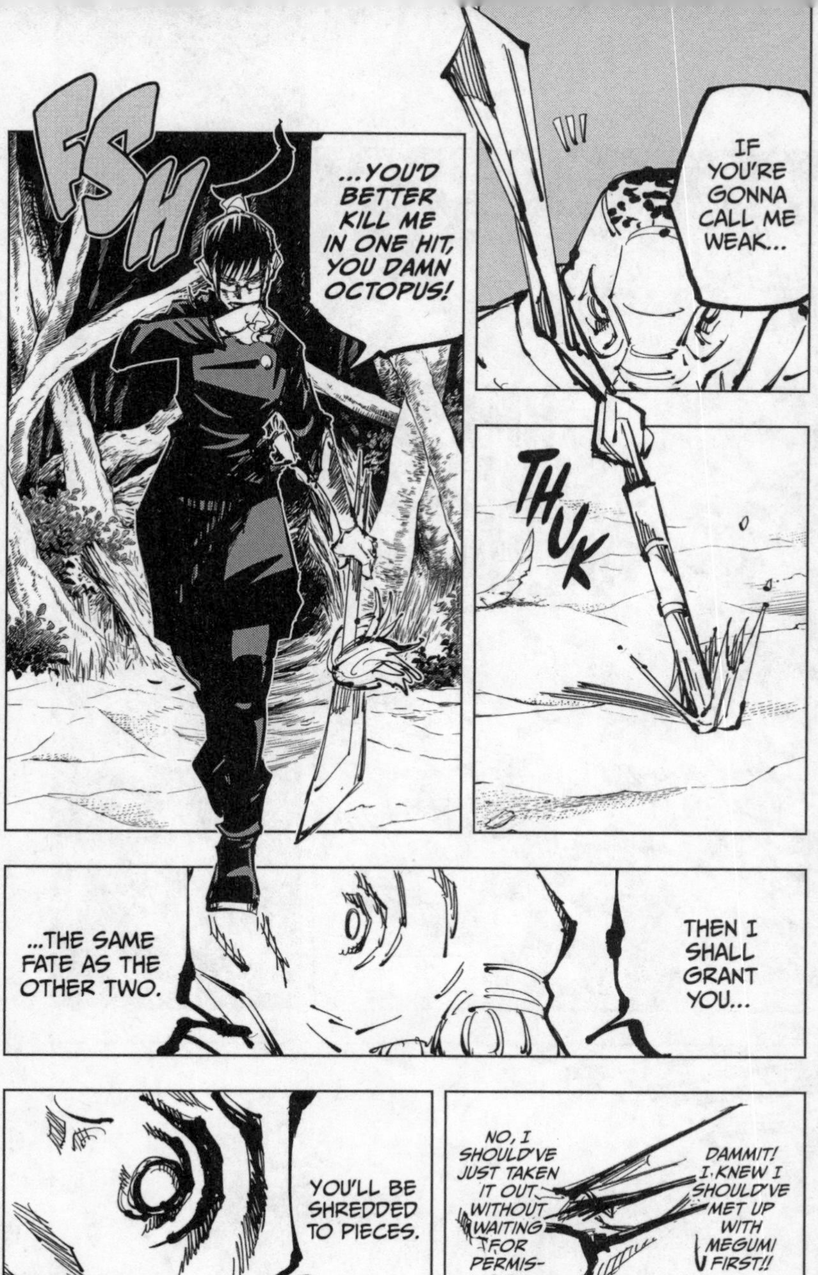
!!!
IF YOU'RE GONNA CALL ME WEAK...
THUK
FSH
...YOU'D BETTER KILL ME IN ONE HIT, YOU DAMN OCTOPUS!
THEN I SHALL GRANT YOU...
...THE SAME FATE AS THE OTHER TWO.
DAMMIT! I KNEW I SHOULD'VE MET UP WITH MEGUMI FIRST!!
NO, I SHOULD'VE JUST TAKEN IT OUT WITHOUT WAITING FOR PERMISSION.
YOU'LL BE SHREDDED TO PIECES.

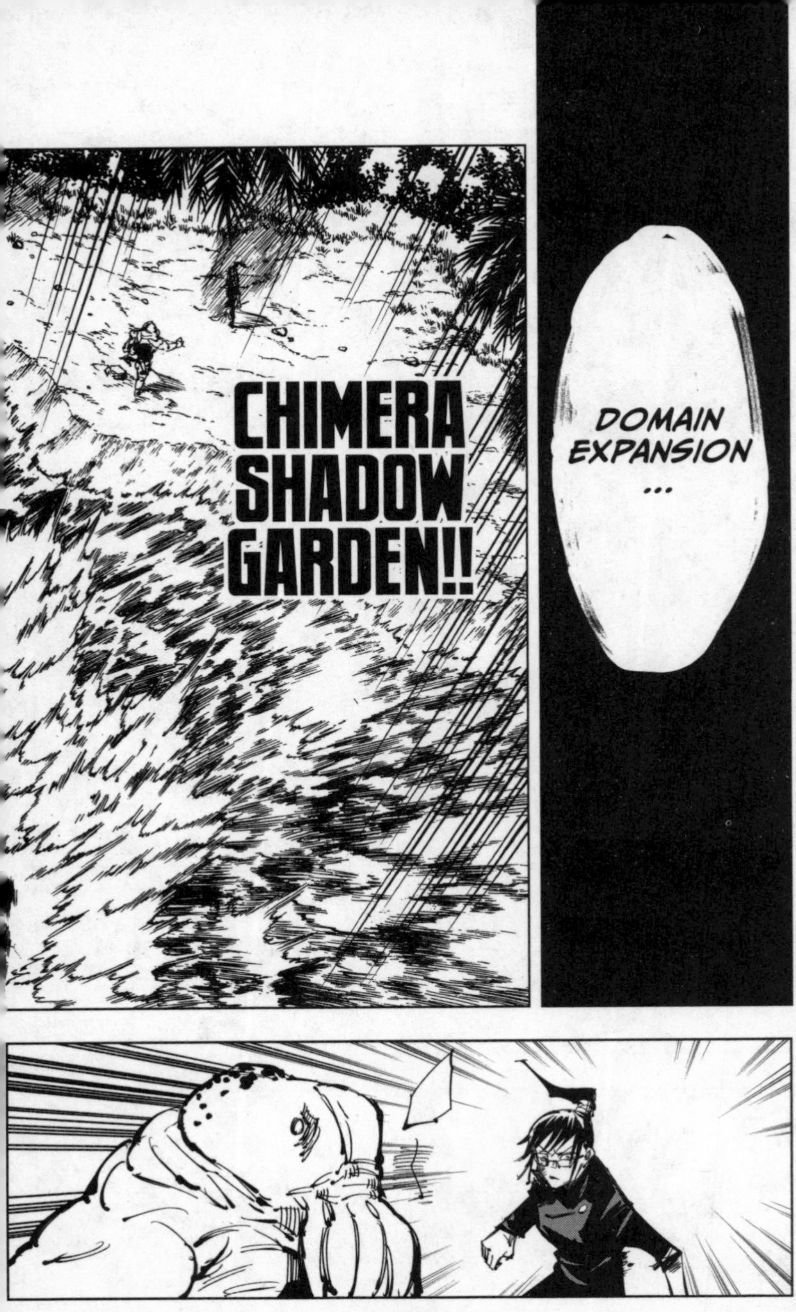
DOMAIN EXPANSION ...
CHIMERA SHADOW GARDEN!!

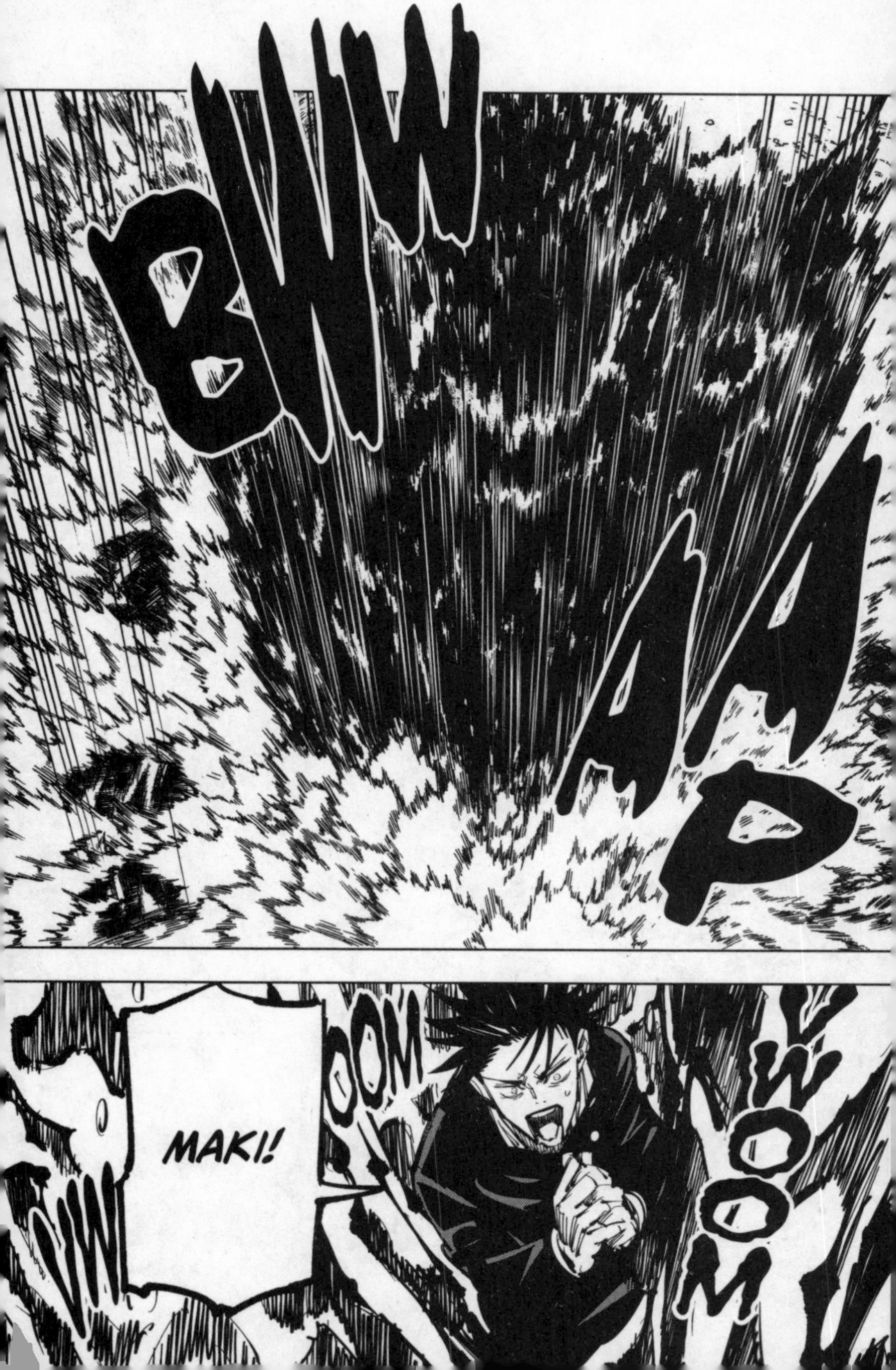
WOOOM
MAKI!

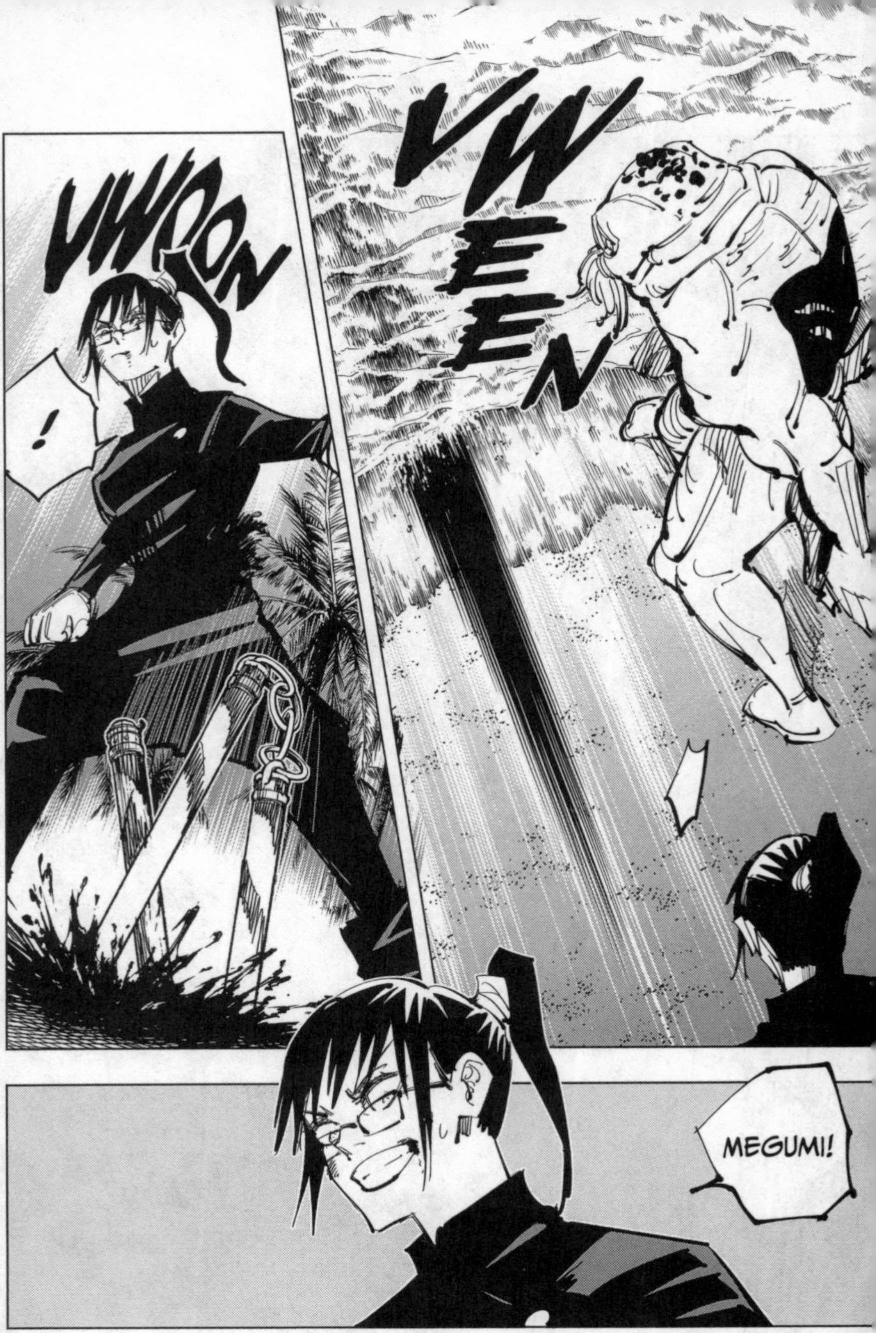
VWEEEN
VWOON
!
MEGUMI!

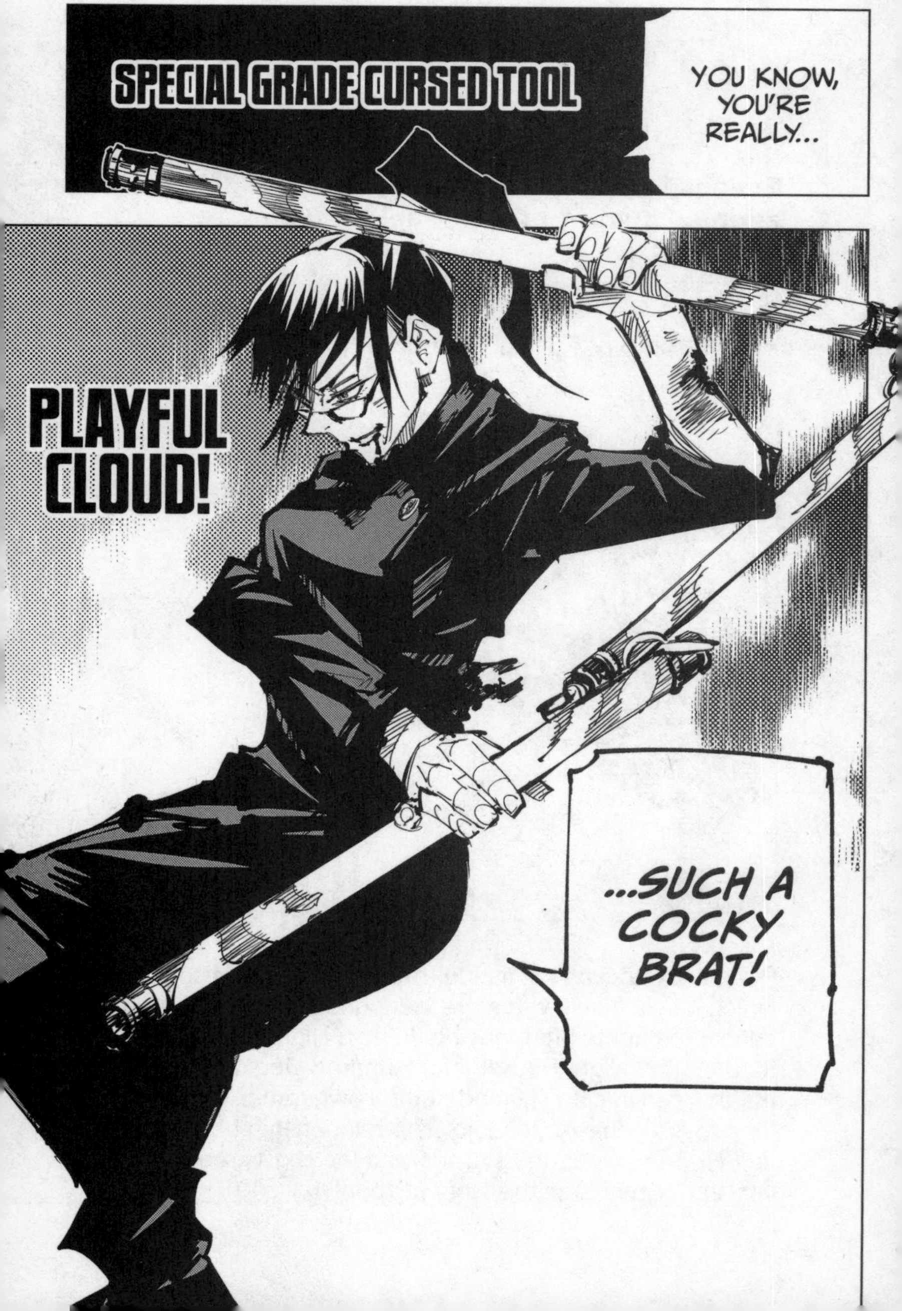
YOU KNOW, YOU'RE REALLY...
SPECIAL GRADE CURSED TOOL
PLAYFUL CLOUD!
...SUCH A COCKY BRAT!

Scenes I was planning to address but forgot about until now, part 2

• Ownership of Playful Cloud

Playful Cloud was left inside Papaguro's cursed spirit, which has the ability to store weapons, and Geto used it in critical moments after leaving Jujutsu High. Gojo reclaimed it during the Night Parade of a Hundred Demons (vol. 0), but the Zen'in clan claimed rightful ownership. Now it's on loan to Maki thanks to Gojo. The relationship between Jujutsu High weapons storage and the Big Three Families will show up later in the story. (Probably.)

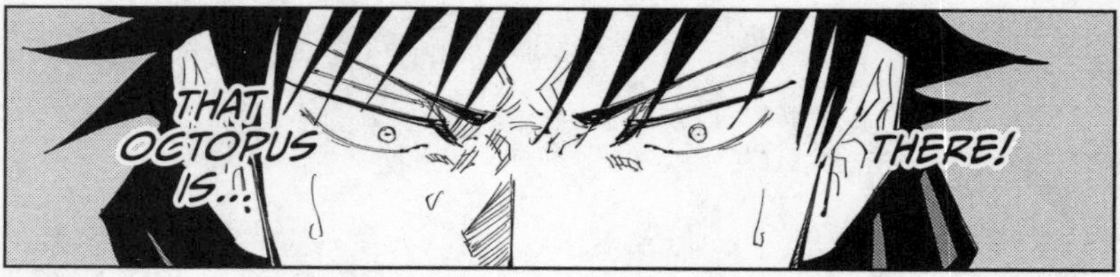
THERE!
THAT OCTOPUS IS...!

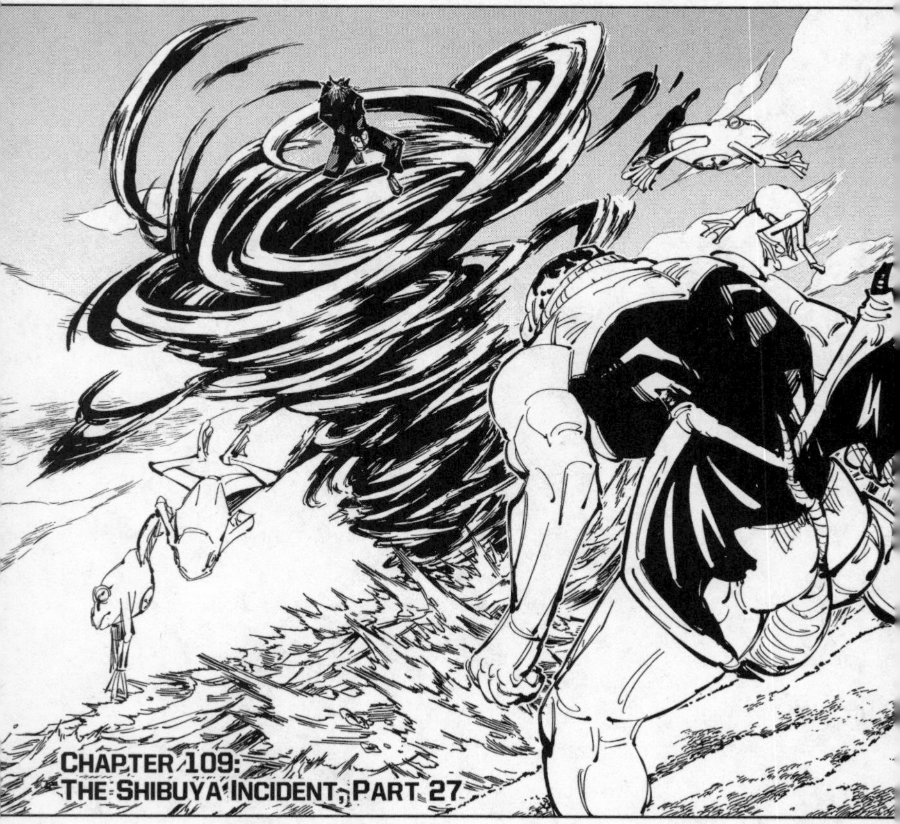
CHAPTER 109:
THE SHIBUYA INCIDENT, PART 27

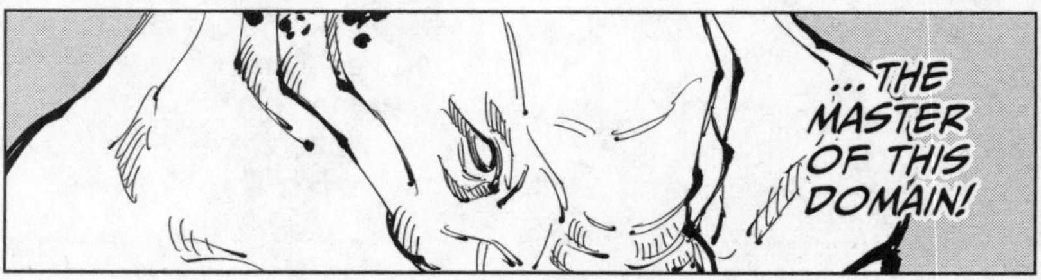
...THE MASTER OF THIS DOMAIN!

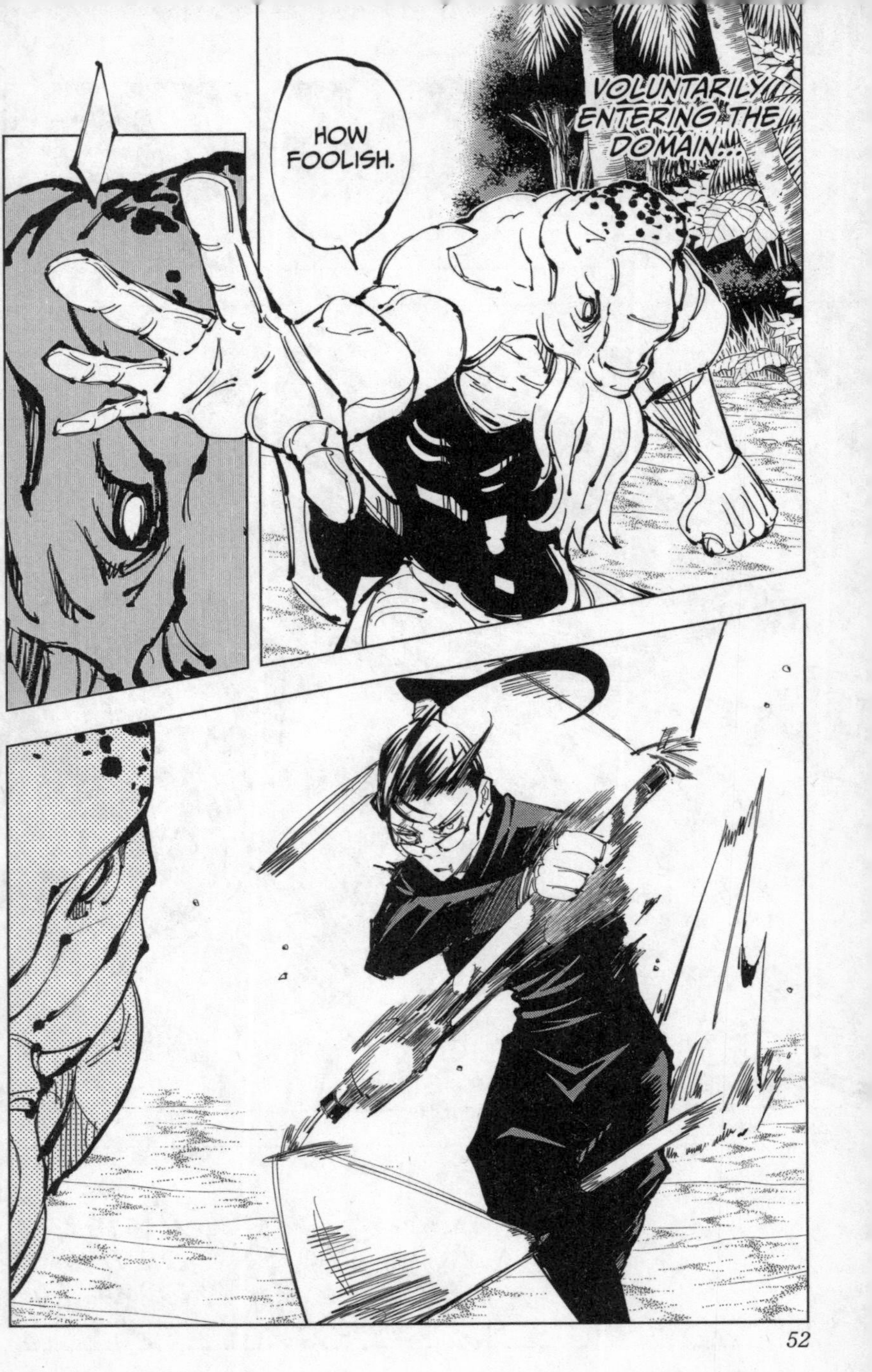
VOLUNTARILY ENTERING THE DOMAIN...
HOW FOOLISH.

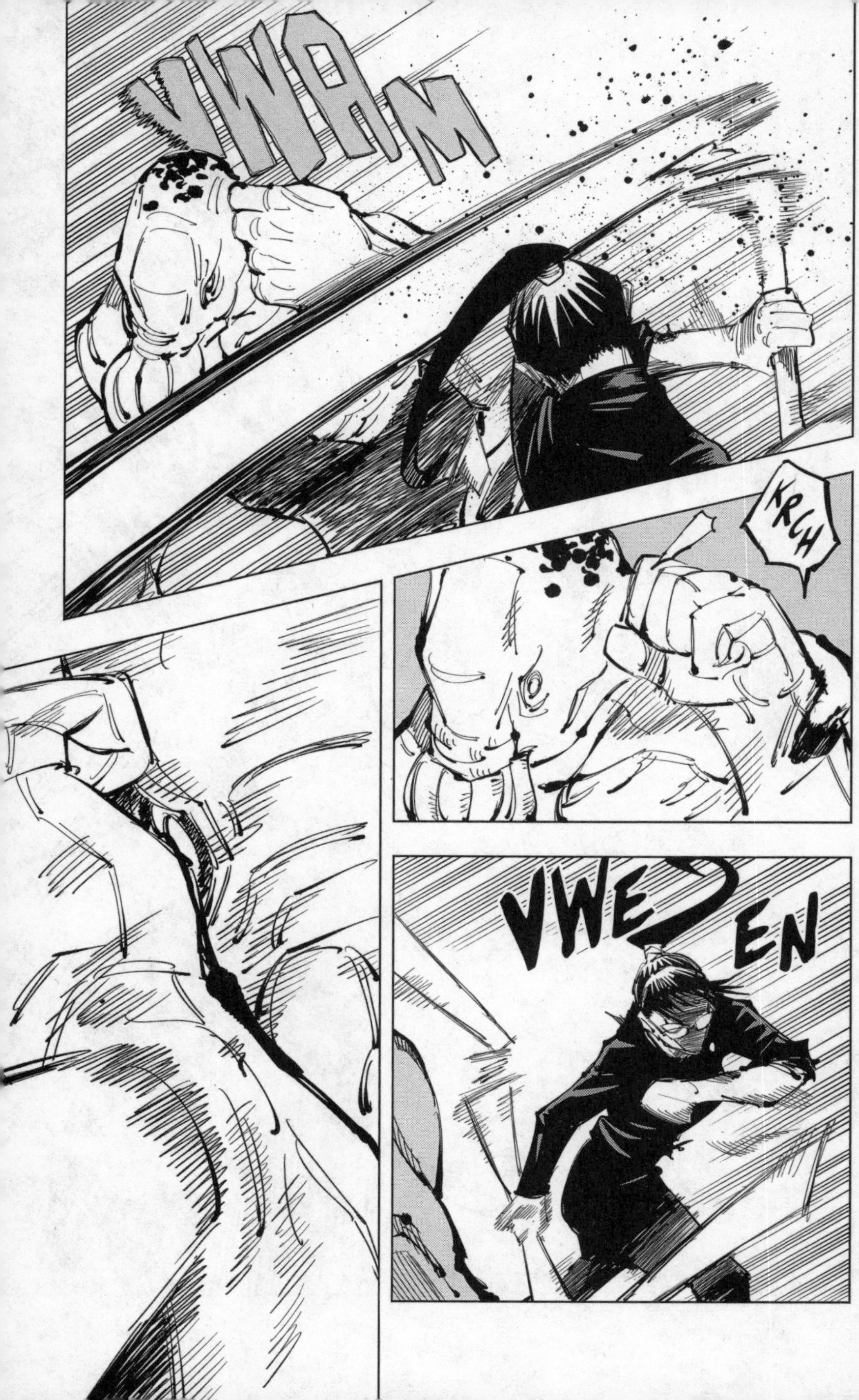
VWAM
KRCH
VWE EN

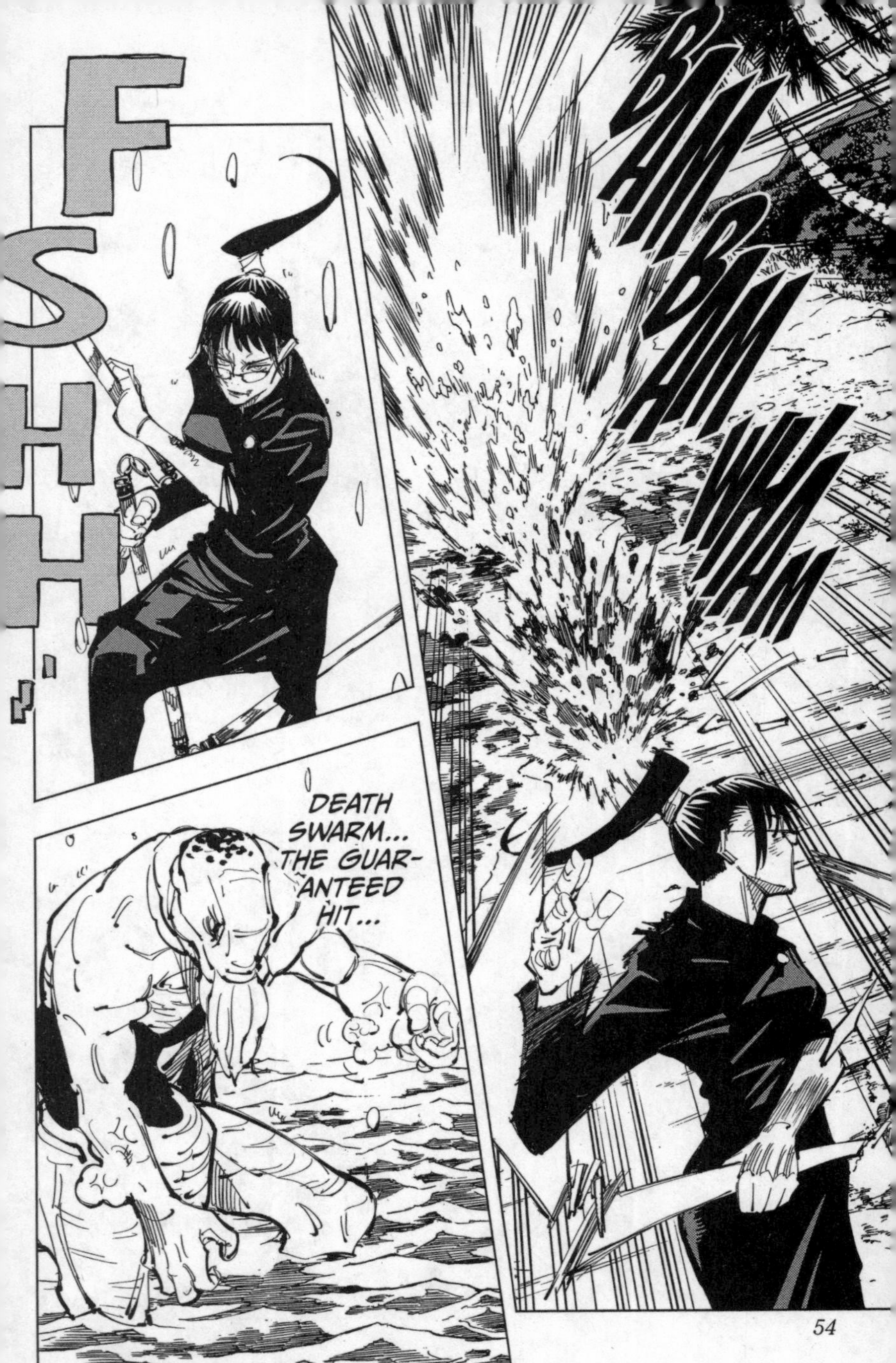
BABAMM
FSHHH
DEATH SWARM... THE GUARANTEED HIT...

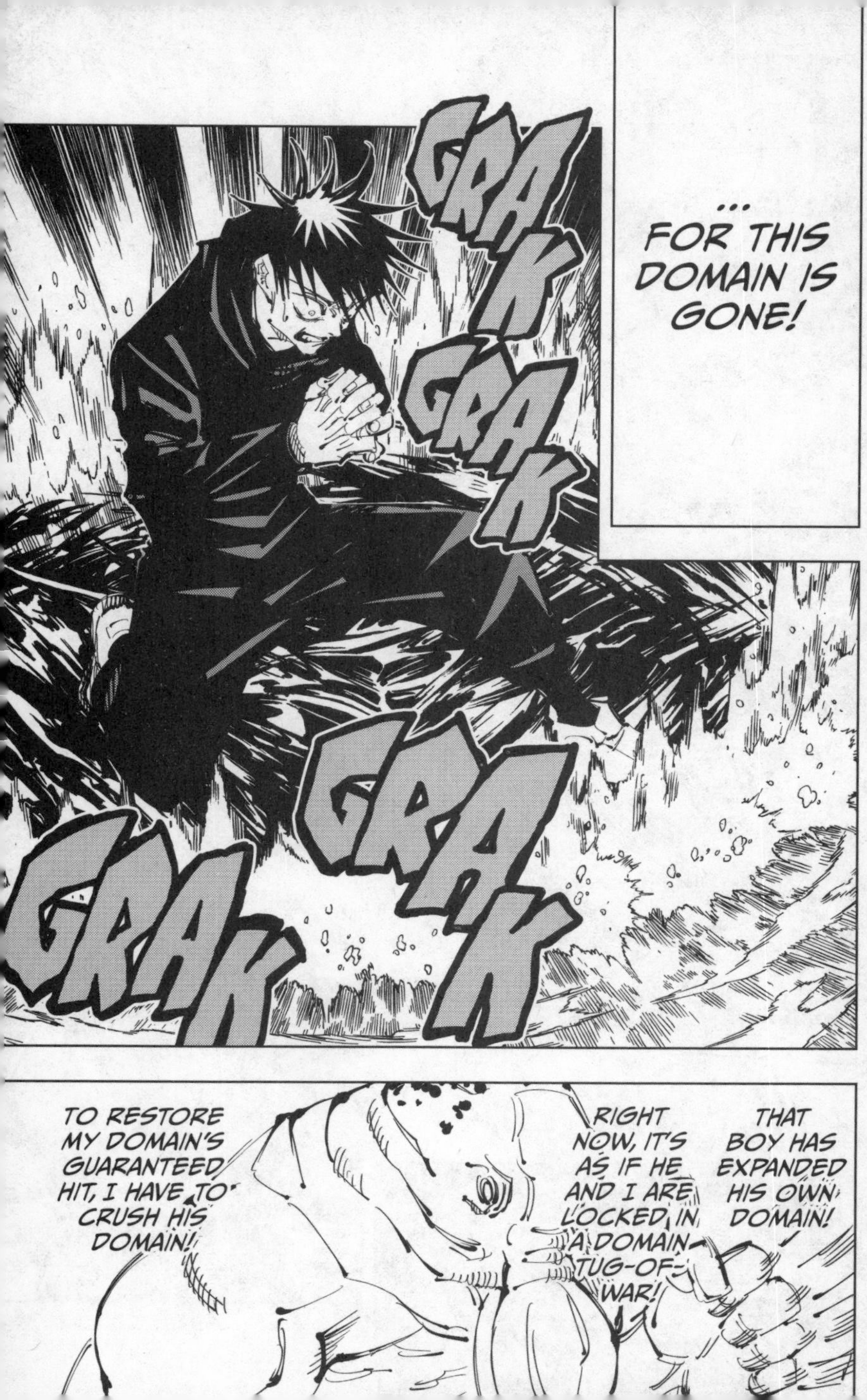

...FOR THIS DOMAIN IS GONE!
GRAK
GRAK
GRAK
GRAK
THAT BOY HAS EXPANDED HIS OWN DOMAIN!
RIGHT NOW, IT'S AS IF HE AND I ARE LOCKED IN A DOMAIN TUG-OF-WAR!
TO RESTORE MY DOMAIN'S GUARANTEED HIT, I HAVE TO CRUSH HIS DOMAIN!

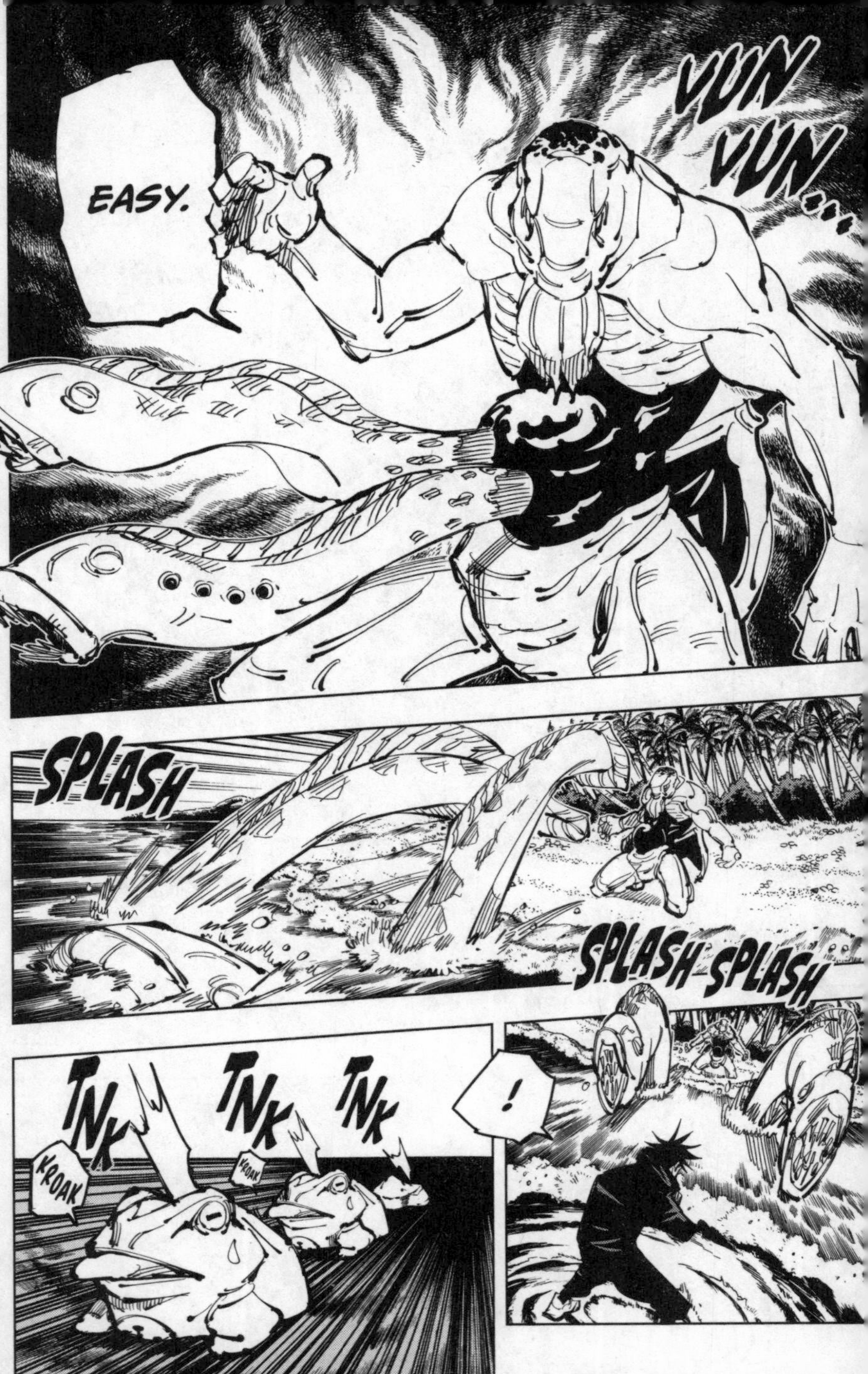
VUN VUN...
EASY.
SPLASH
SPLASH SPLASH
!
TNK
KROAK
TNK
KROAK
TNK

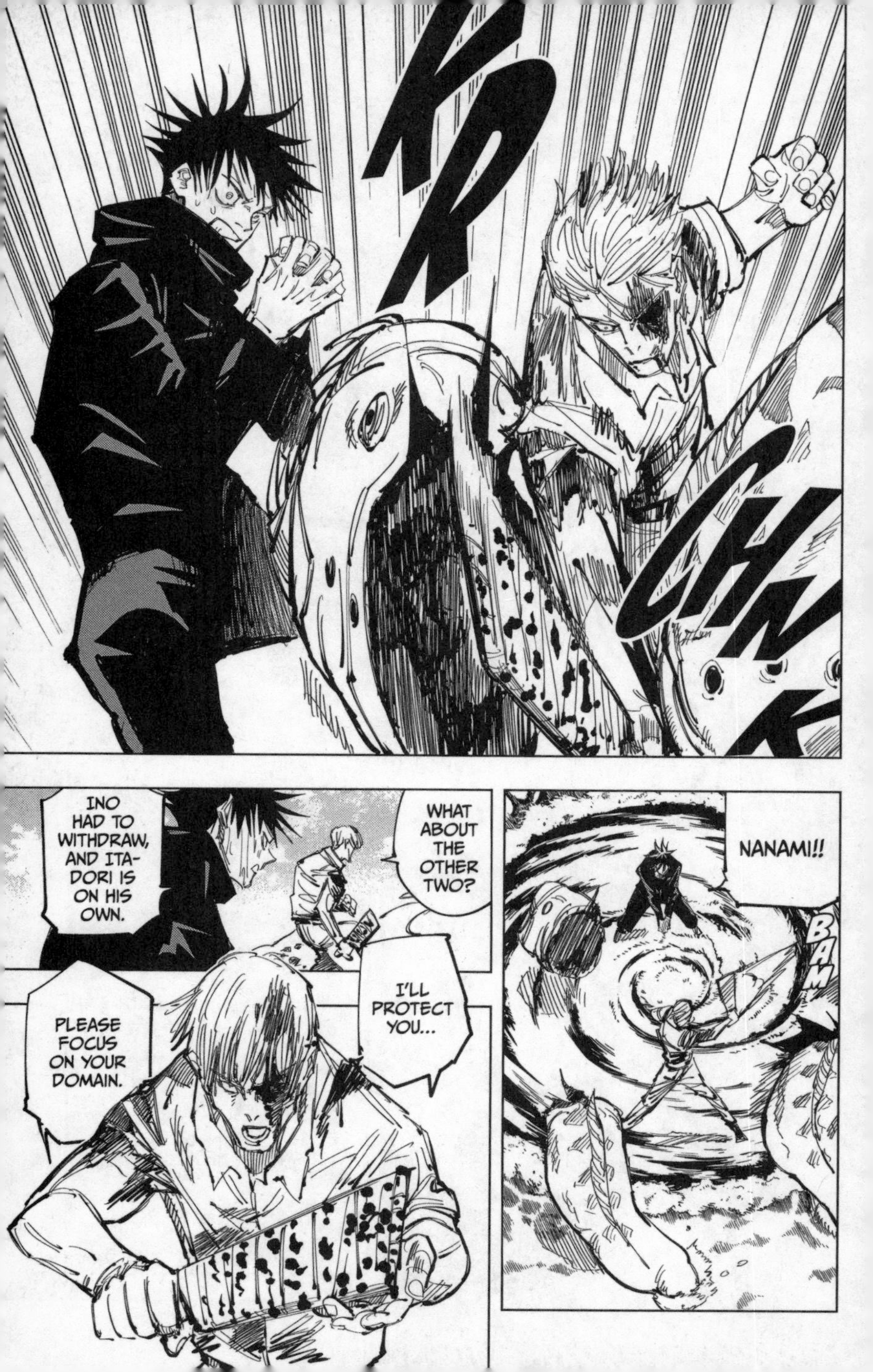

KR
CHNK
NANAMI!!
BAM
WHAT ABOUT THE OTHER TWO?
INO HAD TO WITHDRAW, AND ITA-DORI IS ON HIS OWN.
I'LL PROTECT YOU...
PLEASE FOCUS ON YOUR DOMAIN.

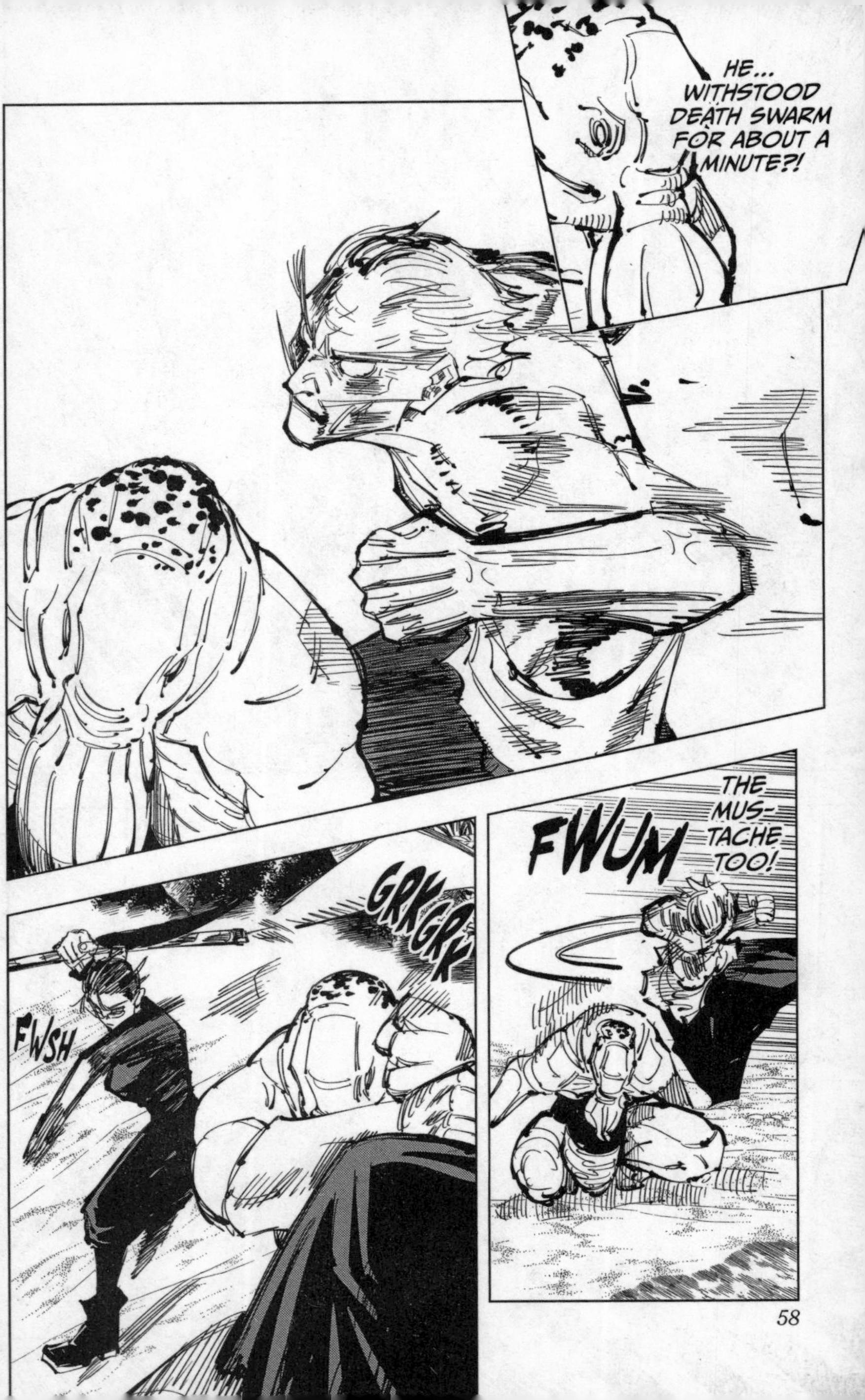
HE... WITHSTOOD DEATH SWARM FOR ABOUT A MINUTE?!
THE MUS-TACHE TOO!
FWUM
GRKGRK
FWSH

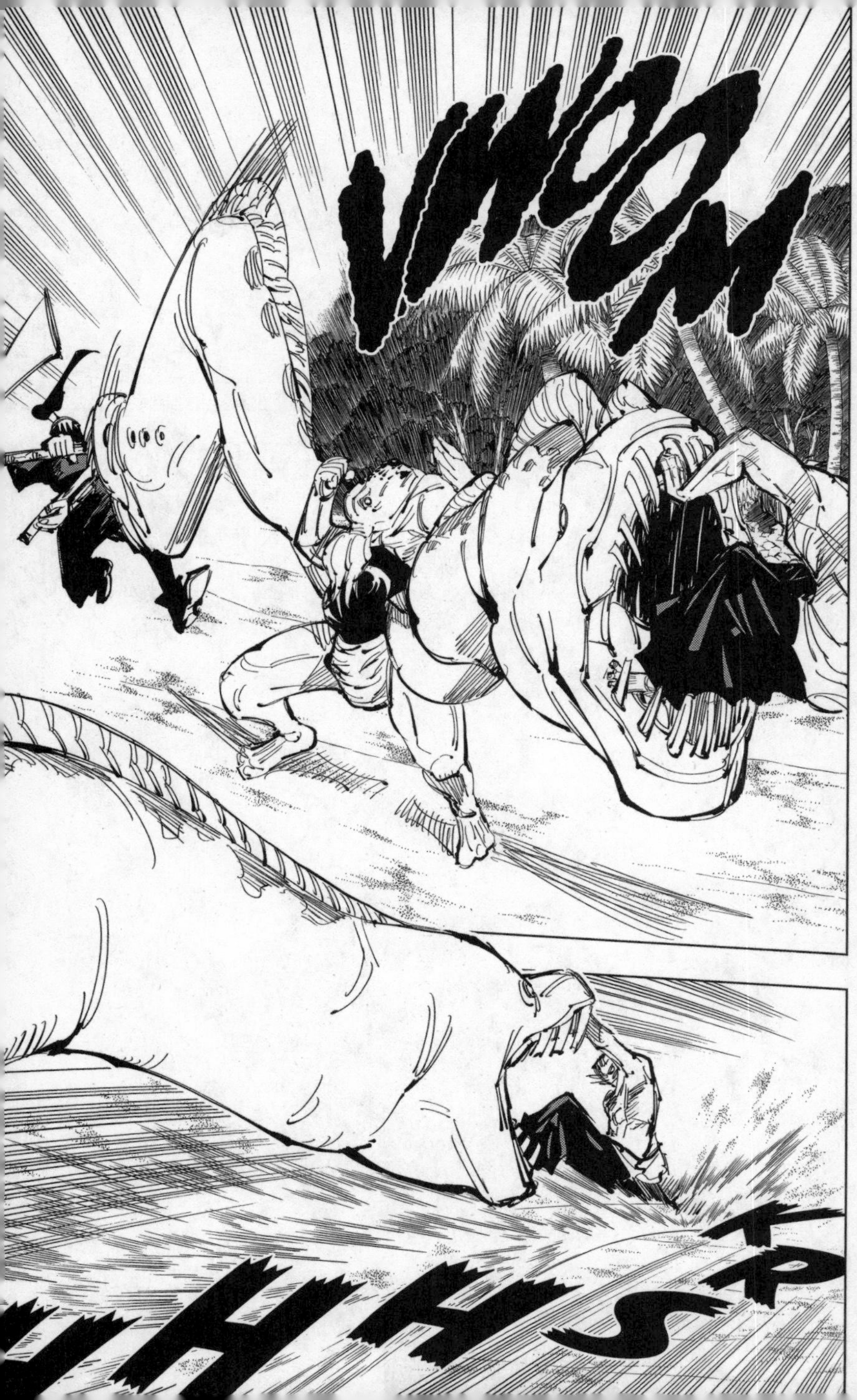
VWOOM
KRSHHH

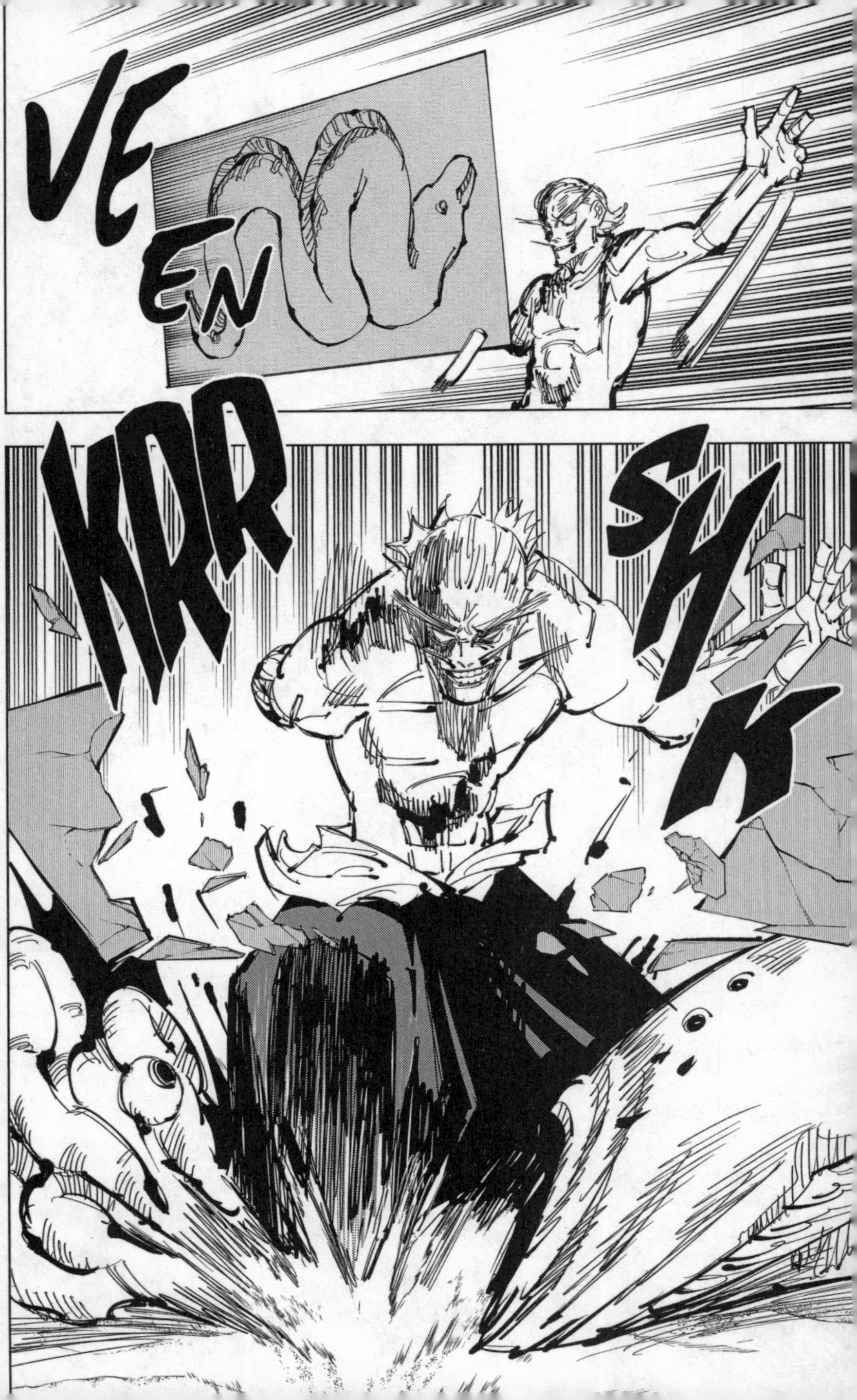
VEEN
KRR
SHK

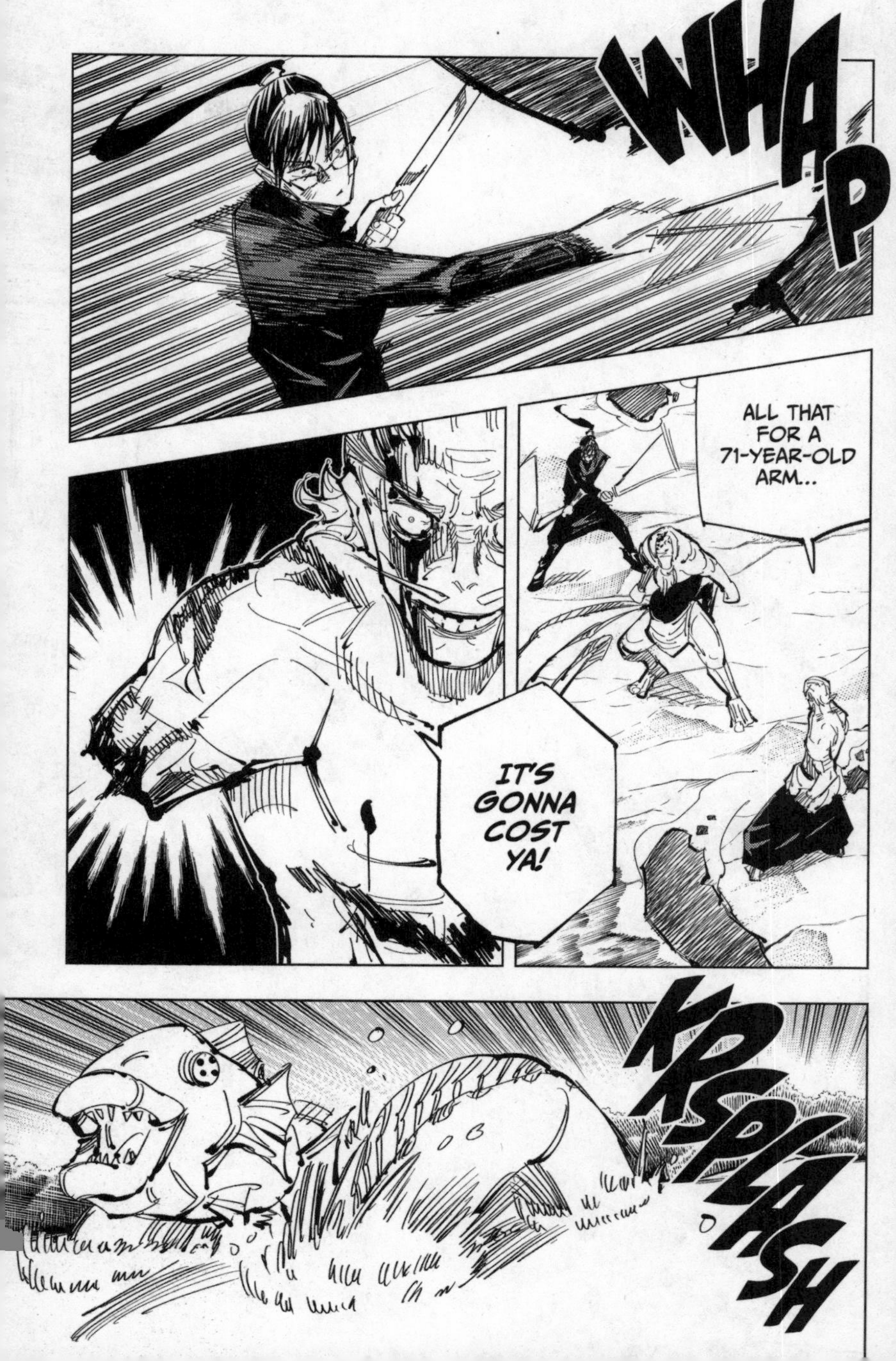
WHAP
ALL THAT FOR A 71-YEAR-OLD ARM...
IT'S GONNA COST YA!
KRSPLASH

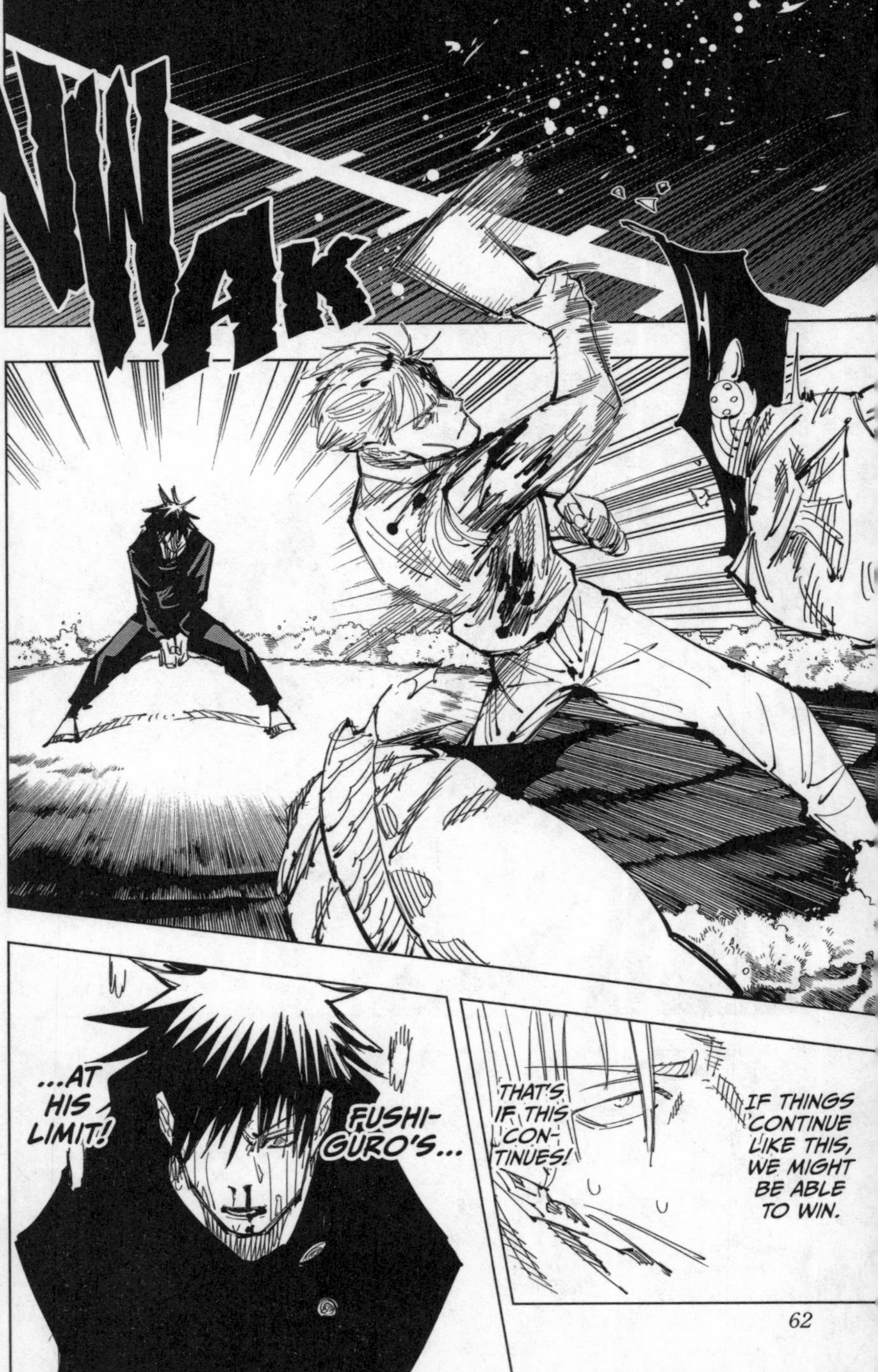
WHAK
IF THINGS CONTINUE LIKE THIS, WE MIGHT BE ABLE TO WIN.
THAT'S IF THIS CON-TINUES!
FUSHI-GURO'S...
...AT HIS LIMIT!

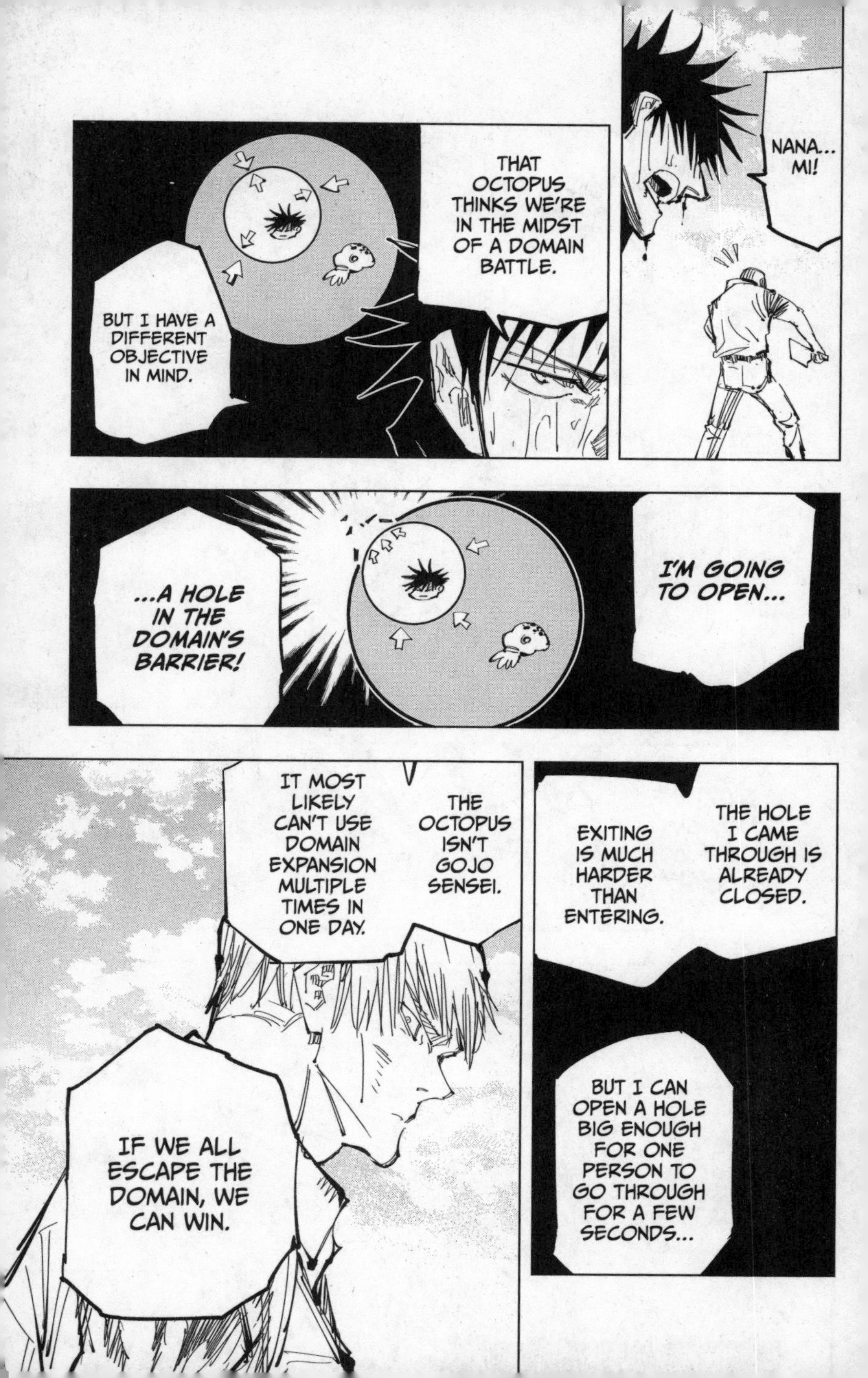
NANA... MI!
THAT OCTOPUS THINKS WE'RE IN THE MIDST OF A DOMAIN BATTLE.
BUT I HAVE A DIFFERENT OBJECTIVE IN MIND.
I'M GOING TO OPEN...
...A HOLE IN THE DOMAIN'S BARRIER!
THE HOLE I CAME THROUGH IS ALREADY CLOSED.
EXITING IS MUCH HARDER THAN ENTERING.
BUT I CAN OPEN A HOLE BIG ENOUGH FOR ONE PERSON TO GO THROUGH FOR A FEW SECONDS...
THE OCTOPUS ISN'T GOJO SENSEI.
IT MOST LIKELY CAN'T USE DOMAIN EXPANSION MULTIPLE TIMES IN ONE DAY.
IF WE ALL ESCAPE THE DOMAIN, WE CAN WIN.

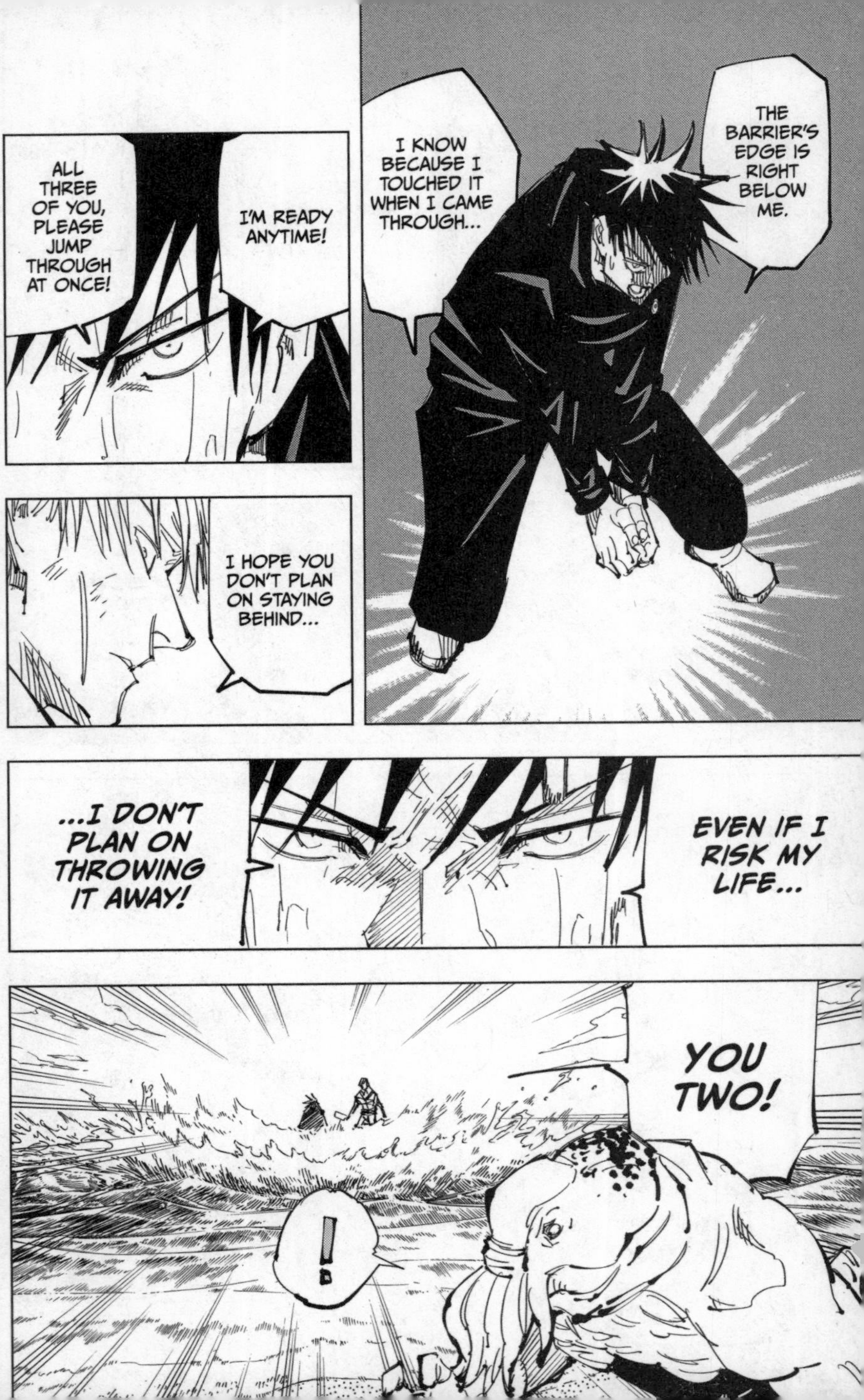
THE BARRIER'S EDGE IS RIGHT BELOW ME.
I KNOW BECAUSE I TOUCHED IT WHEN I CAME THROUGH...
I'M READY ANYTIME!
ALL THREE OF YOU, PLEASE JUMP THROUGH AT ONCE!
I HOPE YOU DON'T PLAN ON STAYING BEHIND...
EVEN IF I RISK MY LIFE...
...I DON'T PLAN ON THROWING IT AWAY!
YOU TWO!
!

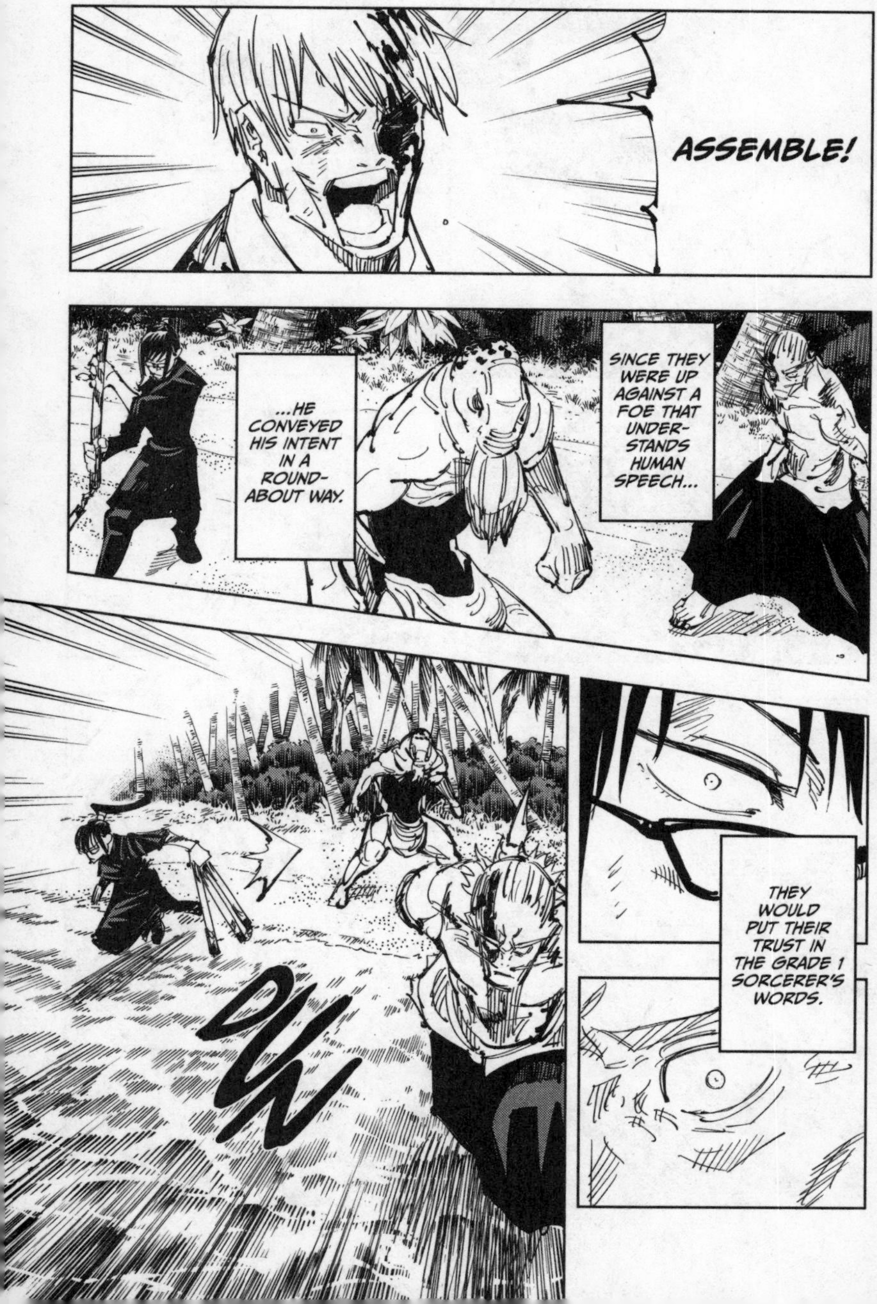
ASSEMBLE!
SINCE THEY WERE UP AGAINST A FOE THAT UNDER-STANDS HUMAN SPEECH...
...HE CONVEYED HIS INTENT IN A ROUND-ABOUT WAY.
THEY WOULD PUT THEIR TRUST IN THE GRADE 1 SORCERER'S WORDS.

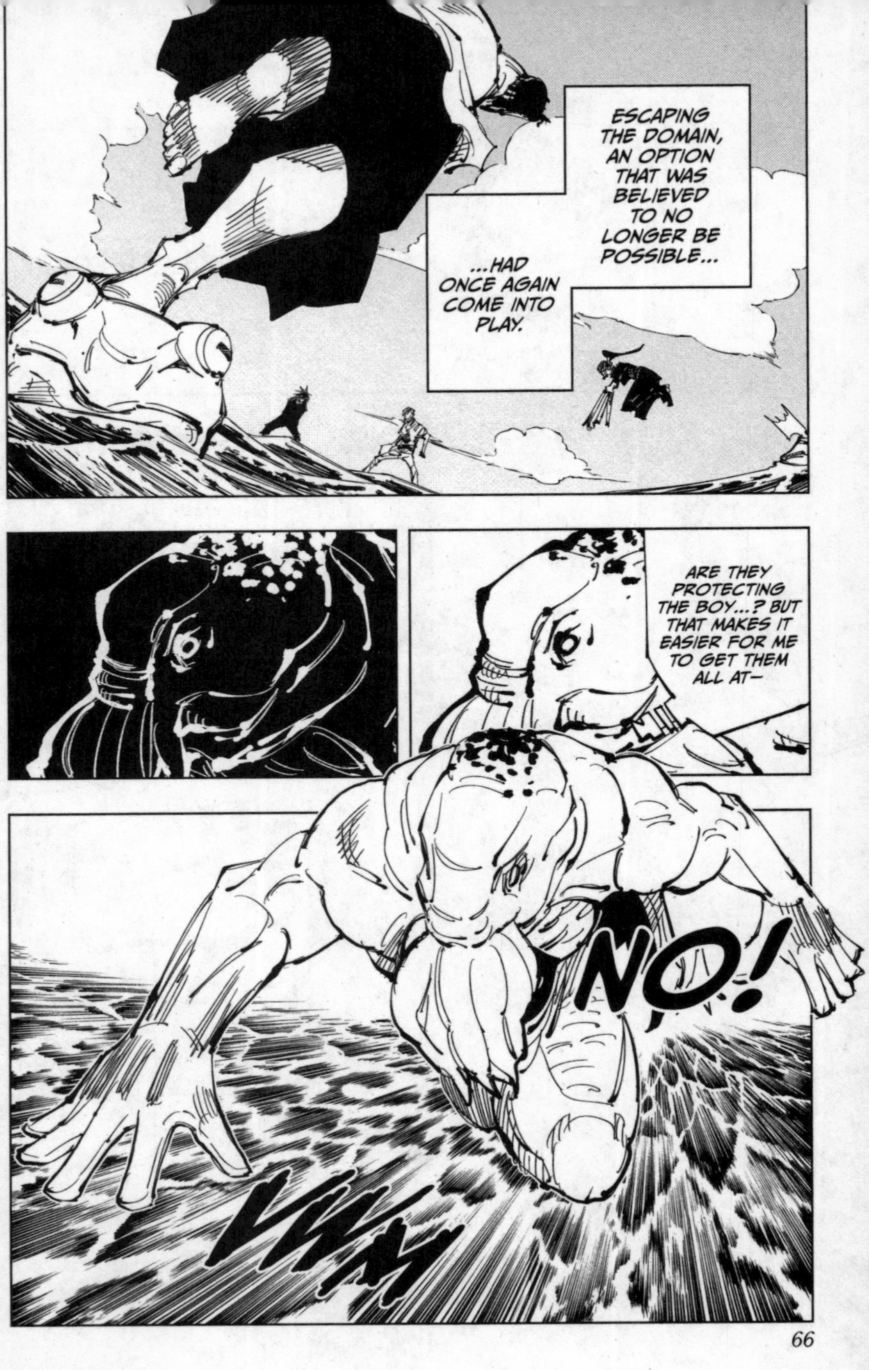
ESCAPING THE DOMAIN, AN OPTION THAT WAS BELIEVED TO NO LONGER BE POSSIBLE...
...HAD ONCE AGAIN COME INTO PLAY.
ARE THEY PROTECTING THE BOY...? BUT THAT MAKES IT EASIER FOR ME TO GET THEM ALL AT—
NO!

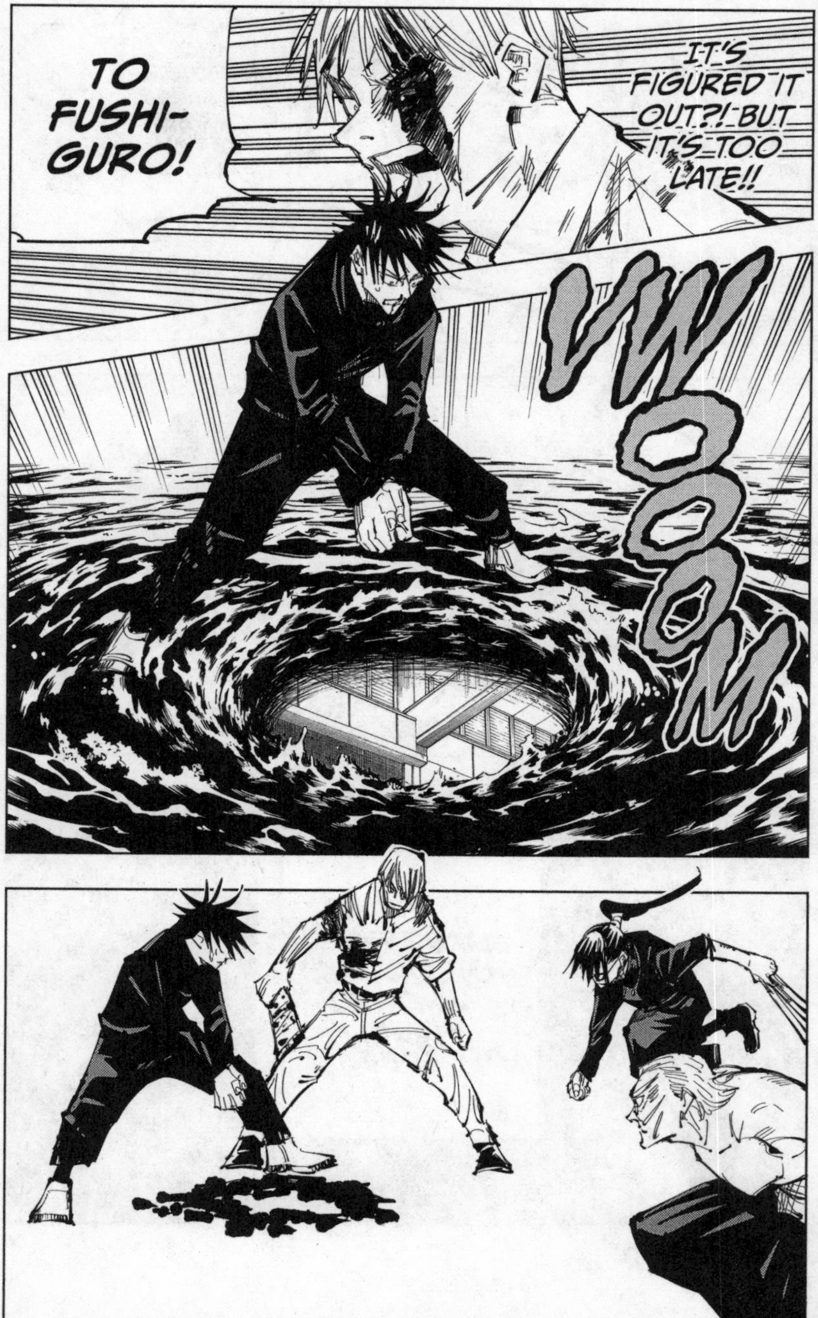
IT'S FIGURED IT OUT?! BUT IT'S TOO LATE!!
TO FUSHI-GURO!
VWOOOM

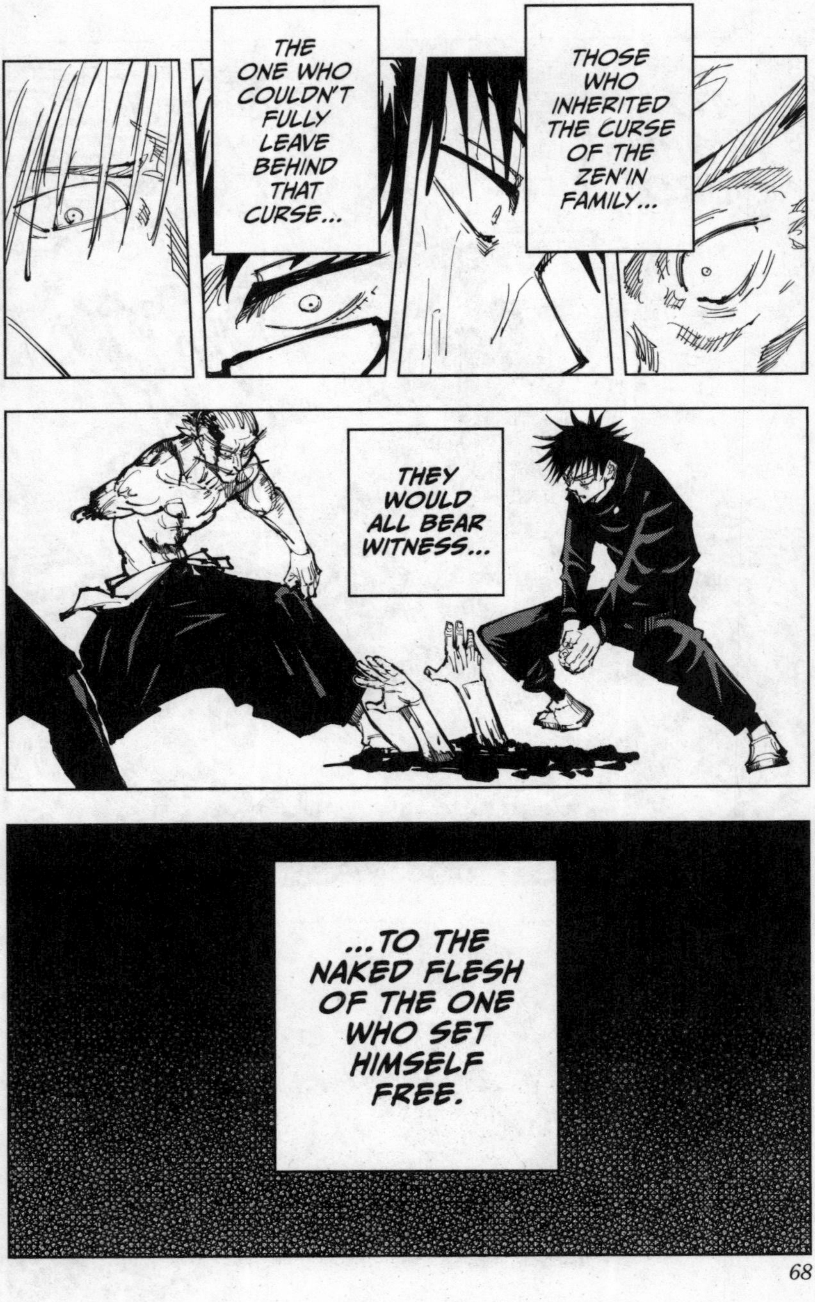
THOSE WHO INHERITED THE CURSE OF THE ZEN'IN FAMILY...
THE ONE WHO COULDN'T FULLY LEAVE BEHIND THAT CURSE...
THEY WOULD ALL BEAR WITNESS...
...TO THE NAKED FLESH OF THE ONE WHO SET HIMSELF FREE.

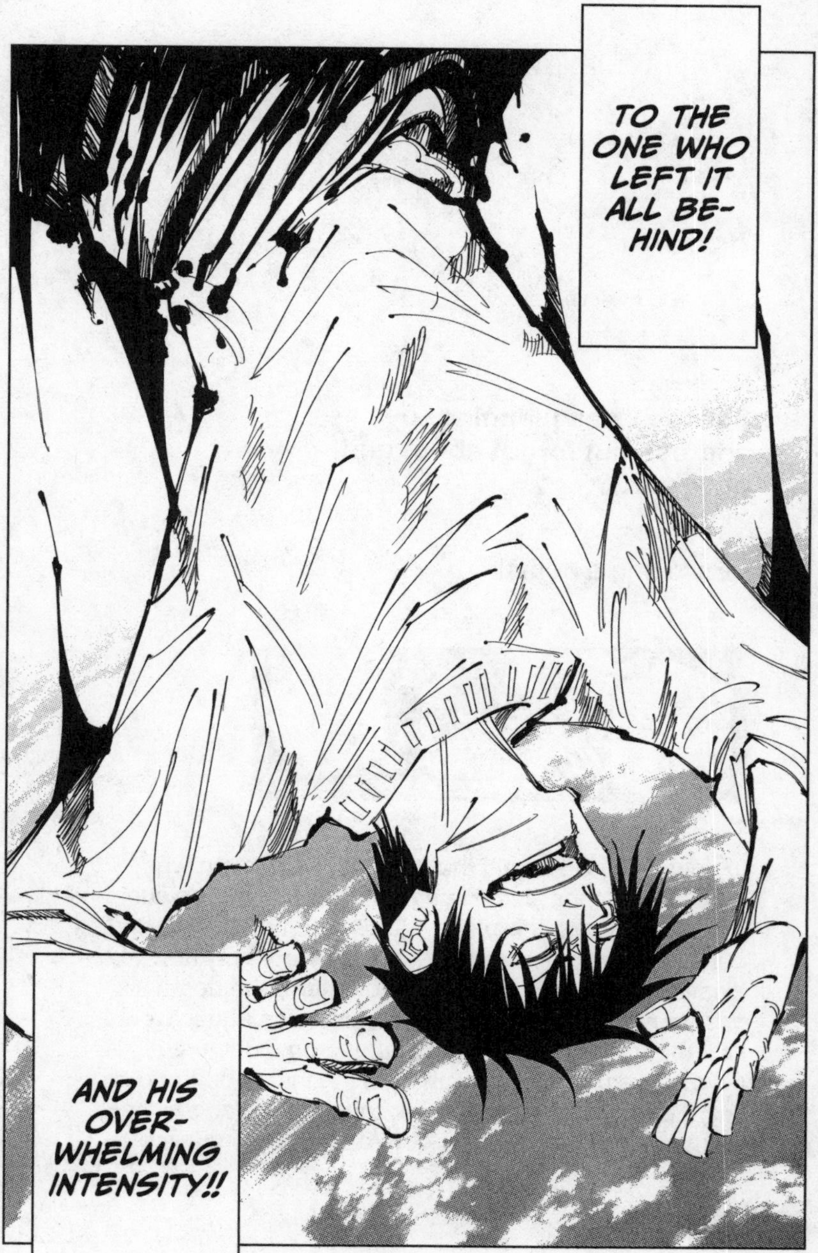
TO THE ONE WHO LEFT IT ALL BE-HIND!
AND HIS OVER-WHELMING INTENSITY!!

Scenes I was planning to address but forgot about until now, part 3

• Escaping a domain

In volume 2, Gojo said that escaping a domain was practically impossible. He meant that a domain's cubic volume appears completely different on the inside and outside, so someone trapped inside wouldn't know the location of the boundaries. (Also, before the domain's prisoner could figure it out, the can't-miss attack would kill that person; and even if that person did figure it out, it would be difficult to break from the inside out; and so on.) But as Fushiguro said, he touched the edge when he came through, so they were able to try out this plan.

Chapter 110: The Shibuya Incident, Part 28

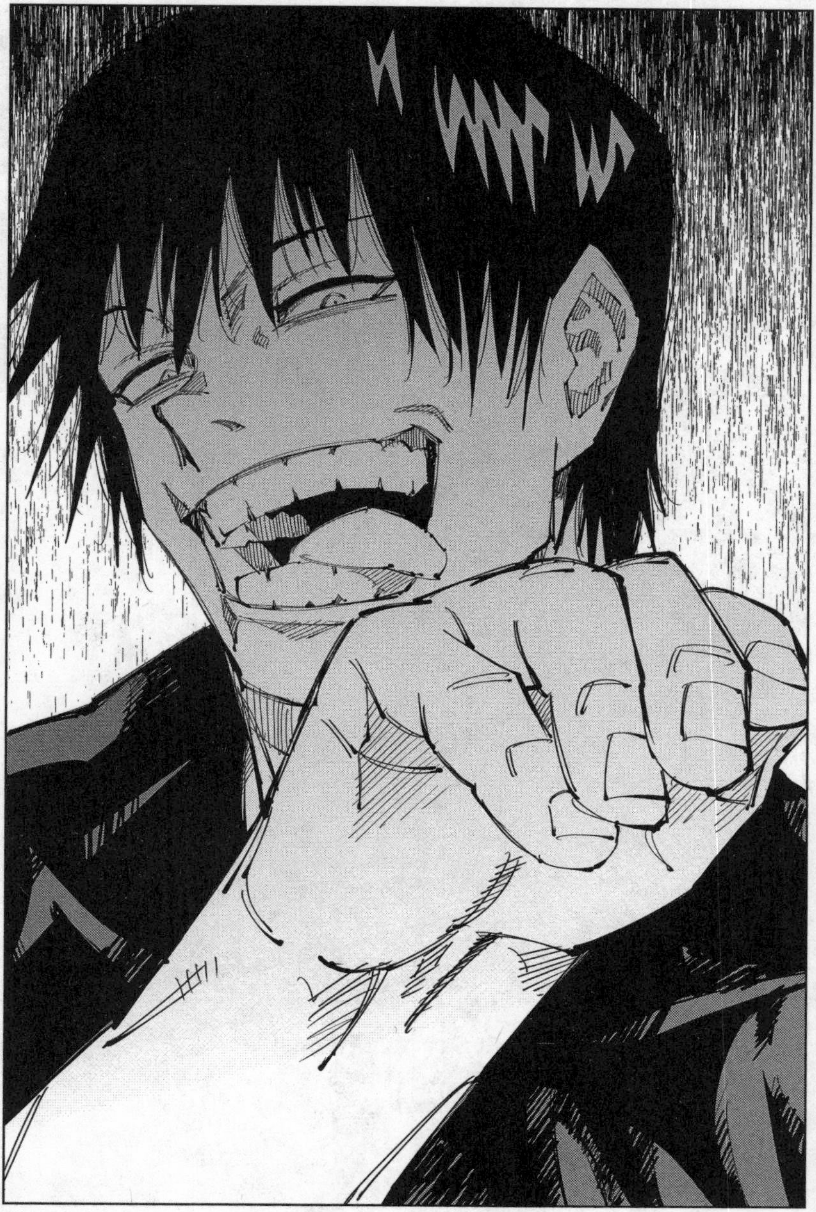

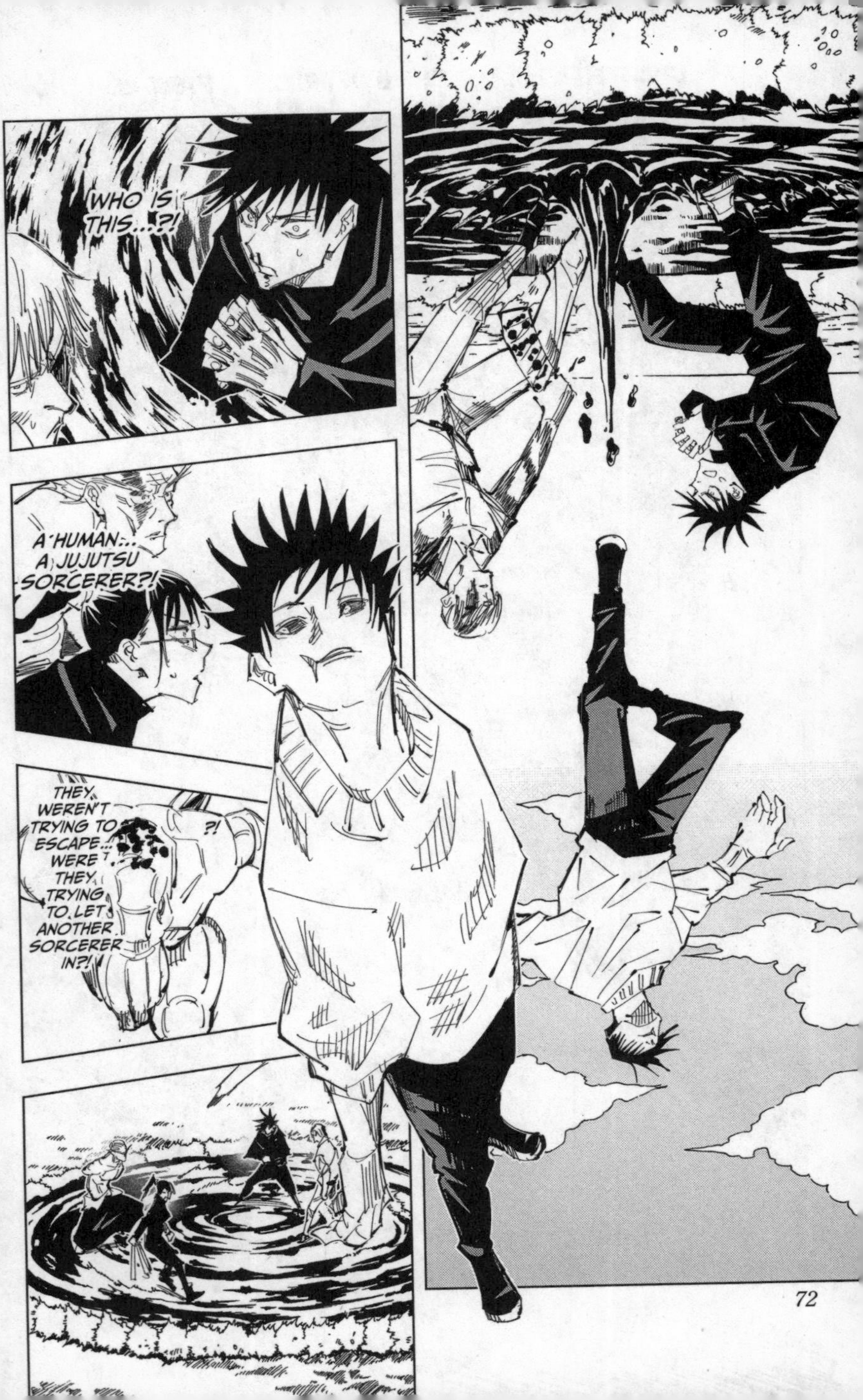
WHO IS THIS...?!
A HUMAN... A JUJUTSU SORCERER?!
?!
THEY WEREN'T TRYING TO ESCAPE... WERE THEY TRYING TO LET ANOTHER SORCERER IN?!

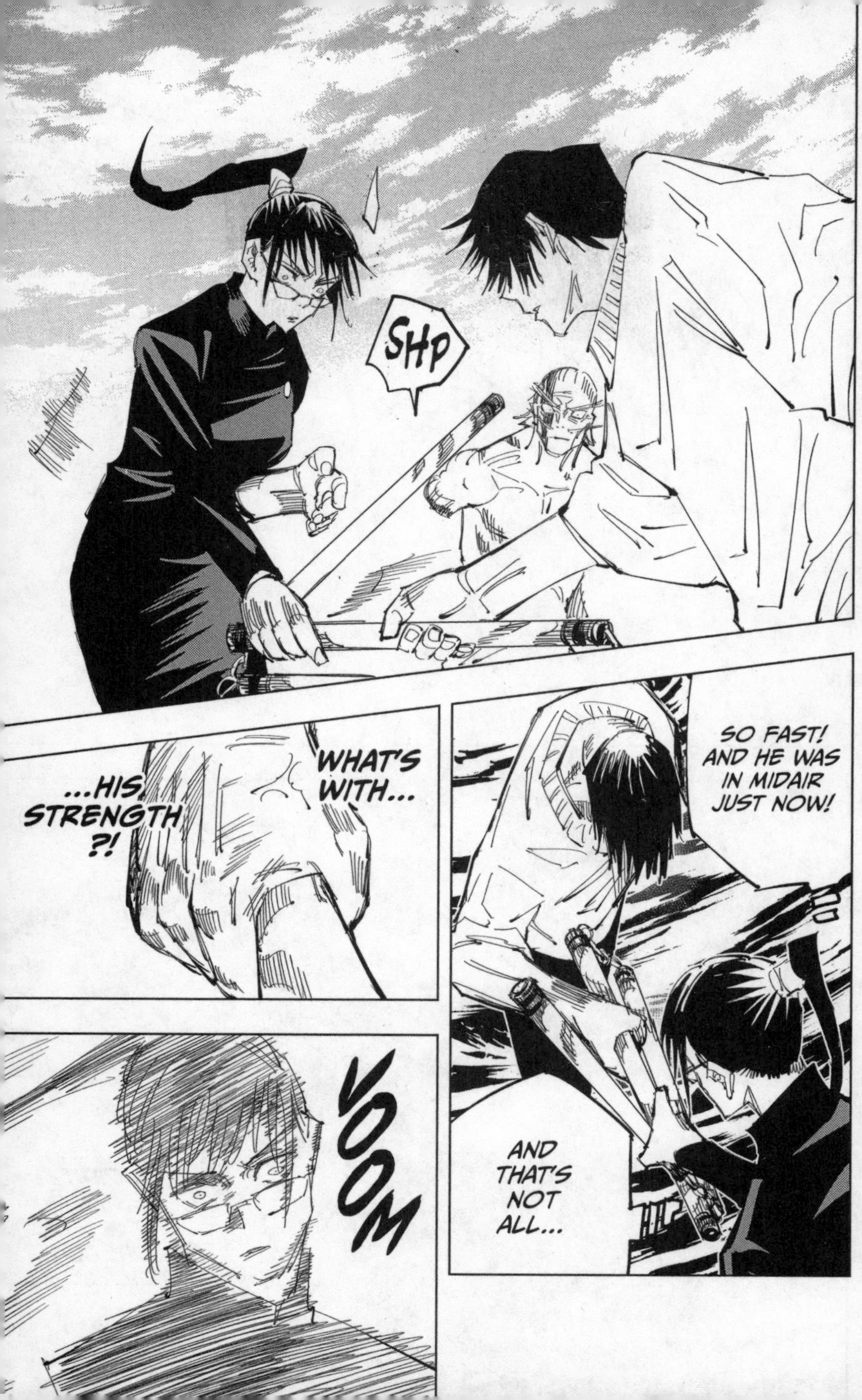
SHP
SO FAST! AND HE WAS IN MIDAIR JUST NOW!
AND THAT'S NOT ALL...
WHAT'S WITH...
...HIS STRENGTH?!
VOOM

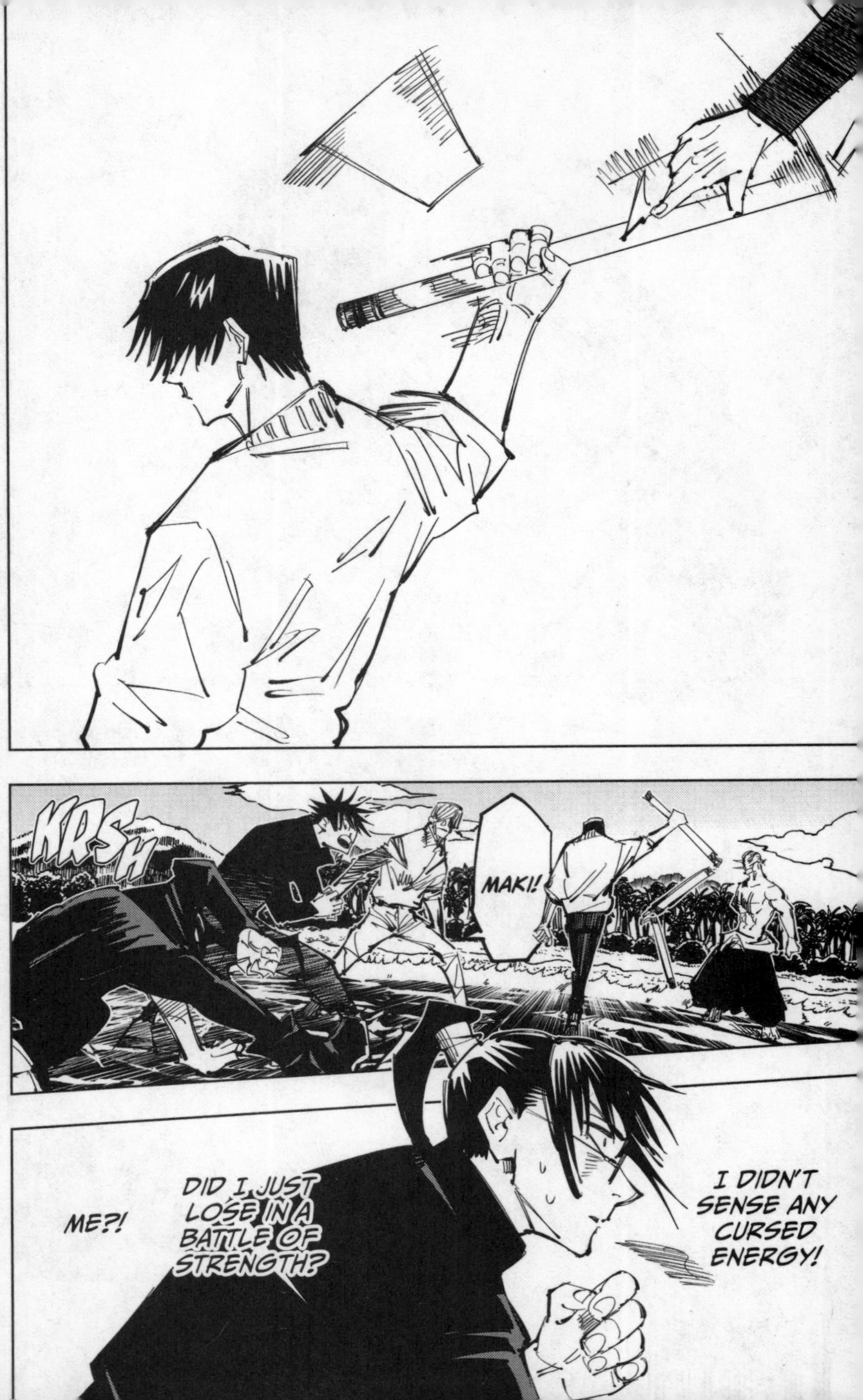
MAKI!
KRSH
I DIDN'T SENSE ANY CURSED ENERGY!
DID I JUST LOSE IN A BATTLE OF STRENGTH?
ME?!

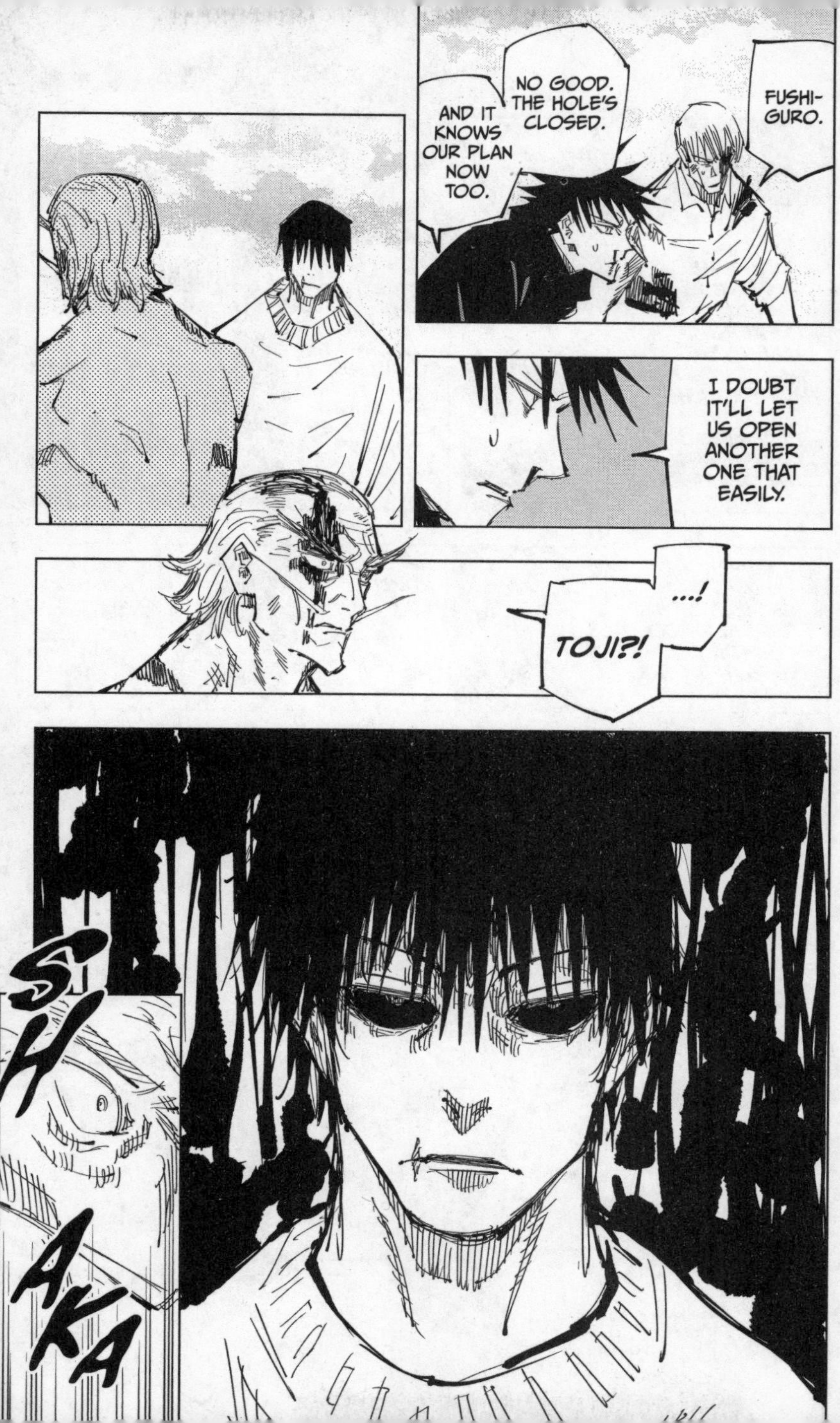
FUSHI-GURO.
NO GOOD. THE HOLE'S CLOSED.
AND IT KNOWS OUR PLAN NOW TOO.
I DOUBT IT'LL LET US OPEN ANOTHER ONE THAT EASILY.
...!
TOJI?!
SHAKA

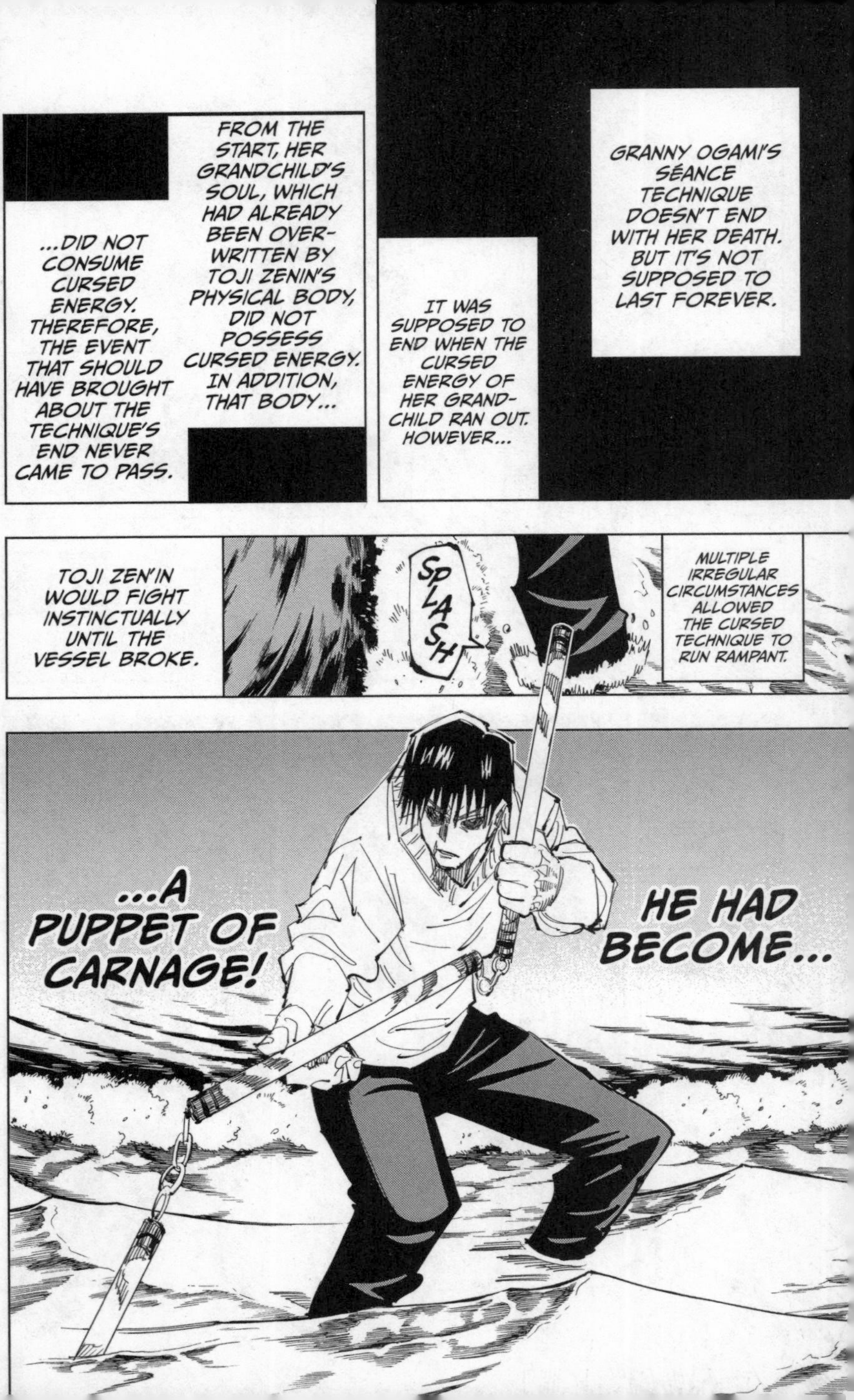
GRANNY OGAMI'S SÉANCE TECHNIQUE DOESN'T END WITH HER DEATH. BUT IT'S NOT SUPPOSED TO LAST FOREVER.
IT WAS SUPPOSED TO END WHEN THE CURSED ENERGY OF HER GRAND-CHILD RAN OUT. HOWEVER...
FROM THE START, HER GRANDCHILD'S SOUL, WHICH HAD ALREADY BEEN OVER-WRITTEN BY TOJI ZENIN'S PHYSICAL BODY, DID NOT POSSESS CURSED ENERGY. IN ADDITION, THAT BODY...
...DID NOT CONSUME CURSED ENERGY. THEREFORE, THE EVENT THAT SHOULD HAVE BROUGHT ABOUT THE TECHNIQUE'S END NEVER CAME TO PASS.
MULTIPLE IRREGULAR CIRCUMSTANCES ALLOWED THE CURSED TECHNIQUE TO RUN RAMPANT.
SPLASH
TOJI ZEN'IN WOULD FIGHT INSTINCTUALLY UNTIL THE VESSEL BROKE.
HE HAD BECOME...
...A PUPPET OF CARNAGE!

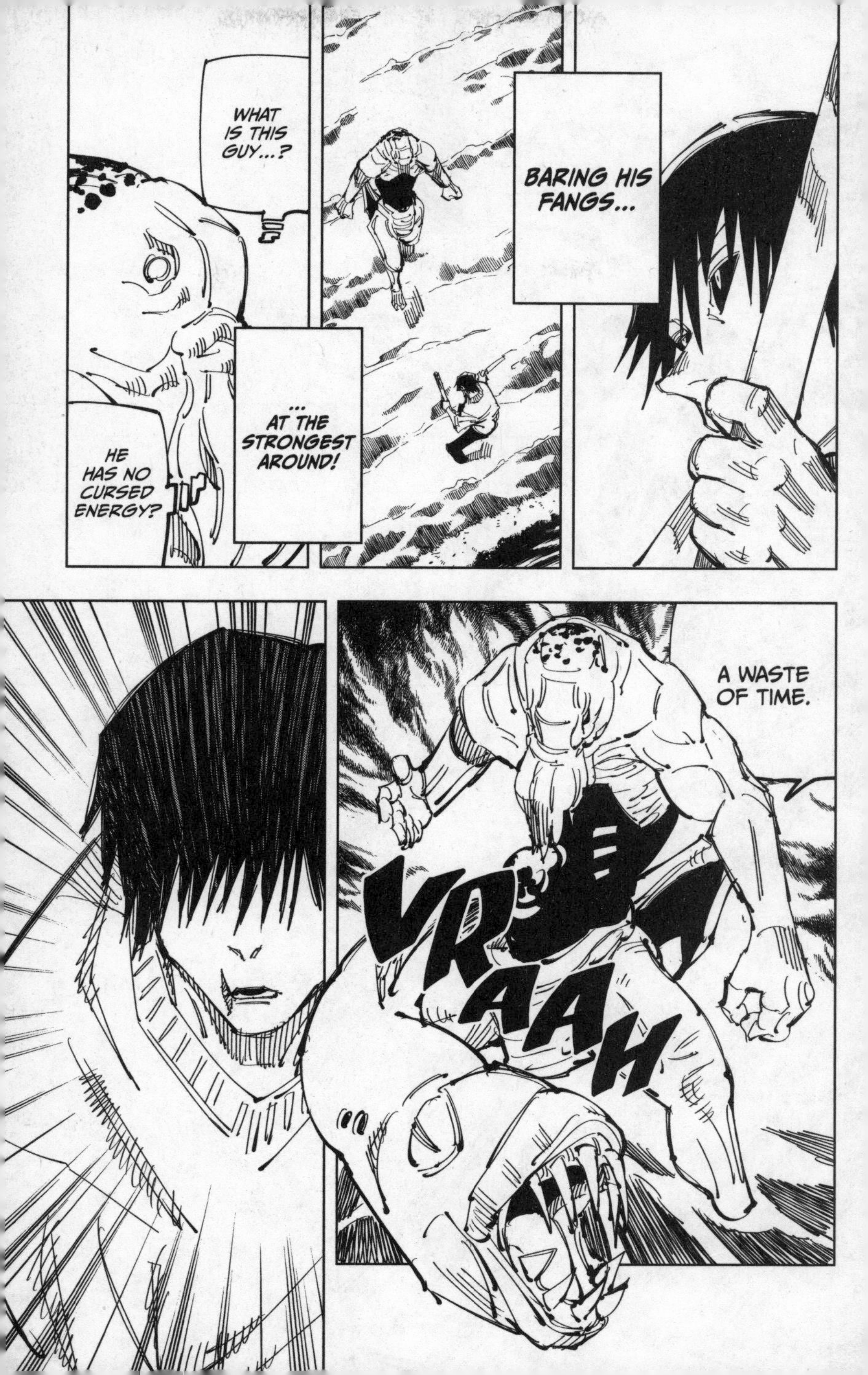
BARING HIS FANGS...
... AT THE STRONGEST AROUND!
WHAT IS THIS GUY...?
HE HAS NO CURSED ENERGY?
A WASTE OF TIME.
VRAAH

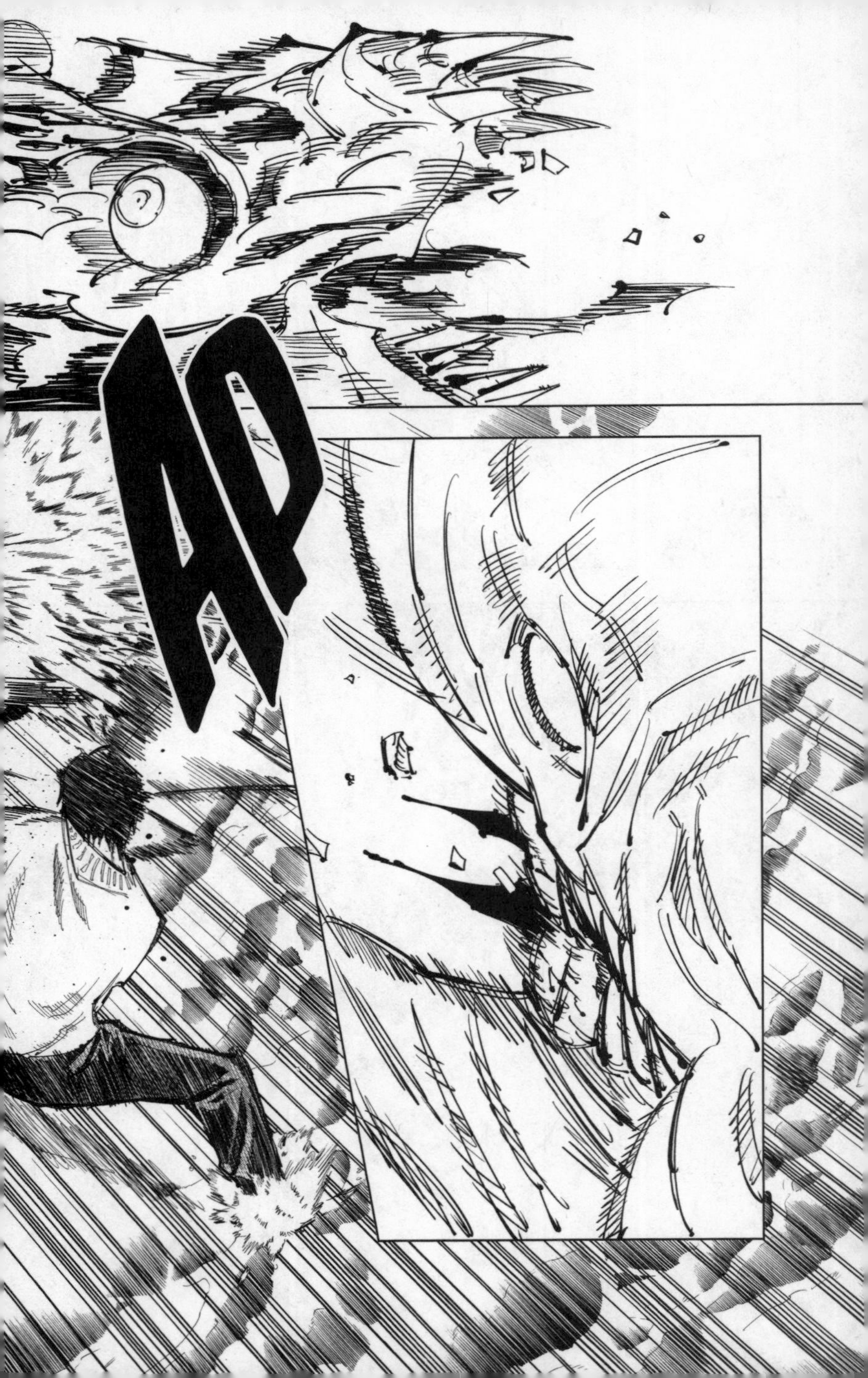

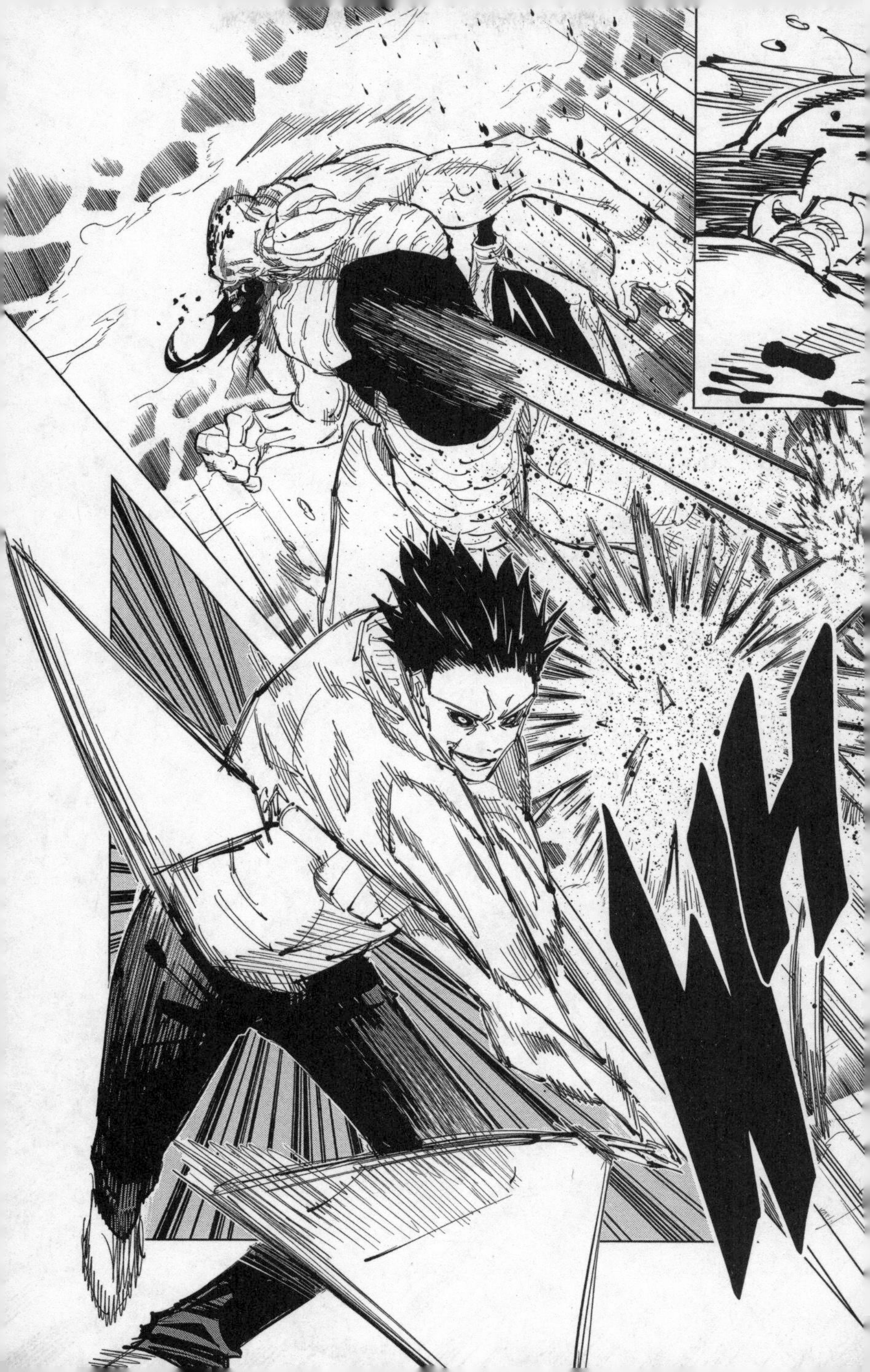

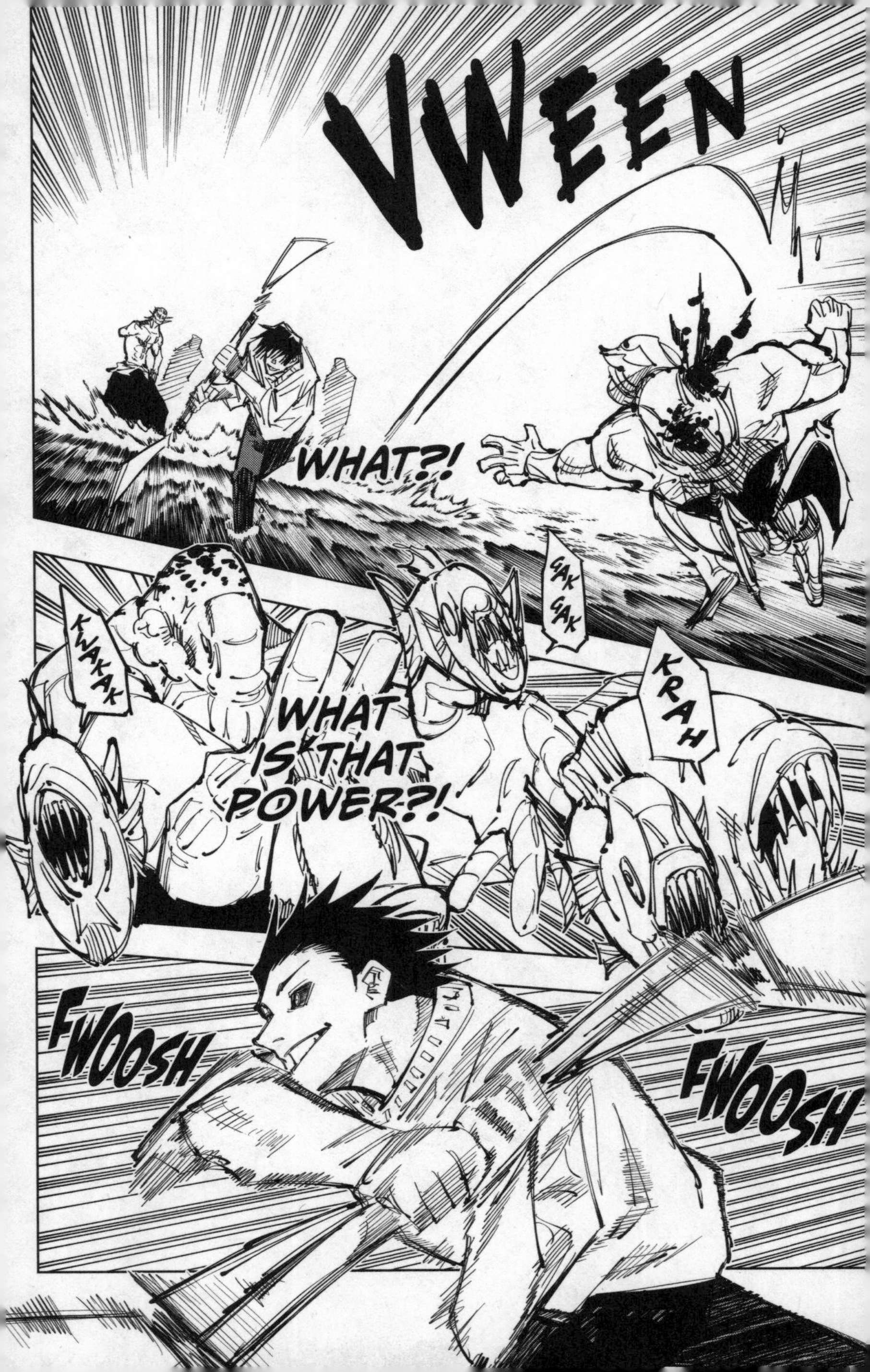
VWEEN
WHAT?!
KRAH
GAK GAK
WHAT IS THAT POWER?!
KWAKAK
FWOOSH
FWOOSH

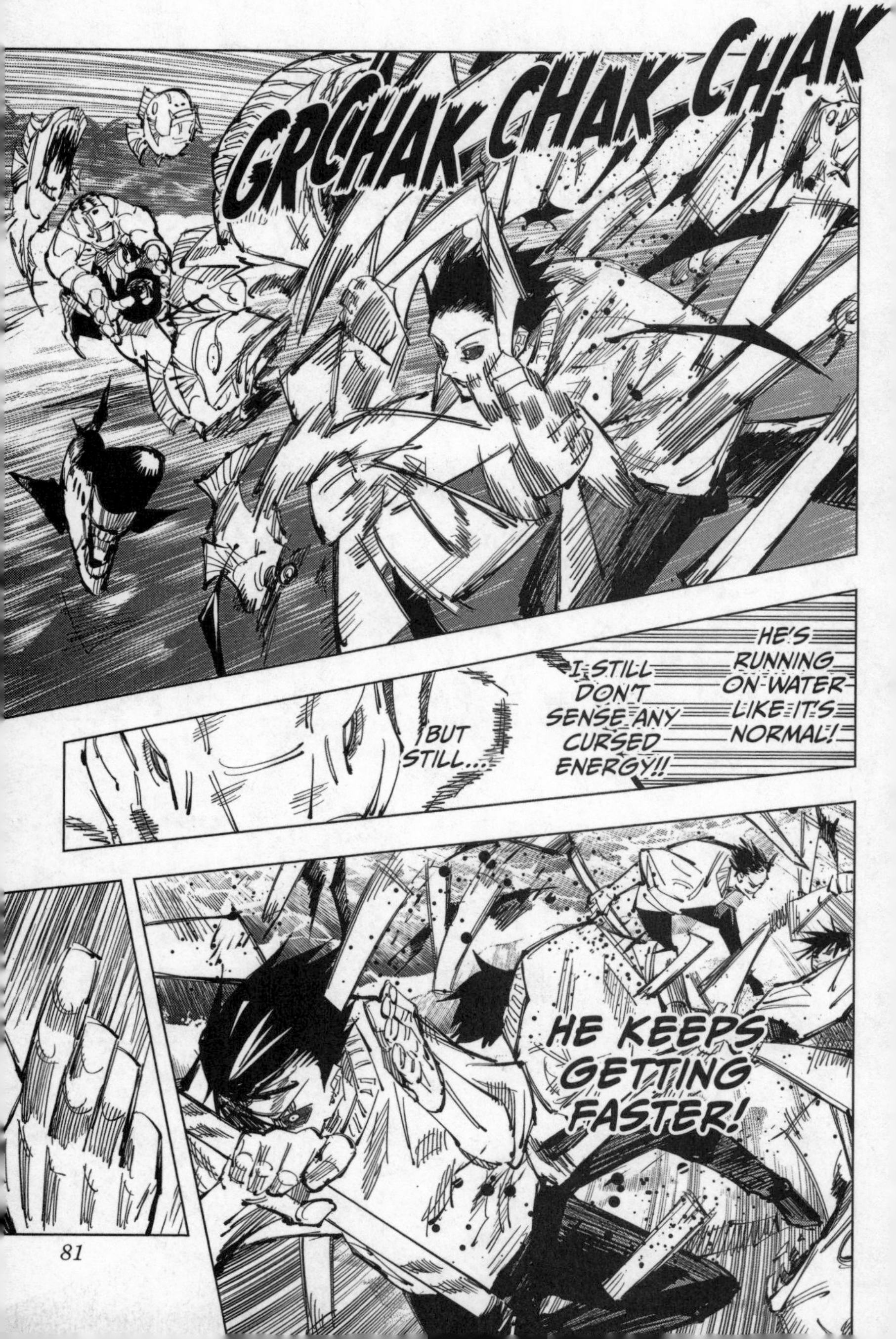
GRCHAK CHAK CHAK
HE'S RUNNING ON WATER LIKE IT'S NORMAL!
I STILL DON'T SENSE ANY CURSED ENERGY!!
BUT STILL...
HE KEEPS GETTING FASTER!

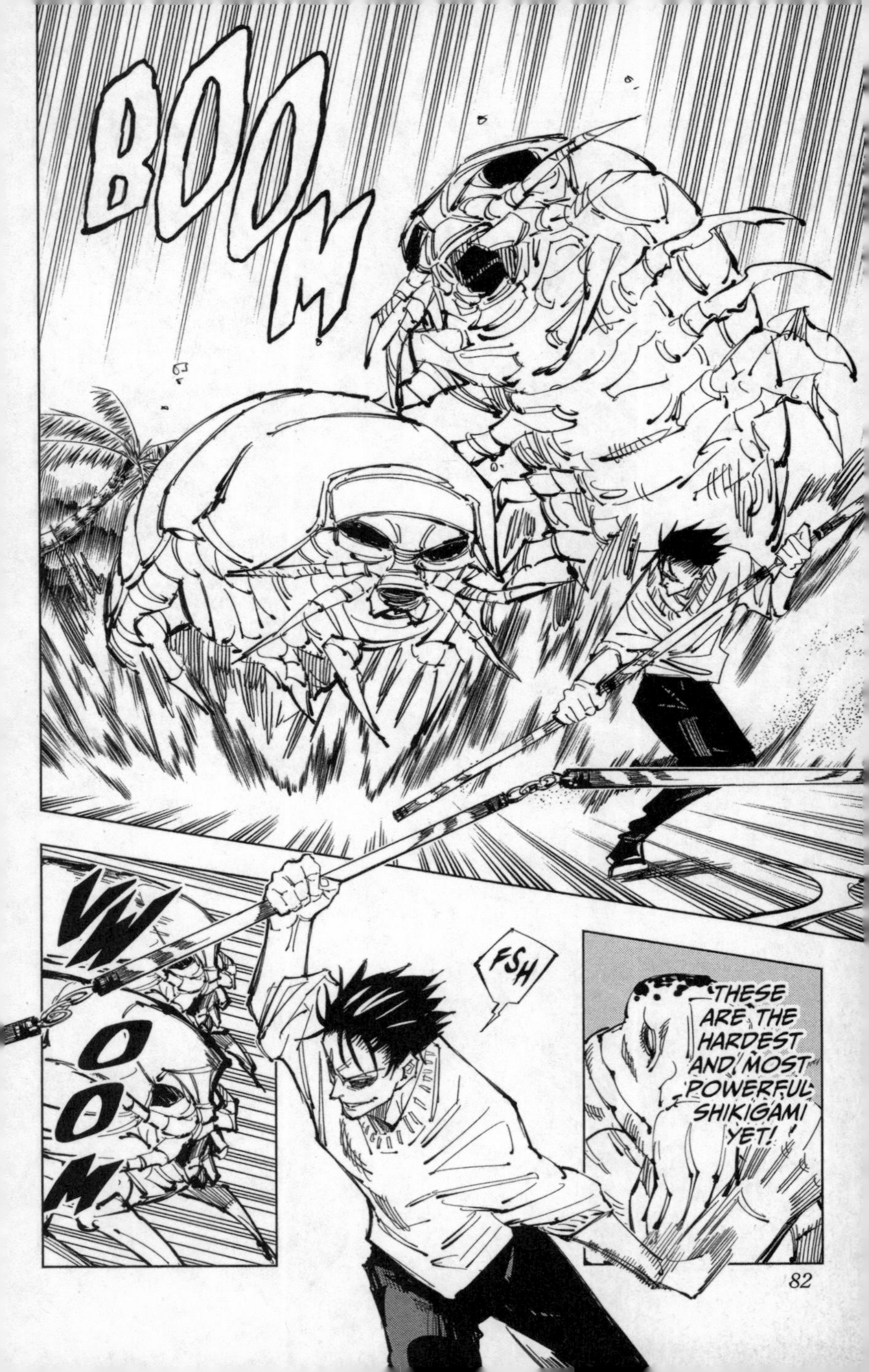
BOOOM
THESE ARE THE HARDEST AND MOST POWERFUL SHIKIGAMI YET!
FSH
VWOOOM

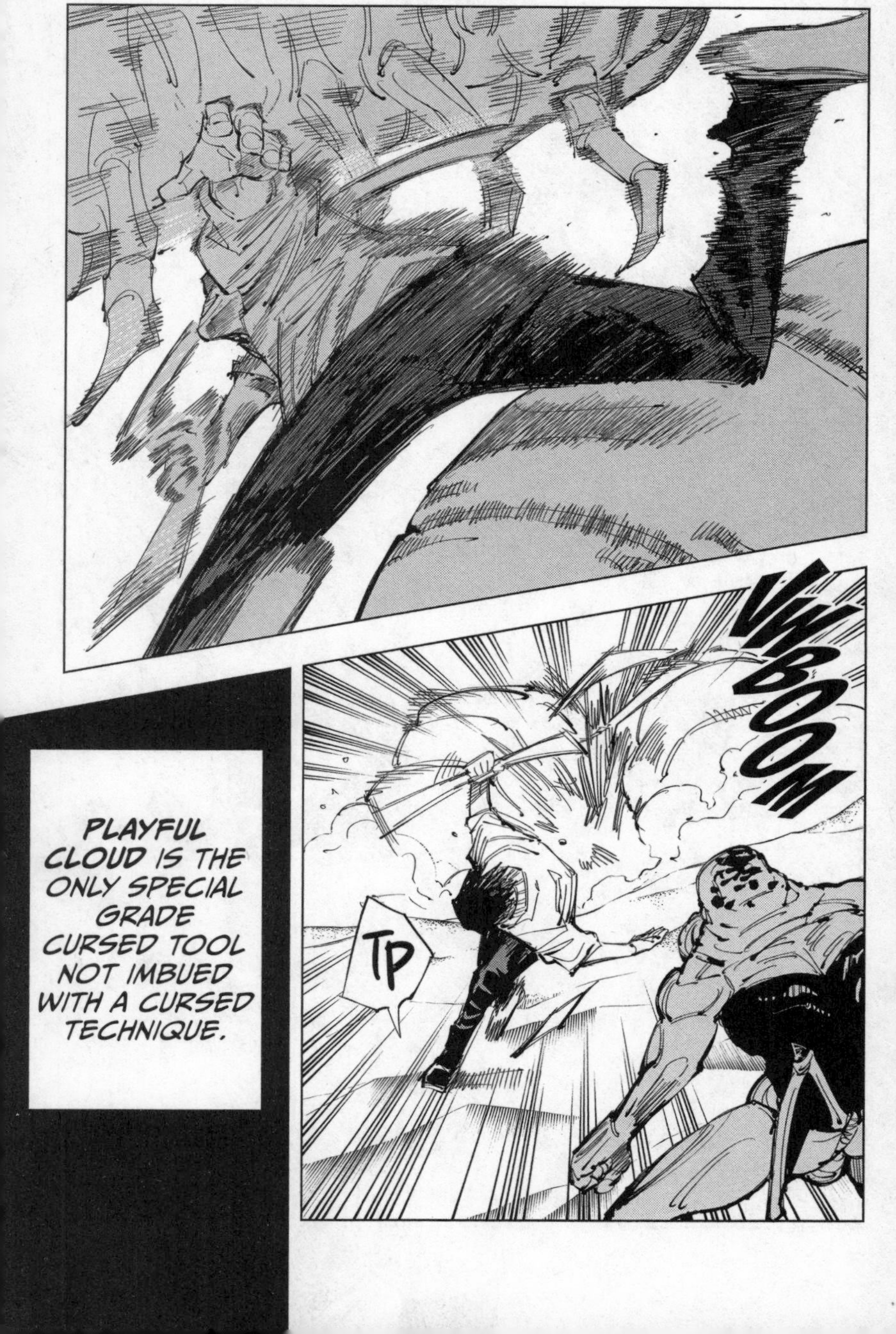
VWBOOM
TP
PLAYFUL CLOUD IS THE ONLY SPECIAL GRADE CURSED TOOL NOT IMBUED WITH A CURSED TECHNIQUE.

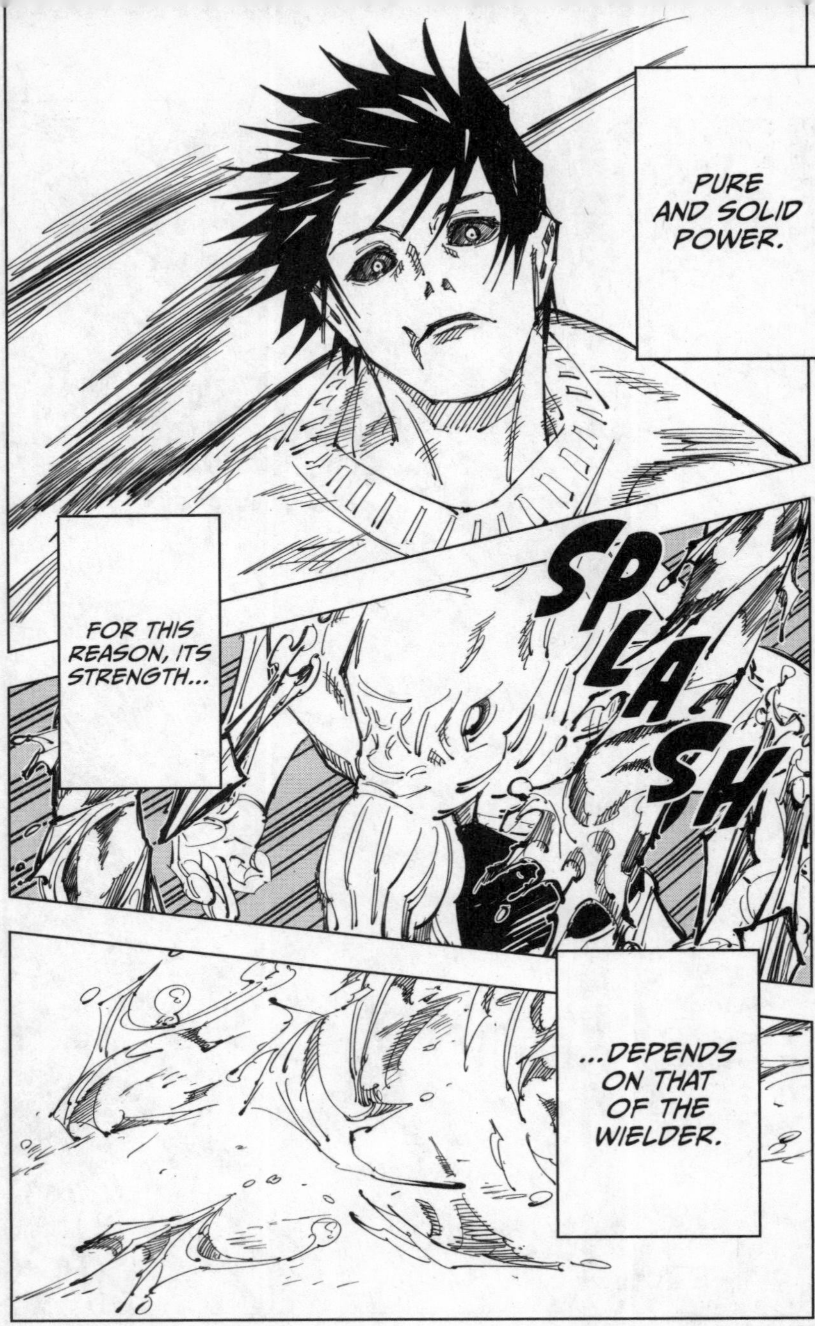
PURE AND SOLID POWER.
FOR THIS REASON, ITS STRENGTH...
SPLASH
...DEPENDS ON THAT OF THE WIELDER.

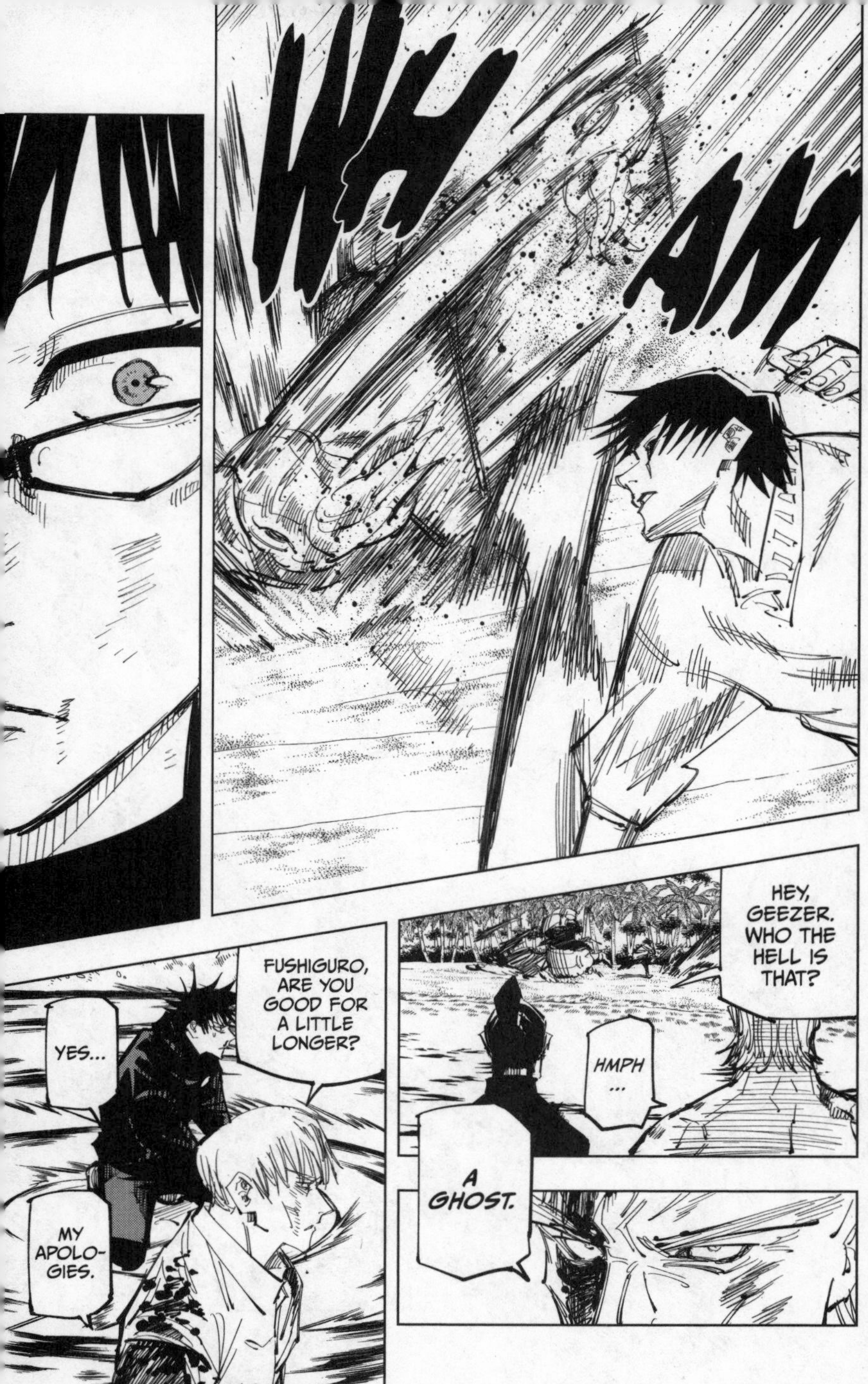
WHAM
HEY, GEEZER. WHO THE HELL IS THAT?
HMPH...
A GHOST.
FUSHIGURO, ARE YOU GOOD FOR A LITTLE LONGER?
YES...
MY APOLOGIES.

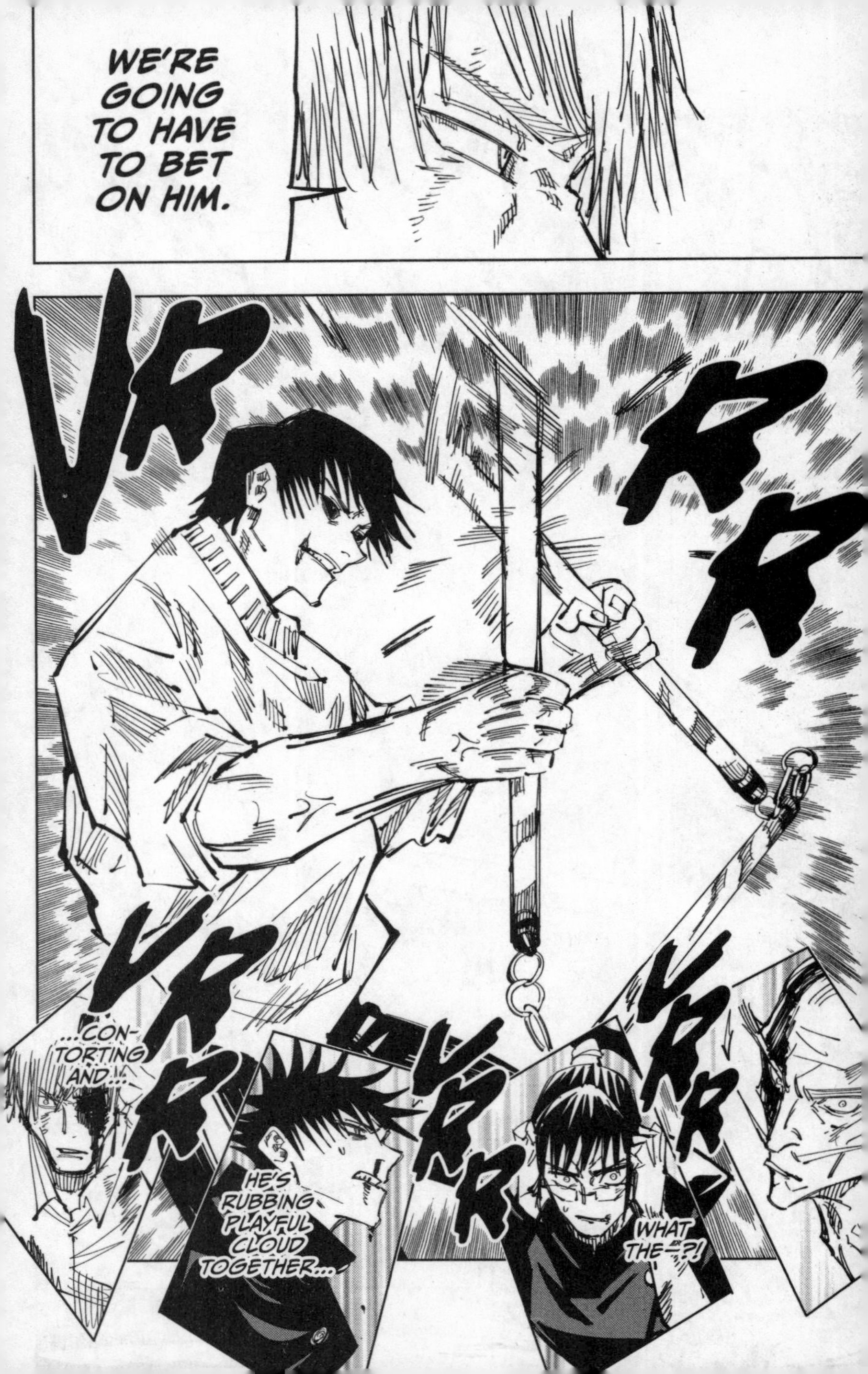

WE'RE GOING TO HAVE TO BET ON HIM.
VRRRR
VRRR
WHAT THE—?!
VRRR
HE'S RUBBING PLAYFUL CLOUD TOGETHER...
VRRR
...CONTORTING AND...

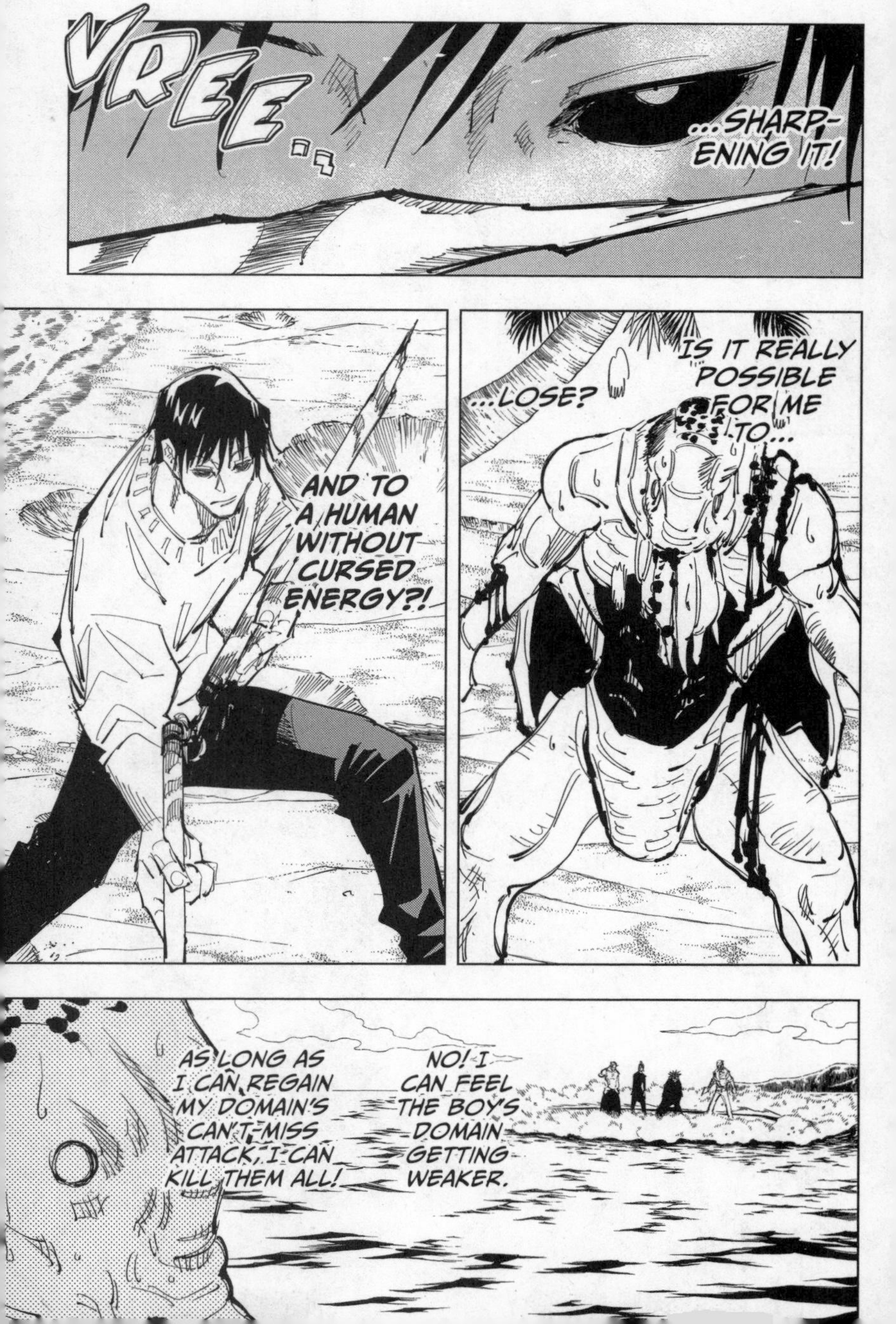
...SHARPENING IT!
VREE...
IS IT REALLY POSSIBLE FOR ME TO...
...LOSE?
AND TO A HUMAN WITHOUT CURSED ENERGY?!
NO! I CAN FEEL THE BOY'S DOMAIN GETTING WEAKER.
AS LONG AS I CAN REGAIN MY DOMAIN'S CAN'T-MISS ATTACK, I CAN KILL THEM ALL!

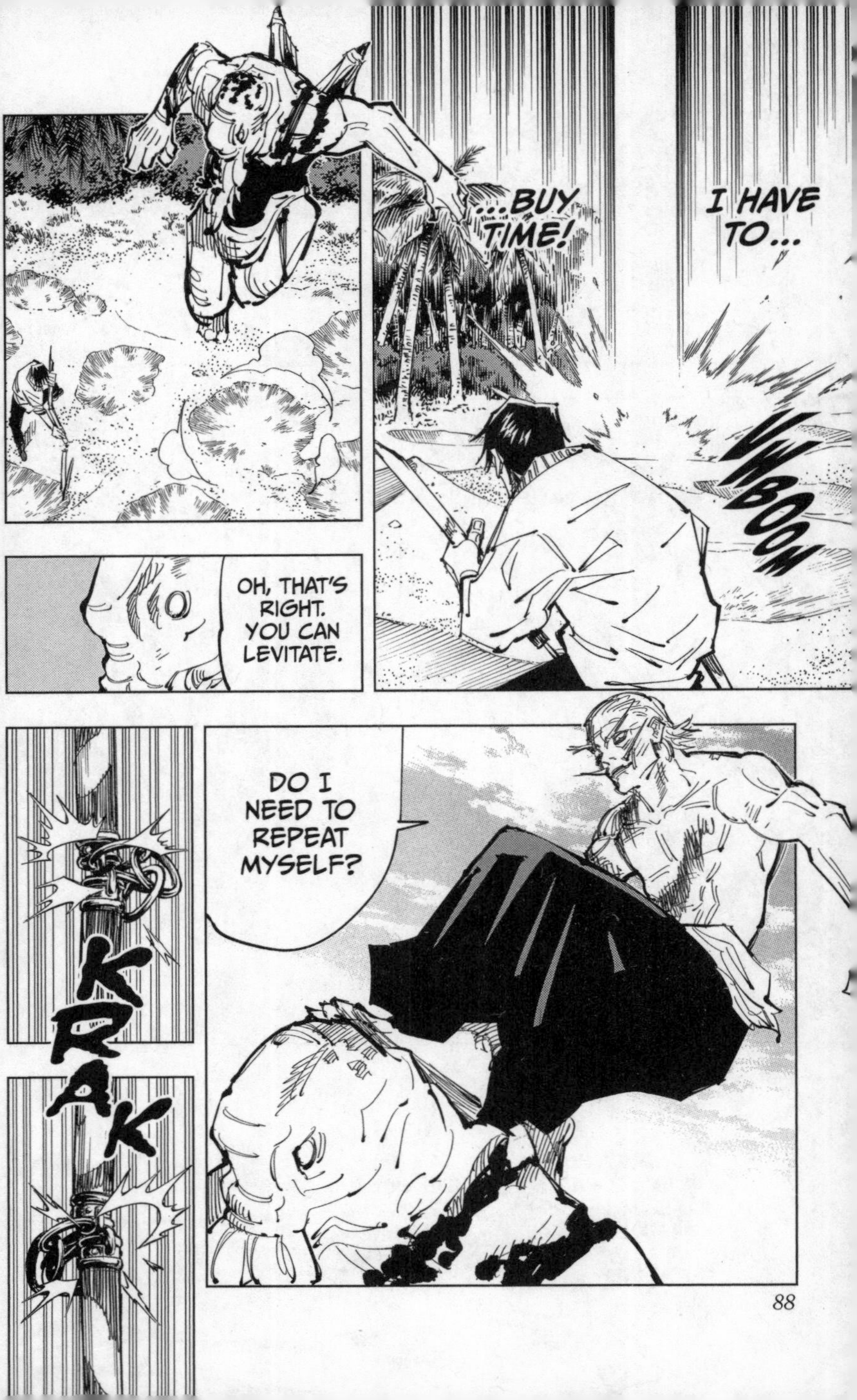
I HAVE TO...
...BUY TIME!
VWBOOM
OH, THAT'S RIGHT. YOU CAN LEVITATE.
DO I NEED TO REPEAT MYSELF?
KRAK

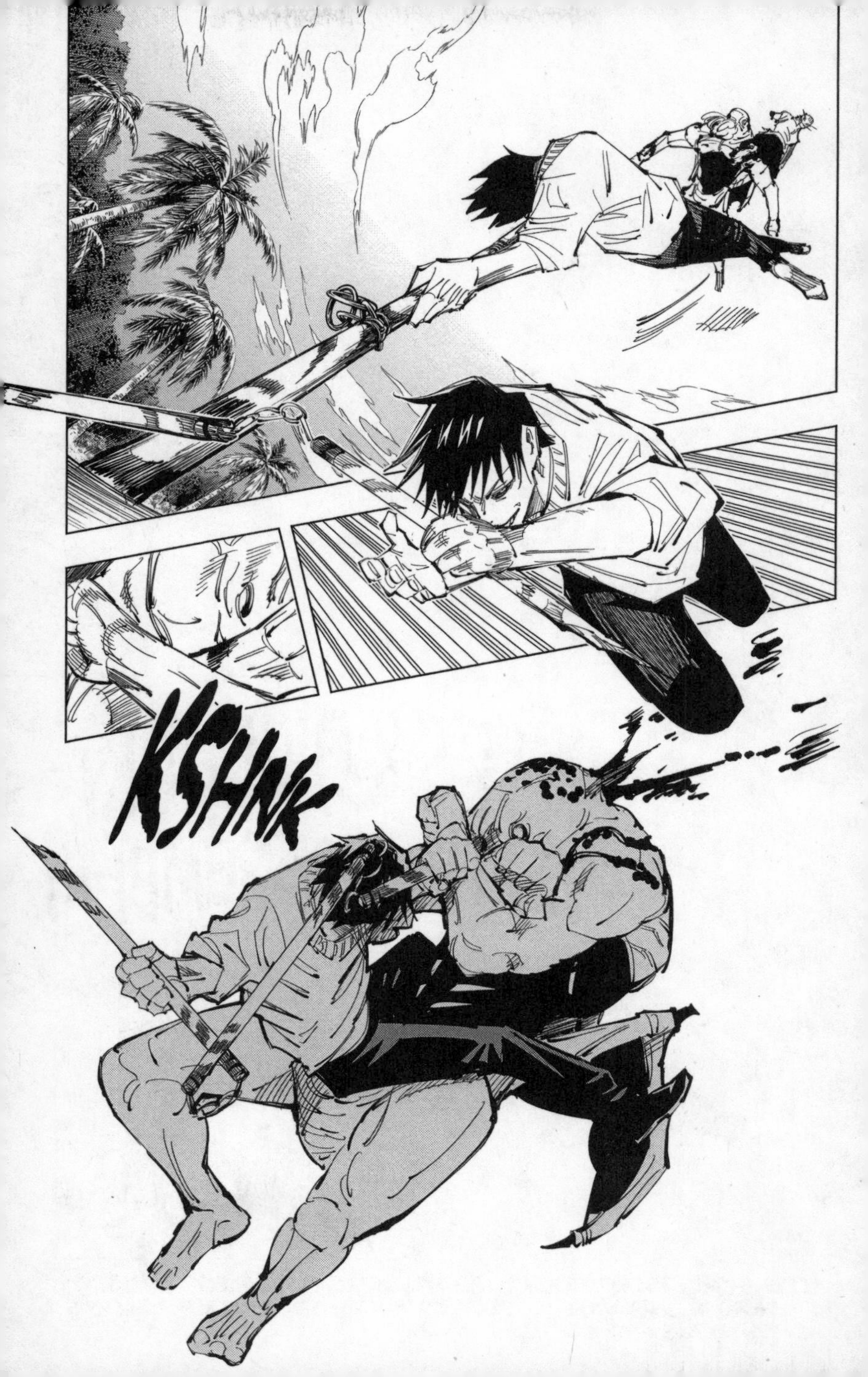
KSHNK

IT'S 8 O'CLOCK! ZEN'INS, ASSEMBLE!

THAT'S NOT WHAT IT MEANS...

*IT'S 8 O'CLOCK! EVERYONE, ASSEMBLE! IS THE NAME OF A VARIETY TV SHOW IN JAPAN. THE WORD FOR "EVERYONE" IS ZENIN, WHICH IS HOMONYMOUS WITH ZEN'IN.

Chapter 111: The Shibuya Incident, Part 29

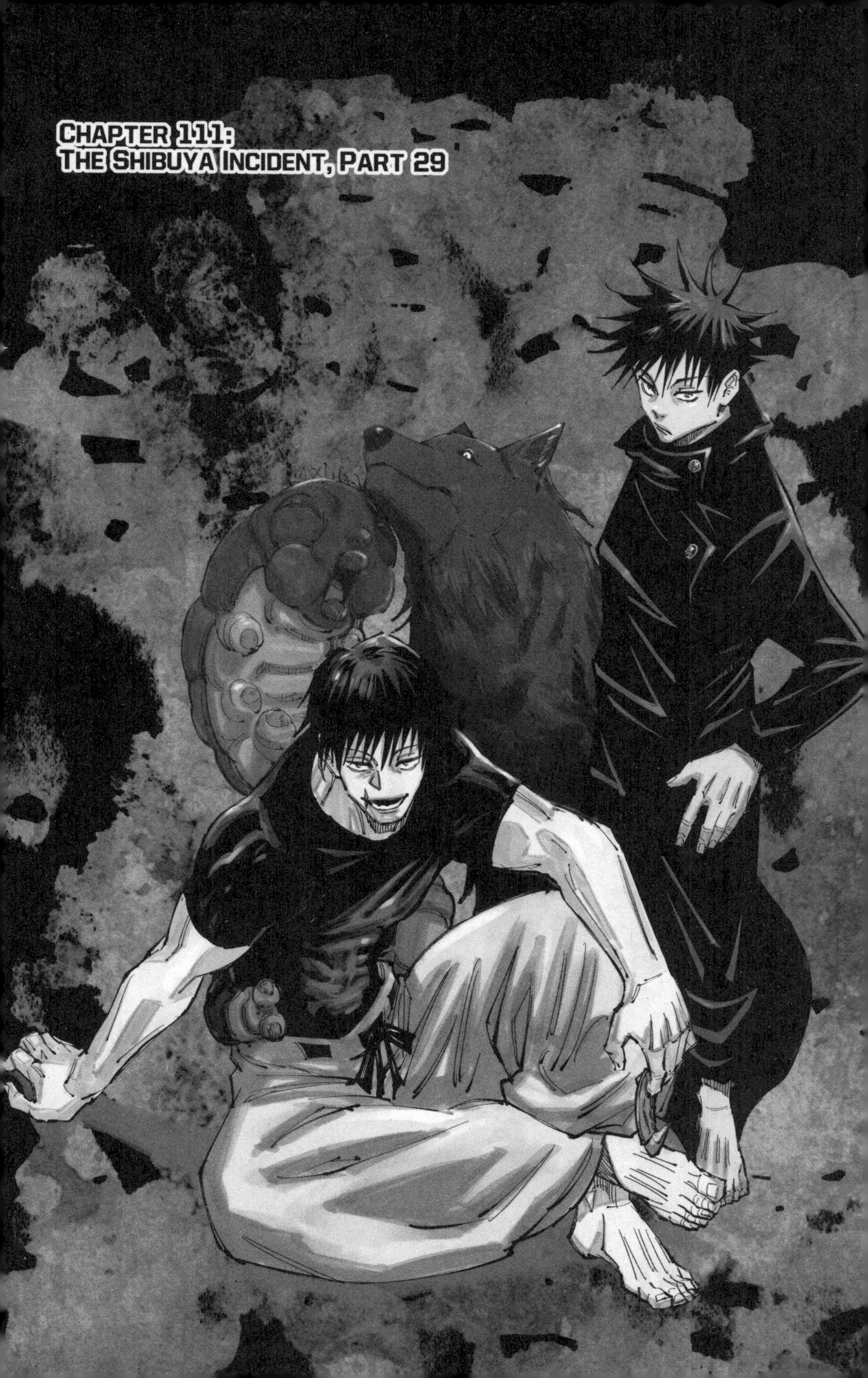

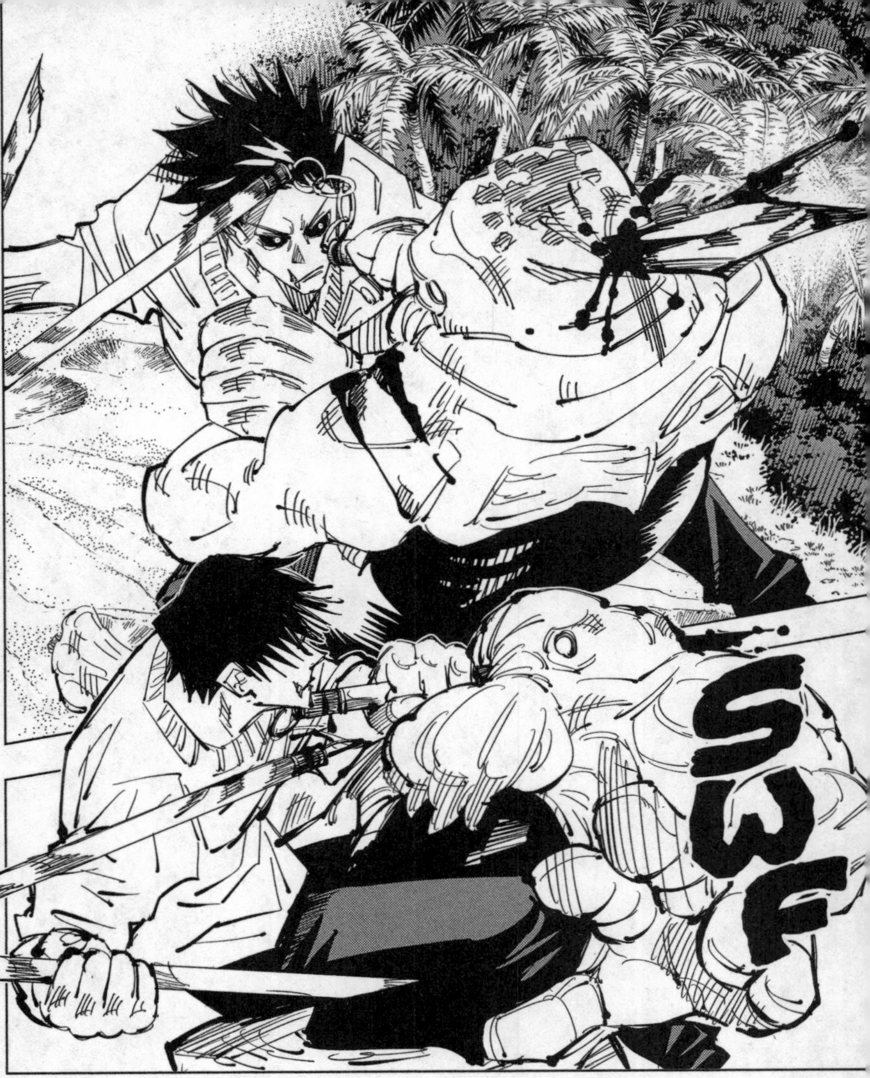
SWF
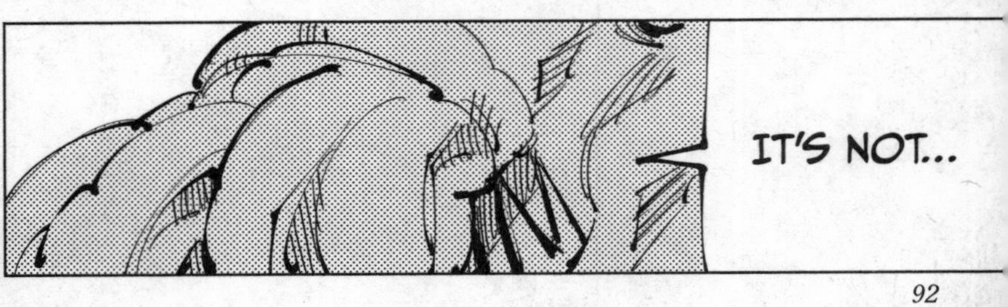
IT'S NOT...

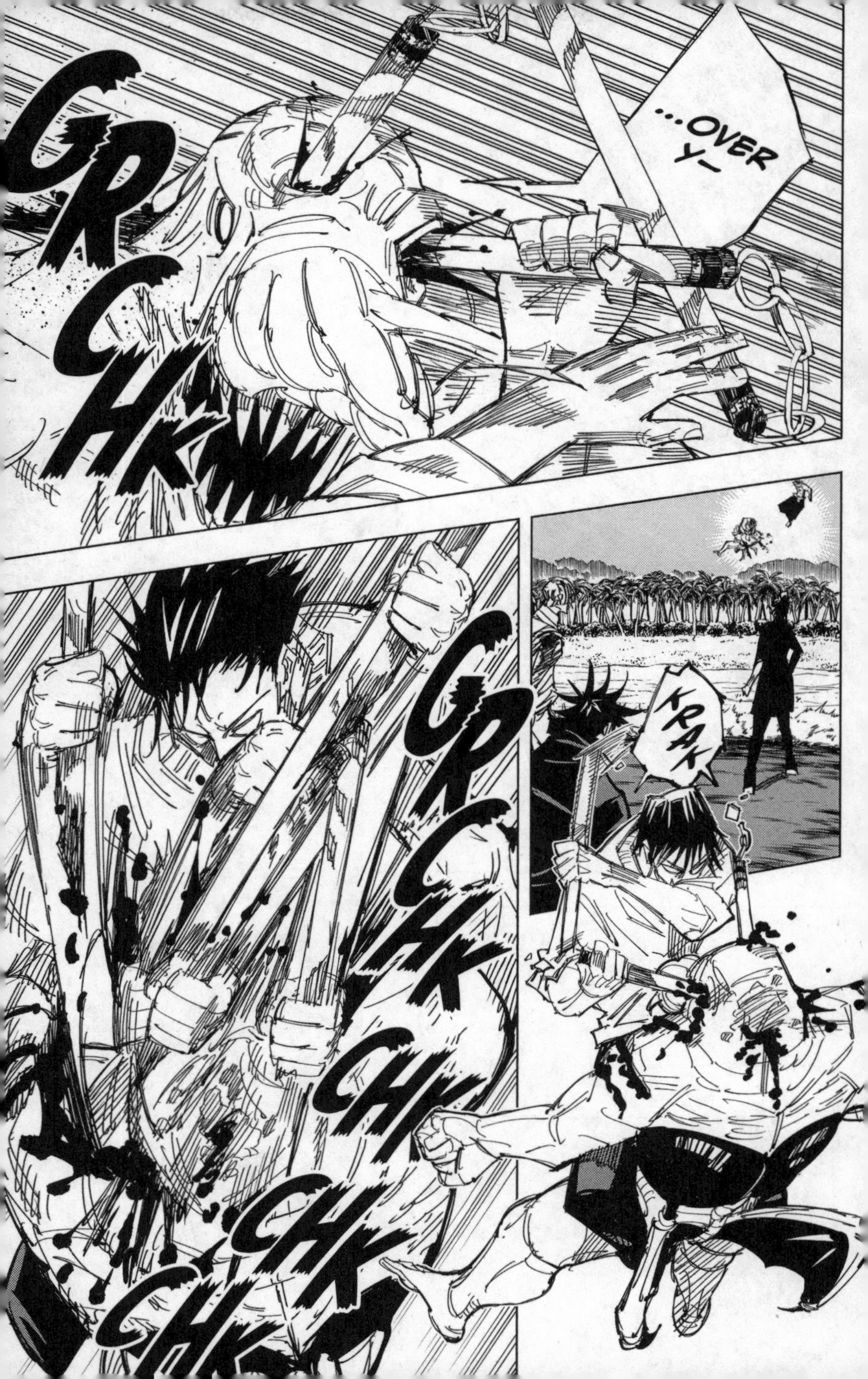
...OVER Y—
GRCHK
KRAK
GRCHK CHK CHK

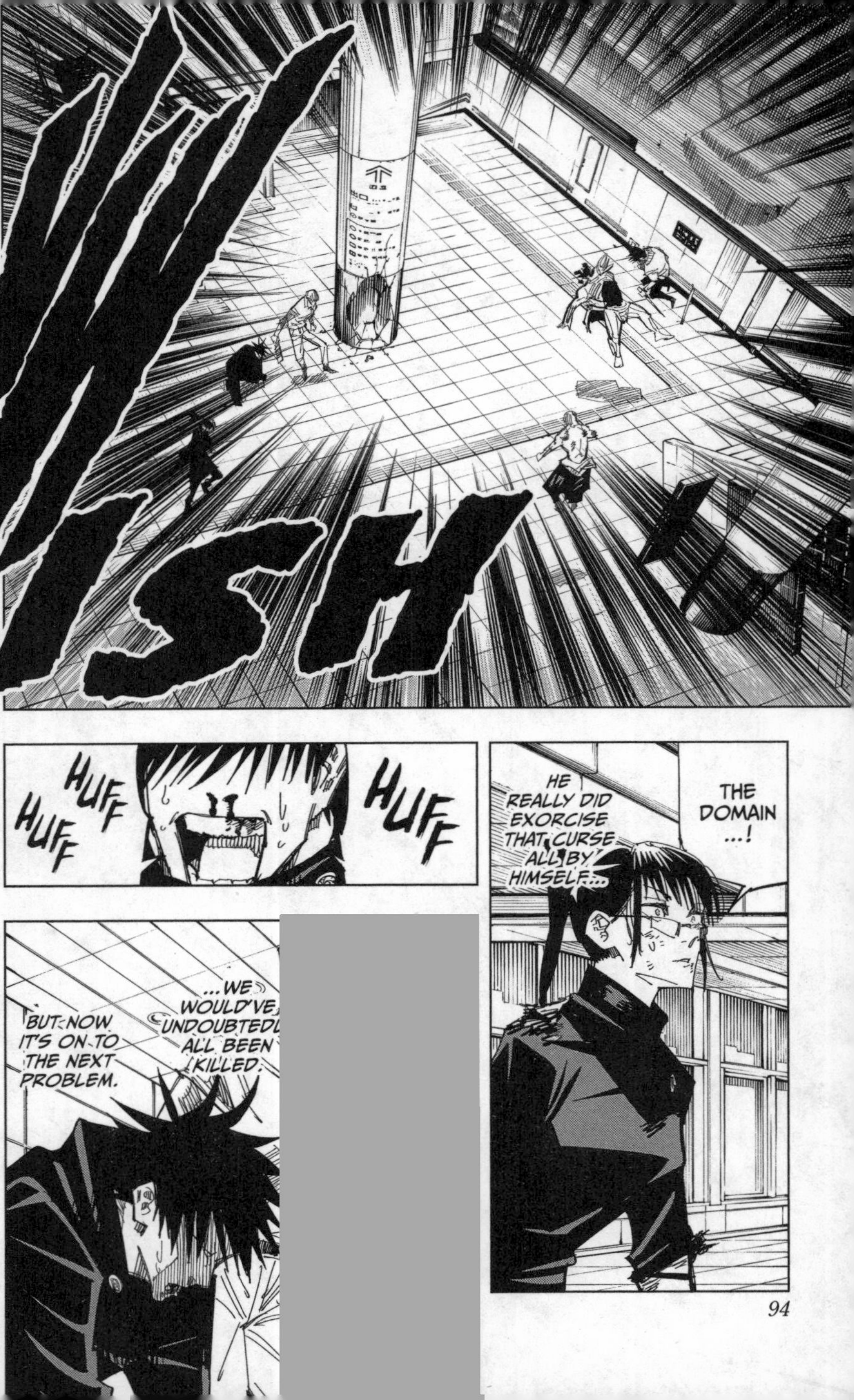
SH
THE DOMAIN ...!
HE REALLY DID EXORCISE THAT CURSE ALL BY HIMSELF...
HUFF
HUFF
HUFF
...WE WOULD'VE UNDOUBTEDL ALL BEEN KILLED.
BUT NOW IT'S ON TO THE NEXT PROBLEM.

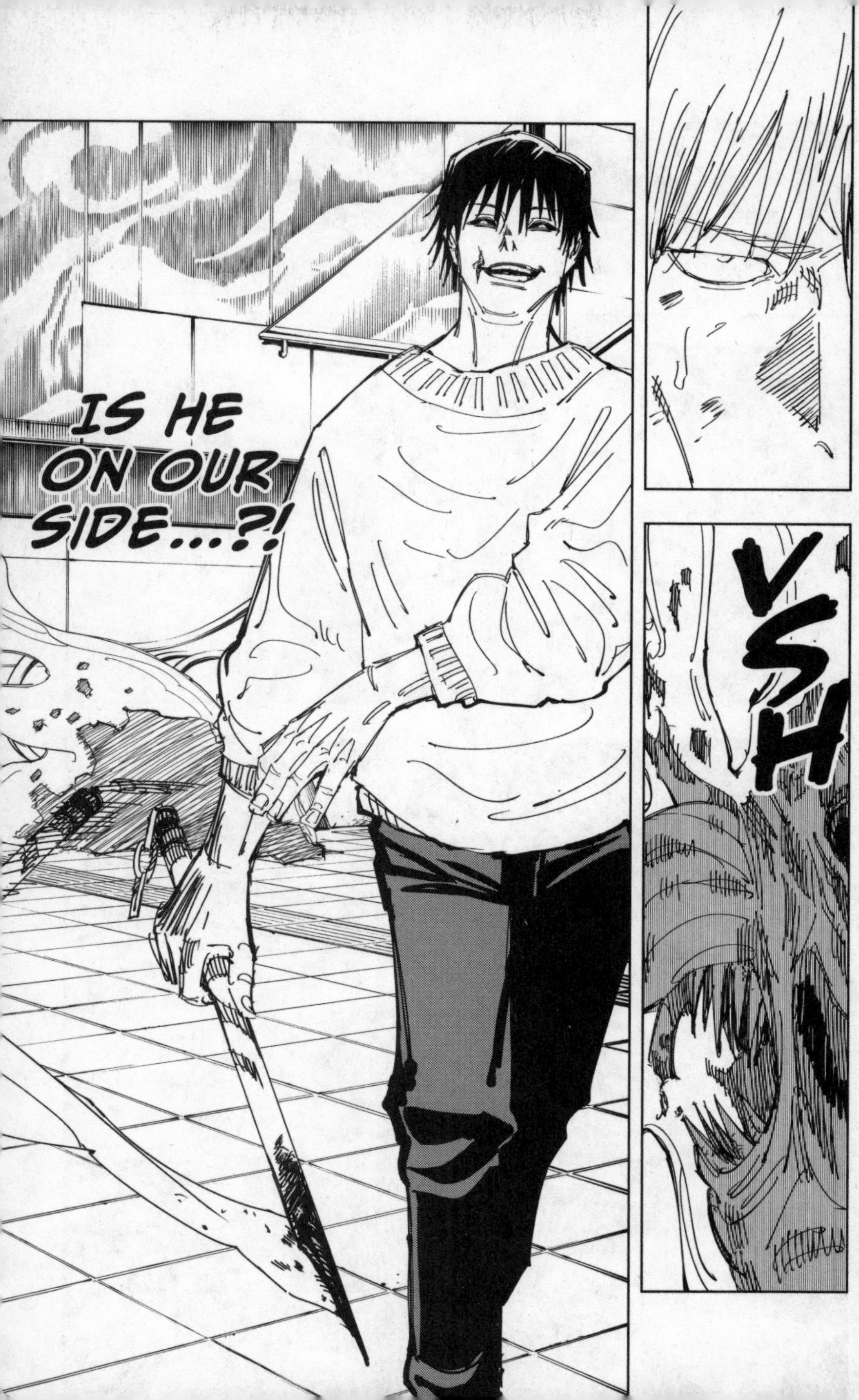
VSH
IS HE ON OUR SIDE...?!

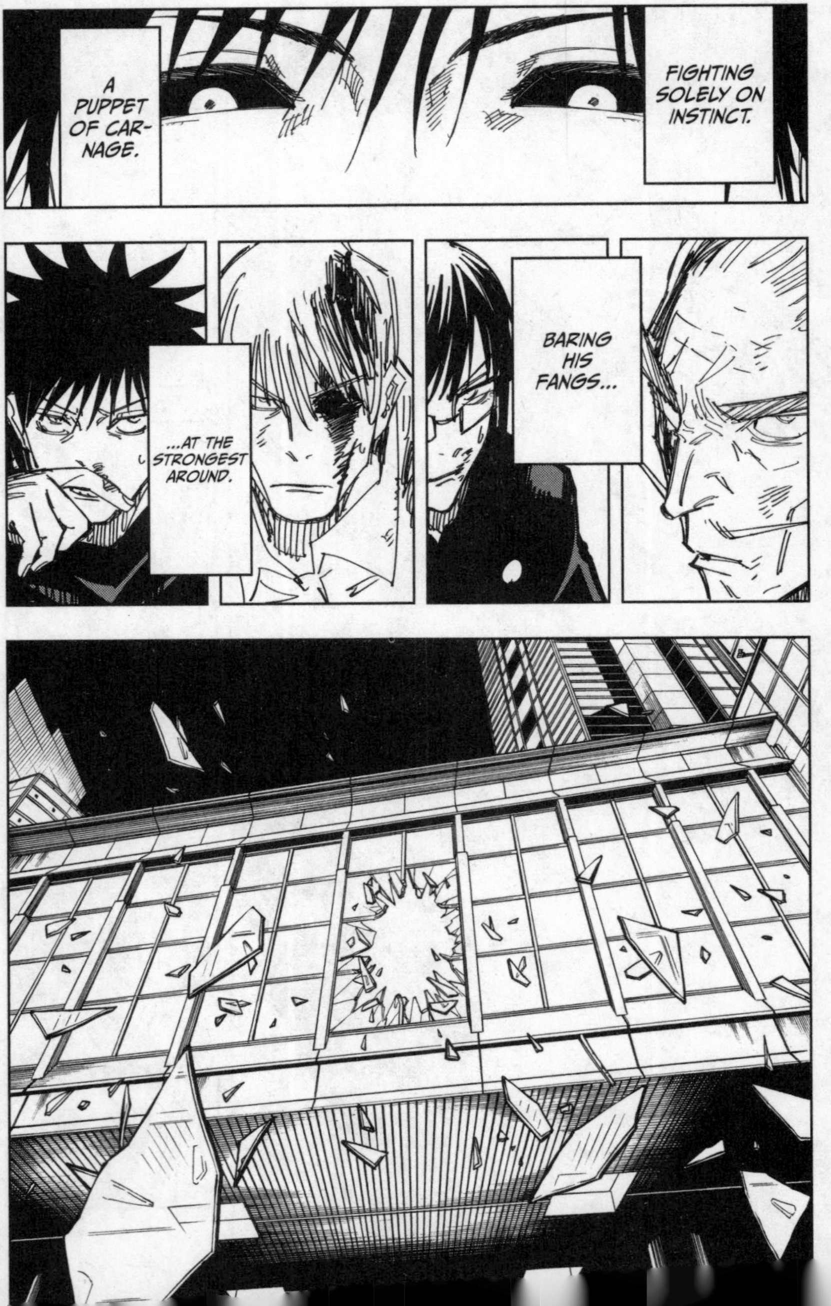
FIGHTING SOLELY ON INSTINCT.
A PUPPET OF CAR-NAGE.
BARING HIS FANGS...
...AT THE STRONGEST AROUND.

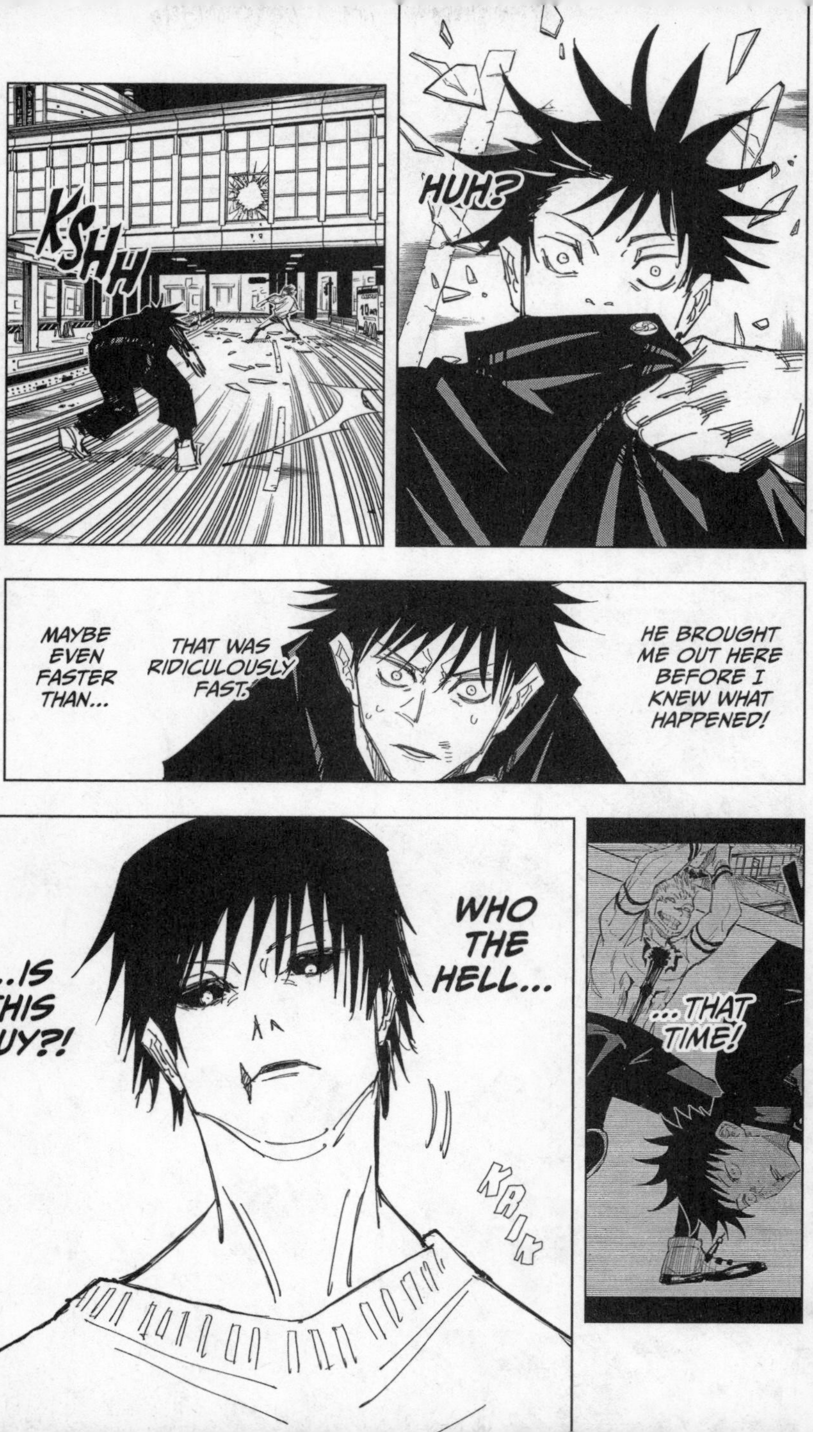
HUH?
KSHH
HE BROUGHT ME OUT HERE BEFORE I KNEW WHAT HAPPENED!
THAT WAS RIDICULOUSLY FAST.
MAYBE EVEN FASTER THAN...
...THAT TIME!
WHO THE HELL...
...IS THIS GUY?!
KRIK

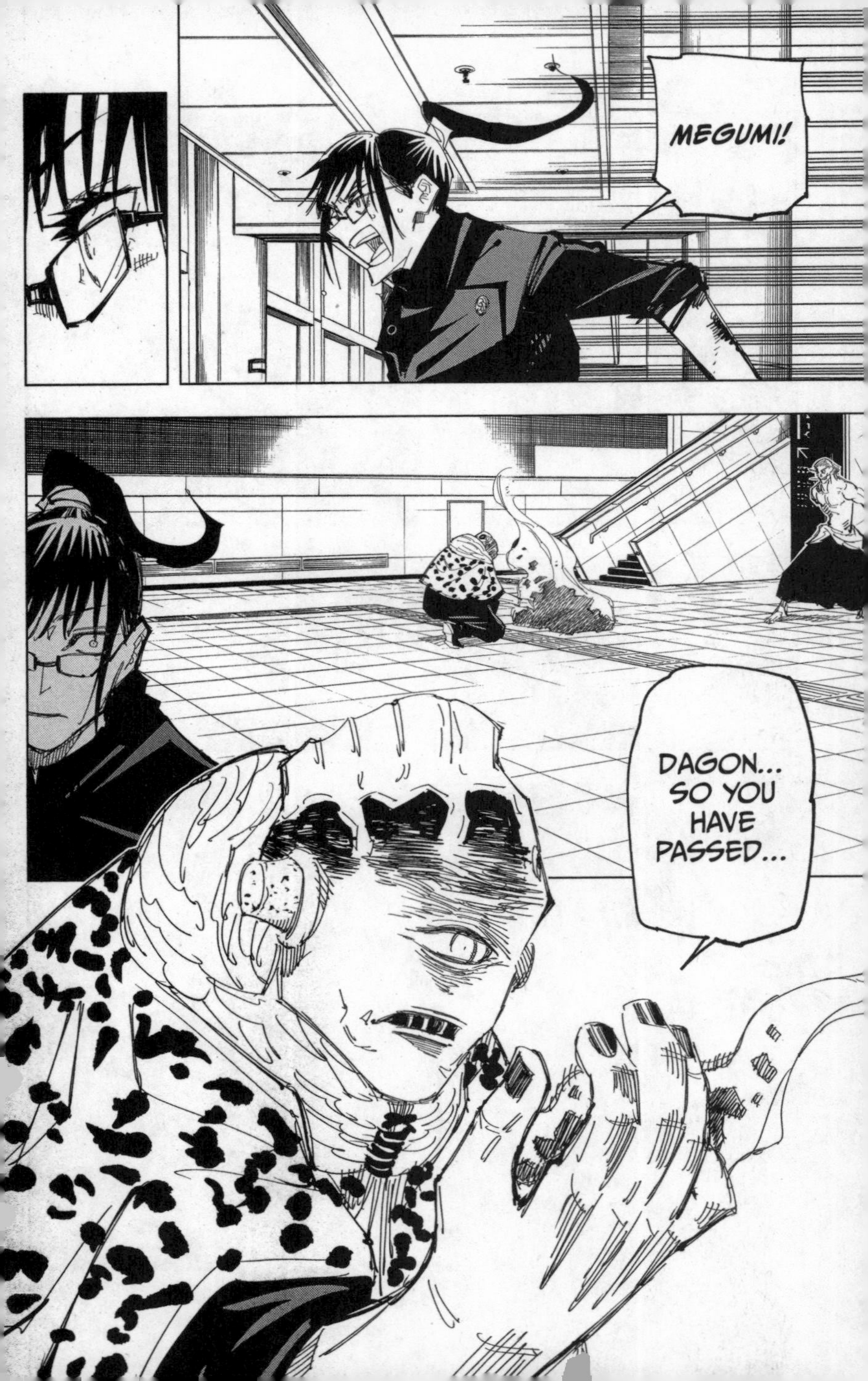
MEGUMI!
DAGON... SO YOU HAVE PASSED...

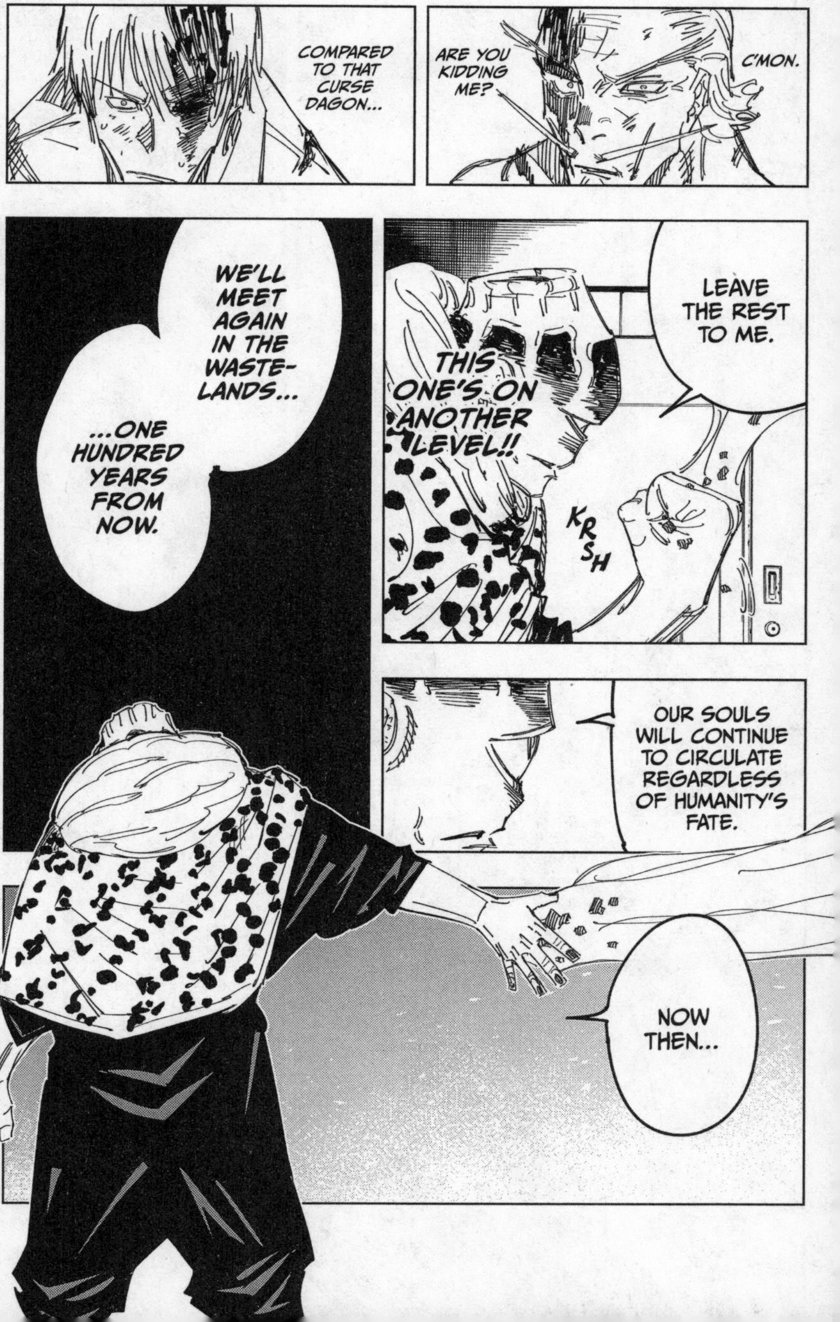
C'MON.
ARE YOU KIDDING ME?
COMPARED TO THAT CURSE DAGON...
LEAVE THE REST TO ME.
THIS ONE'S ON ANOTHER LEVEL!!
KRSH
OUR SOULS WILL CONTINUE TO CIRCULATE REGARDLESS OF HUMANITY'S FATE.
WE'LL MEET AGAIN IN THE WASTE-LANDS...
...ONE HUNDRED YEARS FROM NOW.
NOW THEN...

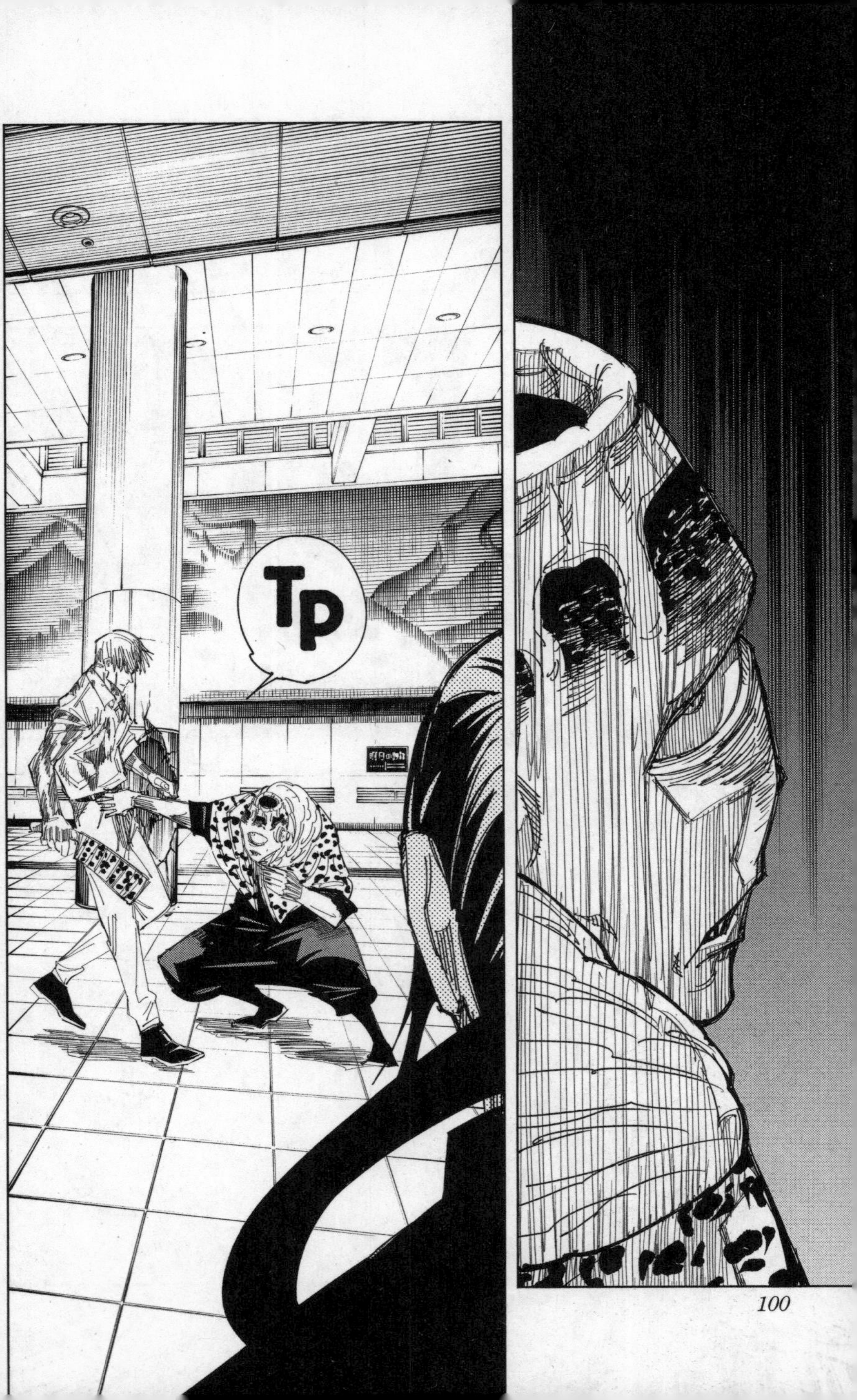
TP

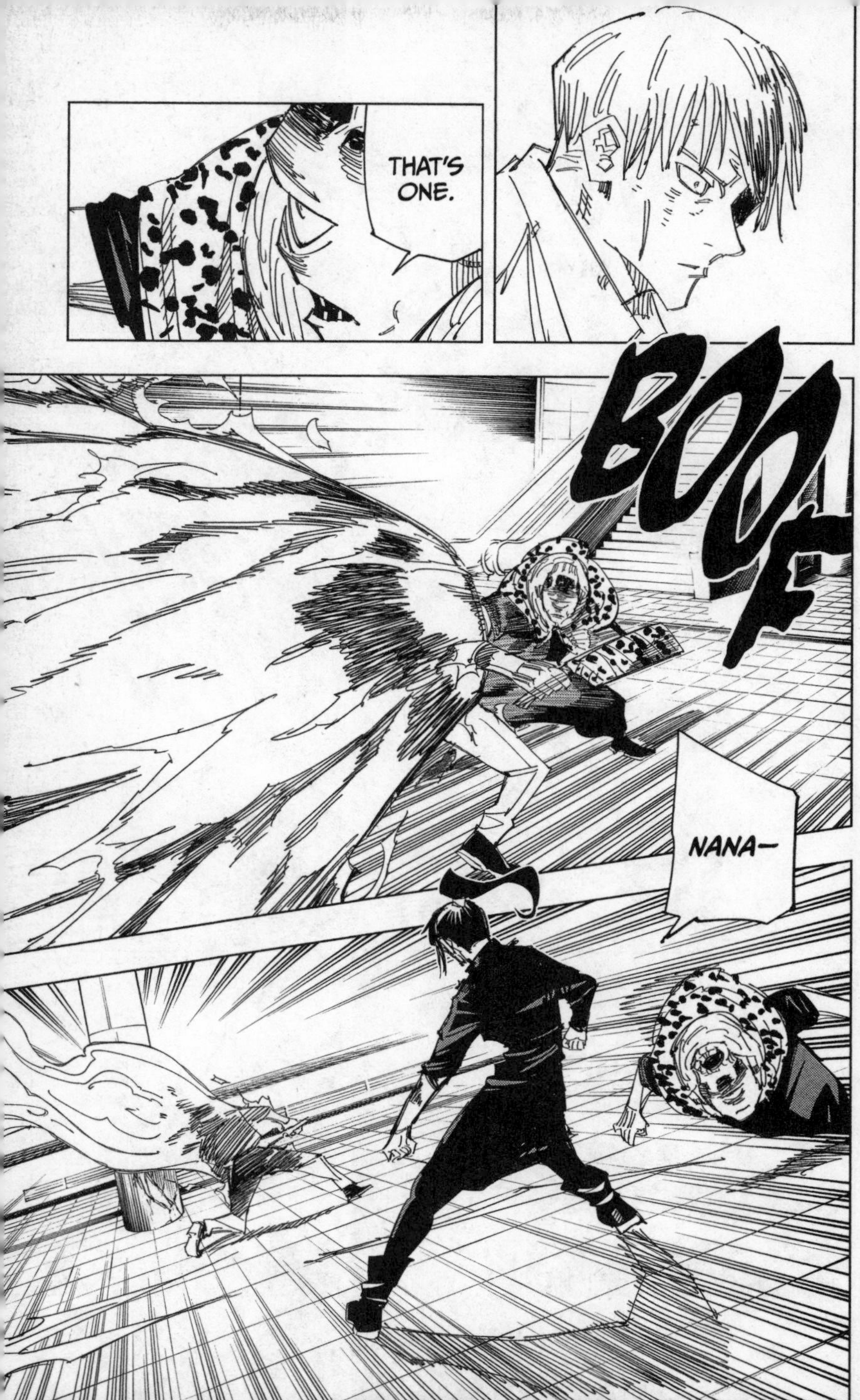
THAT'S ONE.
BOOF
NANA—

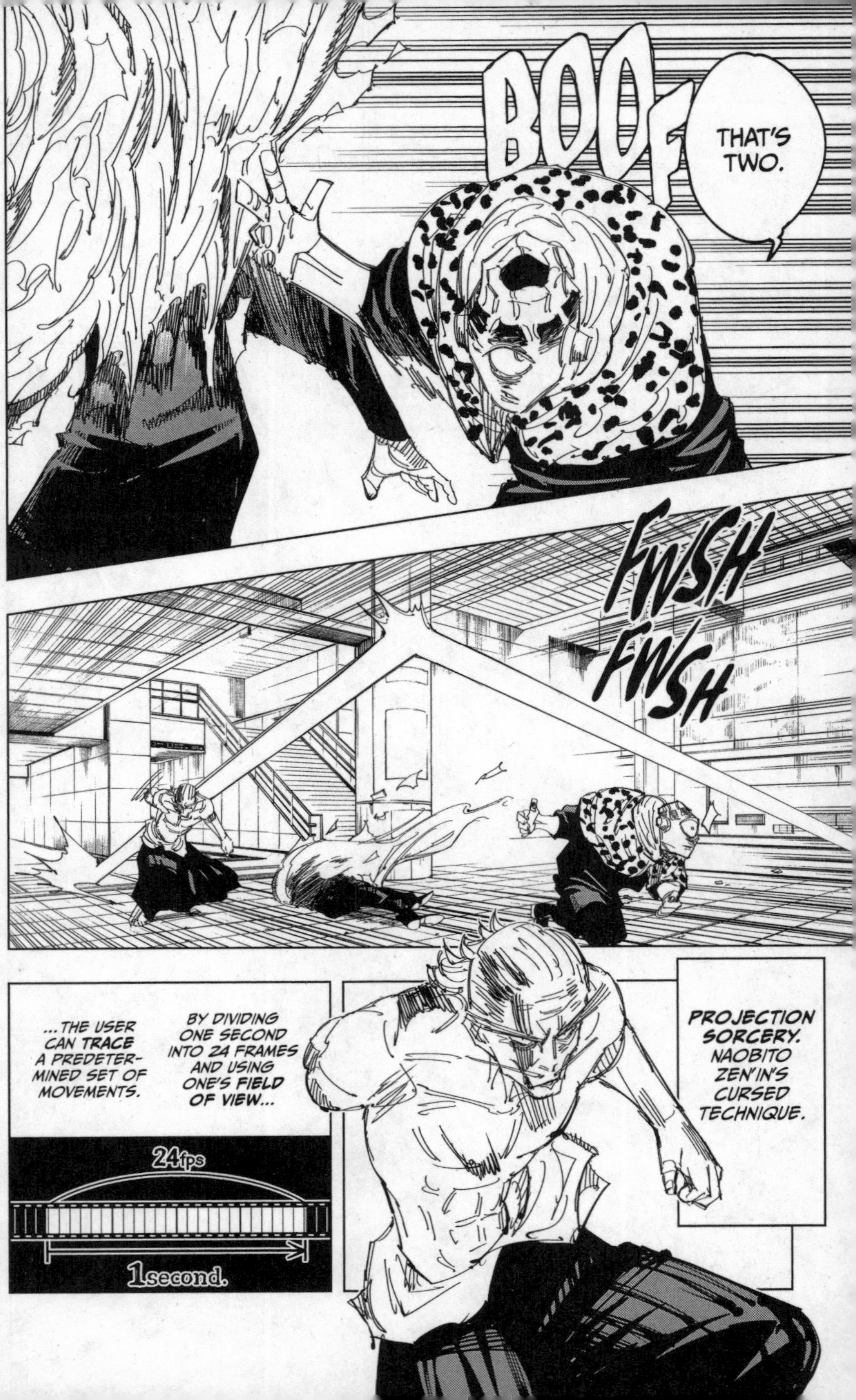
BOOF
THAT'S TWO.
FWSH FWSH
PROJECTION SORCERY. NAOBITO ZEN'IN'S CURSED TECHNIQUE.
BY DIVIDING ONE SECOND INTO 24 FRAMES AND USING ONE'S FIELD OF VIEW...
...THE USER CAN TRACE A PREDETERMINED SET OF MOVEMENTS.
24fps
1second.

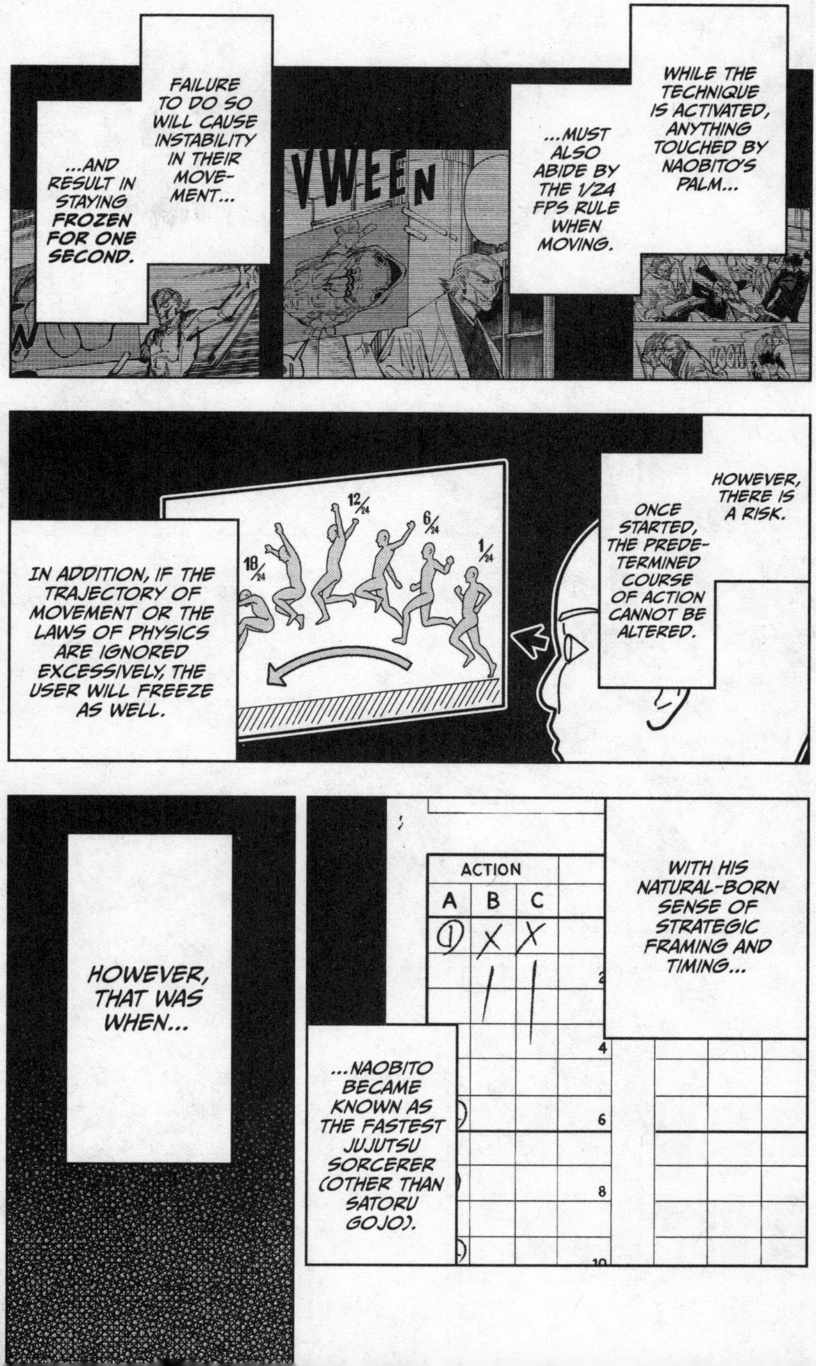
WHILE THE TECHNIQUE IS ACTIVATED, ANYTHING TOUCHED BY NAOBITO'S PALM...
...MUST ALSO ABIDE BY THE 1/24 FPS RULE WHEN MOVING.
VWEEN
FAILURE TO DO SO WILL CAUSE INSTABILITY IN THEIR MOVE-MENT...
...AND RESULT IN STAYING FROZEN FOR ONE SECOND.
HOWEVER, THERE IS A RISK.
ONCE STARTED, THE PREDE-TERMINED COURSE OF ACTION CANNOT BE ALTERED.
1/24
6/24
12/24
18/24
IN ADDITION, IF THE TRAJECTORY OF MOVEMENT OR THE LAWS OF PHYSICS ARE IGNORED EXCESSIVELY, THE USER WILL FREEZE AS WELL.
WITH HIS NATURAL-BORN SENSE OF STRATEGIC FRAMING AND TIMING...
ACTION
A B C
4
6
8
...NAOBITO BECAME KNOWN AS THE FASTEST JUJUTSU SORCERER (OTHER THAN SATORU GOJO).
HOWEVER, THAT WAS WHEN...

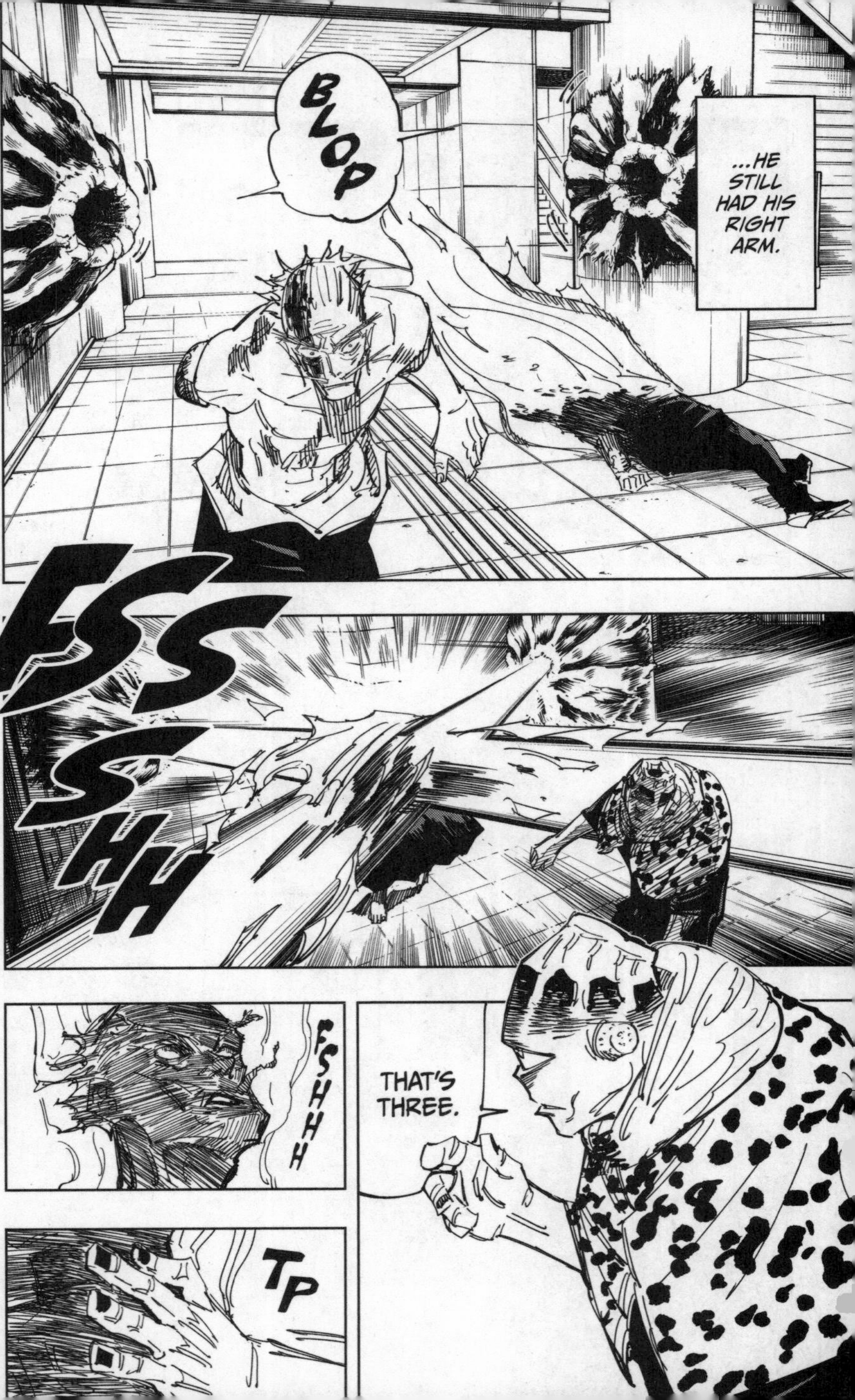
...HE STILL HAD HIS RIGHT ARM.
BLOP
FSSSHH
THAT'S THREE.
FSHHH
TP

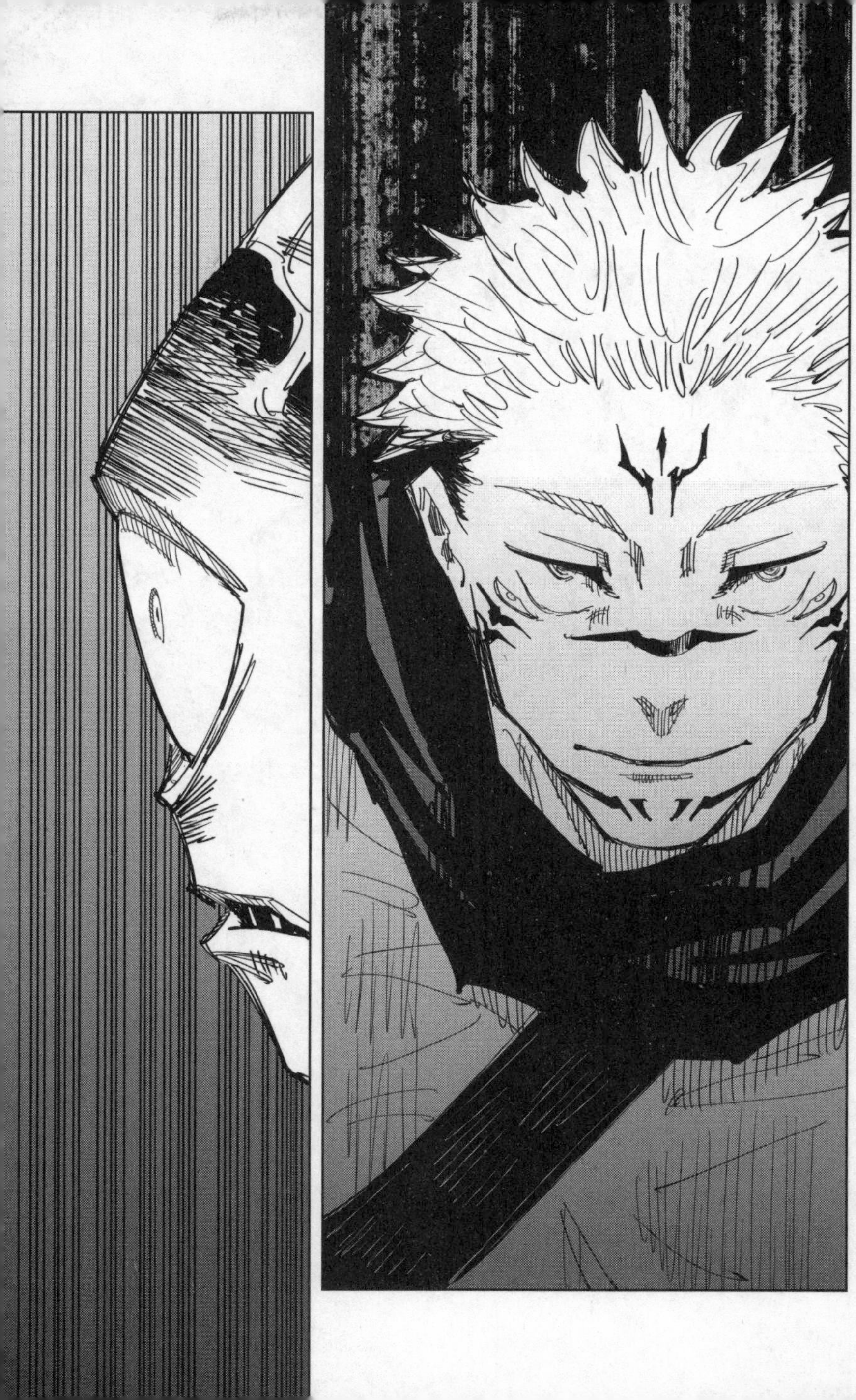

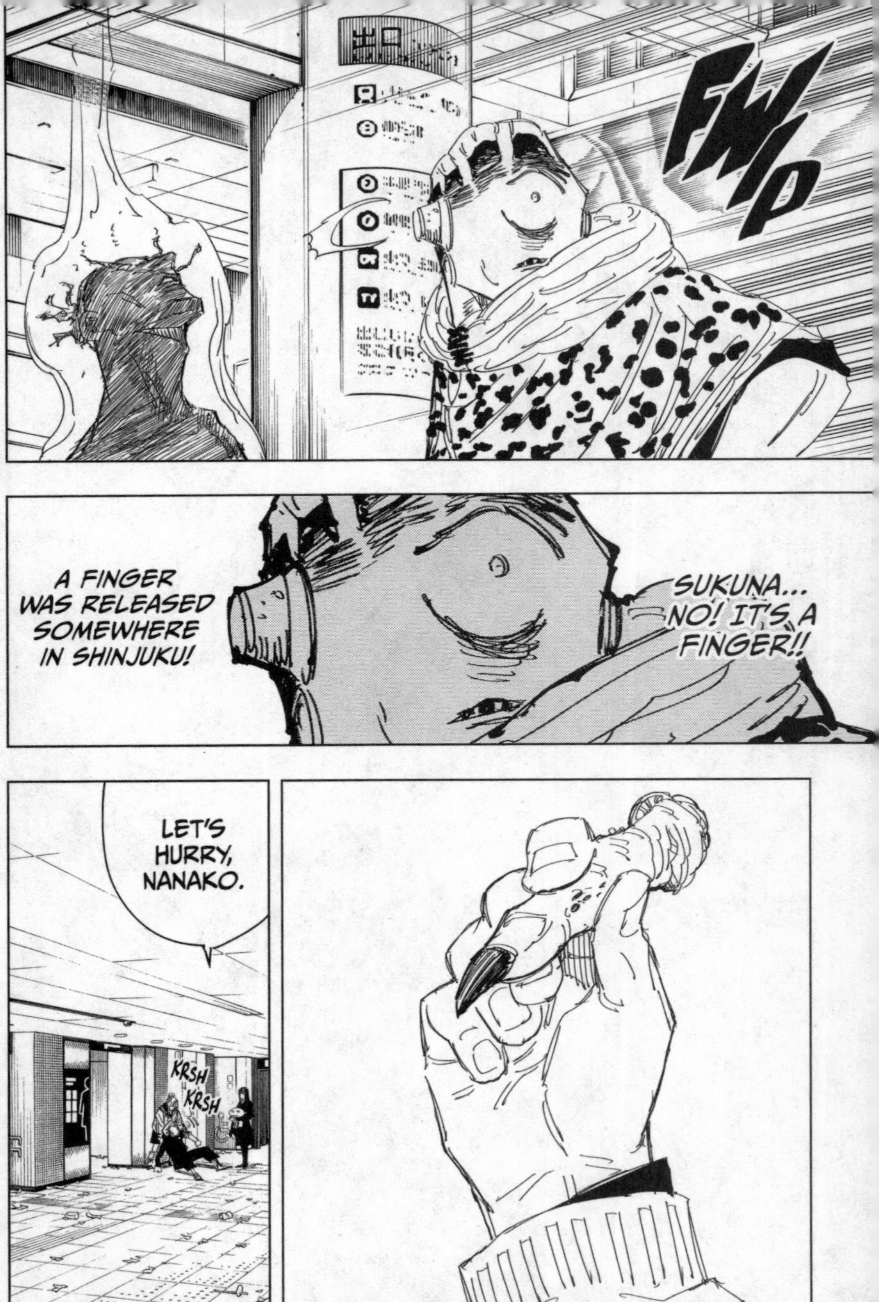
FWIP
出口
SUKUNA... NO! IT'S A FINGER!!
A FINGER WAS RELEASED SOMEWHERE IN SHINJUKU!
LET'S HURRY, NANAKO.
KRSH KRSH

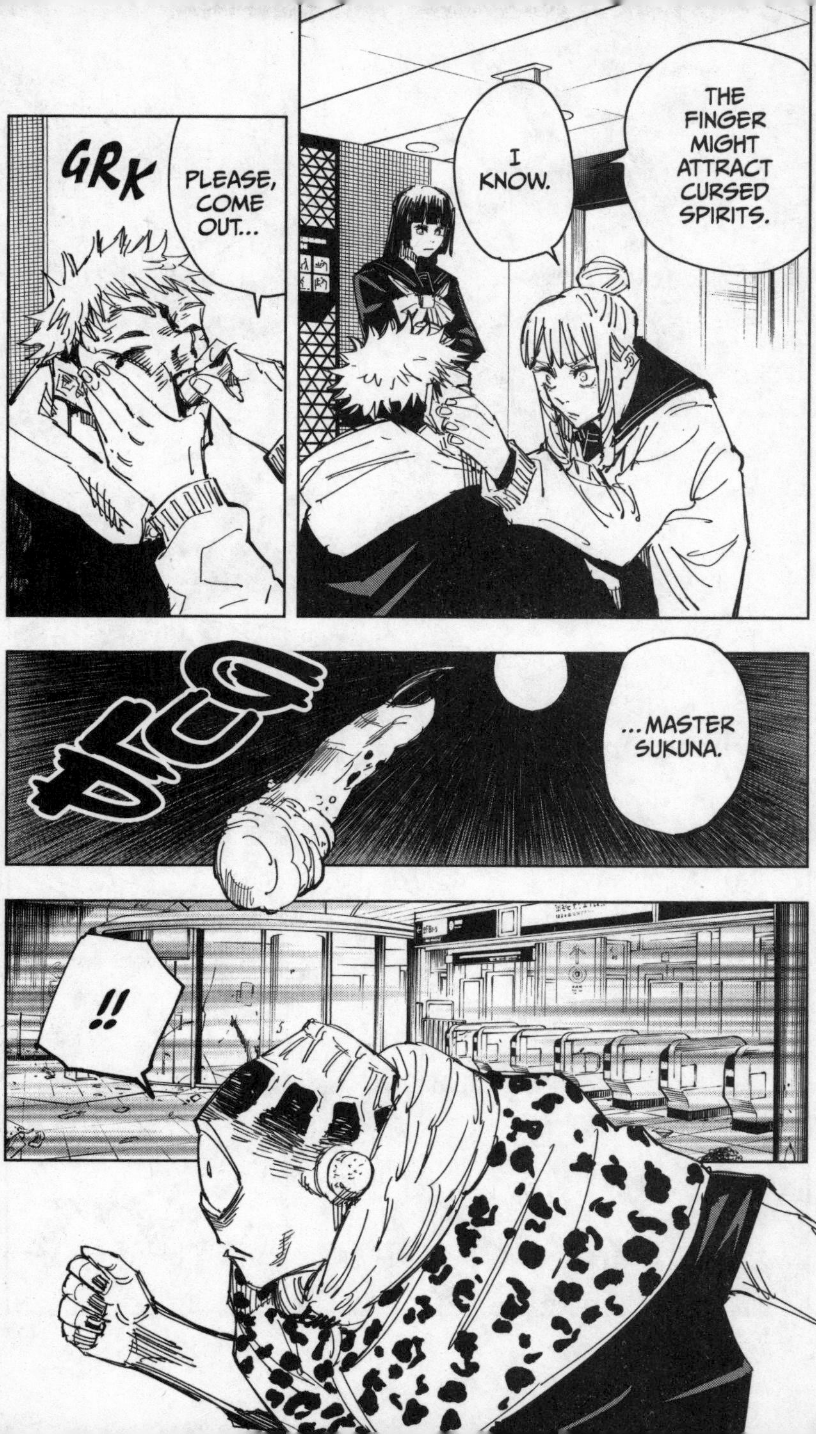
THE FINGER MIGHT ATTRACT CURSED SPIRITS.
I KNOW.
PLEASE, COME OUT...
GRK
...MASTER SUKUNA.
!!

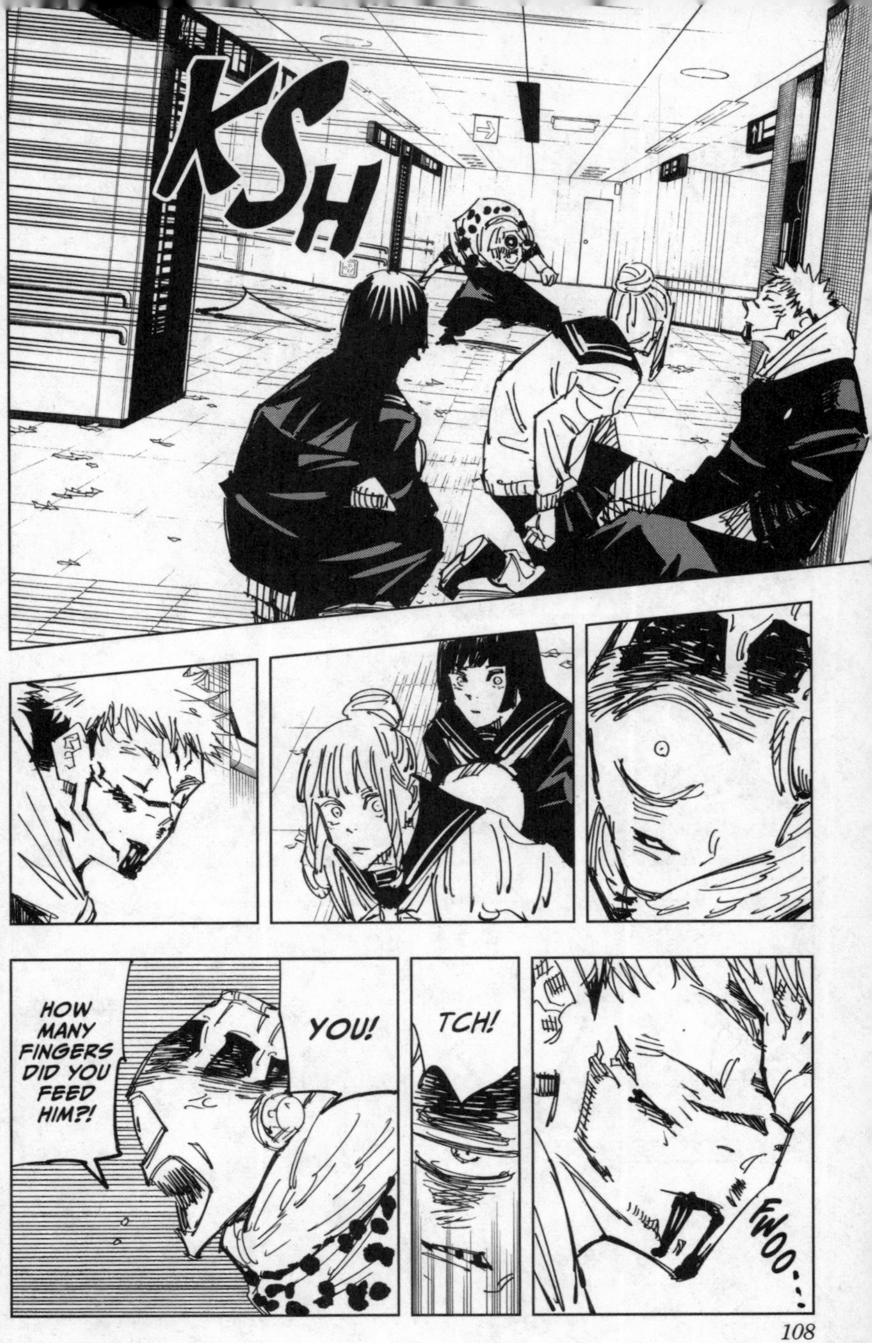
KSH
FWOO...
TCH!
YOU!
HOW MANY FINGERS DID YOU FEED HIM?!

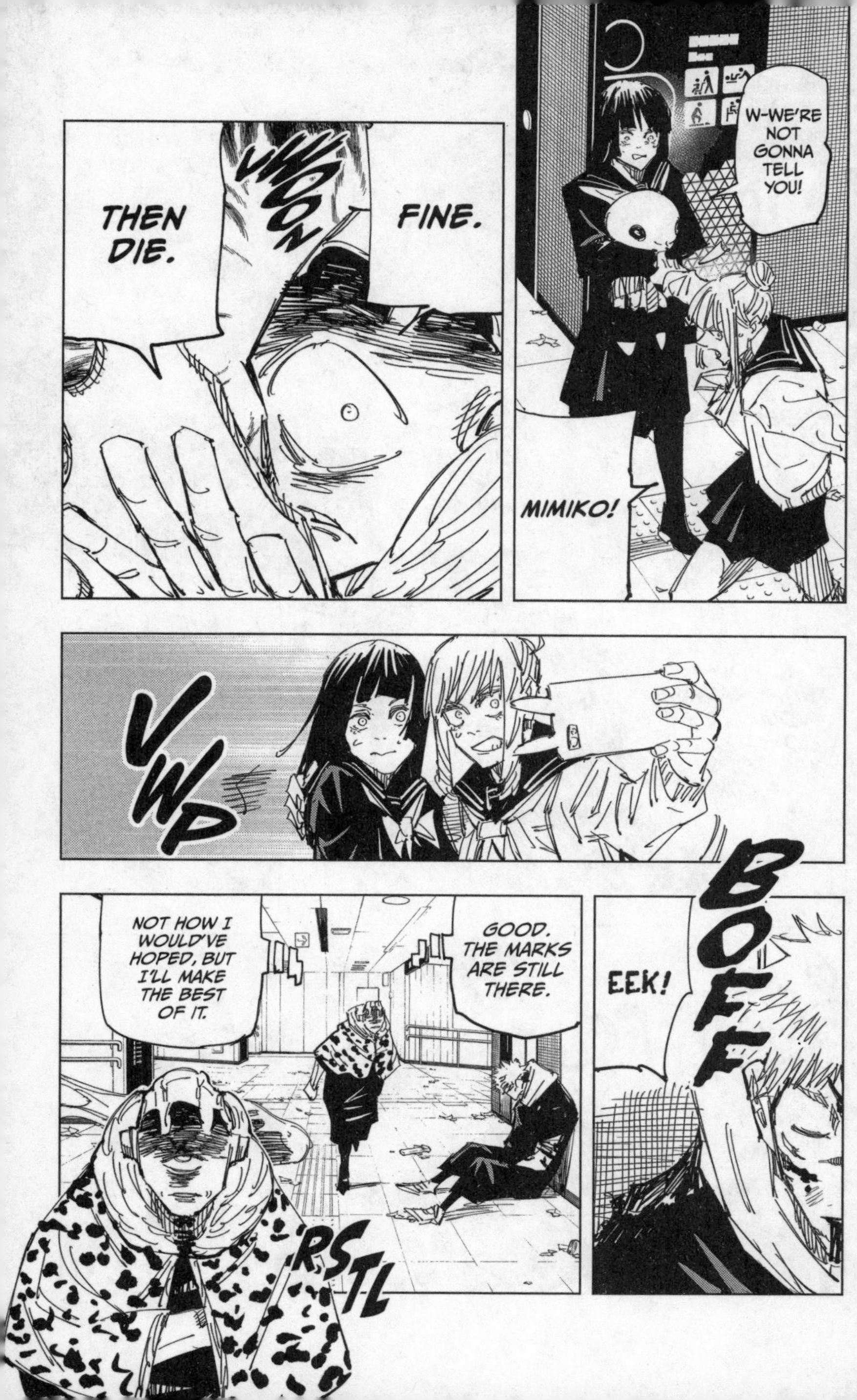
W-WE'RE NOT GONNA TELL YOU!
MIMIKO!
FINE.
VWOOM
THEN DIE.
VWP
BOFF
EEK!
GOOD. THE MARKS ARE STILL THERE.
NOT HOW I WOULD'VE HOPED, BUT I'LL MAKE THE BEST OF IT.
RSTL

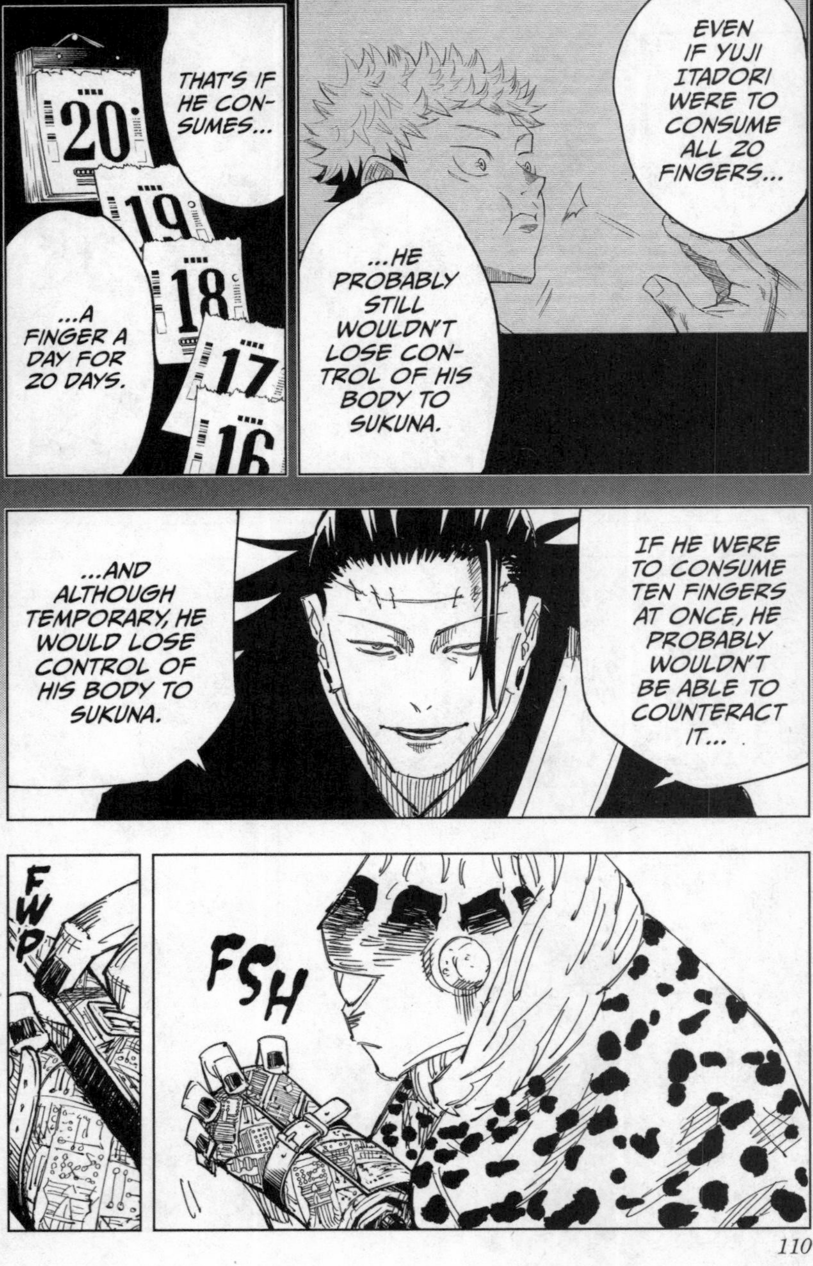
EVEN IF YUJI ITADORI WERE TO CONSUME ALL 20 FINGERS...
...HE PROBABLY STILL WOULDN'T LOSE CONTROL OF HIS BODY TO SUKUNA.
THAT'S IF HE CONSUMES...
20
19
18
17
16
...A FINGER A DAY FOR 20 DAYS.
IF HE WERE TO CONSUME TEN FINGERS AT ONCE, HE PROBABLY WOULDN'T BE ABLE TO COUNTERACT IT...
...AND ALTHOUGH TEMPORARY, HE WOULD LOSE CONTROL OF HIS BODY TO SUKUNA.
FSH
FWP

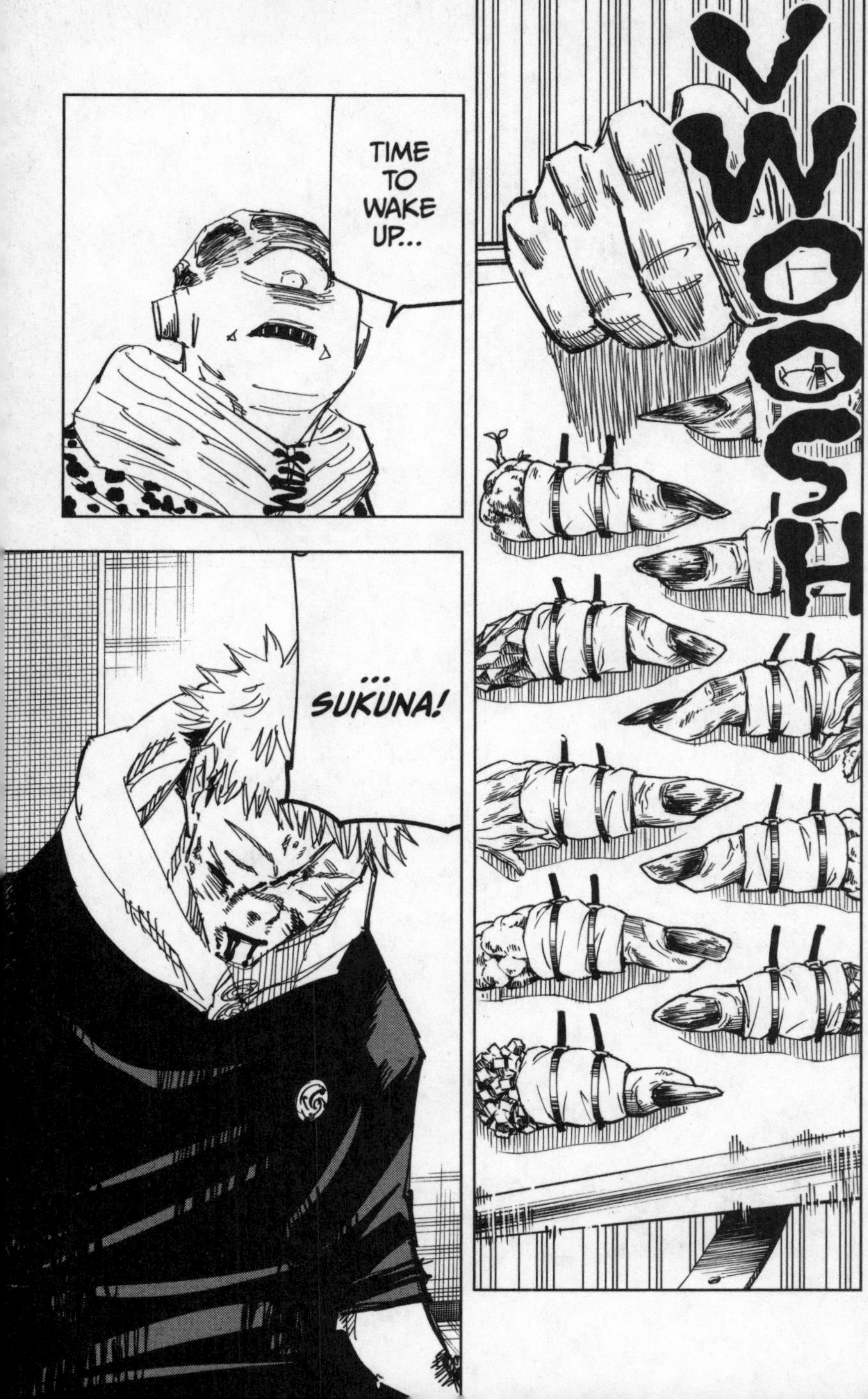
WOOSH
TIME TO WAKE UP...
...SUKUNA!

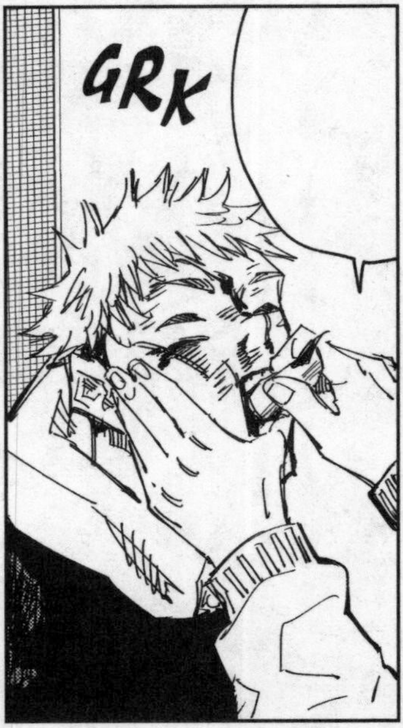
GRK

• Apparently, it's difficult to force-feed someone who's sleeping.
• Something to do with pharyngeal reflex...

Chapter 112: The Shibuya Incident, Part 30

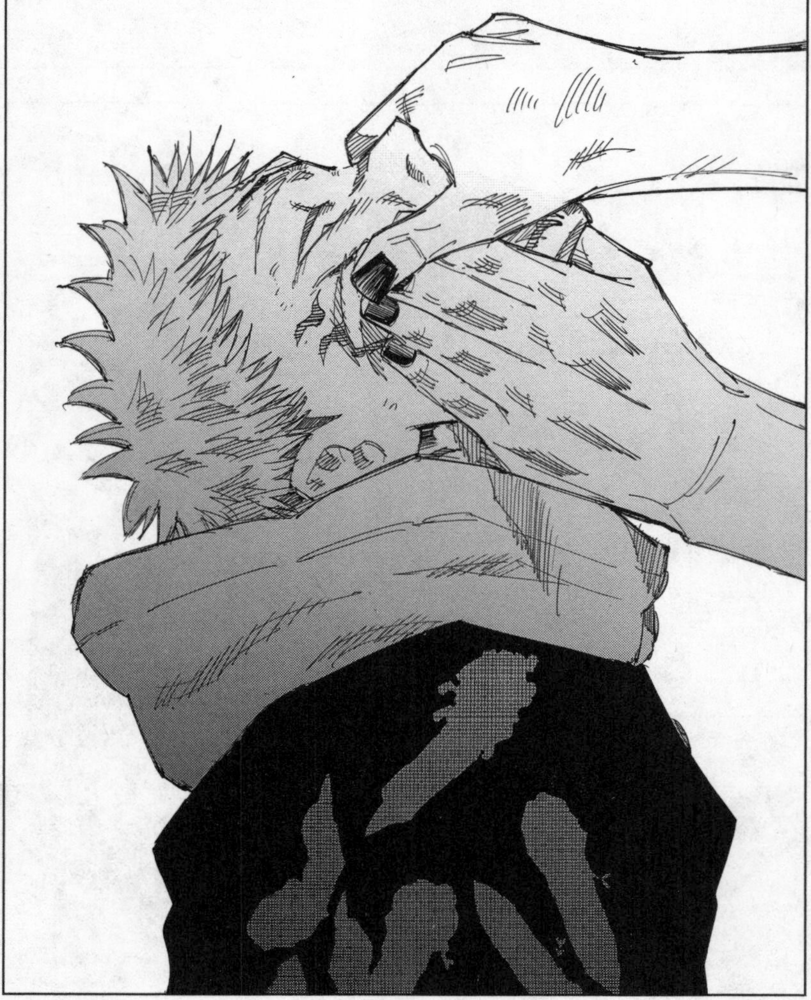

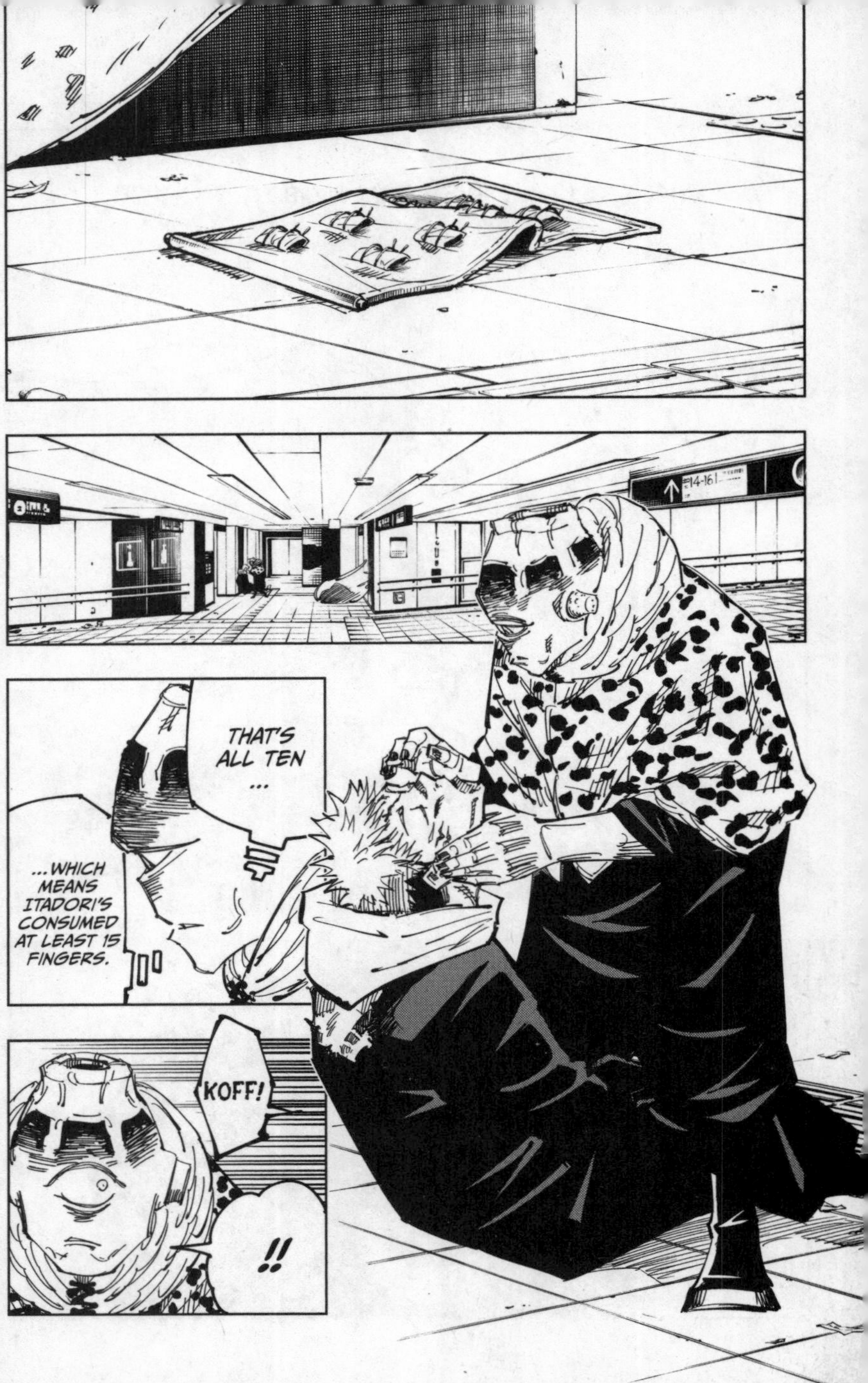
THAT'S ALL TEN ...
...WHICH MEANS ITADORI'S CONSUMED AT LEAST 15 FINGERS.
KOFF!
!!

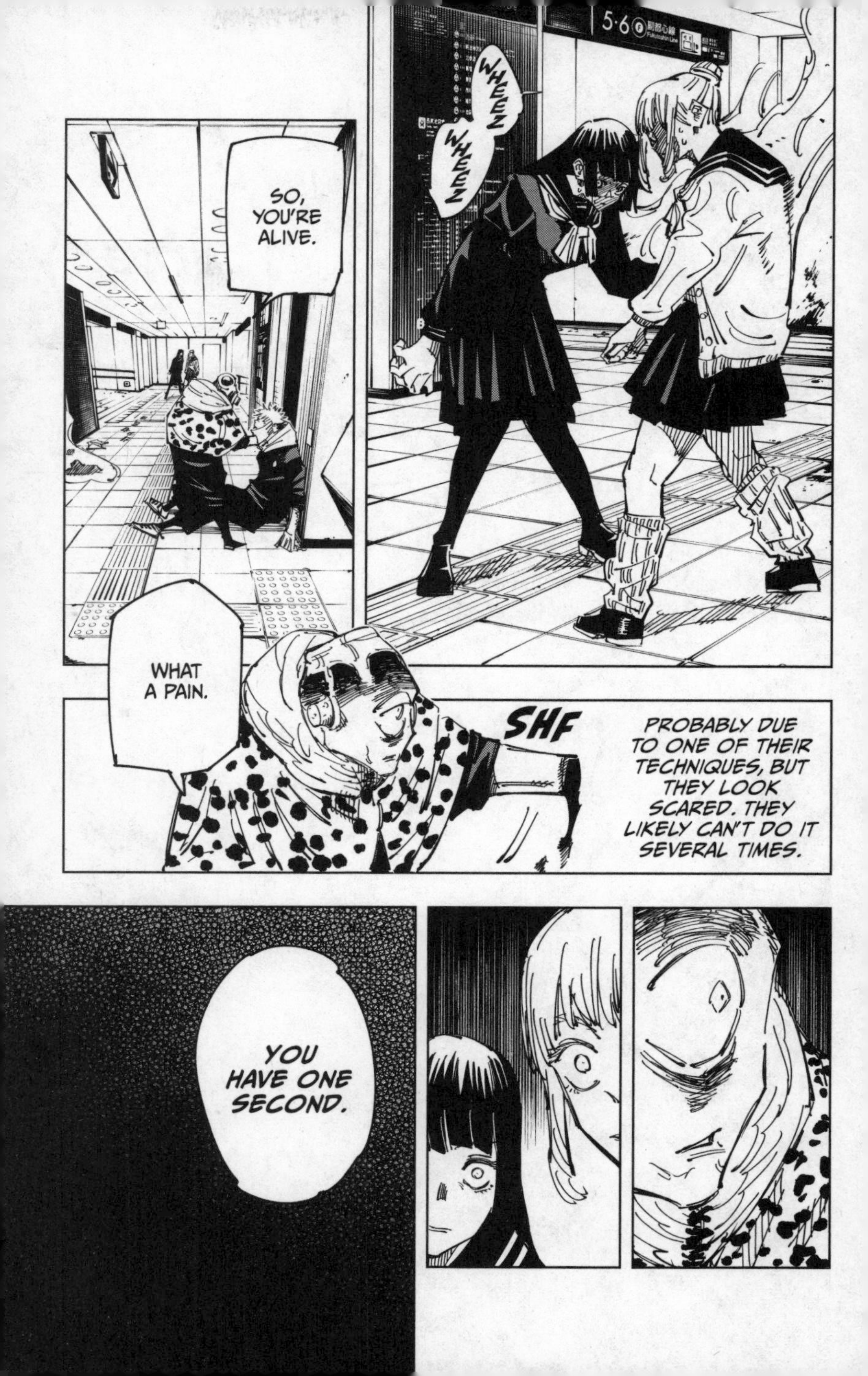
WHEEZ WHEEZ
SO, YOU'RE ALIVE.
WHAT A PAIN.
SHF
PROBABLY DUE TO ONE OF THEIR TECHNIQUES, BUT THEY LOOK SCARED. THEY LIKELY CAN'T DO IT SEVERAL TIMES.
YOU HAVE ONE SECOND.

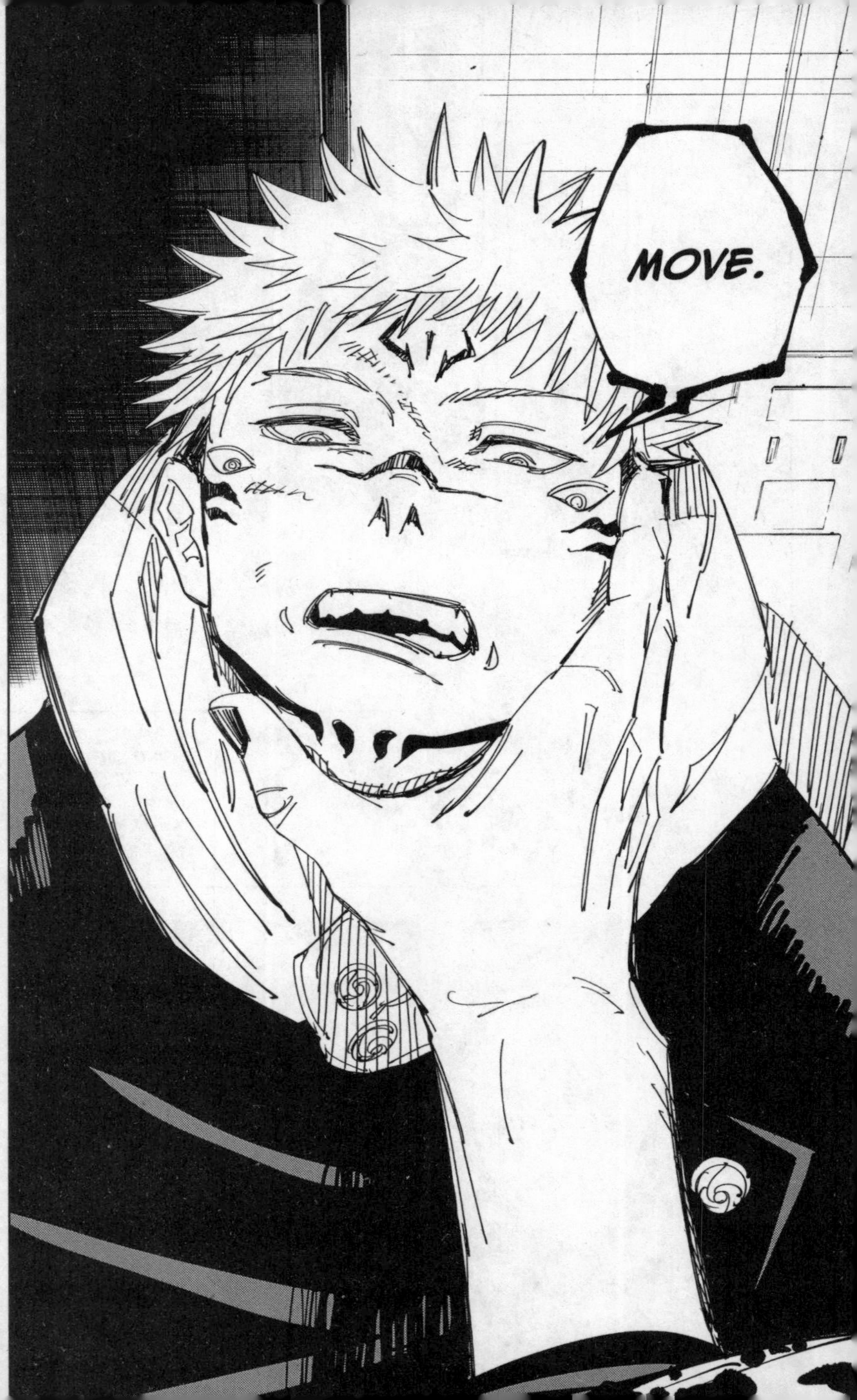
MOVE.

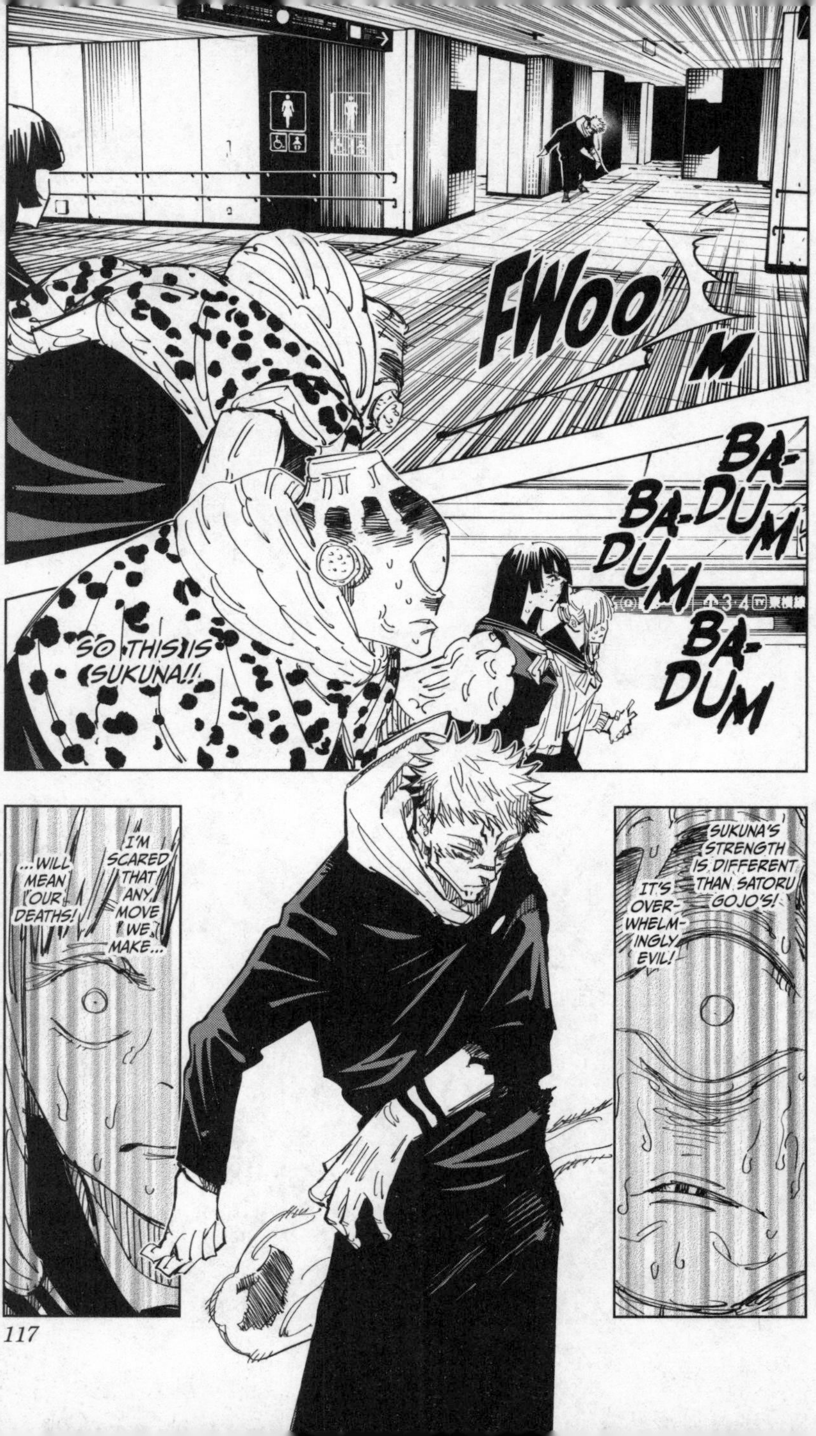
FWOOOM
BA-DUM BA-DUM BA-DUM BA-DUM
SO THIS IS SUKUNA!!
SUKUNA'S STRENGTH IS DIFFERENT THAN SATORU GOJO'S!
IT'S OVER-WHELM-INGLY EVIL!
I'M SCARED THAT ANY MOVE WE MAKE...
...WILL MEAN OUR DEATHS!

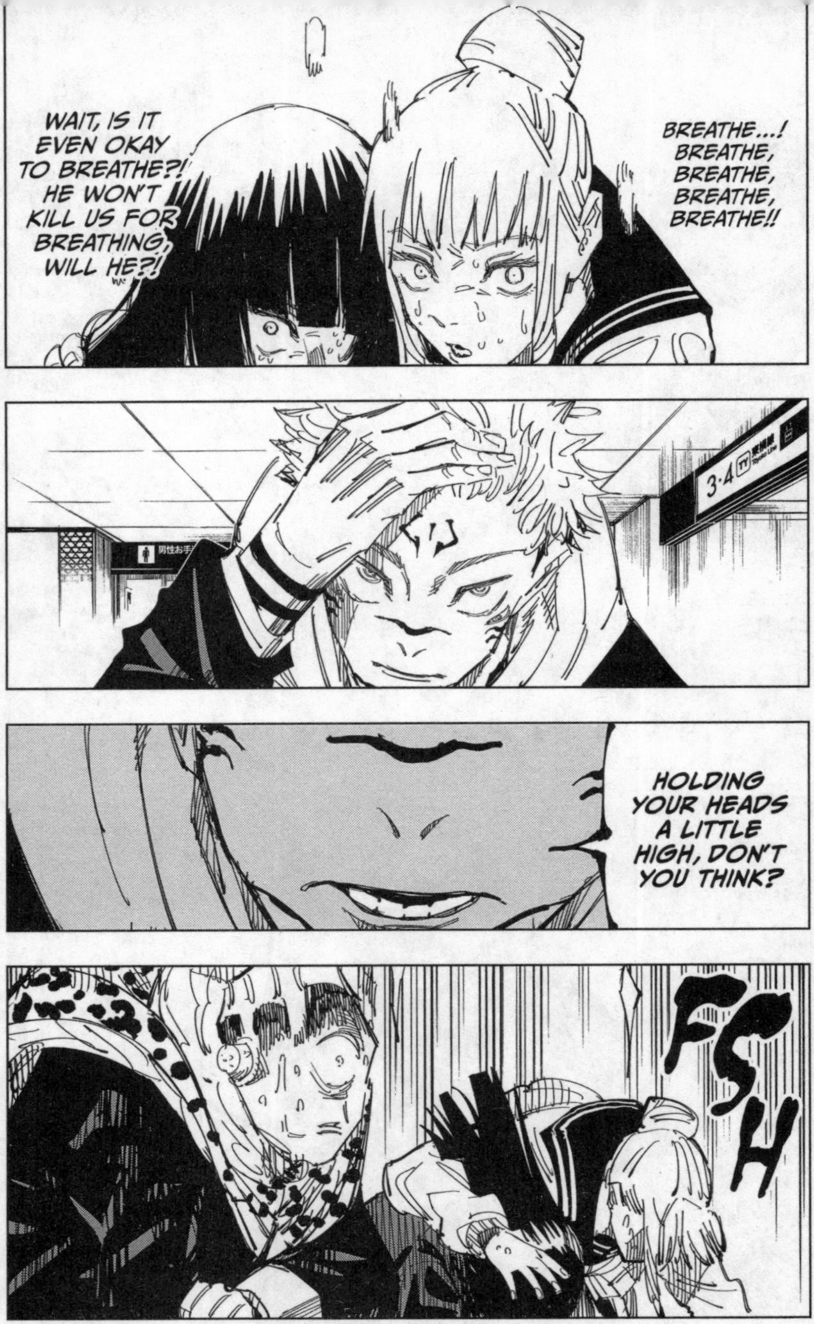
BREATHE...! BREATHE, BREATHE, BREATHE, BREATHE!!
WAIT, IS IT EVEN OKAY TO BREATHE?! HE WON'T KILL US FOR BREATHING, WILL HE?!
3·4
HOLDING YOUR HEADS A LITTLE HIGH, DON'T YOU THINK?
FSH

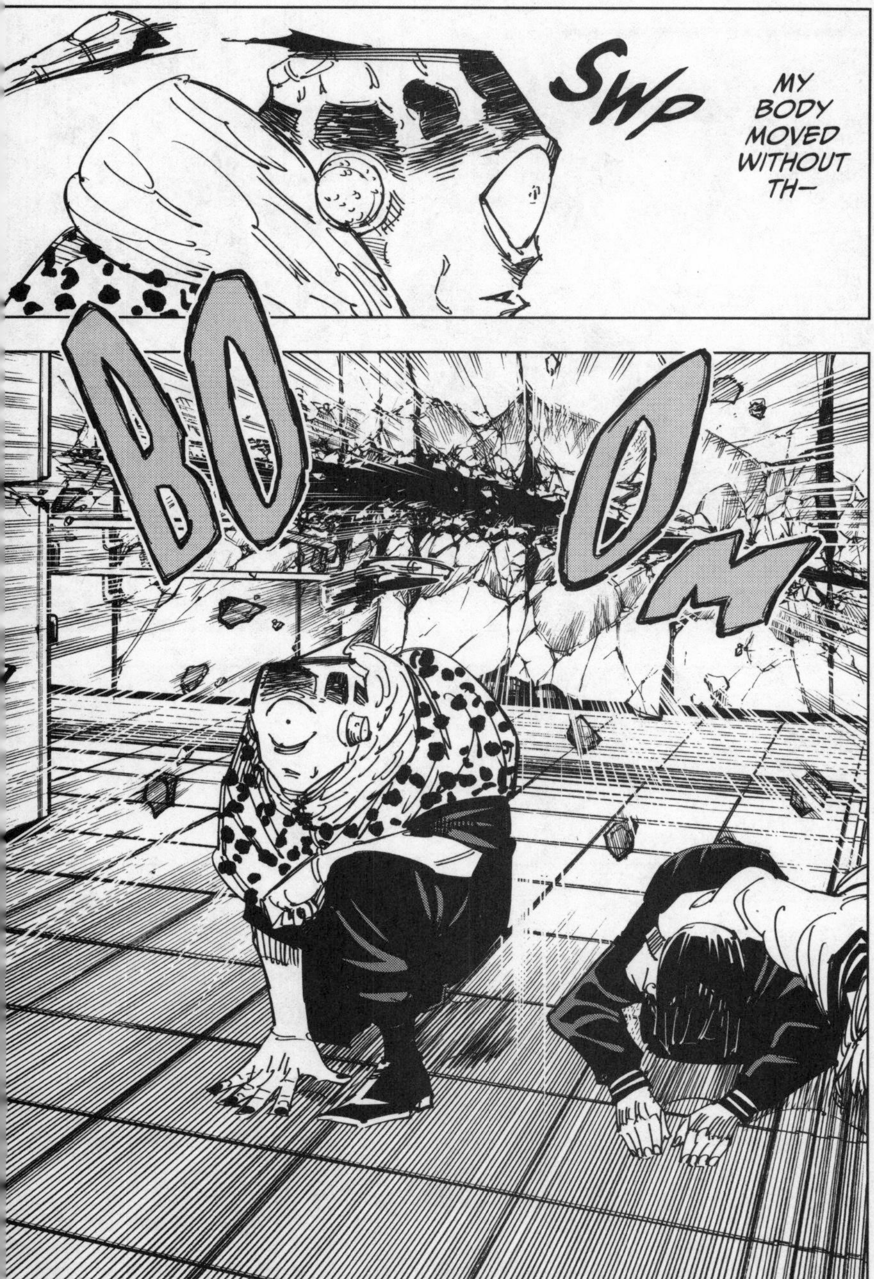
MY BODY MOVED WITHOUT TH—
SWP
BOOM

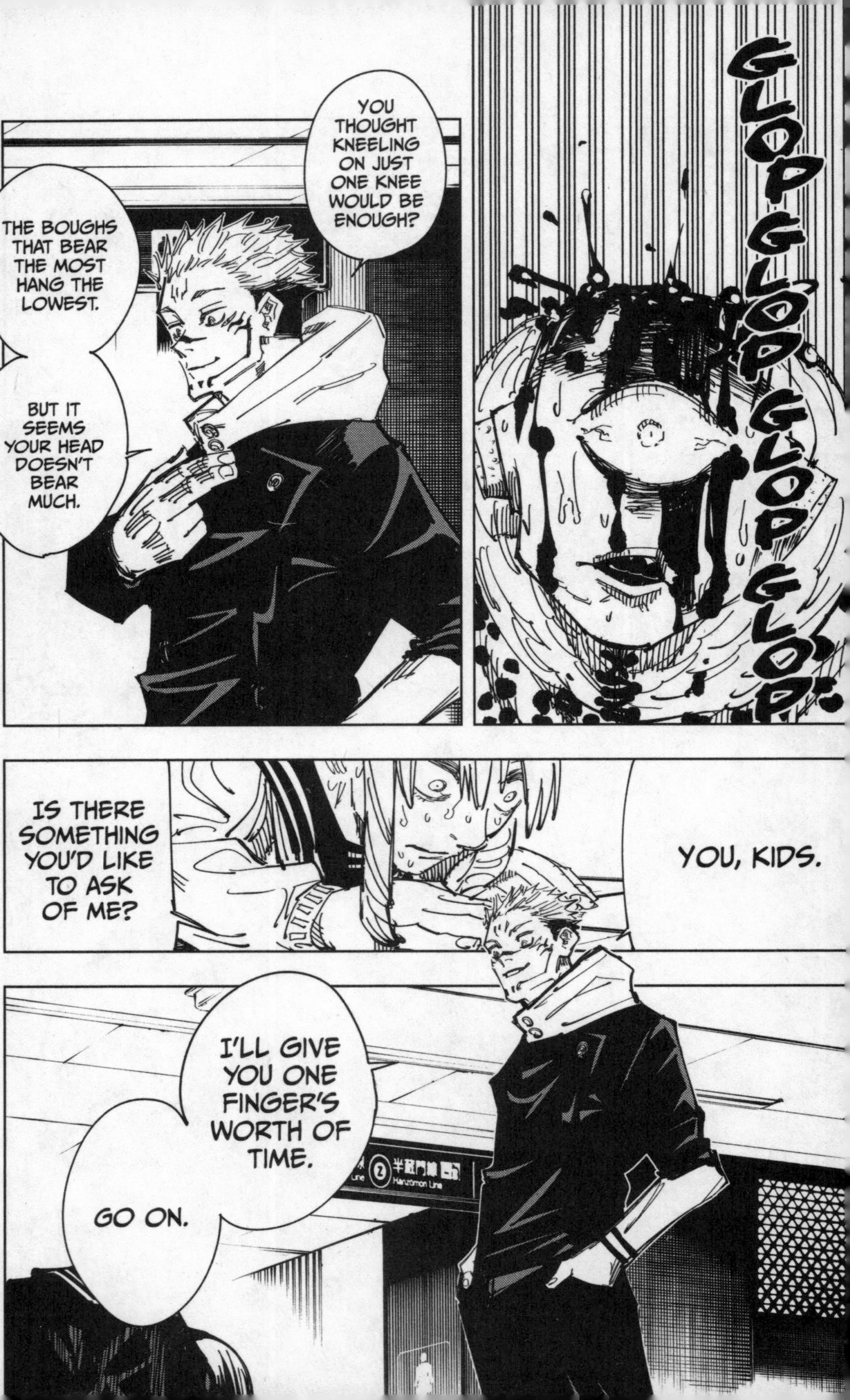
GLOP GLOP GLOP GLOP
YOU THOUGHT KNEELING ON JUST ONE KNEE WOULD BE ENOUGH?
THE BOUGHS THAT BEAR THE MOST HANG THE LOWEST.
BUT IT SEEMS YOUR HEAD DOESN'T BEAR MUCH.
YOU, KIDS.
IS THERE SOMETHING YOU'D LIKE TO ASK OF ME?
I'LL GIVE YOU ONE FINGER'S WORTH OF TIME.
GO ON.

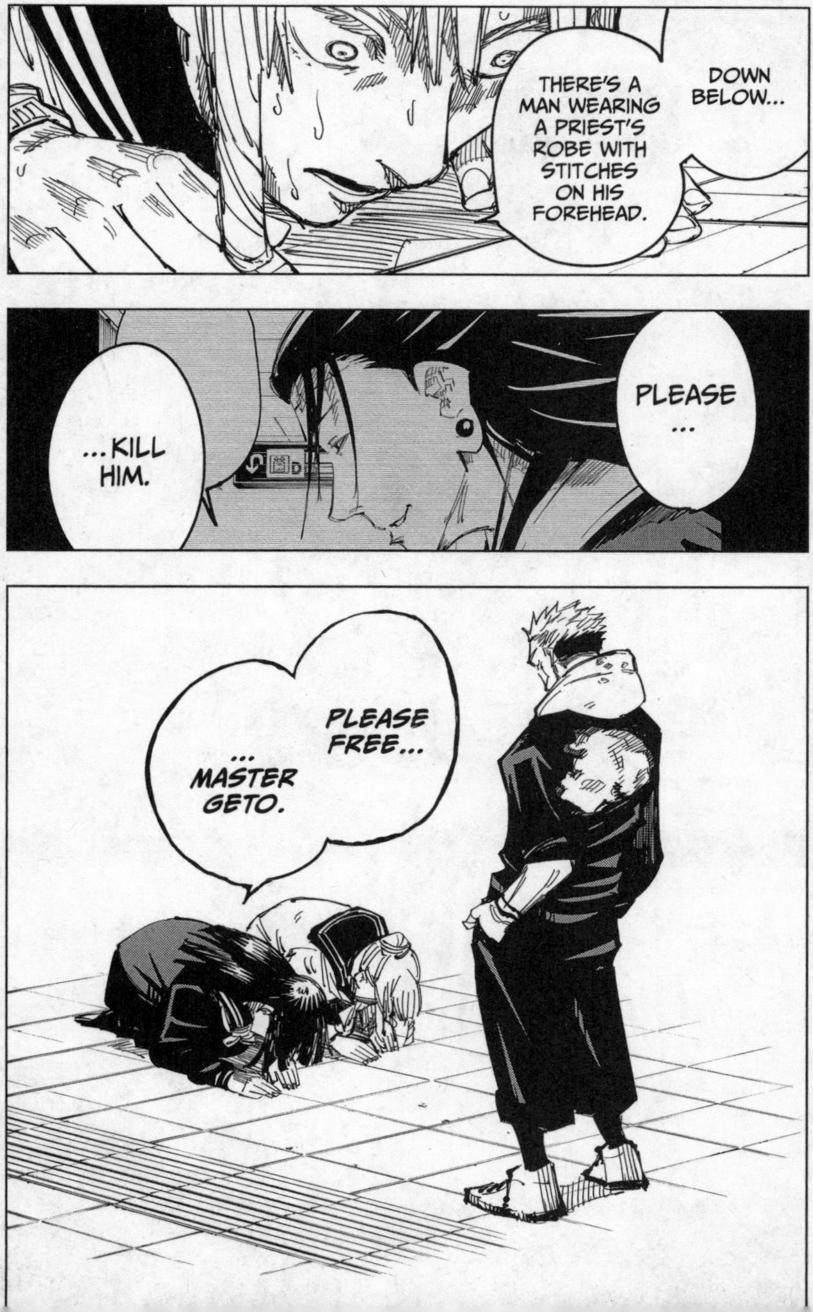
DOWN BELOW...
THERE'S A MAN WEARING A PRIEST'S ROBE WITH STITCHES ON HIS FOREHEAD.
PLEASE ...
...KILL HIM.
PLEASE FREE...
... MASTER GETO.

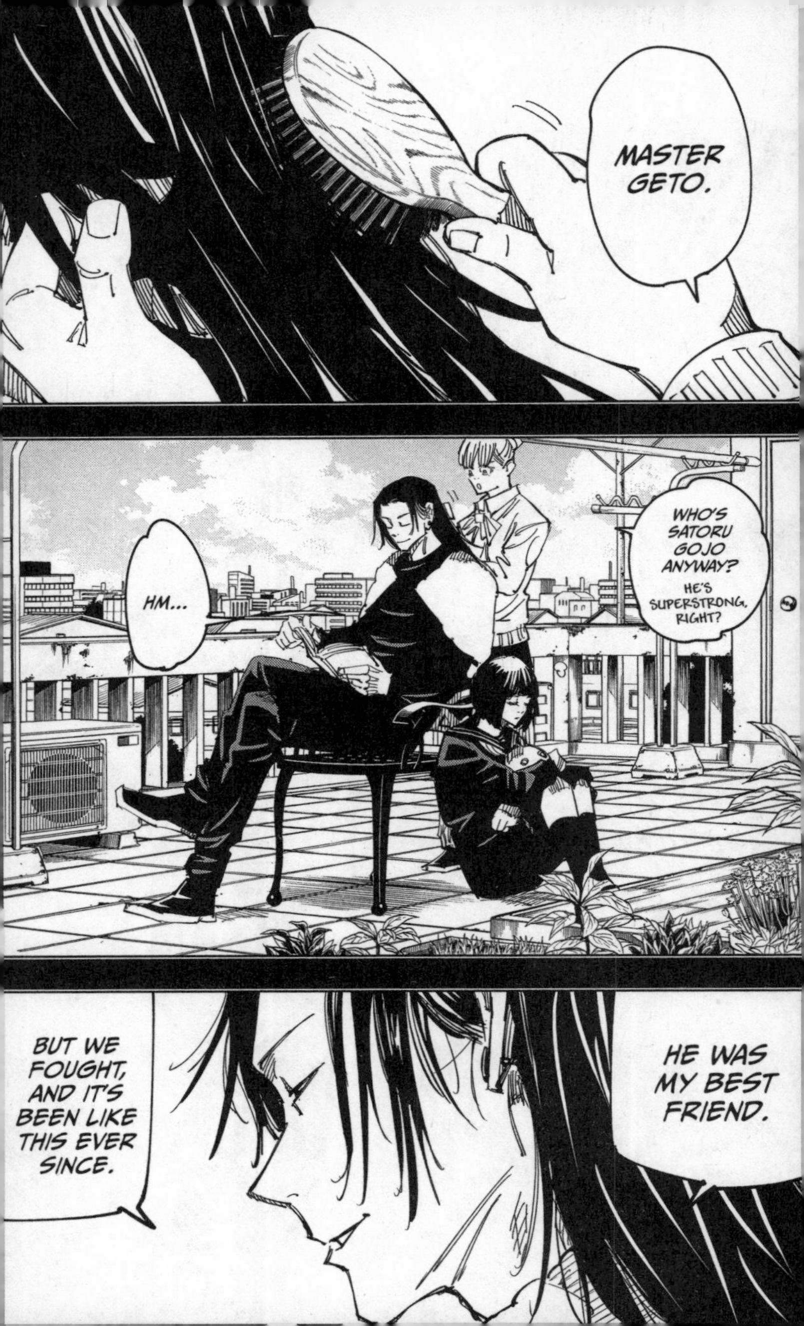
MASTER GETO.
WHO'S SATORU GOJO ANYWAY?
HE'S SUPERSTRONG, RIGHT?
HM...
HE WAS MY BEST FRIEND.
BUT WE FOUGHT, AND IT'S BEEN LIKE THIS EVER SINCE.

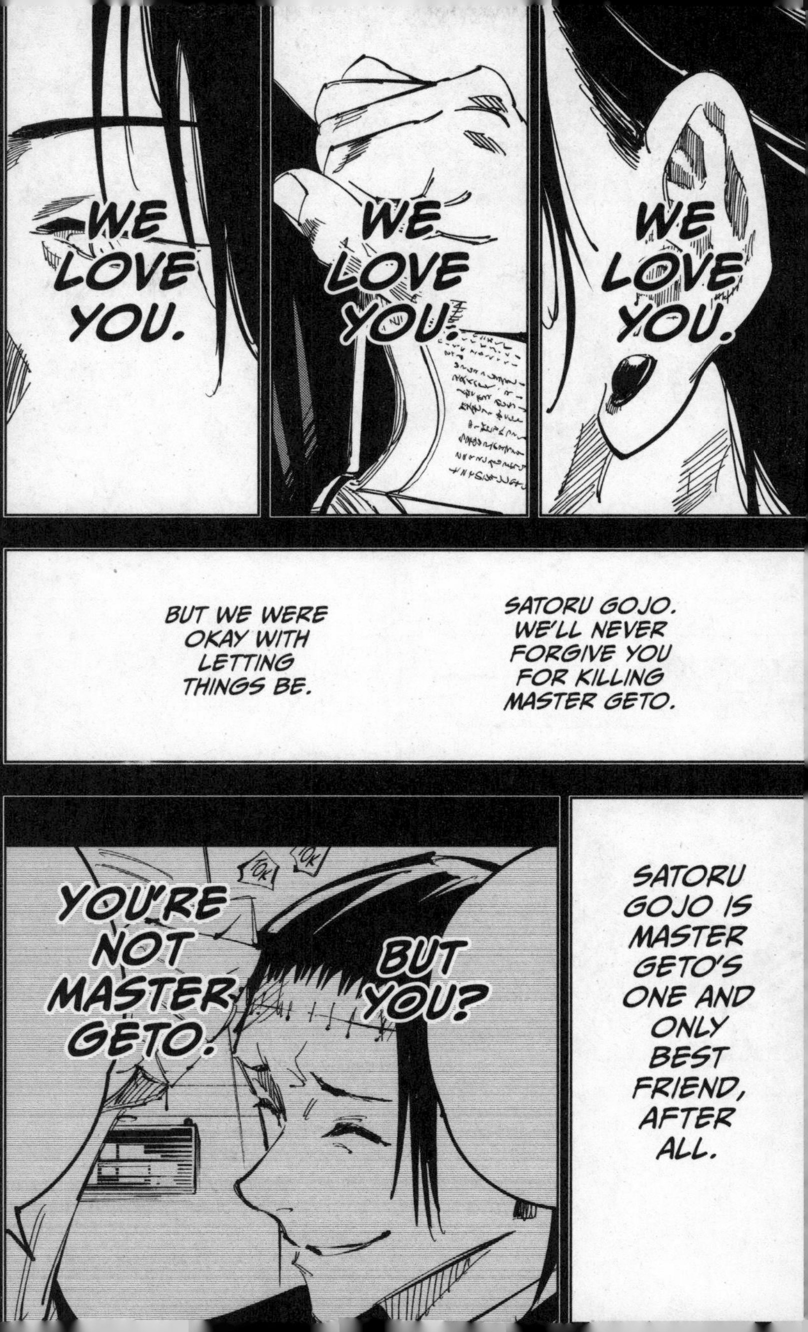
WE LOVE YOU.
WE LOVE YOU.
WE LOVE YOU.
SATORU GOJO. WE'LL NEVER FORGIVE YOU FOR KILLING MASTER GETO.
BUT WE WERE OKAY WITH LETTING THINGS BE.
SATORU GOJO IS MASTER GETO'S ONE AND ONLY BEST FRIEND, AFTER ALL.
BUT YOU?
YOU'RE NOT MASTER GETO.

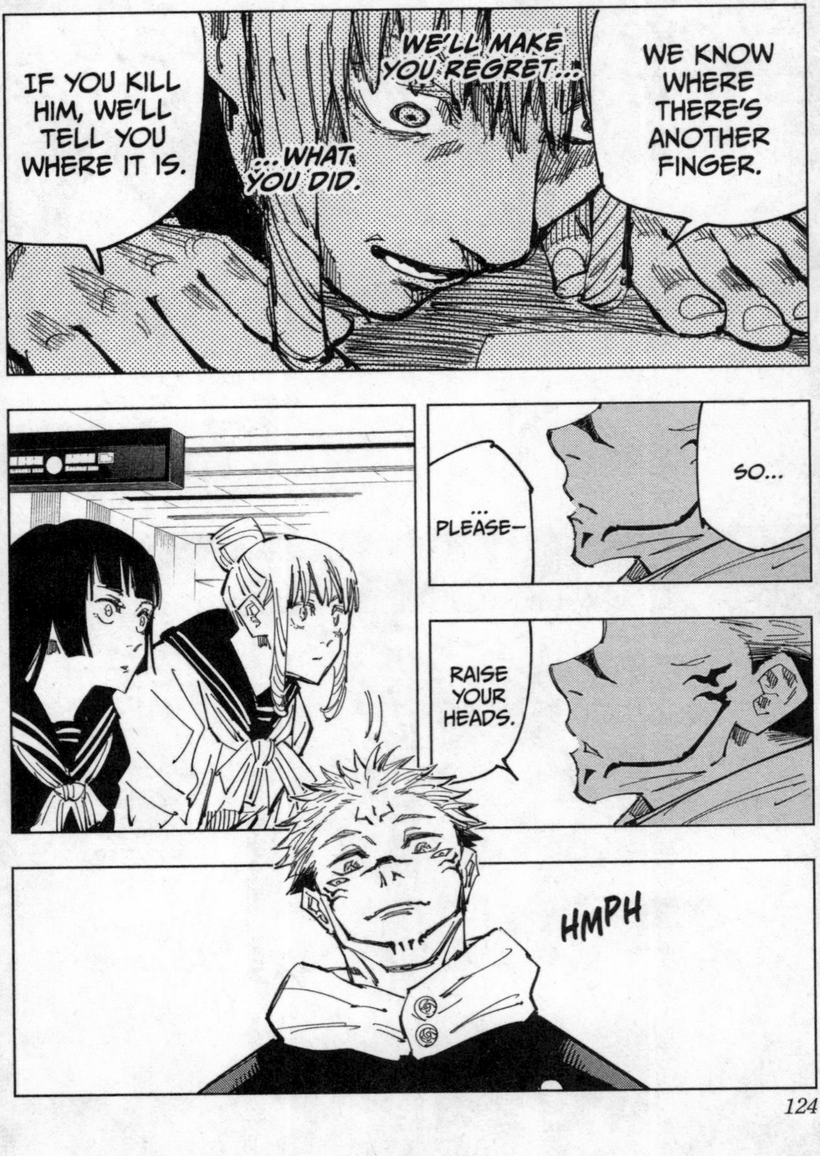
WE KNOW WHERE THERE'S ANOTHER FINGER.
WE'LL MAKE YOU REGRET...
...WHAT YOU DID.
IF YOU KILL HIM, WE'LL TELL YOU WHERE IT IS.
SO...
...PLEASE—
RAISE YOUR HEADS.
HMPH

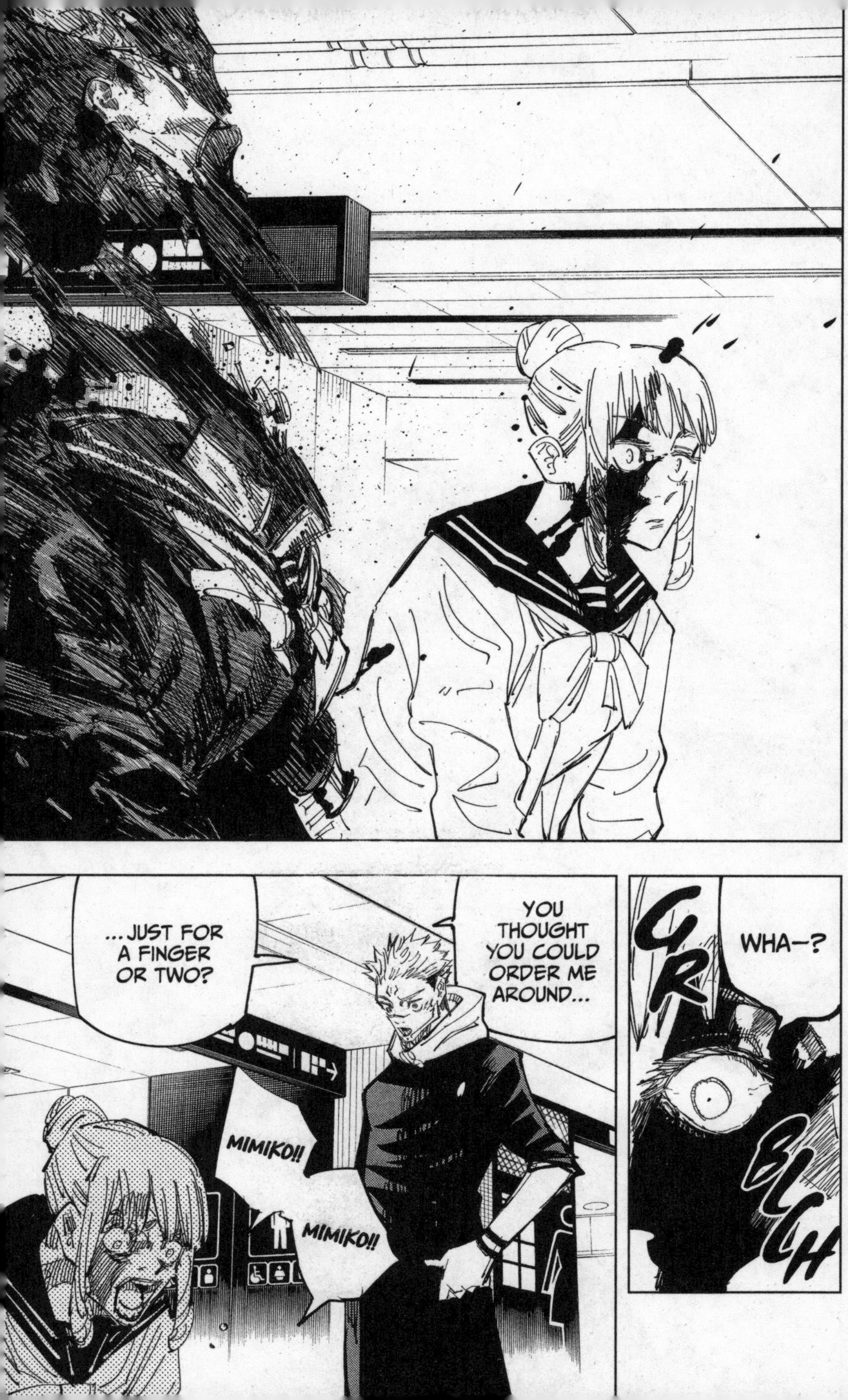
GR
WHA-?
BLCH
YOU THOUGHT YOU COULD ORDER ME AROUND...
...JUST FOR A FINGER OR TWO?
MIMIKO!!
MIMIKO!!

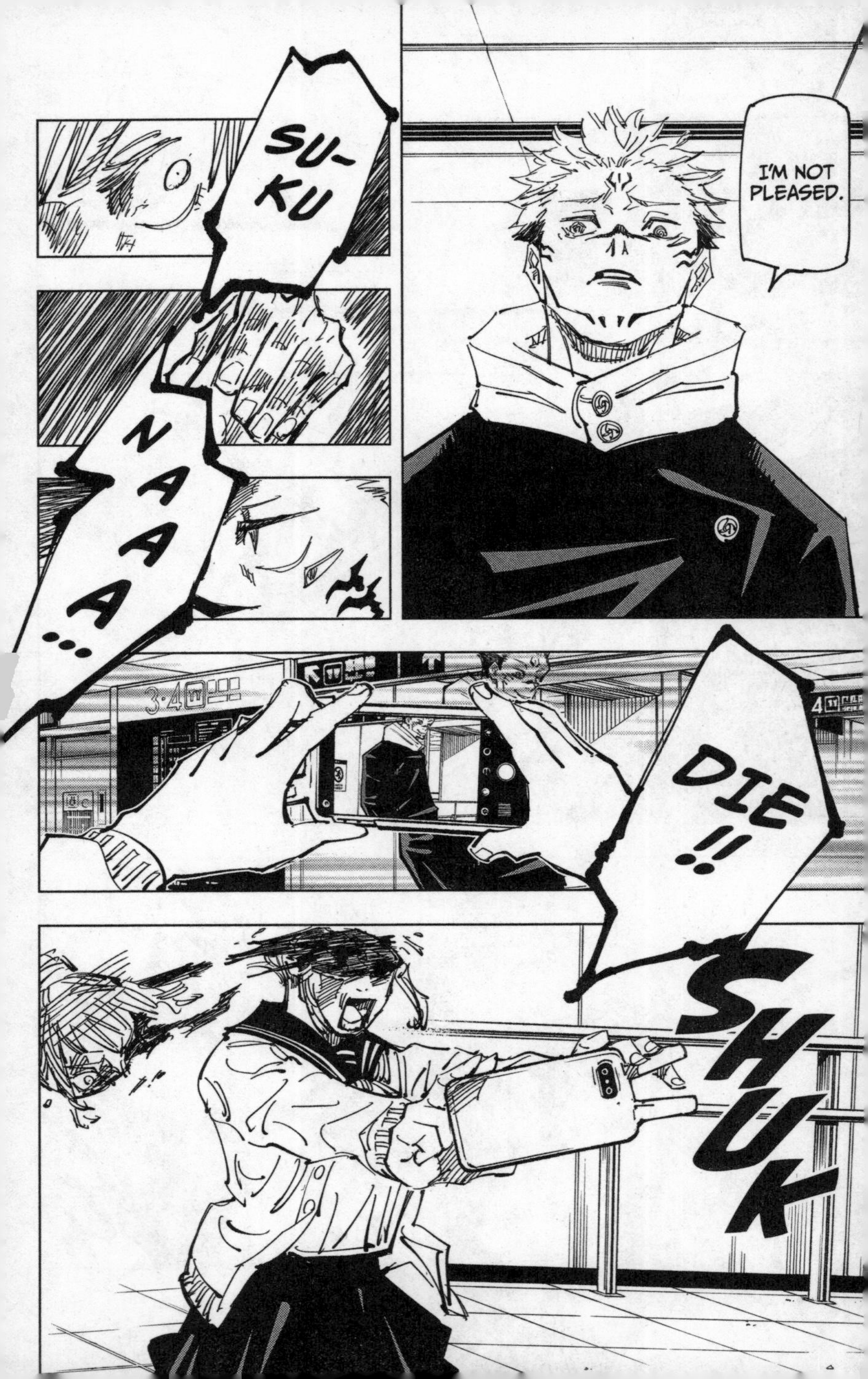
I'M NOT PLEASED.
SU-KU NAAAA...
DIE!!
SHUK

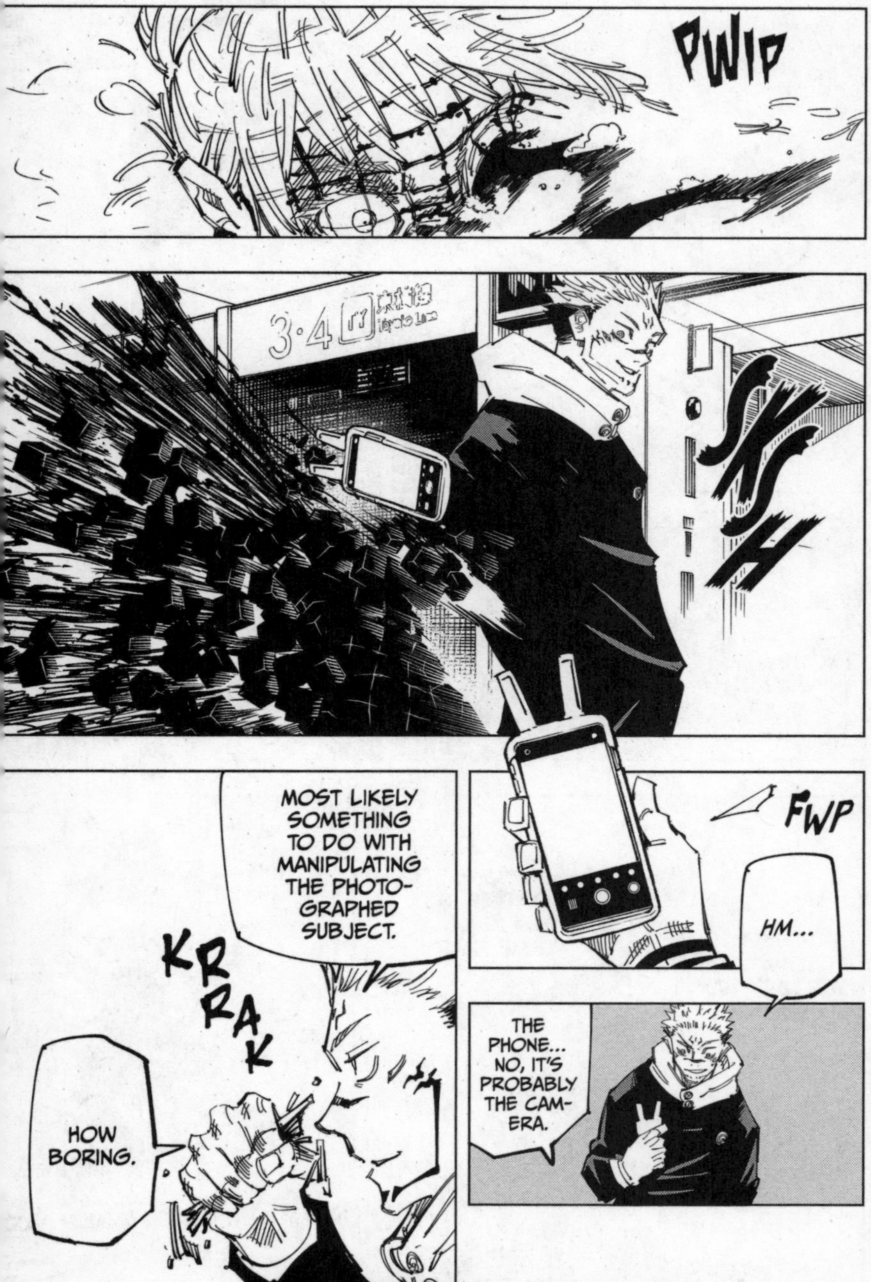
PWIP
3·4
SKSSH
FWP
HM...
THE PHONE... NO, IT'S PROBABLY THE CAMERA.
MOST LIKELY SOMETHING TO DO WITH MANIPULATING THE PHOTOGRAPHED SUBJECT.
KRRAK
HOW BORING.

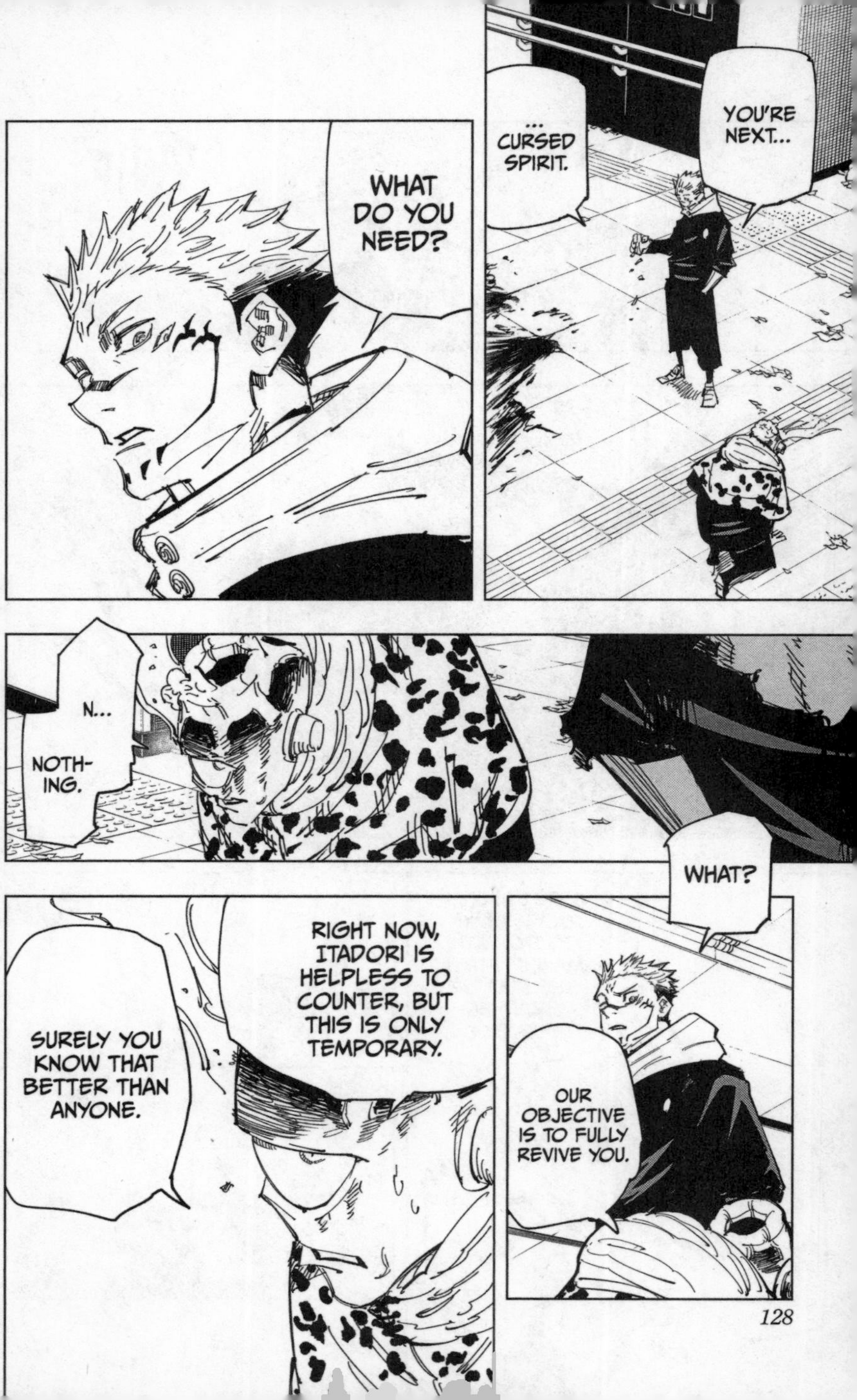
YOU'RE NEXT...
... CURSED SPIRIT.
WHAT DO YOU NEED?
N...
NOTH-ING.
WHAT?
OUR OBJECTIVE IS TO FULLY REVIVE YOU.
RIGHT NOW, ITADORI IS HELPLESS TO COUNTER, BUT THIS IS ONLY TEMPORARY.
SURELY YOU KNOW THAT BETTER THAN ANYONE.

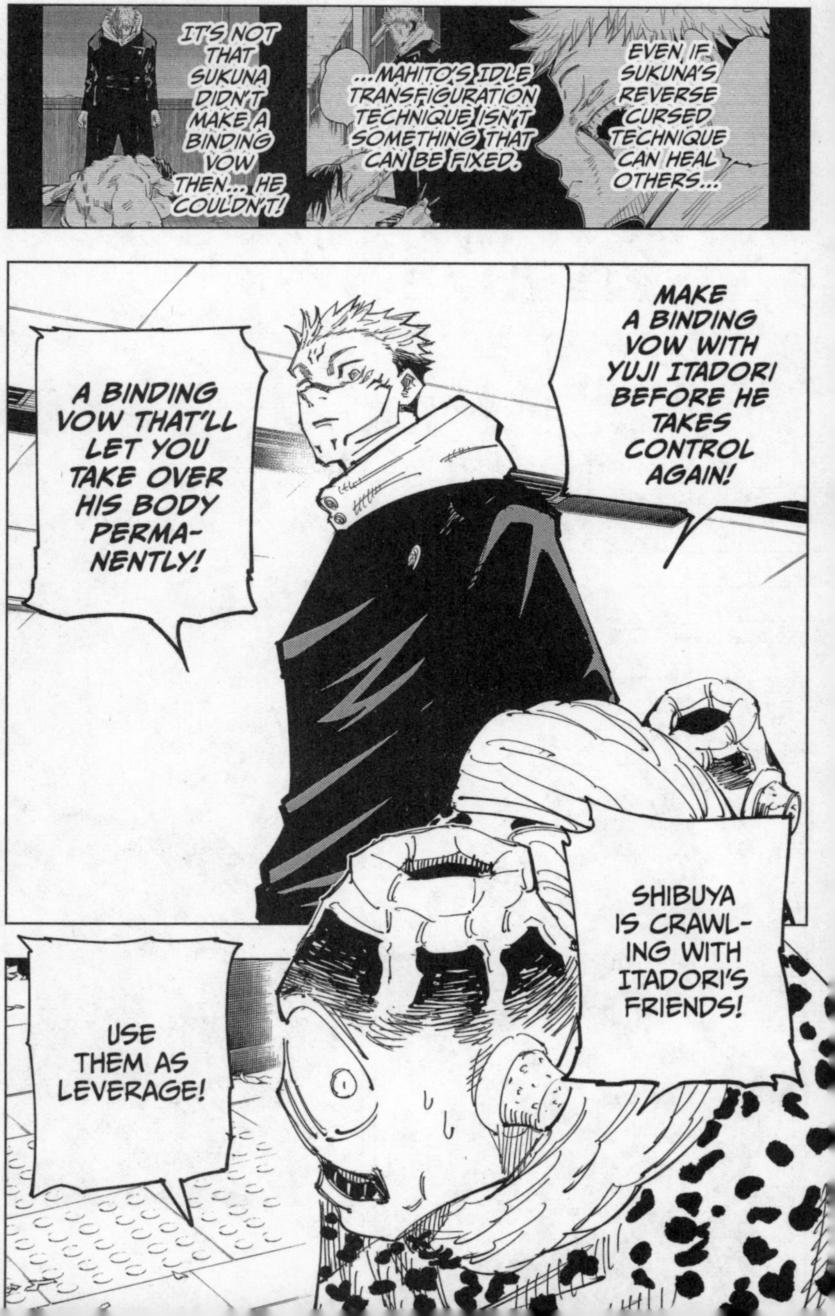
EVEN IF SUKUNA'S REVERSE CURSED TECHNIQUE CAN HEAL OTHERS...
...MAHITO'S IDLE TRANSFIGURATION TECHNIQUE ISN'T SOMETHING THAT CAN BE FIXED.
IT'S NOT THAT SUKUNA DIDN'T MAKE A BINDING VOW THEN... HE COULDN'T!
MAKE A BINDING VOW WITH YUJI ITADORI BEFORE HE TAKES CONTROL AGAIN!
A BINDING VOW THAT'LL LET YOU TAKE OVER HIS BODY PERMA-NENTLY!
SHIBUYA IS CRAWL-ING WITH ITADORI'S FRIENDS!
USE THEM AS LEVERAGE!

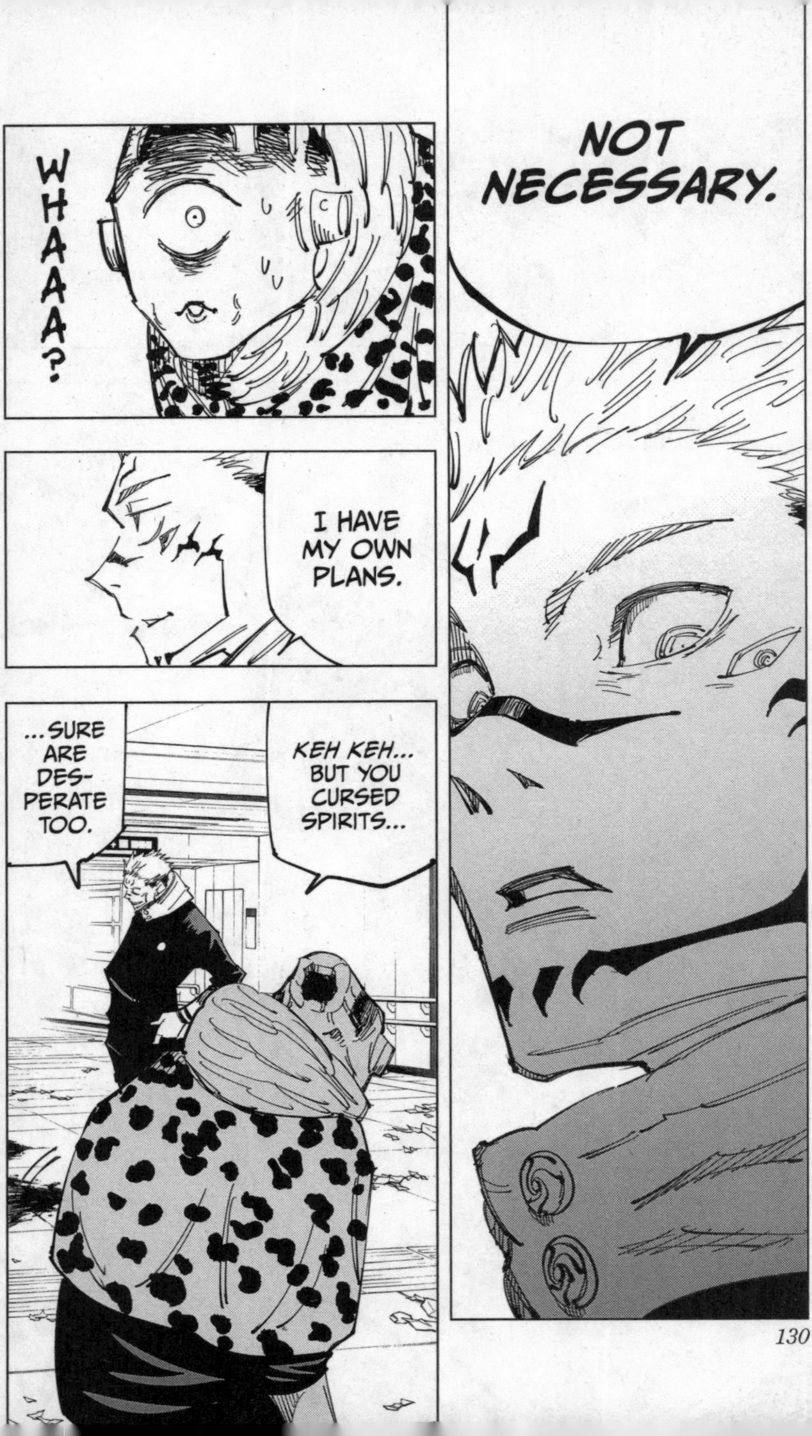
NOT NECESSARY.
WHAAAA?
I HAVE MY OWN PLANS.
KEH KEH... BUT YOU CURSED SPIRITS...
...SURE ARE DES-PERATE TOO.

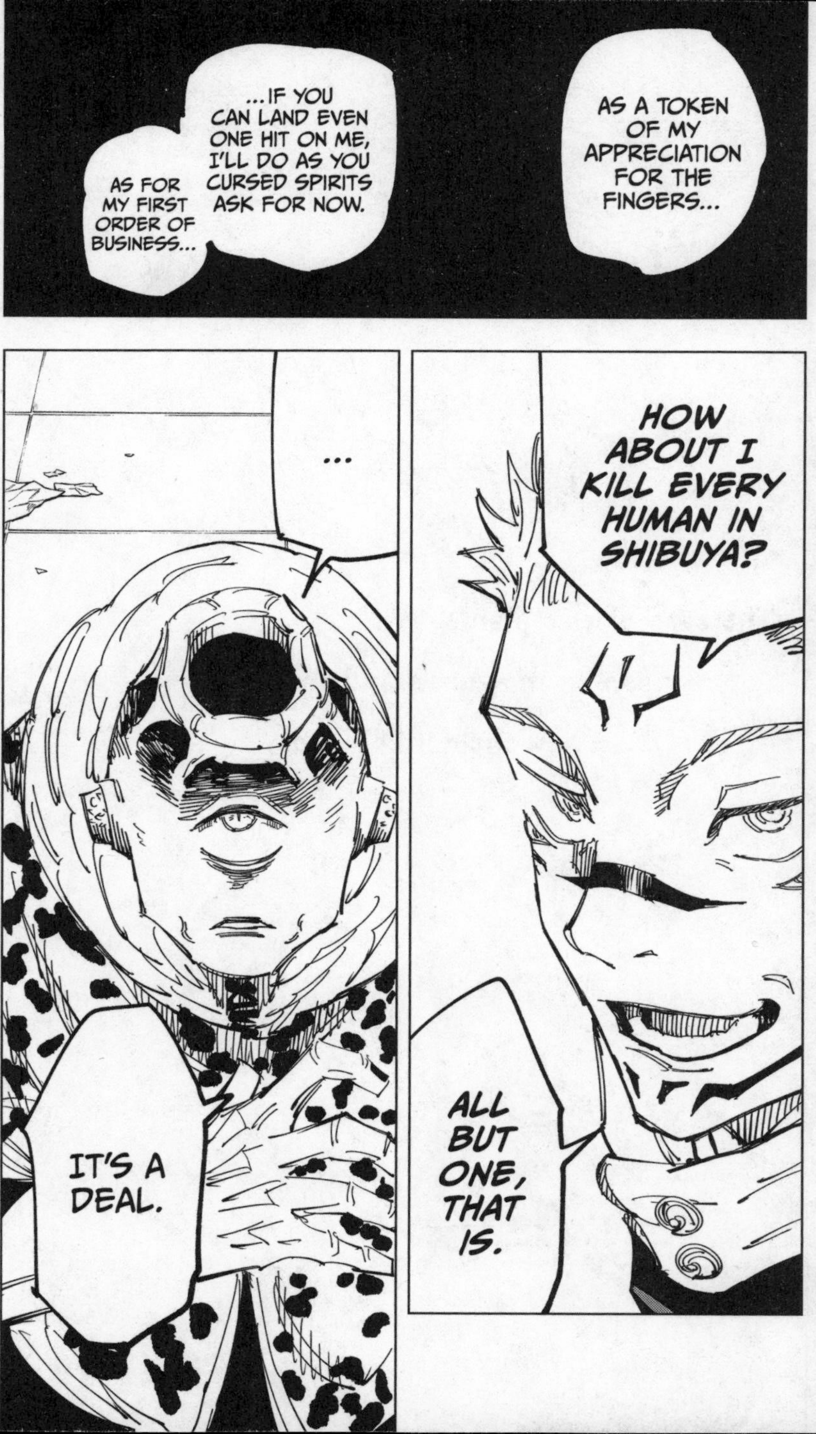
AS A TOKEN OF MY APPRECIATION FOR THE FINGERS...
...IF YOU CAN LAND EVEN ONE HIT ON ME, I'LL DO AS YOU CURSED SPIRITS ASK FOR NOW.
AS FOR MY FIRST ORDER OF BUSINESS...
HOW ABOUT I KILL EVERY HUMAN IN SHIBUYA?
ALL BUT ONE, THAT IS.
...
IT'S A DEAL.

The ears of rice plants

ripen as they grow and then

bow their little heads.

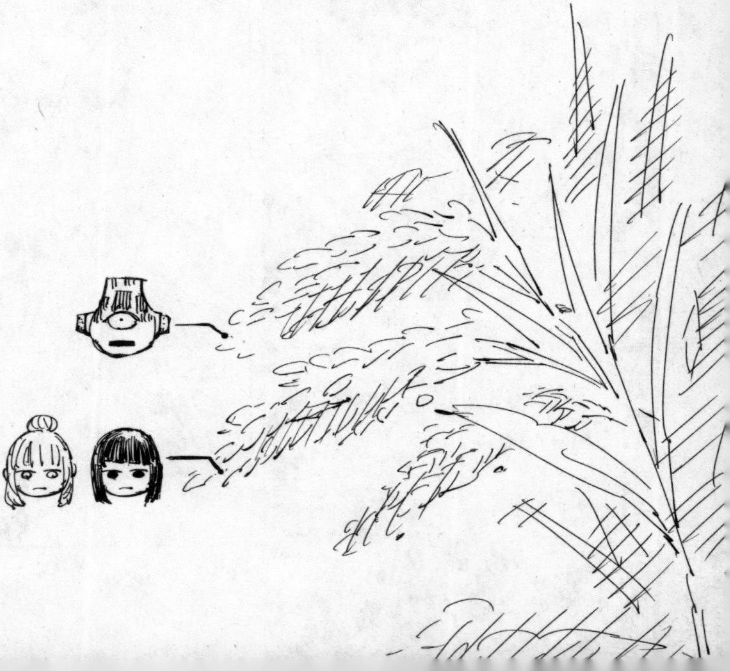

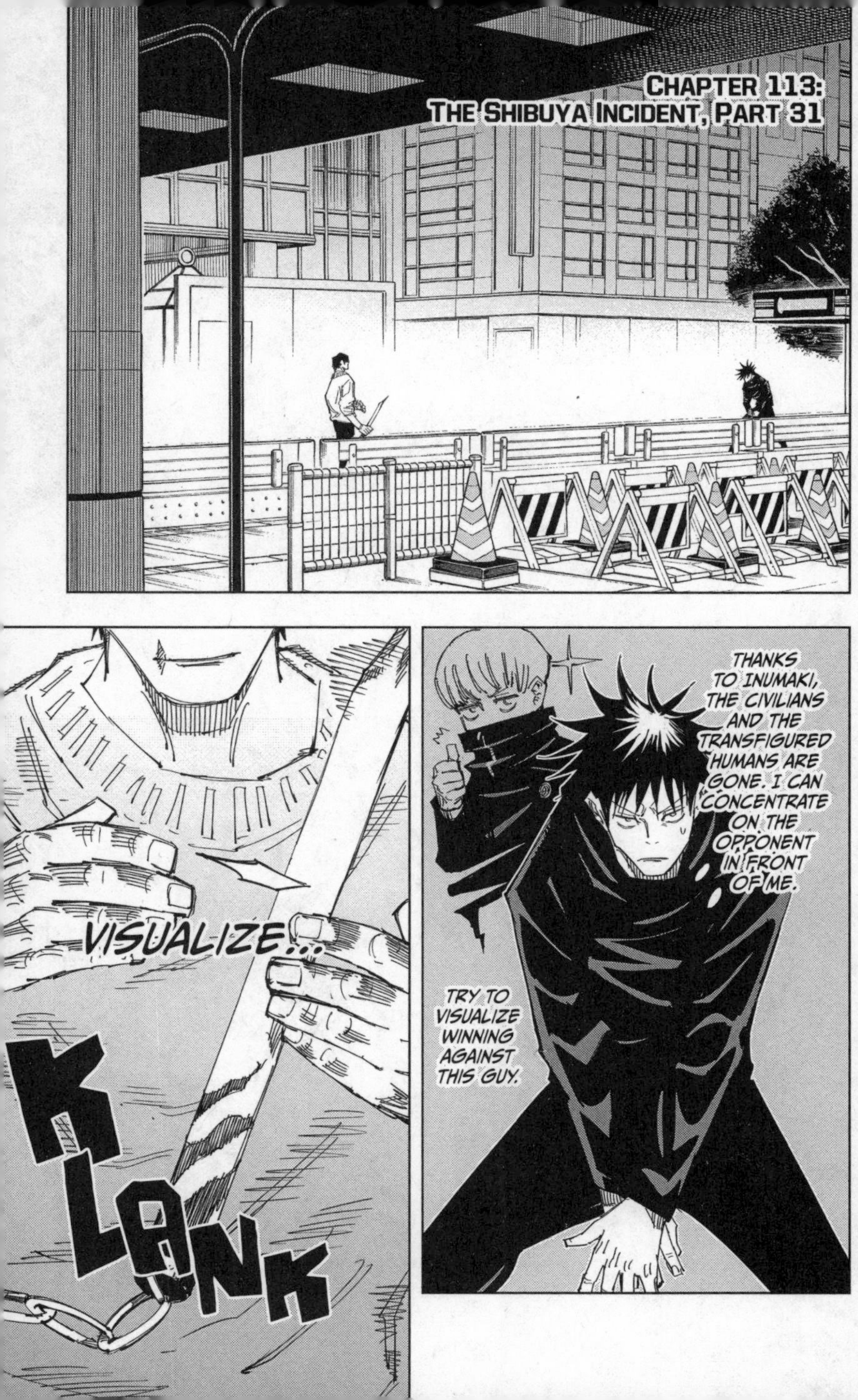
Chapter 113:
The Shibuya Incident, Part 31
THANKS TO INUMAKI, THE CIVILIANS AND THE TRANSFIGURED HUMANS ARE GONE. I CAN CONCENTRATE ON THE OPPONENT IN FRONT OF ME.
TRY TO VISUALIZE WINNING AGAINST THIS GUY.
VISUALIZE...
KLANK

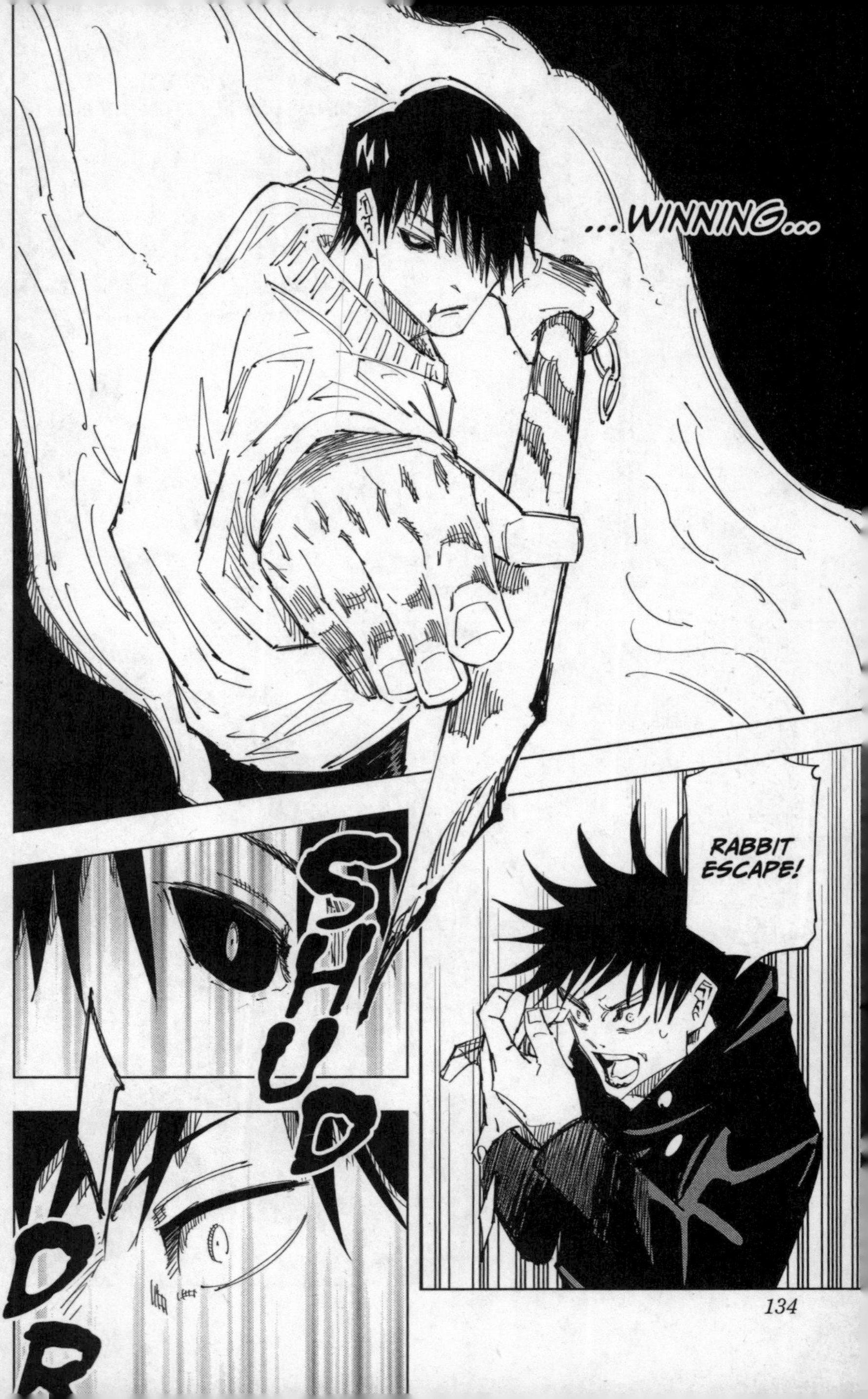
...WINNING...
RABBIT ESCAPE!
SHUD
DR

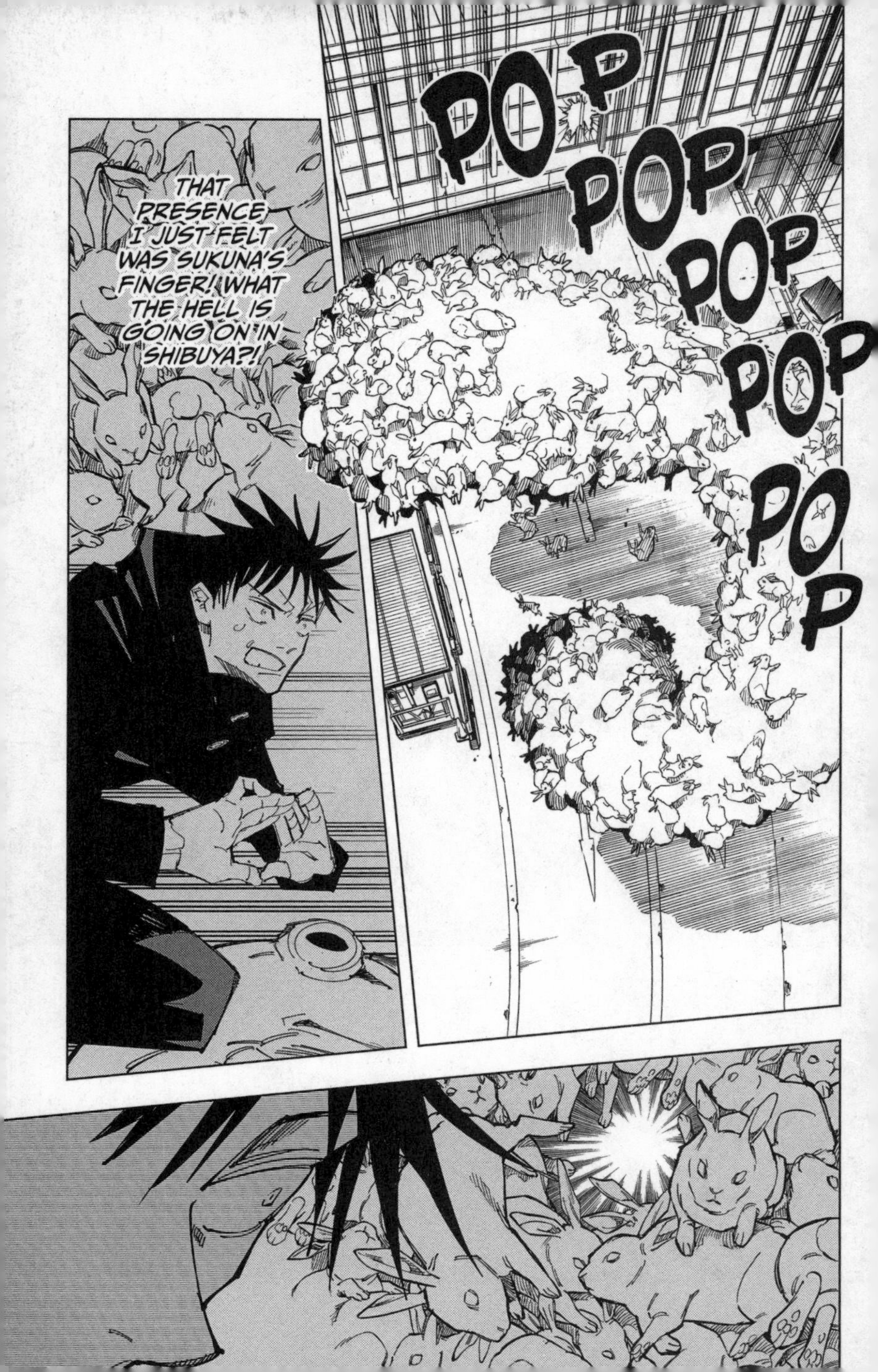
POP POP POP POP POP
THAT PRESENCE I JUST FELT WAS SUKUNA'S FINGER! WHAT THE HELL IS GOING ON IN SHIBUYA?!

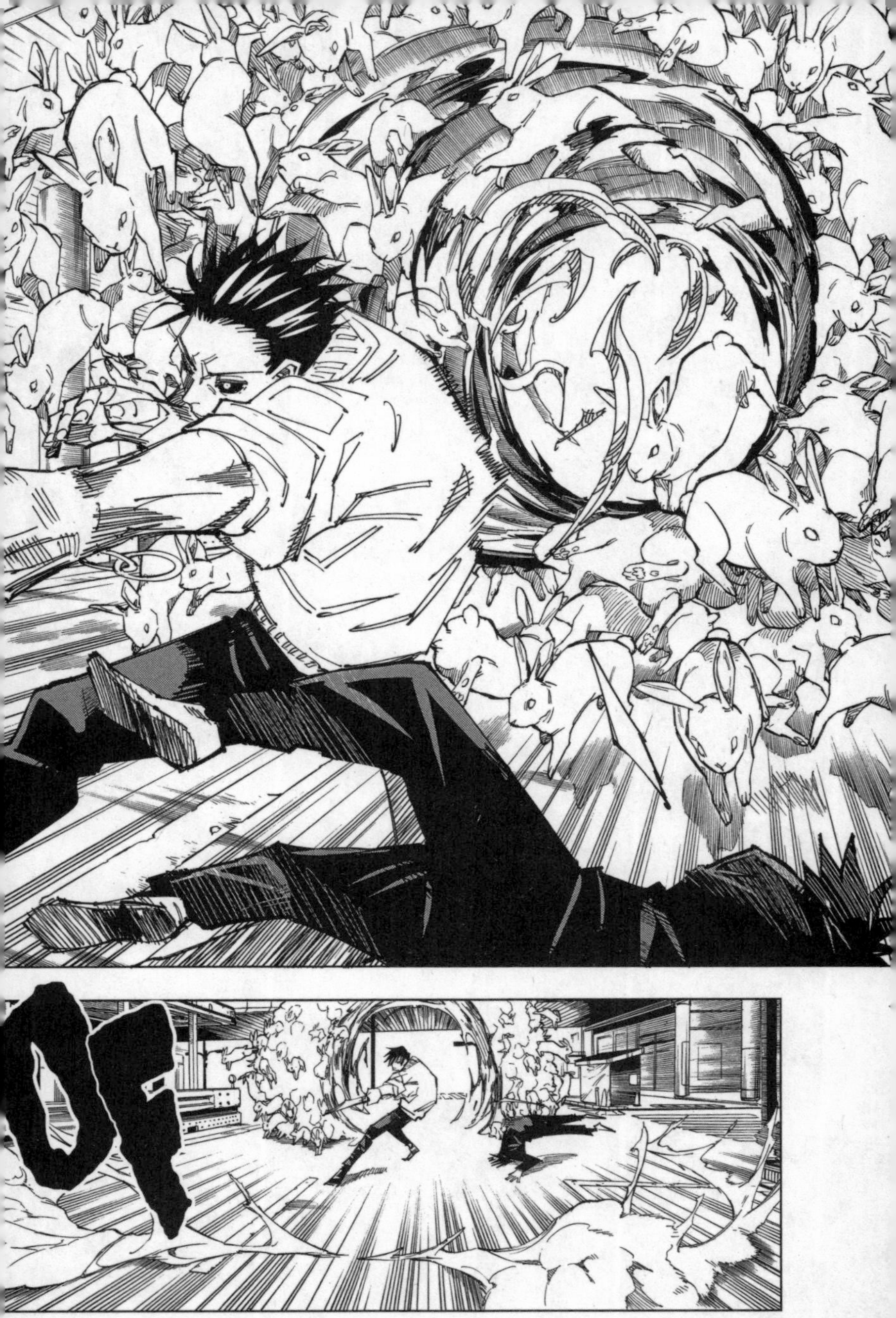
OF

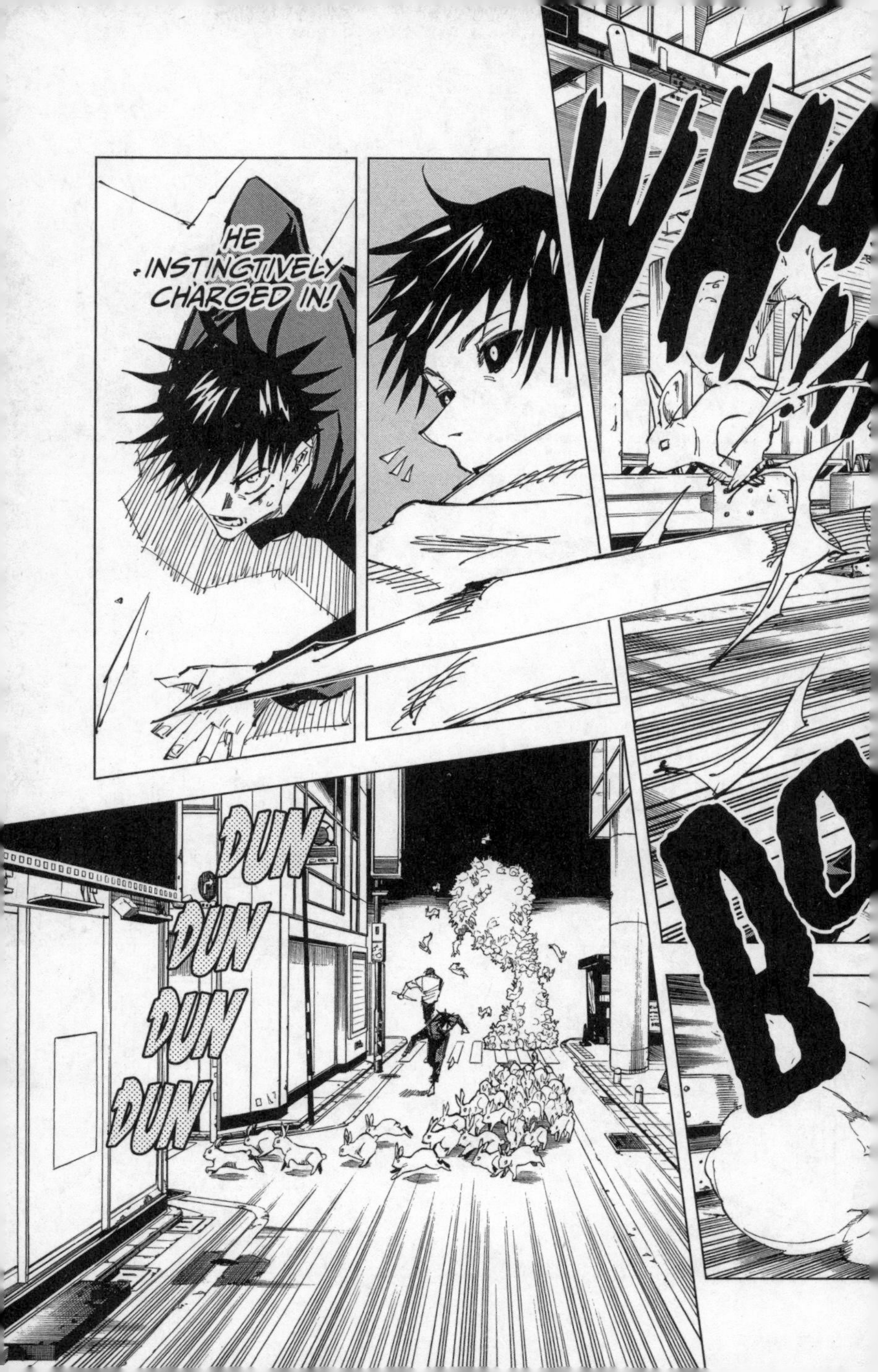
WHA
BO
HE INSTINCTIVELY CHARGED IN!
DUN DUN DUN DUN

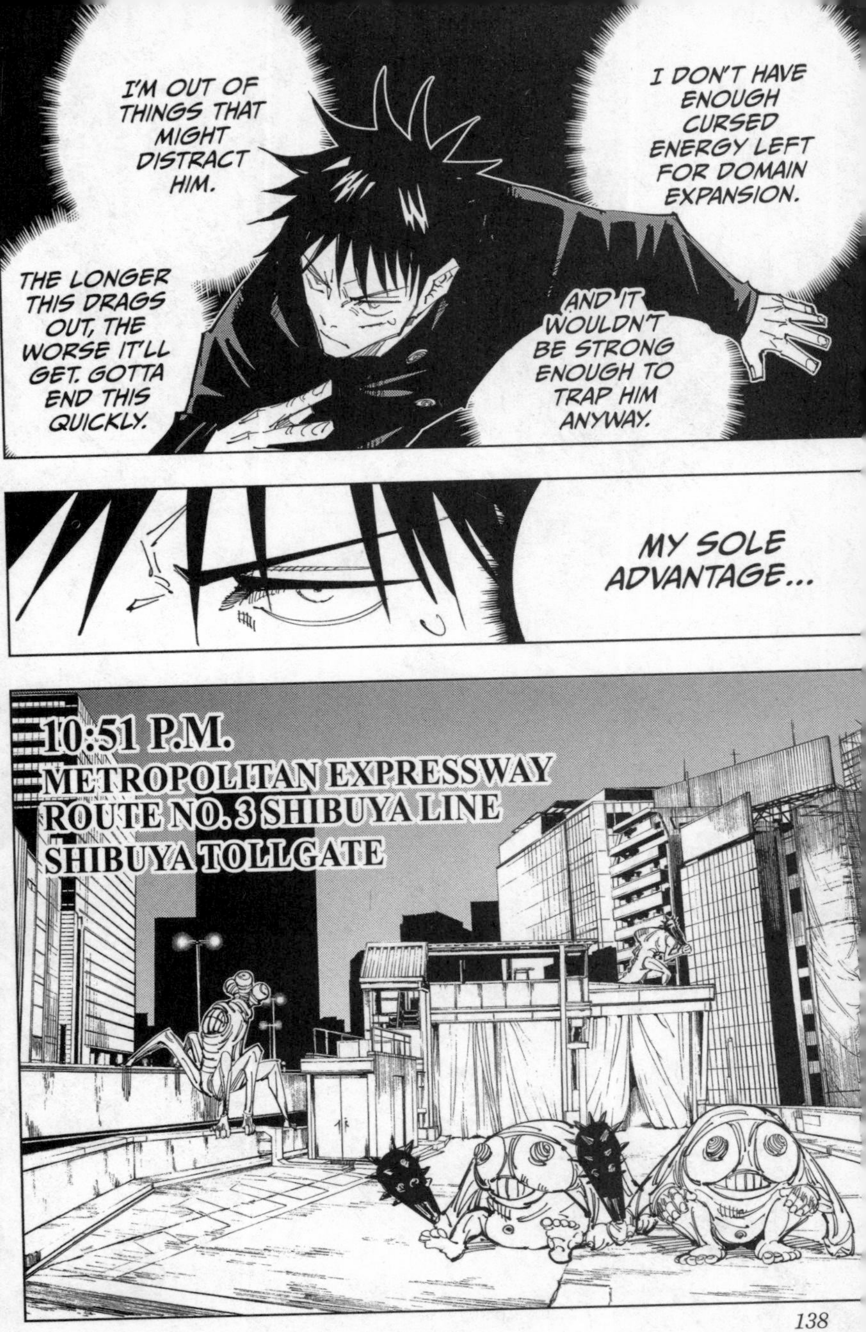
I DON'T HAVE ENOUGH CURSED ENERGY LEFT FOR DOMAIN EXPANSION.
AND IT WOULDN'T BE STRONG ENOUGH TO TRAP HIM ANYWAY.
I'M OUT OF THINGS THAT MIGHT DISTRACT HIM.
THE LONGER THIS DRAGS OUT, THE WORSE IT'LL GET. GOTTA END THIS QUICKLY.
MY SOLE ADVANTAGE...
10:51 P.M.
METROPOLITAN EXPRESSWAY
ROUTE NO. 3 SHIBUYA LINE
SHIBUYA TOLLGATE

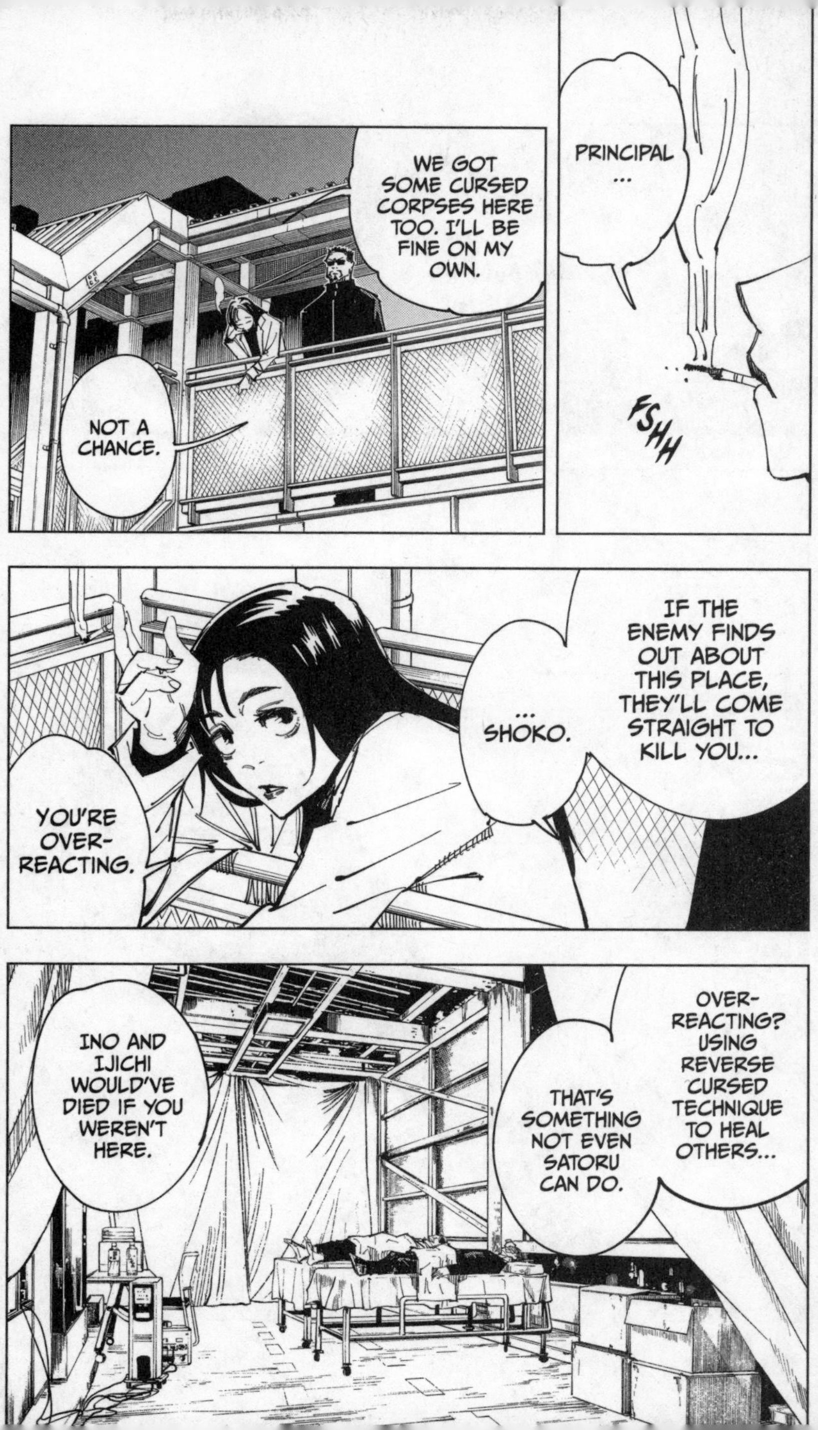
PRINCIPAL ...
FSHH
WE GOT SOME CURSED CORPSES HERE TOO. I'LL BE FINE ON MY OWN.
NOT A CHANCE.
IF THE ENEMY FINDS OUT ABOUT THIS PLACE, THEY'LL COME STRAIGHT TO KILL YOU...
... SHOKO.
YOU'RE OVER-REACTING.
OVER-REACTING? USING REVERSE CURSED TECHNIQUE TO HEAL OTHERS...
THAT'S SOMETHING NOT EVEN SATORU CAN DO.
INO AND IJICHI WOULD'VE DIED IF YOU WEREN'T HERE.

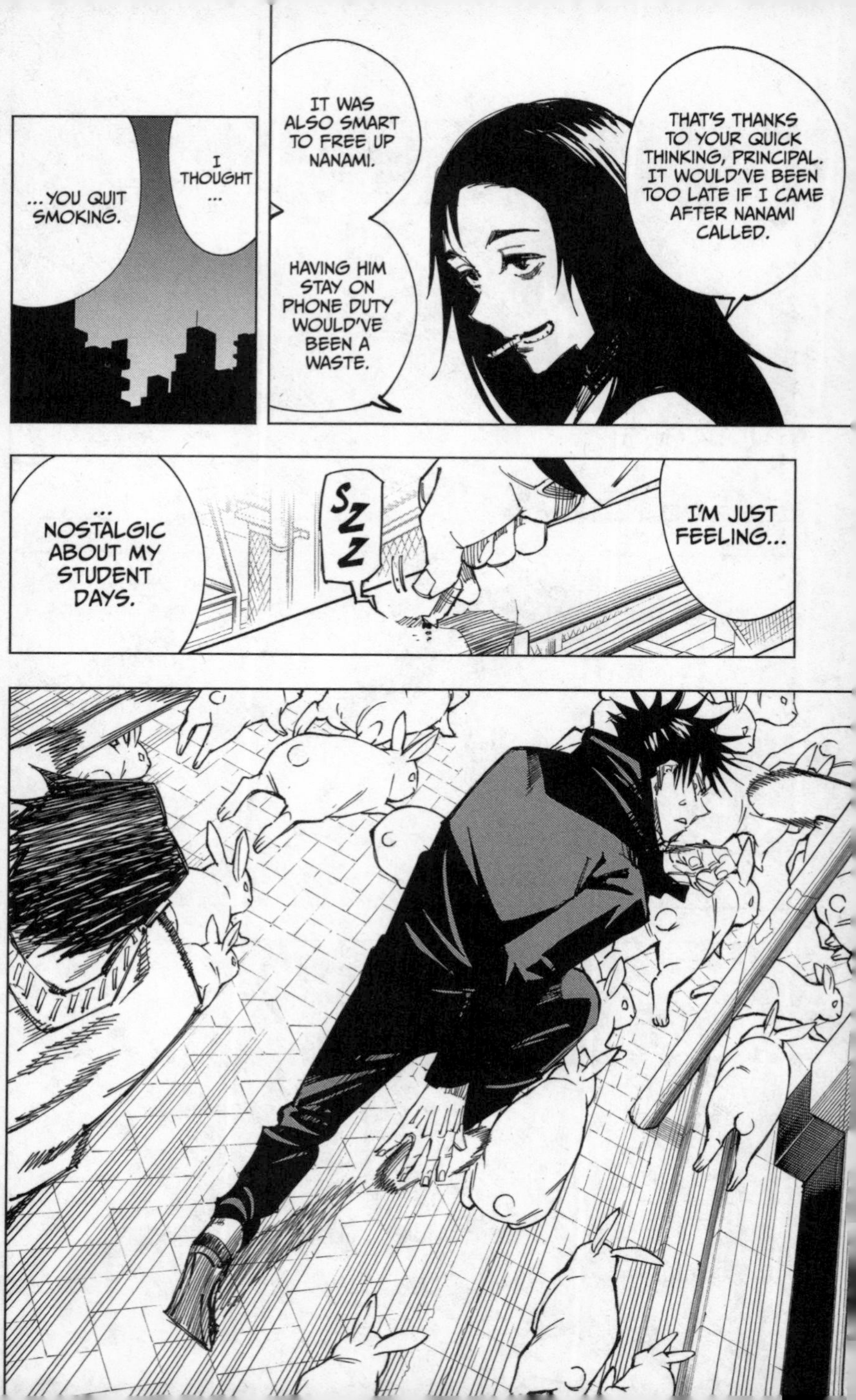
THAT'S THANKS TO YOUR QUICK THINKING, PRINCIPAL. IT WOULD'VE BEEN TOO LATE IF I CAME AFTER NANAMI CALLED.
IT WAS ALSO SMART TO FREE UP NANAMI.
HAVING HIM STAY ON PHONE DUTY WOULD'VE BEEN A WASTE.
I THOUGHT ...
...YOU QUIT SMOKING.
I'M JUST FEELING...
SZZ
... NOSTALGIC ABOUT MY STUDENT DAYS.

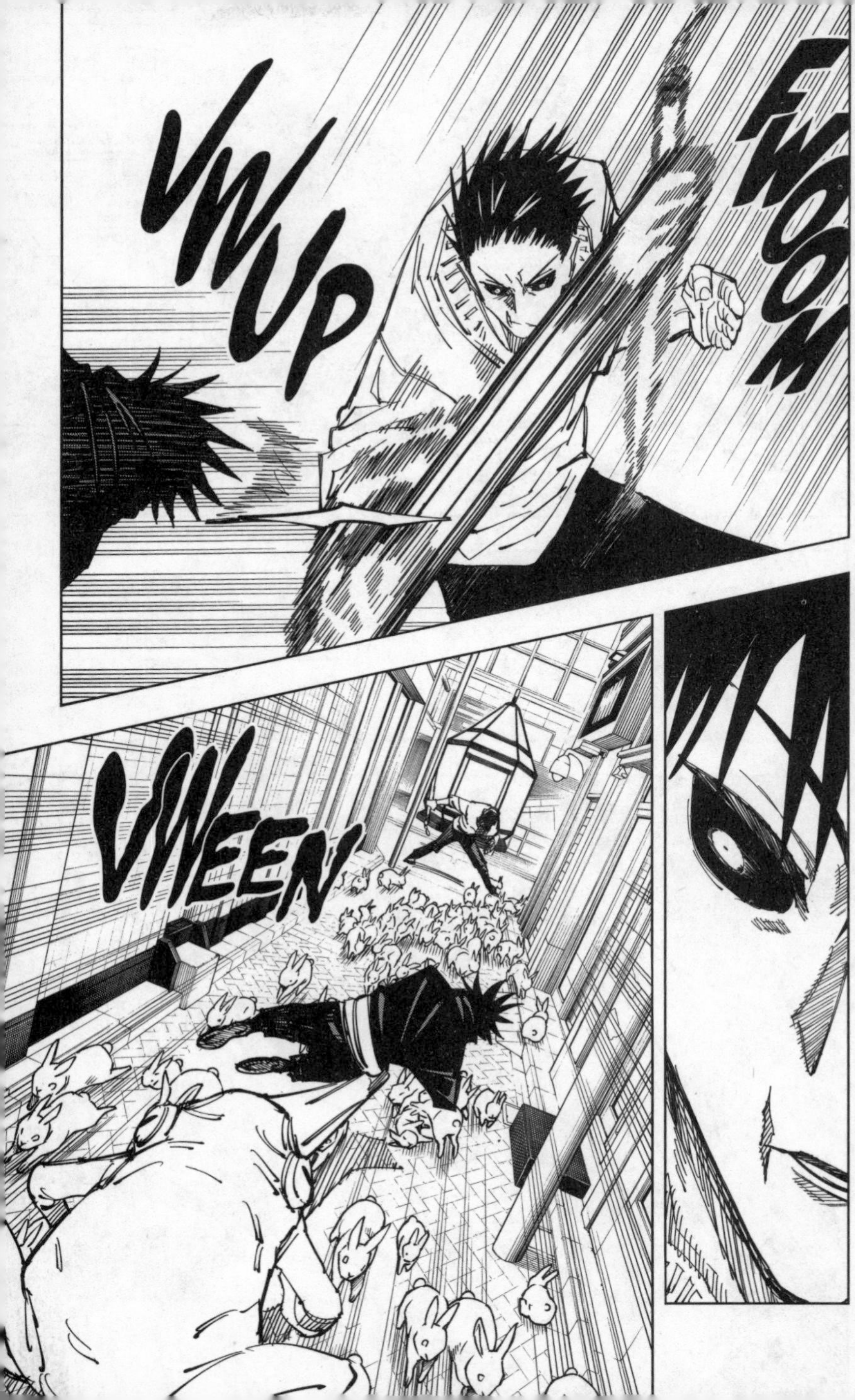
FWOOM
VWUP
VWEEN

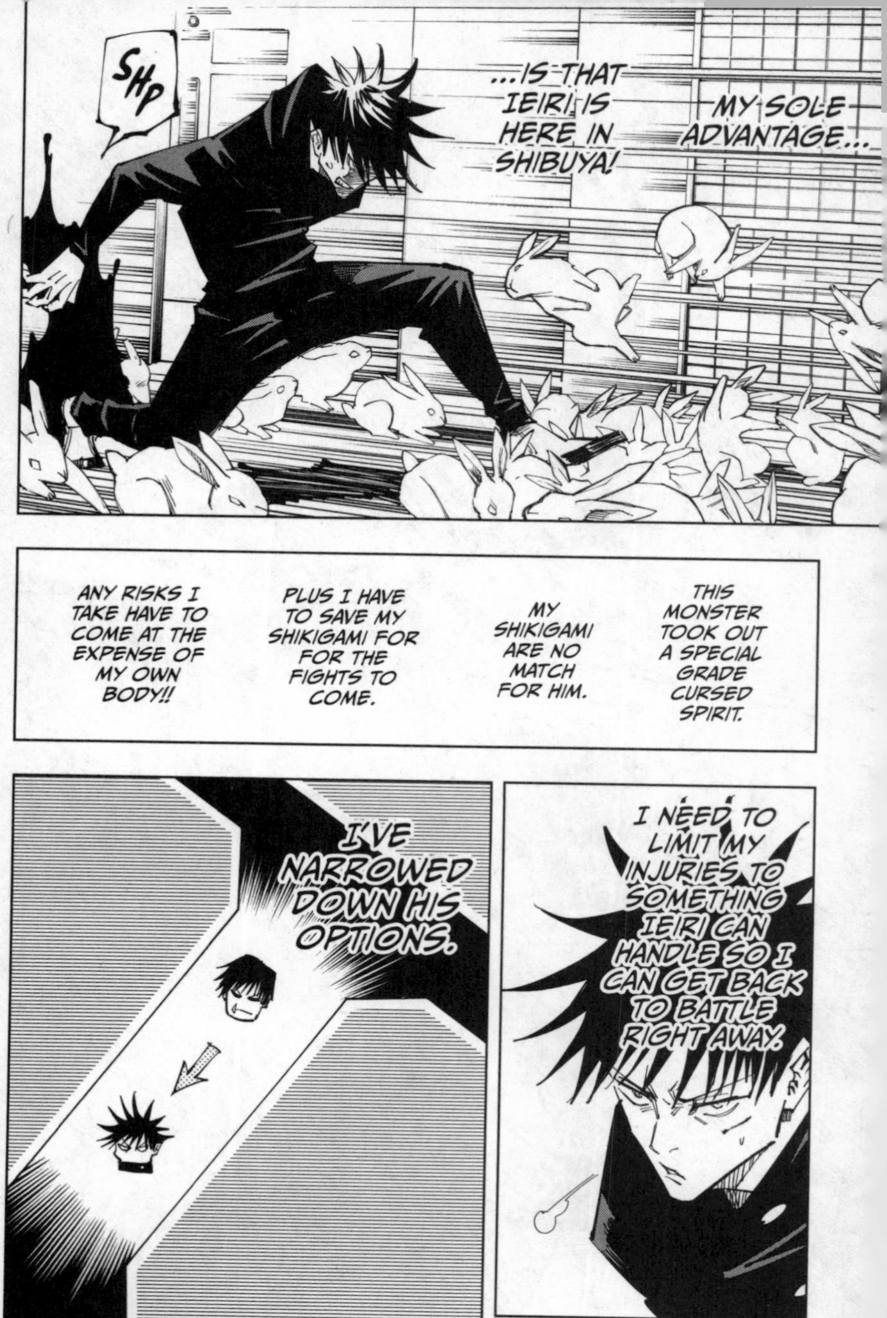
MY SOLE ADVANTAGE...
...IS THAT IEIRI IS HERE IN SHIBUYA!
SHP
THIS MONSTER TOOK OUT A SPECIAL GRADE CURSED SPIRIT.
MY SHIKIGAMI ARE NO MATCH FOR HIM.
PLUS I HAVE TO SAVE MY SHIKIGAMI FOR FOR THE FIGHTS TO COME.
ANY RISKS I TAKE HAVE TO COME AT THE EXPENSE OF MY OWN BODY!!
I NEED TO LIMIT MY INJURIES TO SOMETHING IEIRI CAN HANDLE SO I CAN GET BACK TO BATTLE RIGHT AWAY.
I'VE NARROWED DOWN HIS OPTIONS.

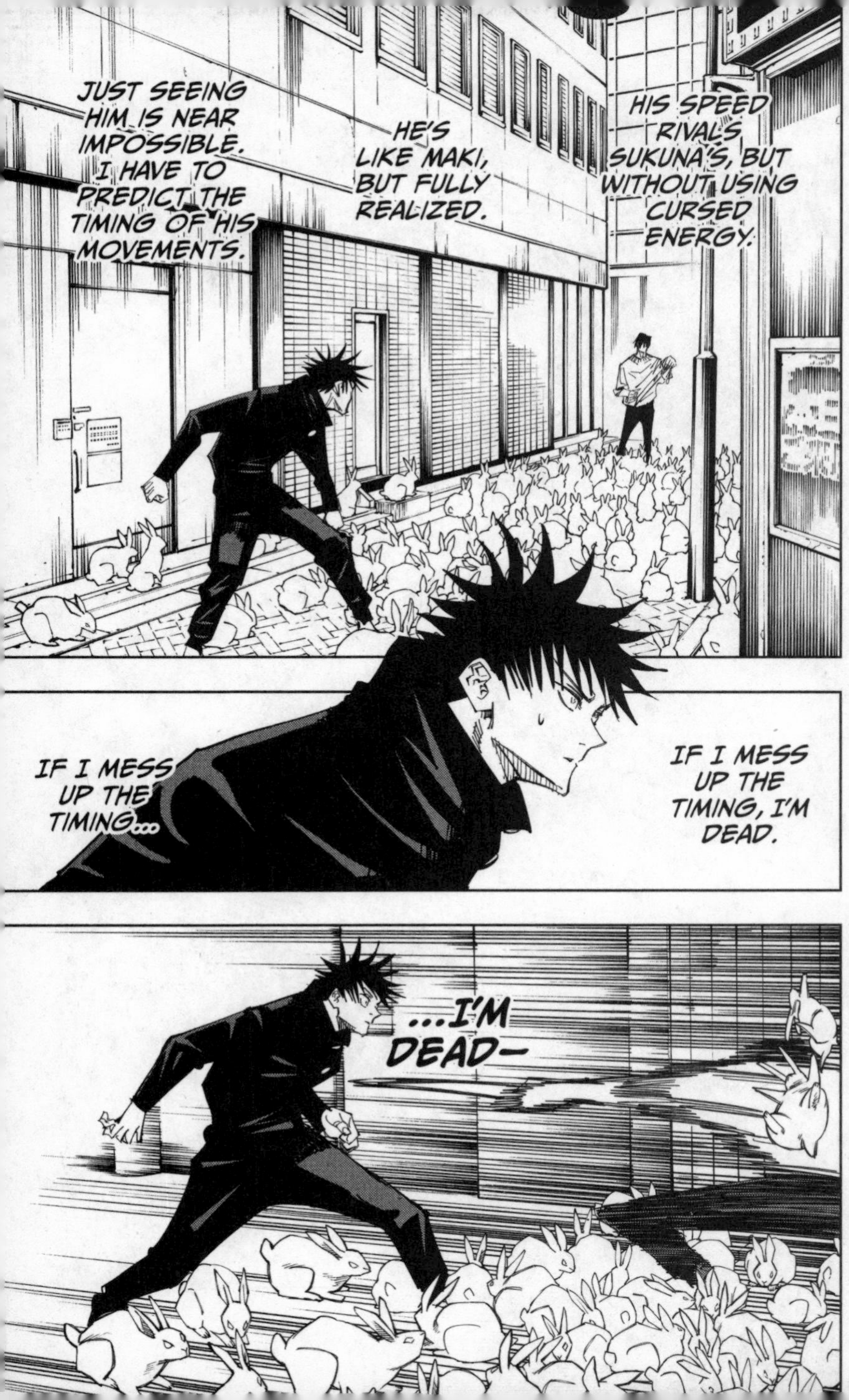
HIS SPEED RIVALS SUKUNA'S, BUT WITHOUT USING CURSED ENERGY.
HE'S LIKE MAKI, BUT FULLY REALIZED.
JUST SEEING HIM IS NEAR IMPOSSIBLE. I HAVE TO PREDICT THE TIMING OF HIS MOVEMENTS.
IF I MESS UP THE TIMING, I'M DEAD.
IF I MESS UP THE TIMING...
...I'M DEAD—

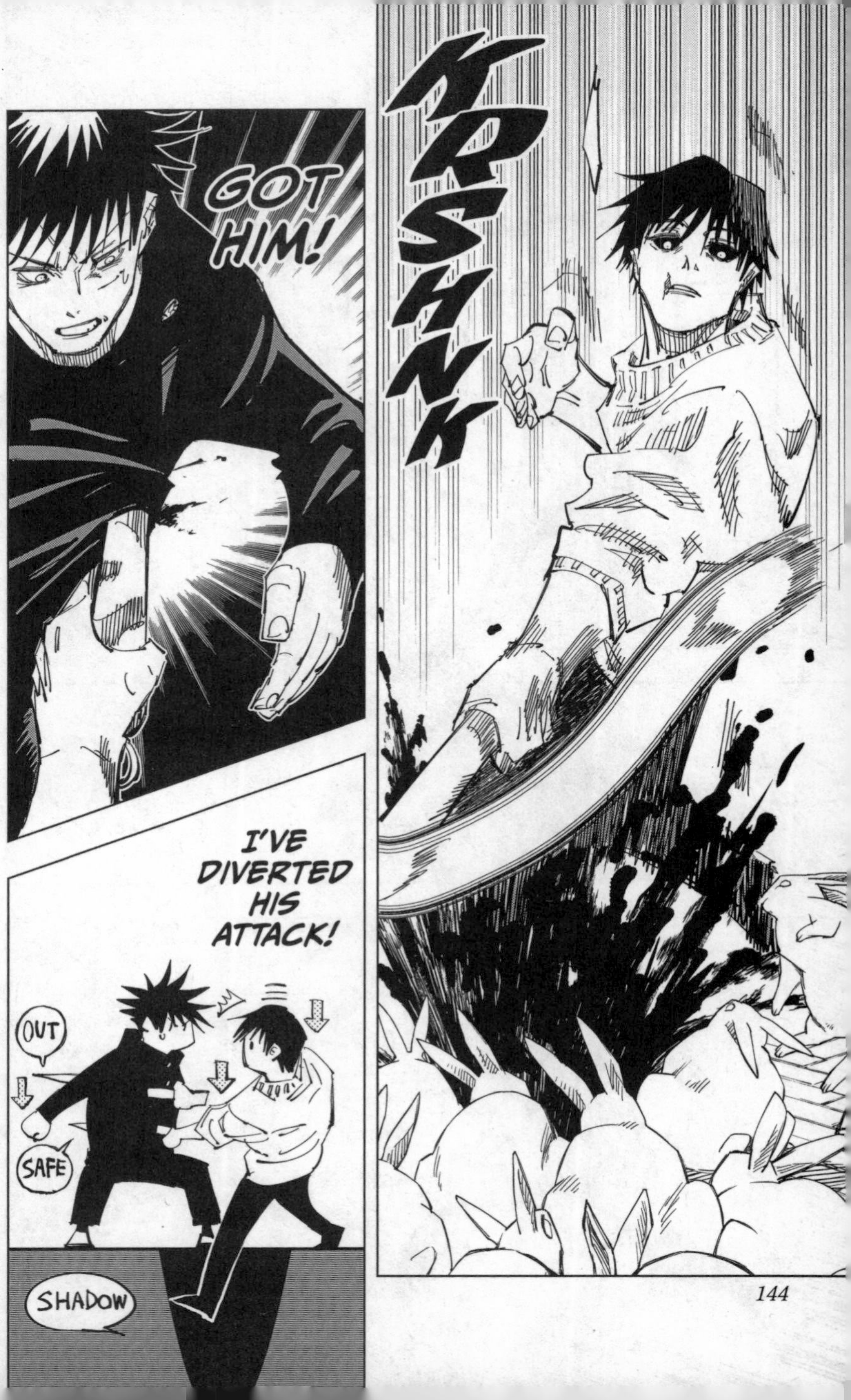
KRSHNK
GOT HIM!
I'VE DIVERTED HIS ATTACK!
OUT
SAFE
SHADOW

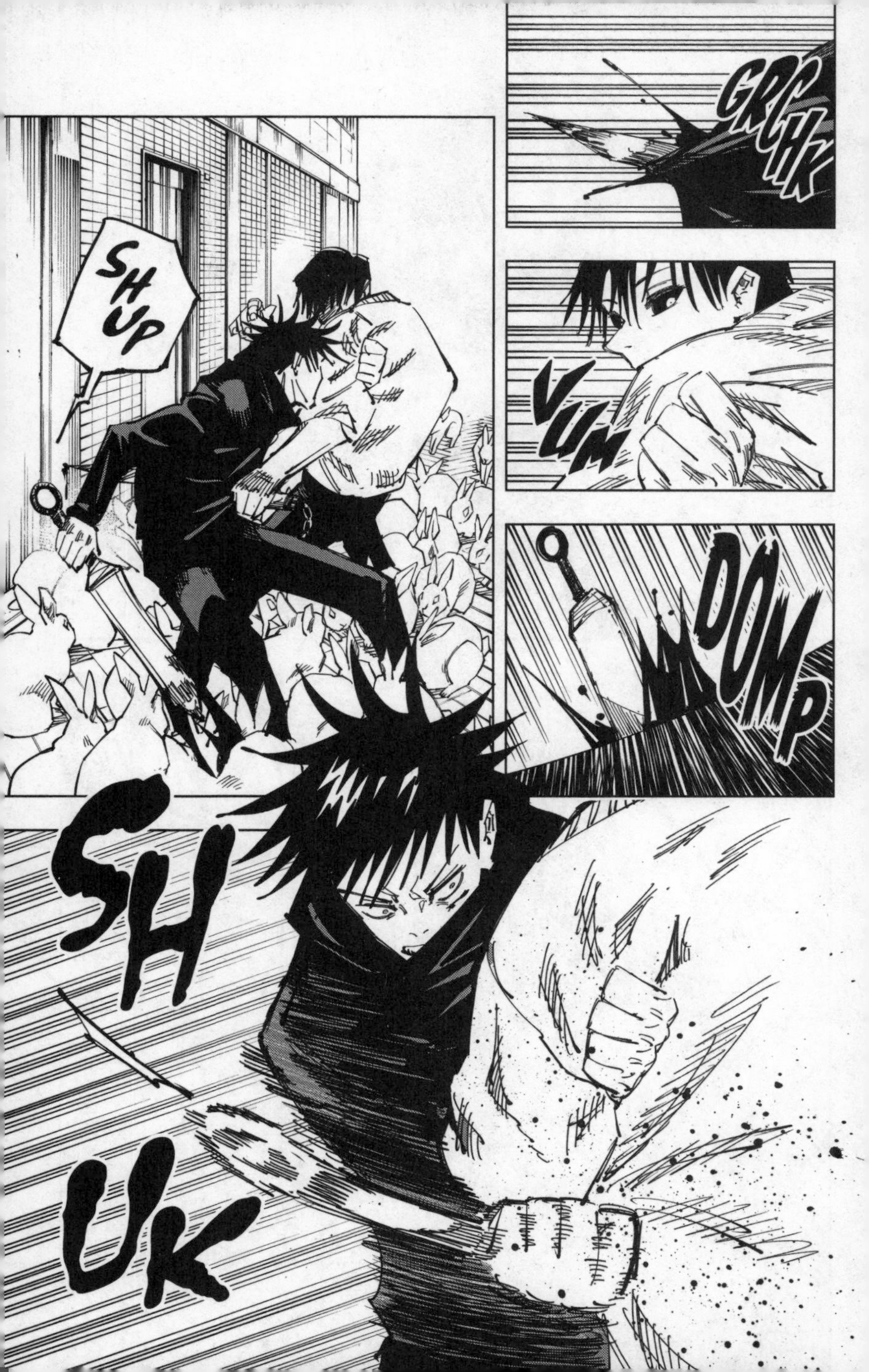
GRCHK
VUM
DOMP
SHUP
SHUK

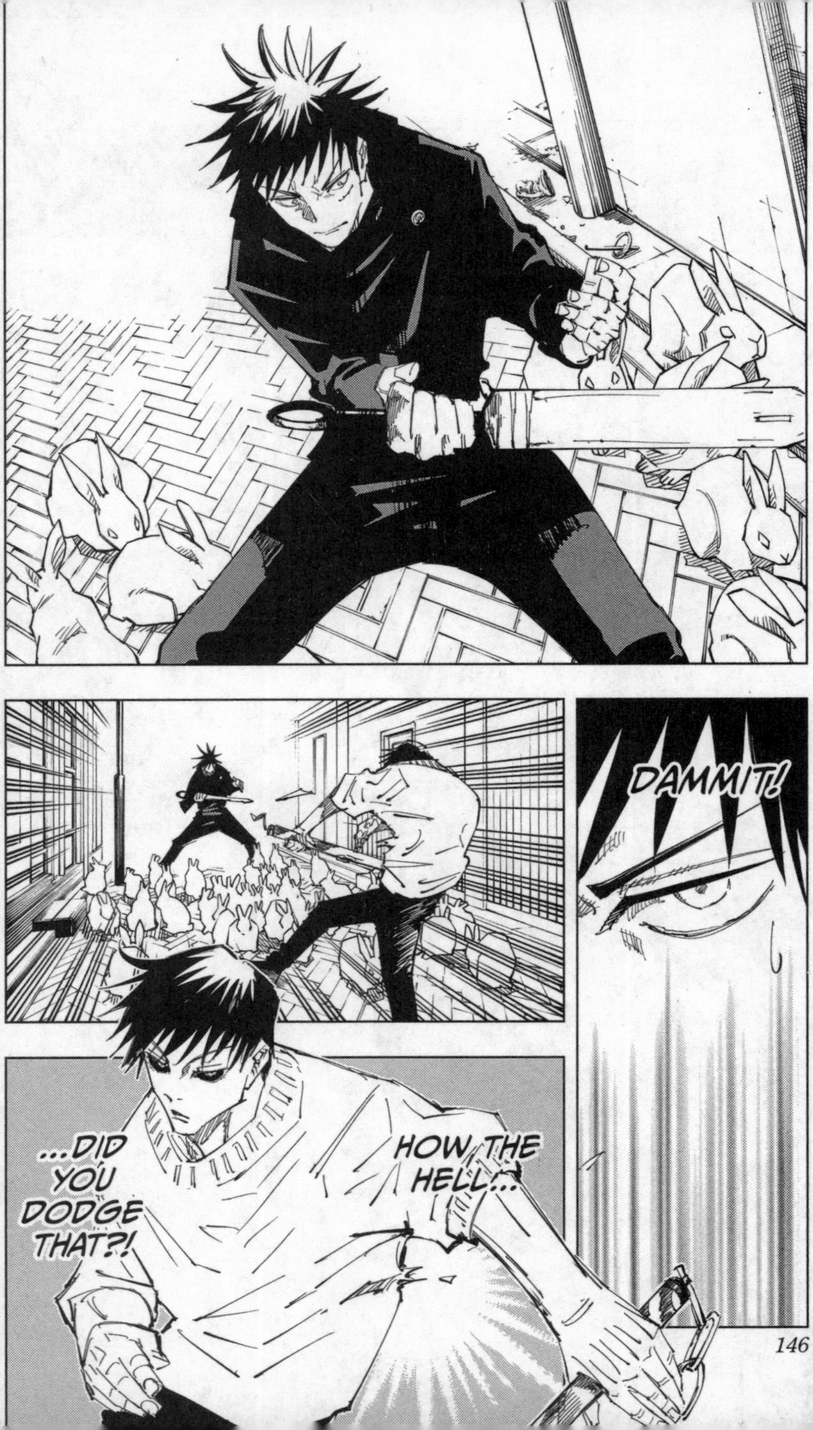
DAMMIT!
HOW THE HELL...
...DID YOU DODGE THAT?!

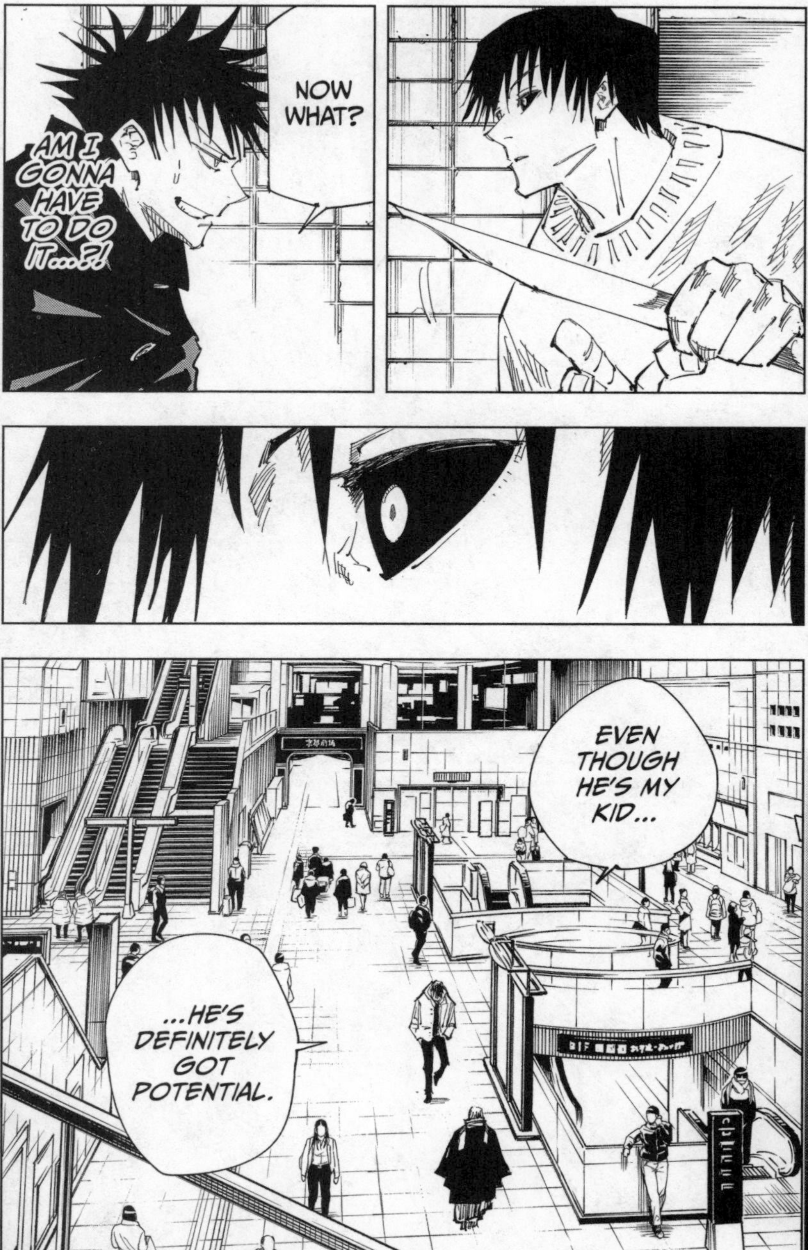
NOW WHAT?
AM I GONNA HAVE TO DO IT...?!
EVEN THOUGH HE'S MY KID...
...HE'S DEFINITELY GOT POTENTIAL.

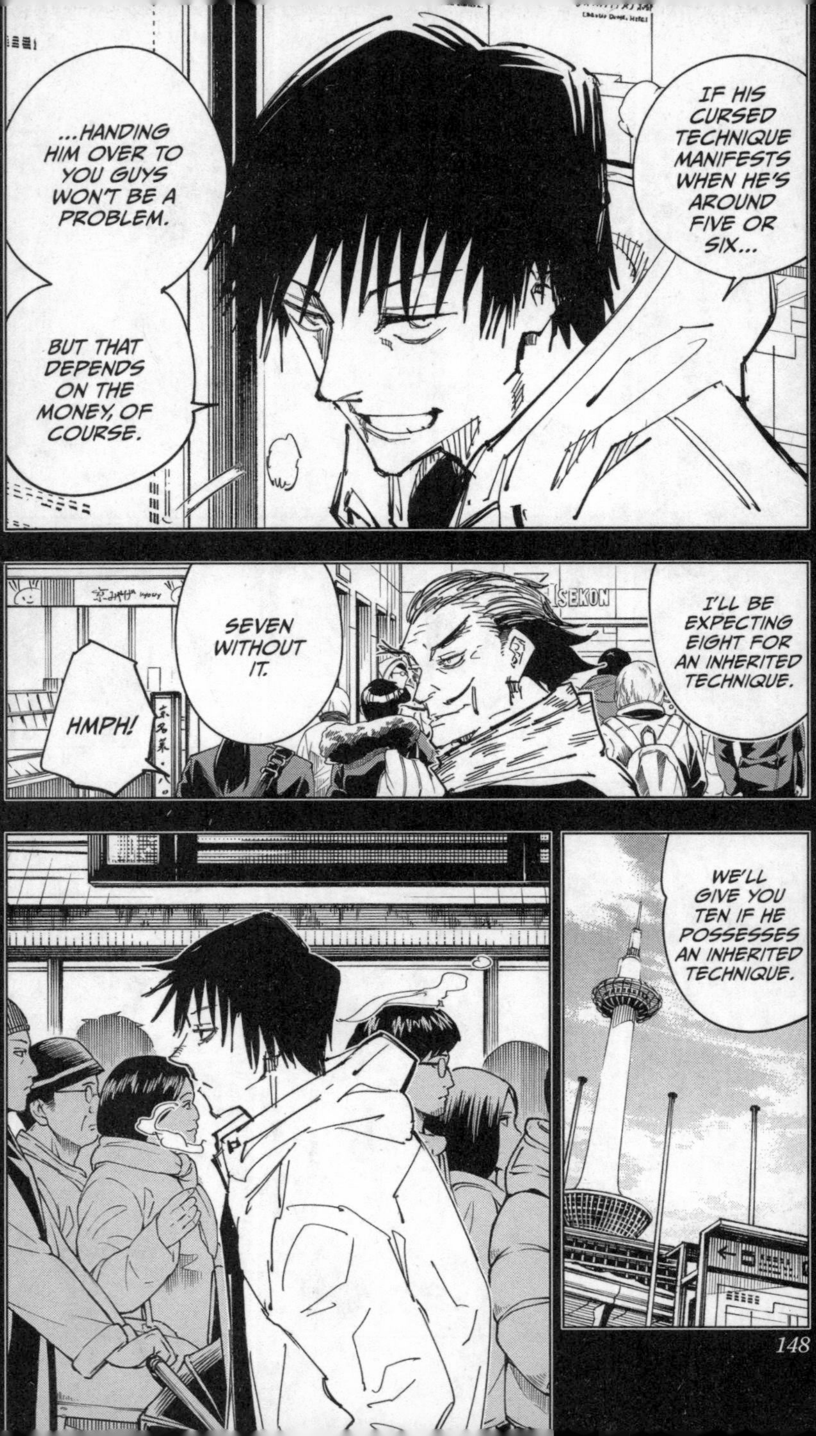
IF HIS CURSED TECHNIQUE MANIFESTS WHEN HE'S AROUND FIVE OR SIX...
...HANDING HIM OVER TO YOU GUYS WON'T BE A PROBLEM.
BUT THAT DEPENDS ON THE MONEY, OF COURSE.
I'LL BE EXPECTING EIGHT FOR AN INHERITED TECHNIQUE.
ISEKON
SEVEN WITHOUT IT.
HMPH!
WE'LL GIVE YOU TEN IF HE POSSESSES AN INHERITED TECHNIQUE.

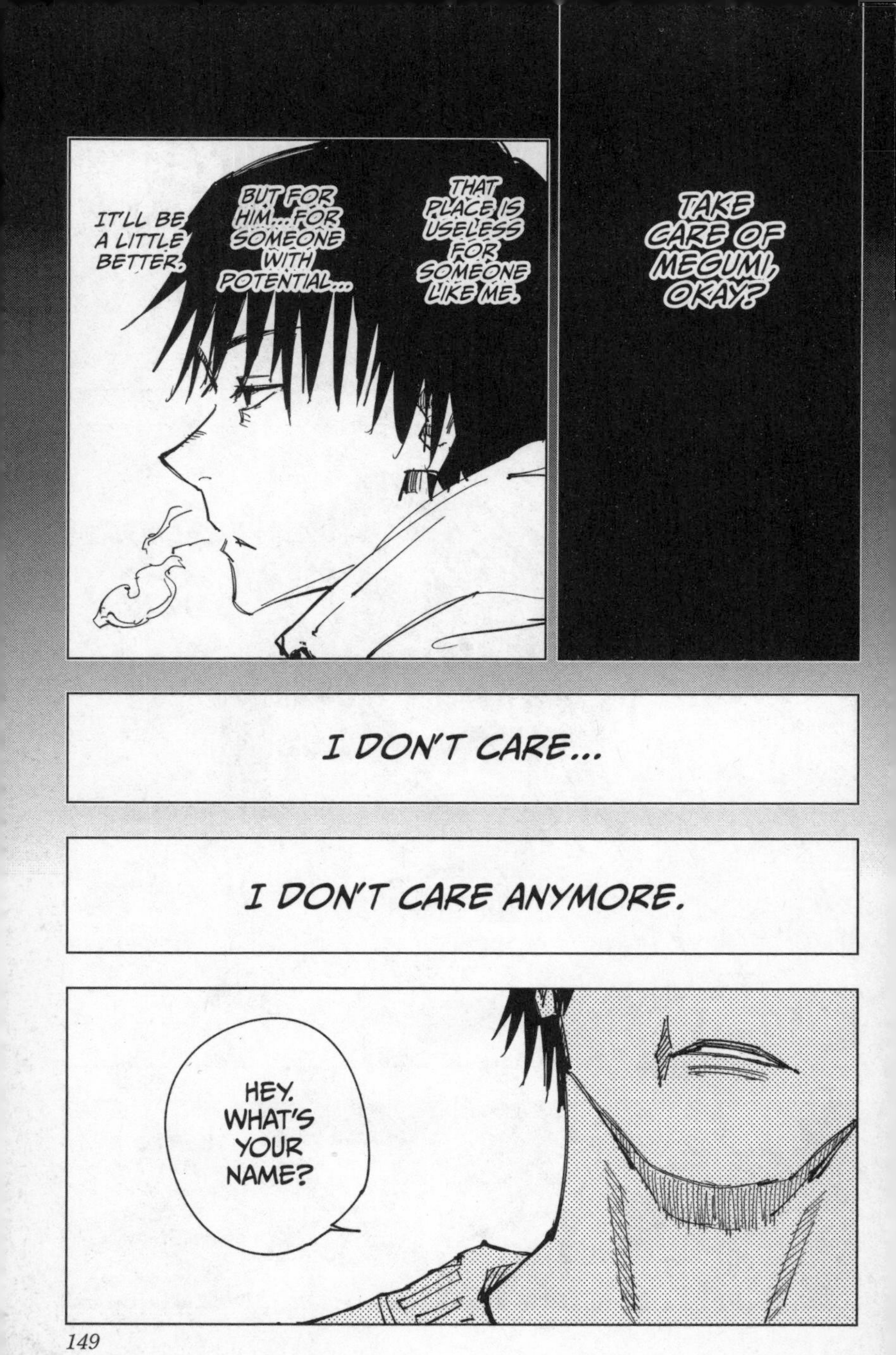
TAKE CARE OF MEGUMI, OKAY?
THAT PLACE IS USELESS FOR SOMEONE LIKE ME.
BUT FOR HIM... FOR SOMEONE WITH POTENTIAL...
IT'LL BE A LITTLE BETTER.
I DON'T CARE...
I DON'T CARE ANYMORE.
HEY. WHAT'S YOUR NAME?

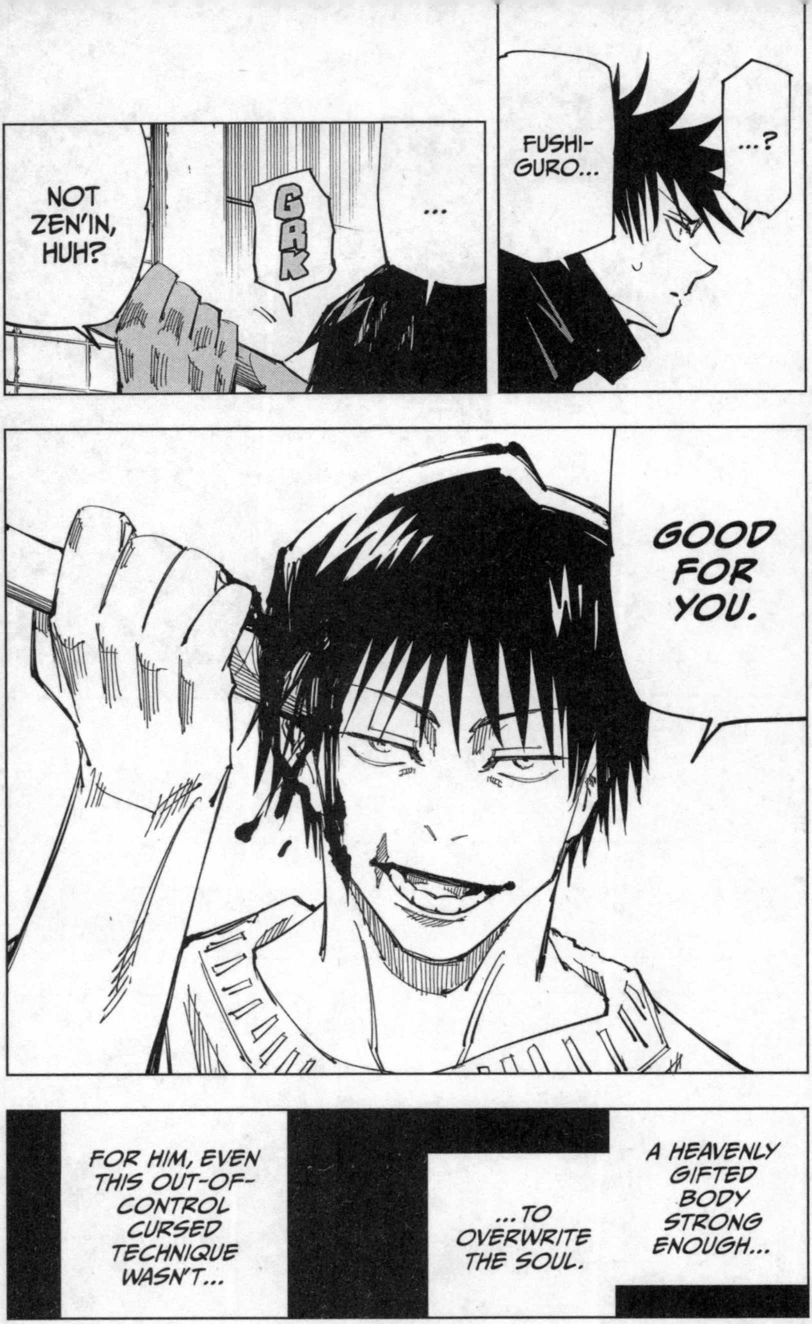
...?
FUSHI-GURO...
...
GRK
NOT ZEN'IN, HUH?
GOOD FOR YOU.
A HEAVENLY GIFTED BODY STRONG ENOUGH...
...TO OVERWRITE THE SOUL.
FOR HIM, EVEN THIS OUT-OF-CONTROL CURSED TECHNIQUE WASN'T...

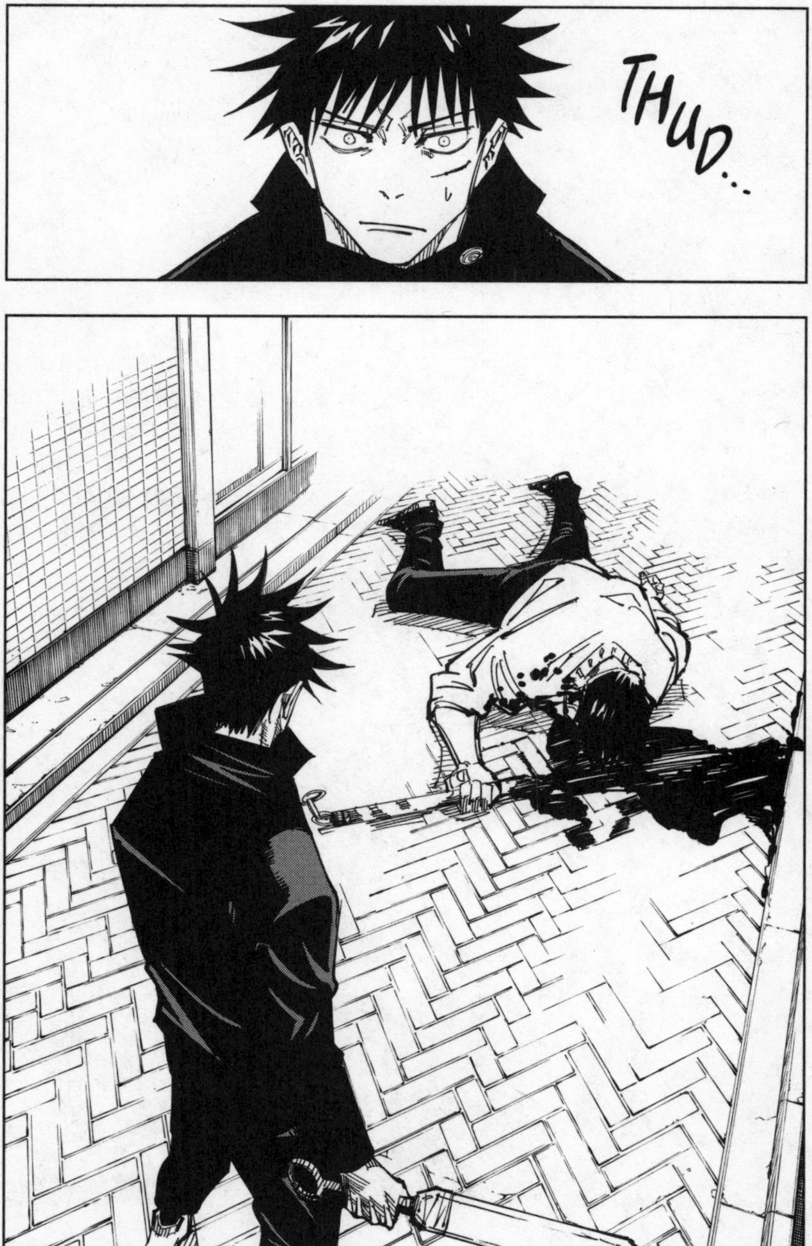
THUD...

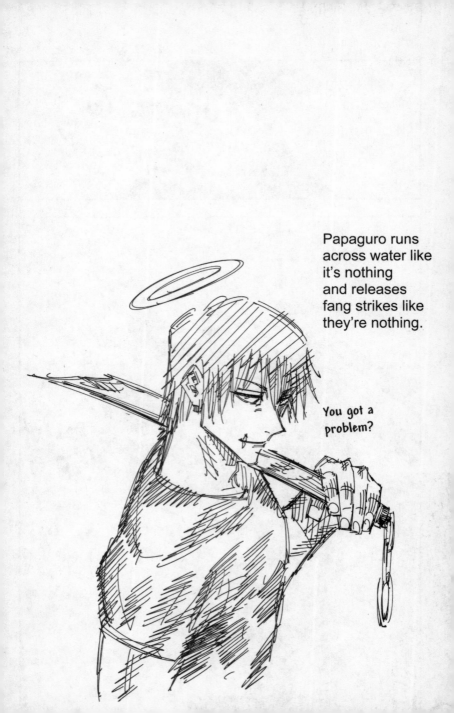

Papaguro runs across water like it's nothing and releases fang strikes like they're nothing.

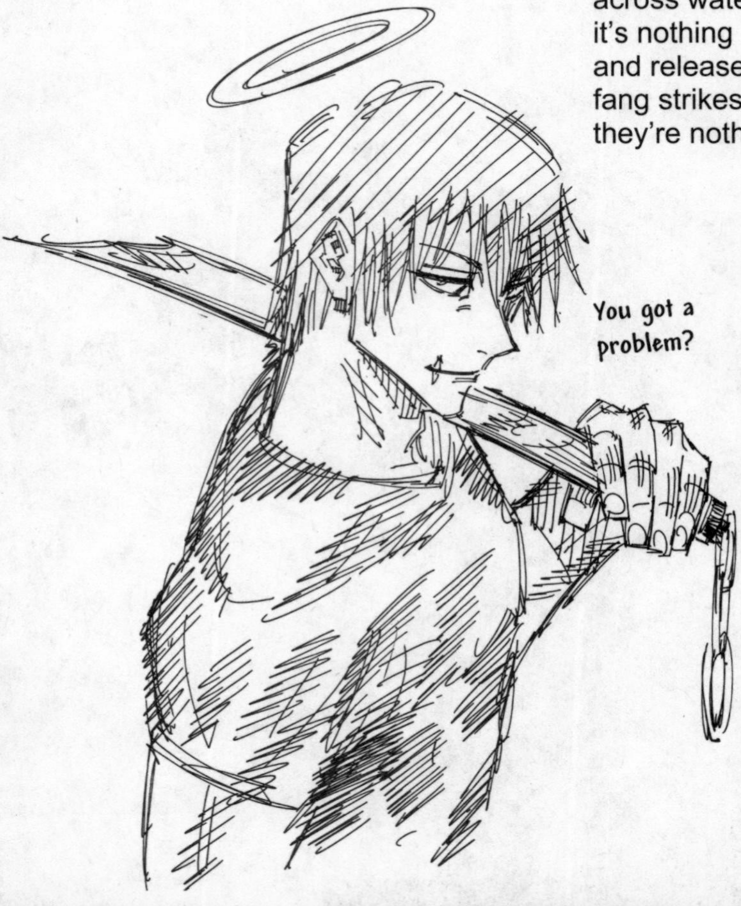
You got a problem?

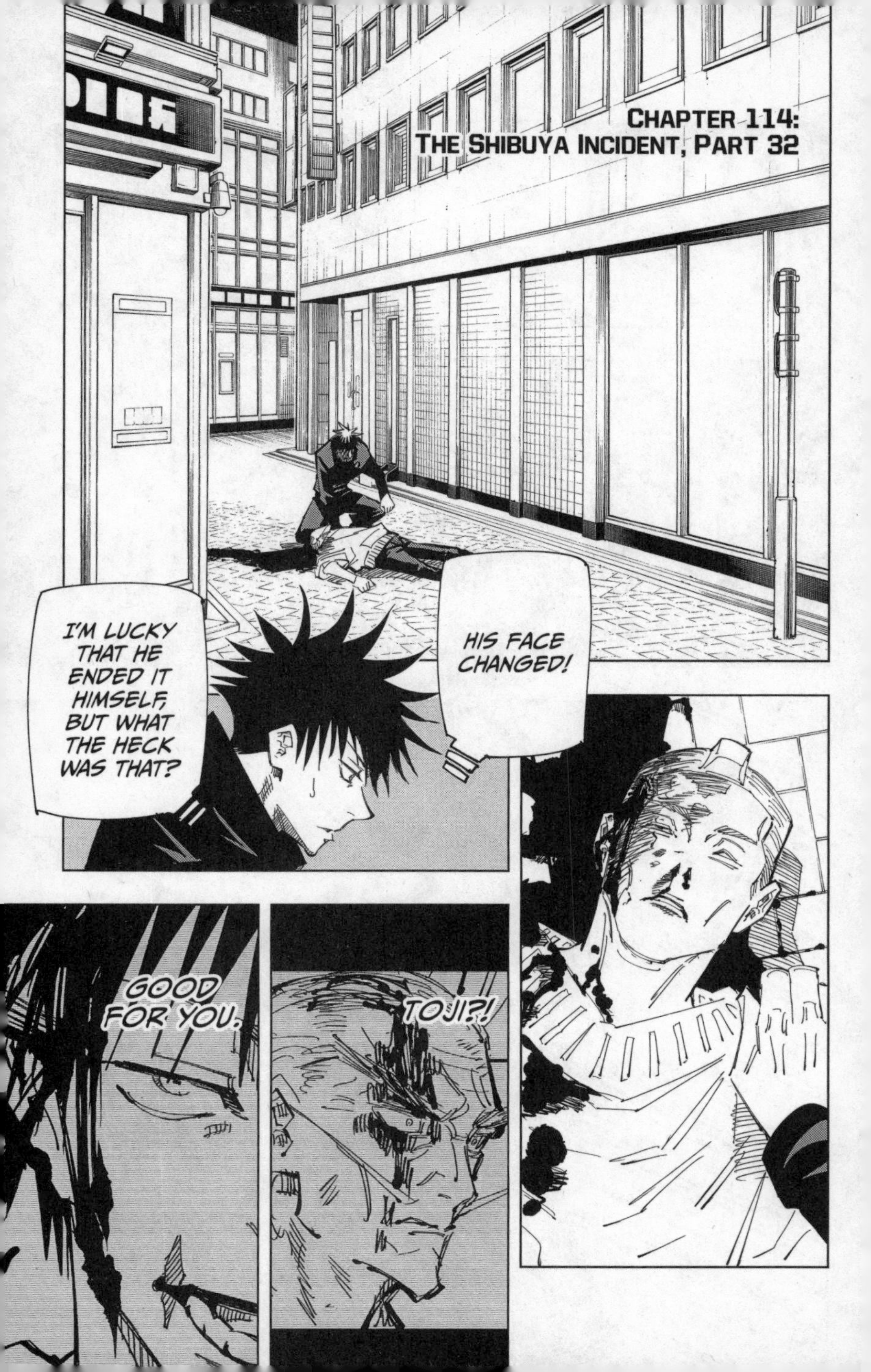
Chapter 114:
The Shibuya Incident, Part 32
HIS FACE CHANGED!
I'M LUCKY THAT HE ENDED IT HIMSELF, BUT WHAT THE HECK WAS THAT?
TOJI?!
GOOD FOR YOU.

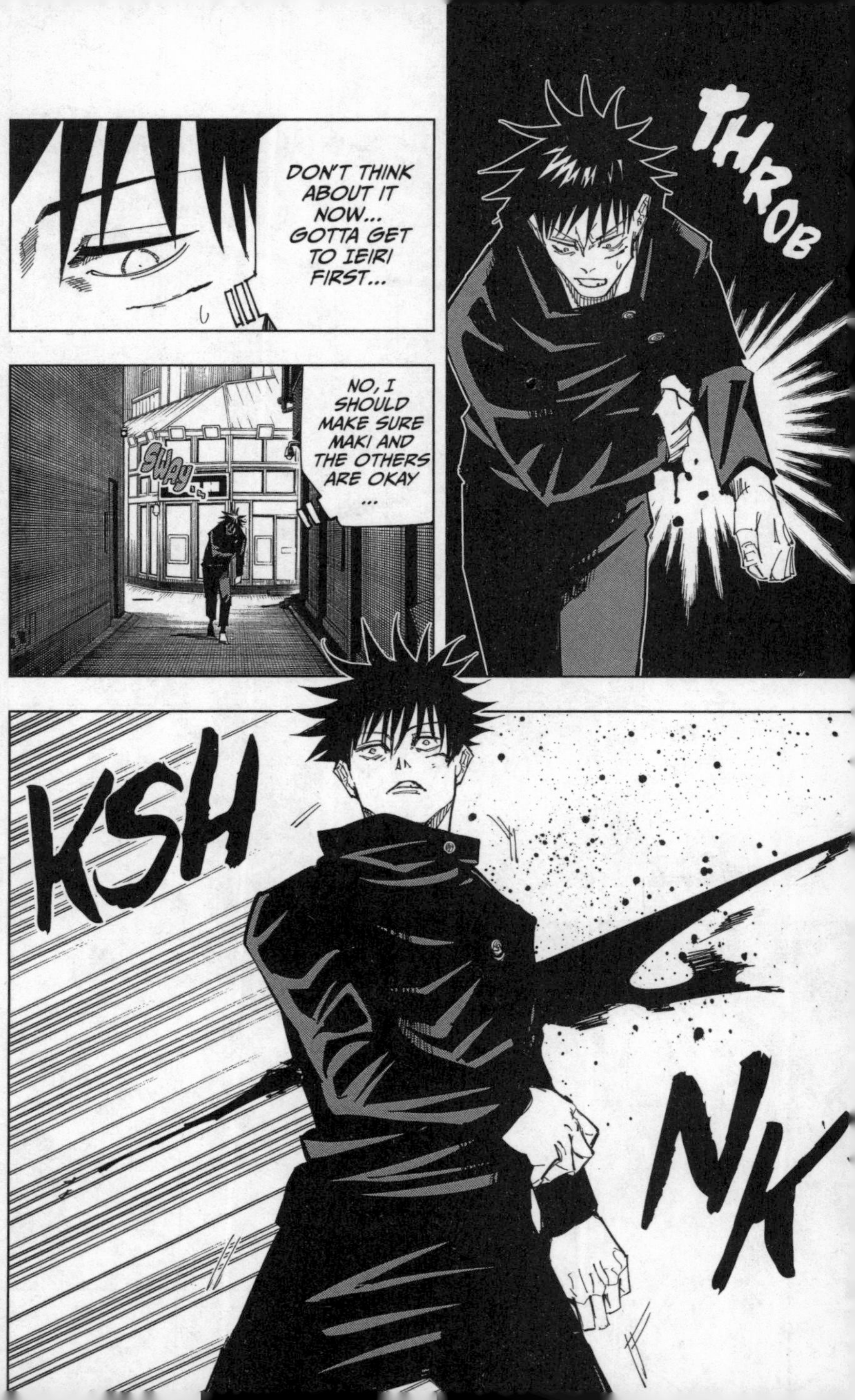
THROB
DON'T THINK ABOUT IT NOW... GOTTA GET TO IEIRI FIRST...
SWAY
NO, I SHOULD MAKE SURE MAKI AND THE OTHERS ARE OKAY ...
KSH
NK

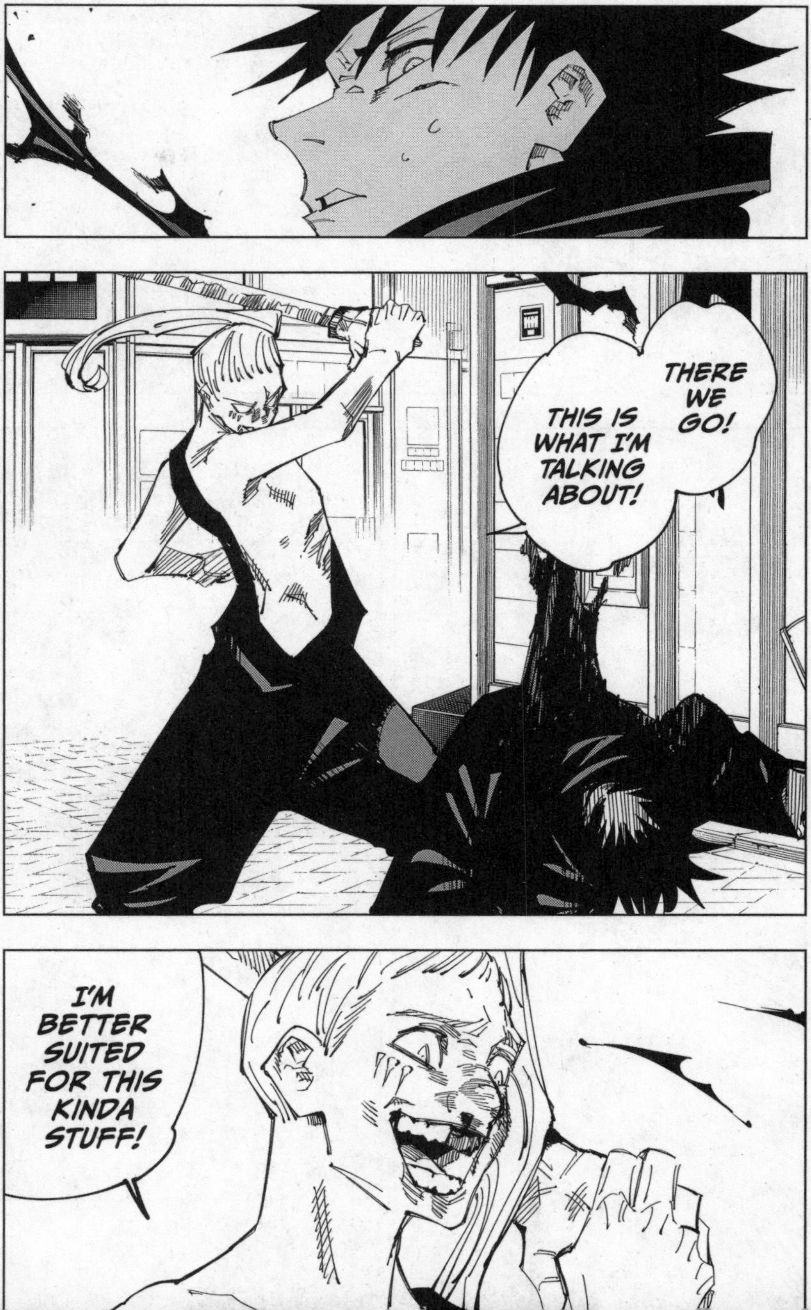
THERE WE GO!
THIS IS WHAT I'M TALKING ABOUT!
I'M BETTER SUITED FOR THIS KINDA STUFF!

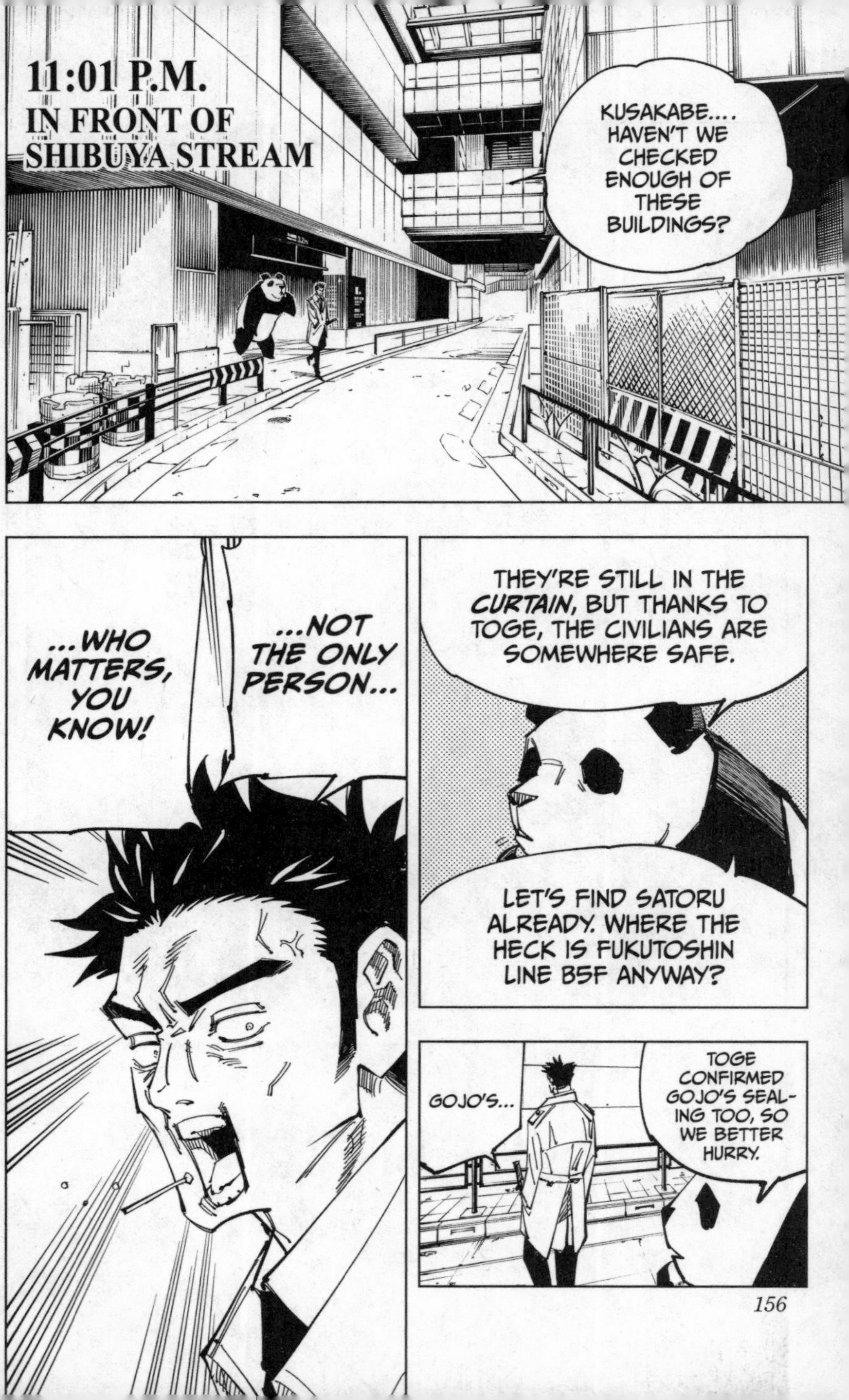
11:01 P.M.
IN FRONT OF SHIBUYA STREAM
KUSAKABE.... HAVEN'T WE CHECKED ENOUGH OF THESE BUILDINGS?
THEY'RE STILL IN THE *CURTAIN*, BUT THANKS TO TOGE, THE CIVILIANS ARE SOMEWHERE SAFE.
LET'S FIND SATORU ALREADY. WHERE THE HECK IS FUKUTOSHIN LINE B5F ANYWAY?
TOGE CONFIRMED GOJO'S SEALING TOO, SO WE BETTER HURRY.
GOJO'S...
...NOT THE ONLY PERSON...
...WHO MATTERS, YOU KNOW!

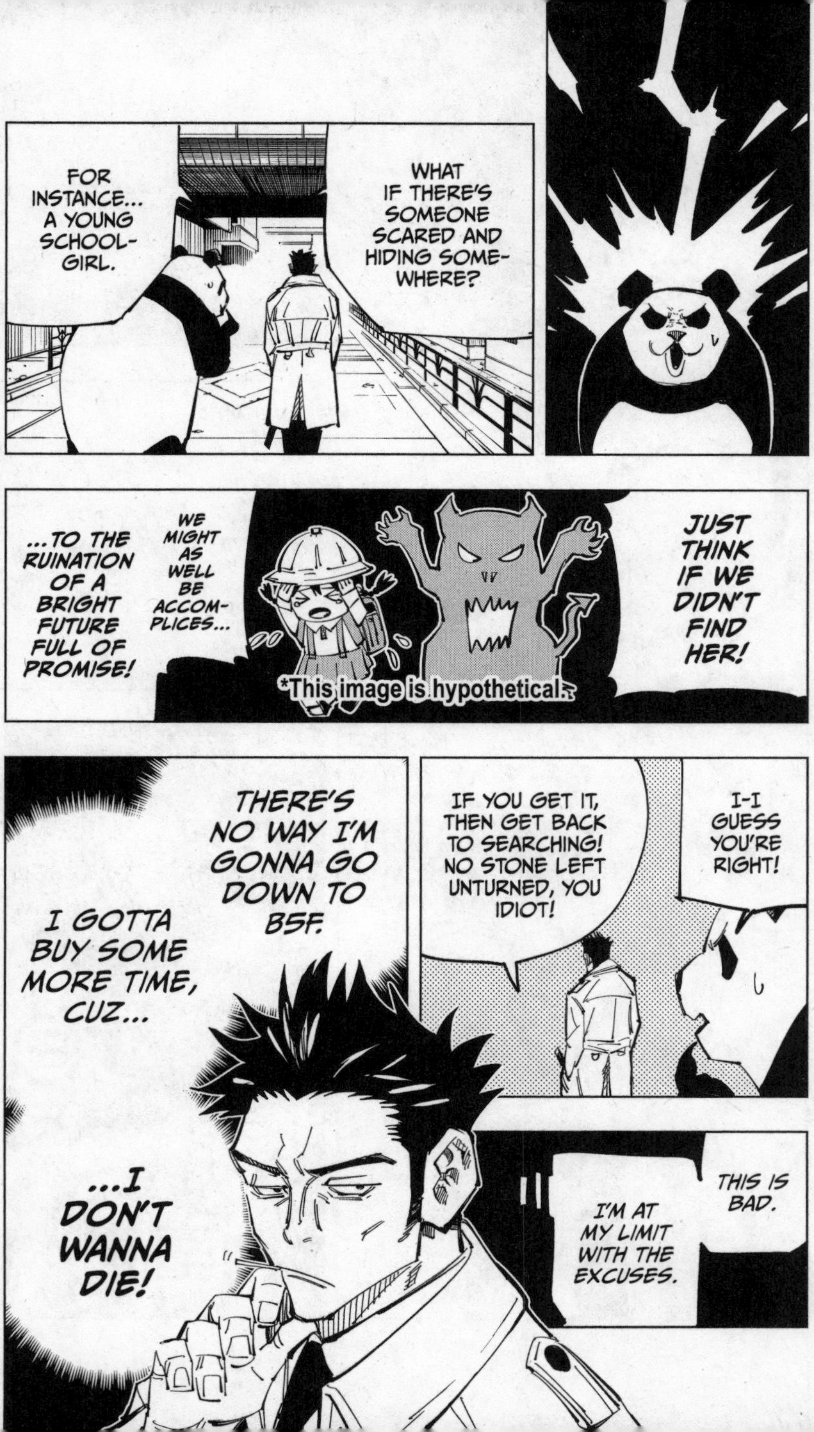
WHAT IF THERE'S SOMEONE SCARED AND HIDING SOMEWHERE?
FOR INSTANCE... A YOUNG SCHOOLGIRL.
JUST THINK IF WE DIDN'T FIND HER!
*This image is hypothetical.
WE MIGHT AS WELL BE ACCOMPLICES...
...TO THE RUINATION OF A BRIGHT FUTURE FULL OF PROMISE!
I-I GUESS YOU'RE RIGHT!
IF YOU GET IT, THEN GET BACK TO SEARCHING! NO STONE LEFT UNTURNED, YOU IDIOT!
THIS IS BAD.
I'M AT MY LIMIT WITH THE EXCUSES.
THERE'S NO WAY I'M GONNA GO DOWN TO B5F.
I GOTTA BUY SOME MORE TIME, CUZ...
...I DON'T WANNA DIE!

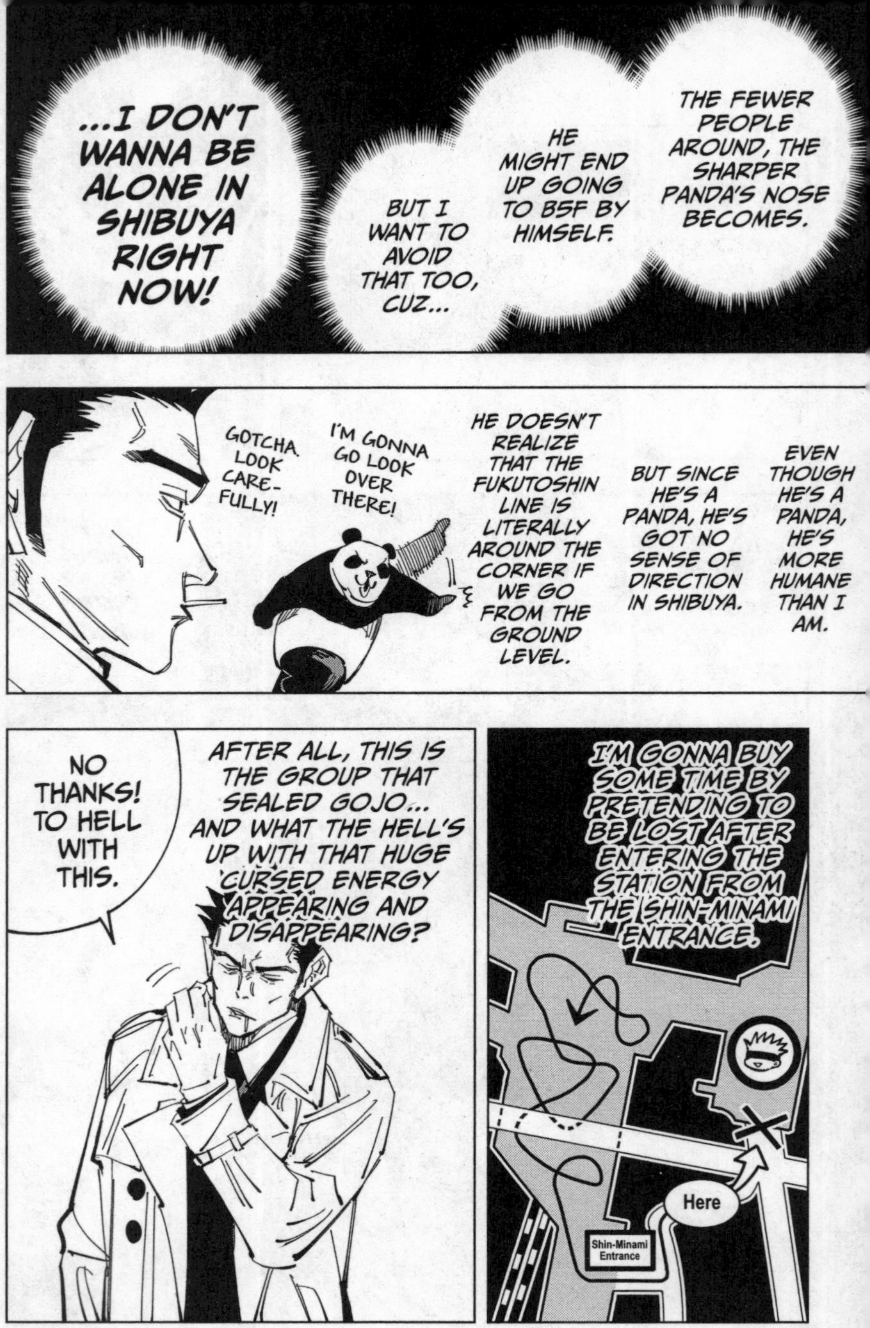
THE FEWER PEOPLE AROUND, THE SHARPER PANDA'S NOSE BECOMES.
HE MIGHT END UP GOING TO B5F BY HIMSELF.
BUT I WANT TO AVOID THAT TOO, CUZ...
...I DON'T WANNA BE ALONE IN SHIBUYA RIGHT NOW!
EVEN THOUGH HE'S A PANDA, HE'S MORE HUMANE THAN I AM.
BUT SINCE HE'S A PANDA, HE'S GOT NO SENSE OF DIRECTION IN SHIBUYA.
HE DOESN'T REALIZE THAT THE FUKUTOSHIN LINE IS LITERALLY AROUND THE CORNER IF WE GO FROM THE GROUND LEVEL.
I'M GONNA GO LOOK OVER THERE!
GOTCHA. LOOK CARE-FULLY!
I'M GONNA BUY SOME TIME BY PRETENDING TO BE LOST AFTER ENTERING THE STATION FROM THE SHIN-MINAMI ENTRANCE.
Here
Shin-Minami Entrance
AFTER ALL, THIS IS THE GROUP THAT SEALED GOJO... AND WHAT THE HELL'S UP WITH THAT HUGE CURSED ENERGY APPEARING AND DISAPPEARING?
NO THANKS! TO HELL WITH THIS.

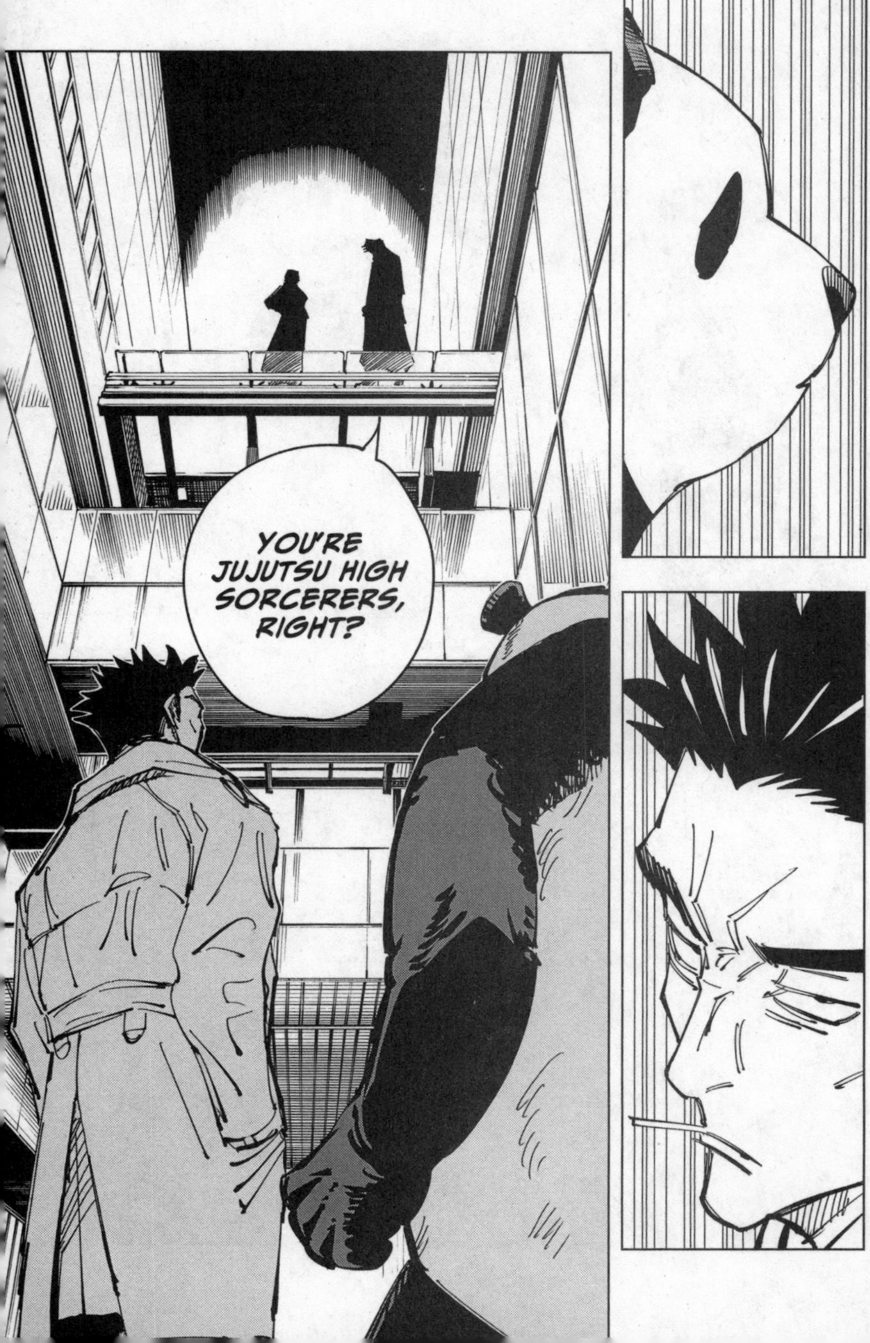
YOU'RE JUJUTSU HIGH SORCERERS, RIGHT?

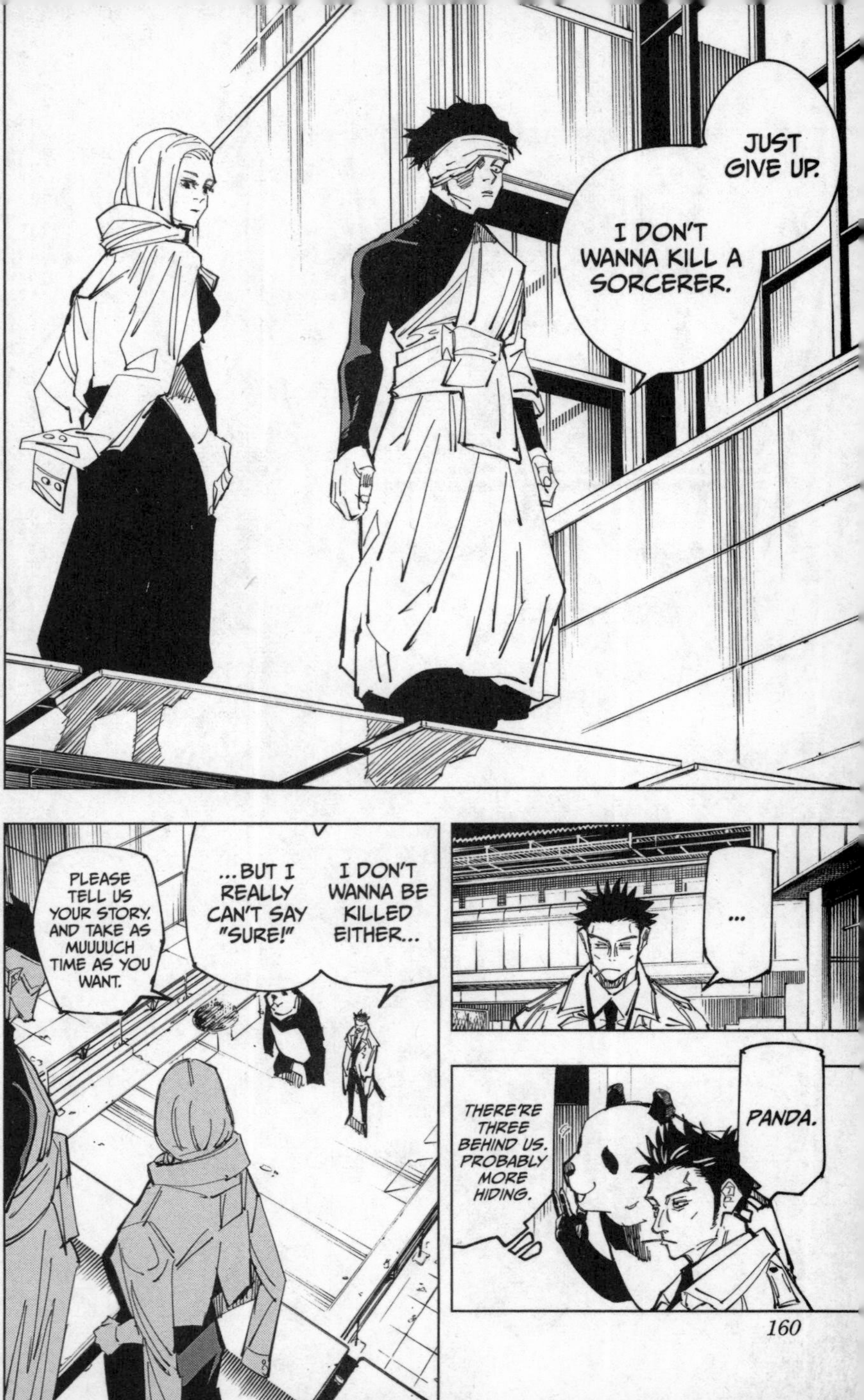
JUST GIVE UP.
I DON'T WANNA KILL A SORCERER.
...
PANDA.
THERE'RE THREE BEHIND US. PROBABLY MORE HIDING.
I DON'T WANNA BE KILLED EITHER...
...BUT I REALLY CAN'T SAY "SURE!"
PLEASE TELL US YOUR STORY. AND TAKE AS MUUUUCH TIME AS YOU WANT.

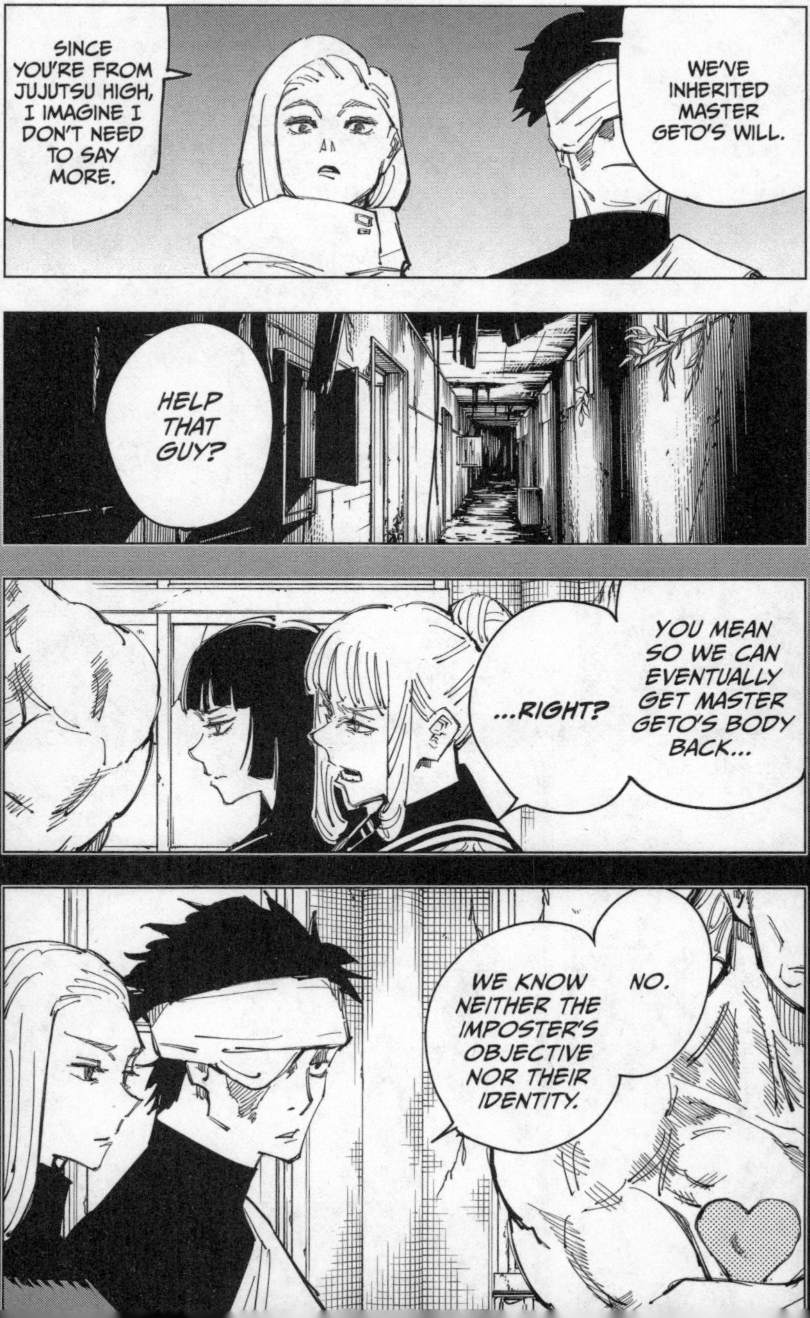
WE'VE INHERITED MASTER GETO'S WILL.
SINCE YOU'RE FROM JUJUTSU HIGH, I IMAGINE I DON'T NEED TO SAY MORE.
HELP THAT GUY?
YOU MEAN SO WE CAN EVENTUALLY GET MASTER GETO'S BODY BACK...
...RIGHT?
NO.
WE KNOW NEITHER THE IMPOSTER'S OBJECTIVE NOR THEIR IDENTITY.

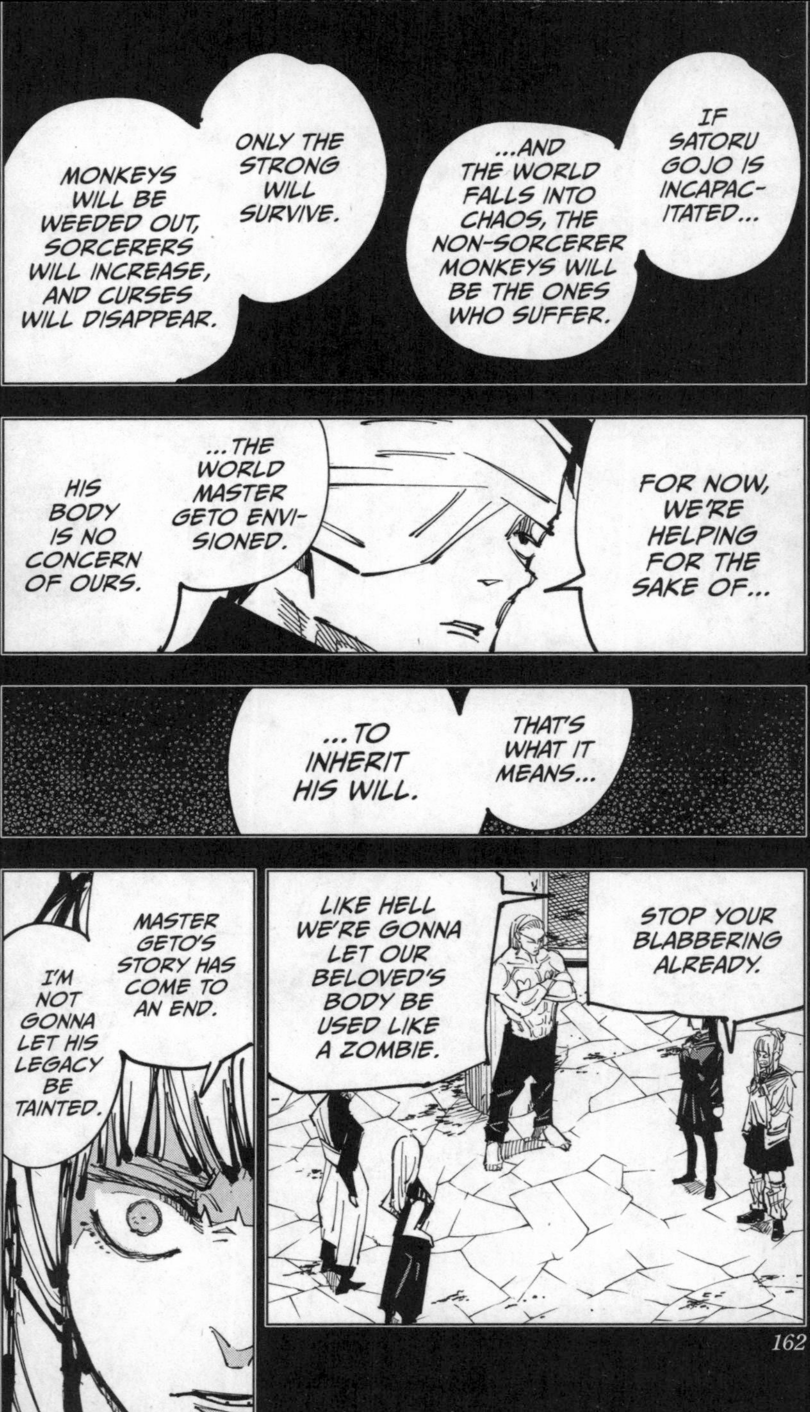
IF SATORU GOJO IS INCAPACITATED...
...AND THE WORLD FALLS INTO CHAOS, THE NON-SORCERER MONKEYS WILL BE THE ONES WHO SUFFER.
ONLY THE STRONG WILL SURVIVE.
MONKEYS WILL BE WEEDED OUT, SORCERERS WILL INCREASE, AND CURSES WILL DISAPPEAR.
FOR NOW, WE'RE HELPING FOR THE SAKE OF...
...THE WORLD MASTER GETO ENVISIONED.
HIS BODY IS NO CONCERN OF OURS.
THAT'S WHAT IT MEANS...
...TO INHERIT HIS WILL.
STOP YOUR BLABBERING ALREADY.
LIKE HELL WE'RE GONNA LET OUR BELOVED'S BODY BE USED LIKE A ZOMBIE.
MASTER GETO'S STORY HAS COME TO AN END.
I'M NOT GONNA LET HIS LEGACY BE TAINTED.

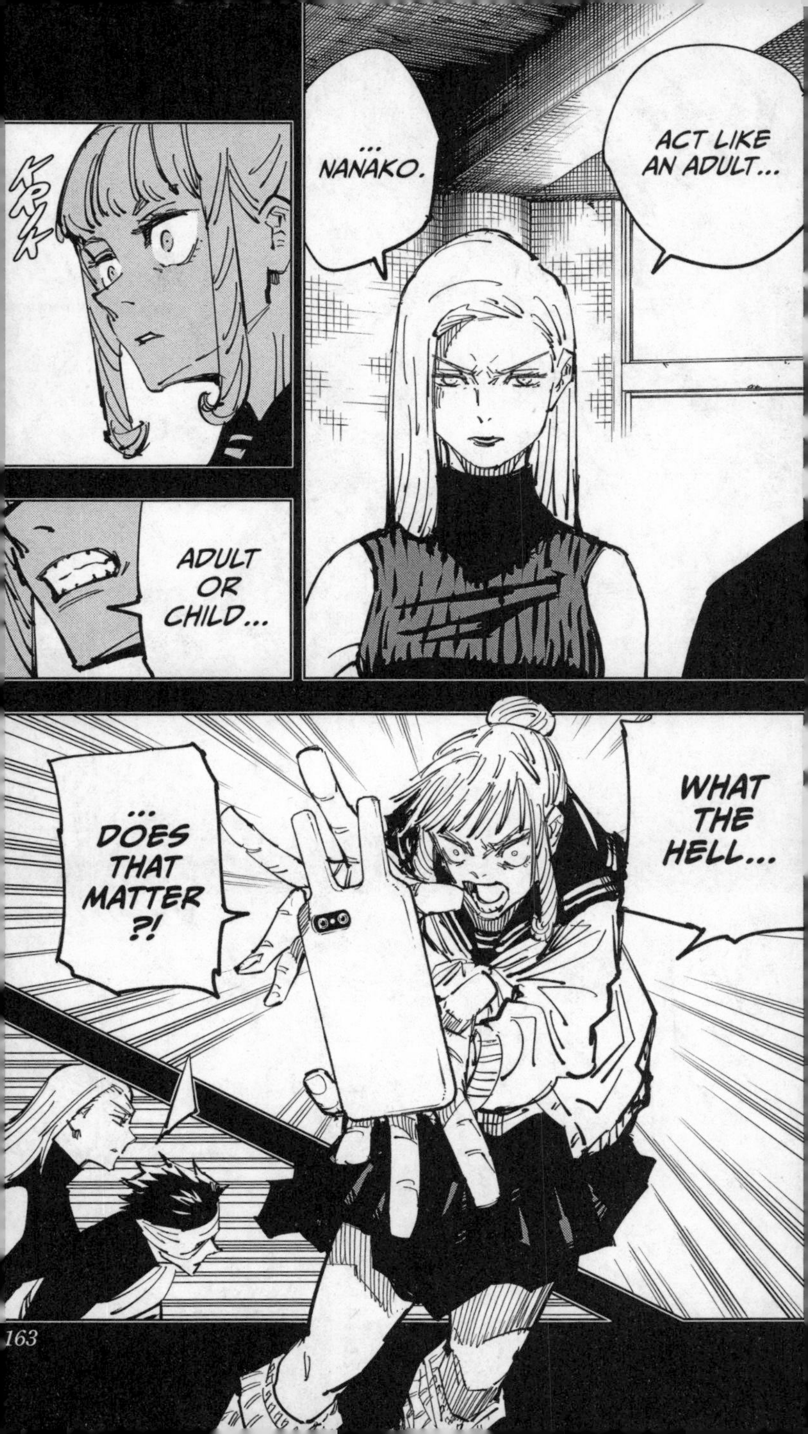
ACT LIKE AN ADULT...
... NANAKO.
KRK
ADULT OR CHILD...
WHAT THE HELL...
... DOES THAT MATTER ?!

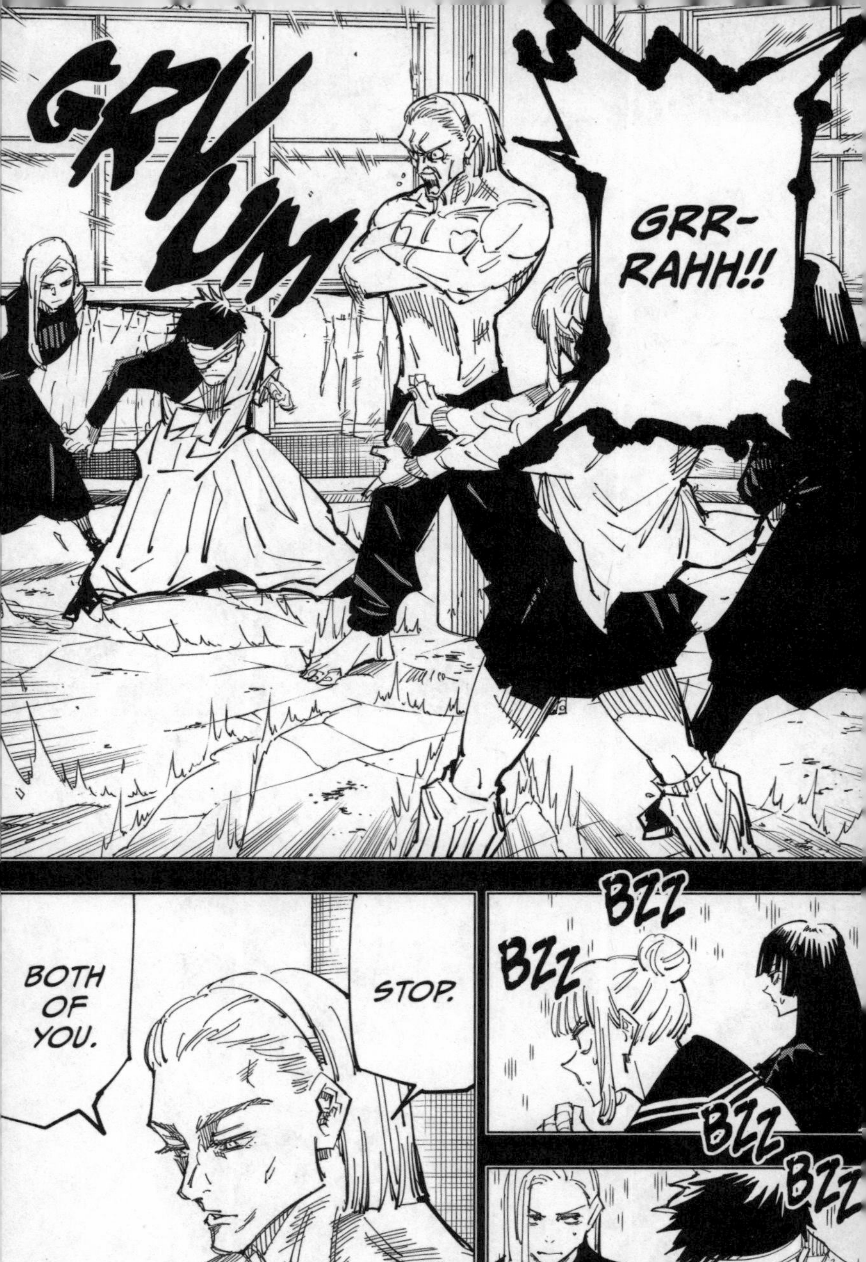
GRR-RAHH!!
BZZ
BZZ
BZZ
BZZ
STOP.
BOTH OF YOU.

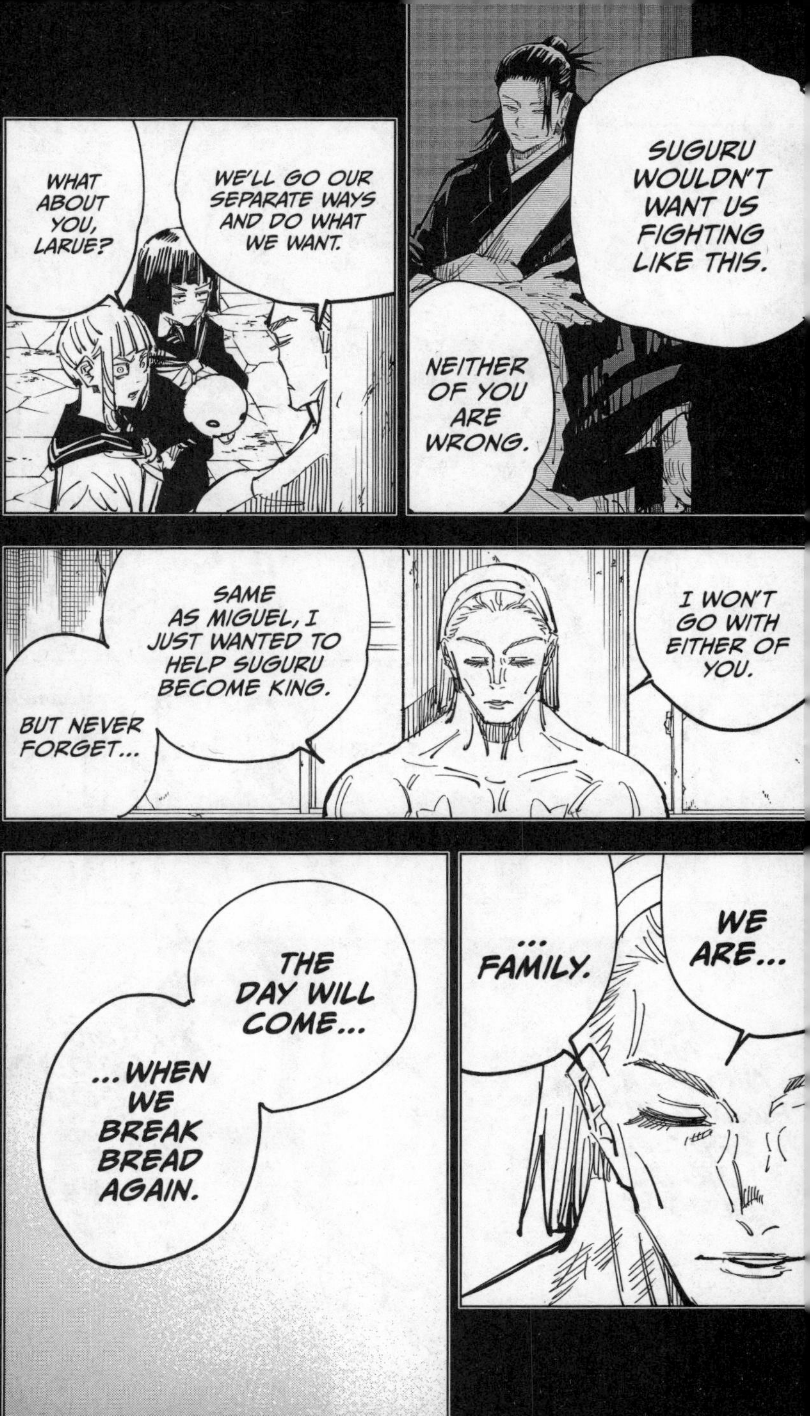
SUGURU WOULDN'T WANT US FIGHTING LIKE THIS.
NEITHER OF YOU ARE WRONG.
WE'LL GO OUR SEPARATE WAYS AND DO WHAT WE WANT.
WHAT ABOUT YOU, LARUE?
I WON'T GO WITH EITHER OF YOU.
SAME AS MIGUEL, I JUST WANTED TO HELP SUGURU BECOME KING.
BUT NEVER FORGET...
WE ARE...
...FAMILY.
THE DAY WILL COME...
...WHEN WE BREAK BREAD AGAIN.

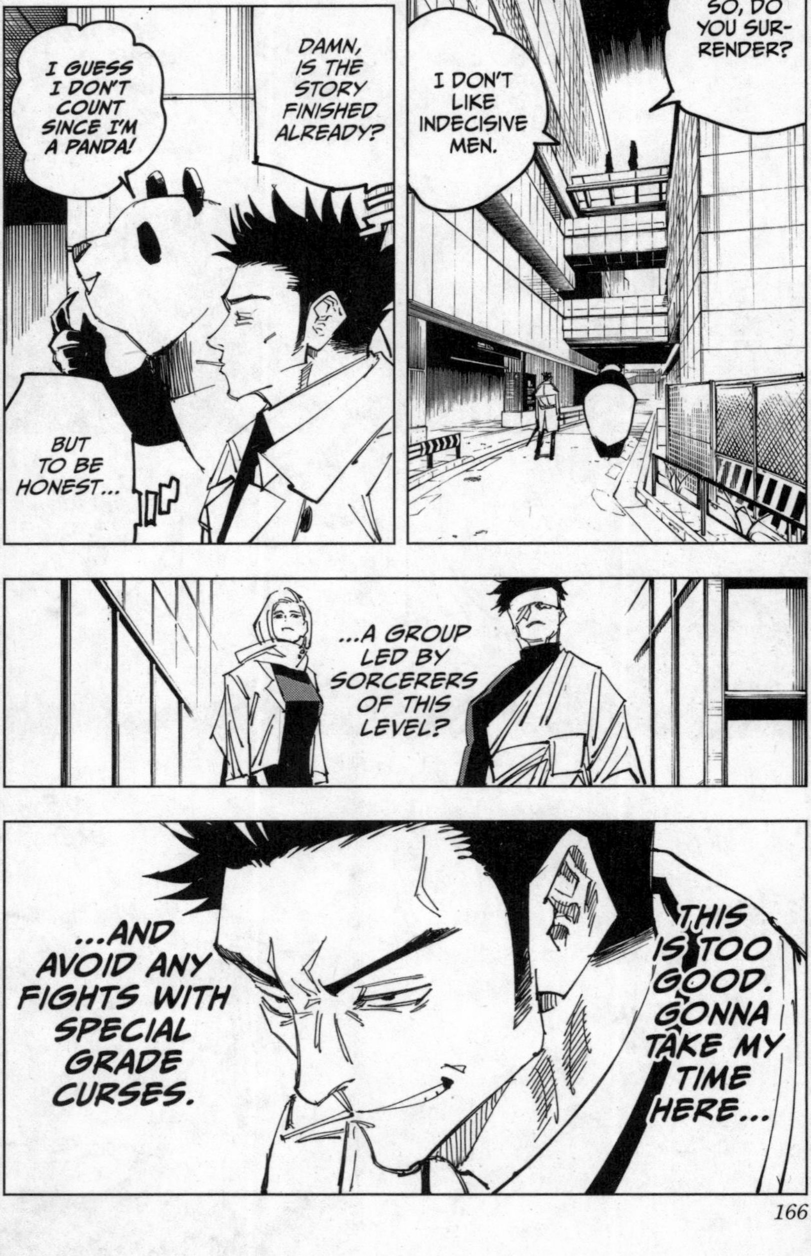
SO, DO YOU SUR-RENDER?
I DON'T LIKE INDECISIVE MEN.
DAMN, IS THE STORY FINISHED ALREADY?
I GUESS I DON'T COUNT SINCE I'M A PANDA!
BUT TO BE HONEST...
...A GROUP LED BY SORCERERS OF THIS LEVEL?
THIS IS TOO GOOD. GONNA TAKE MY TIME HERE...
...AND AVOID ANY FIGHTS WITH SPECIAL GRADE CURSES.

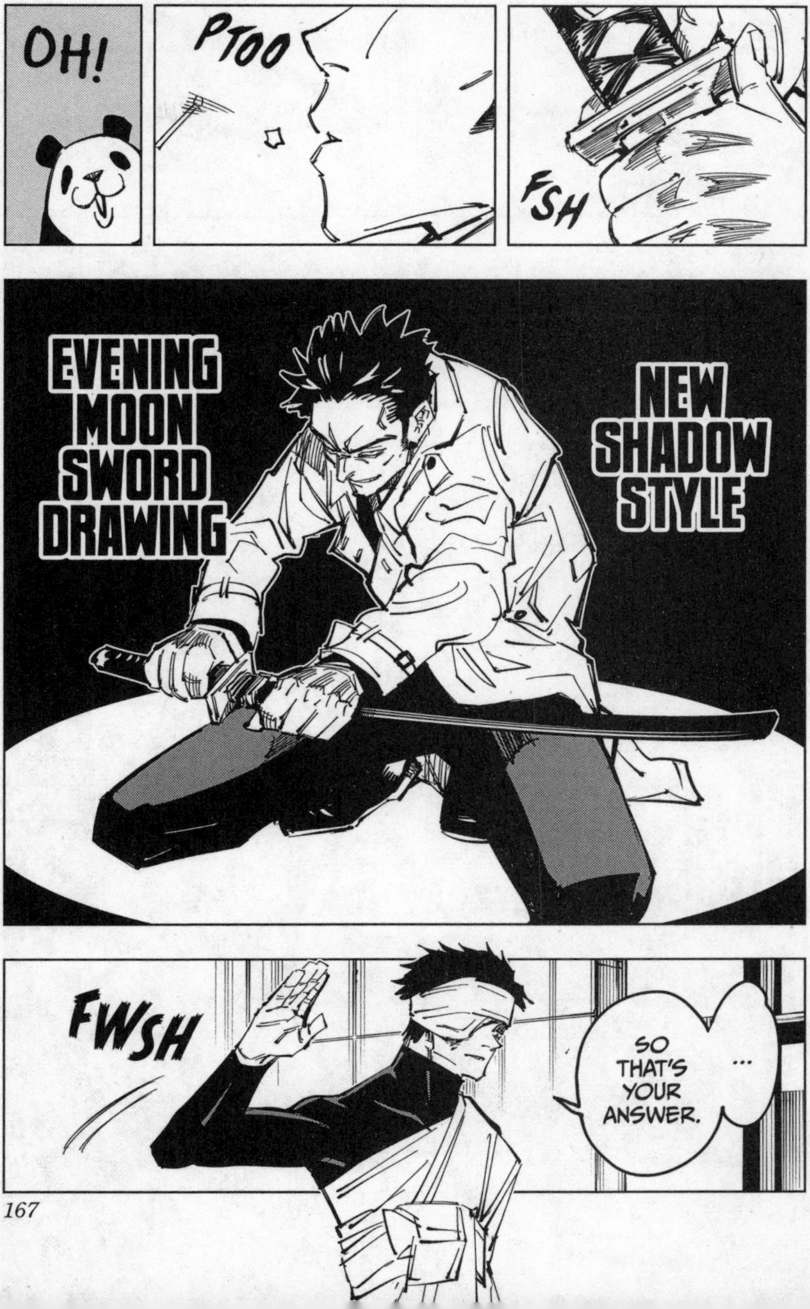
FSH
PTOO
OH!
NEW SHADOW STYLE
EVENING MOON SWORD DRAWING
...
SO THAT'S YOUR ANSWER.
FWSH

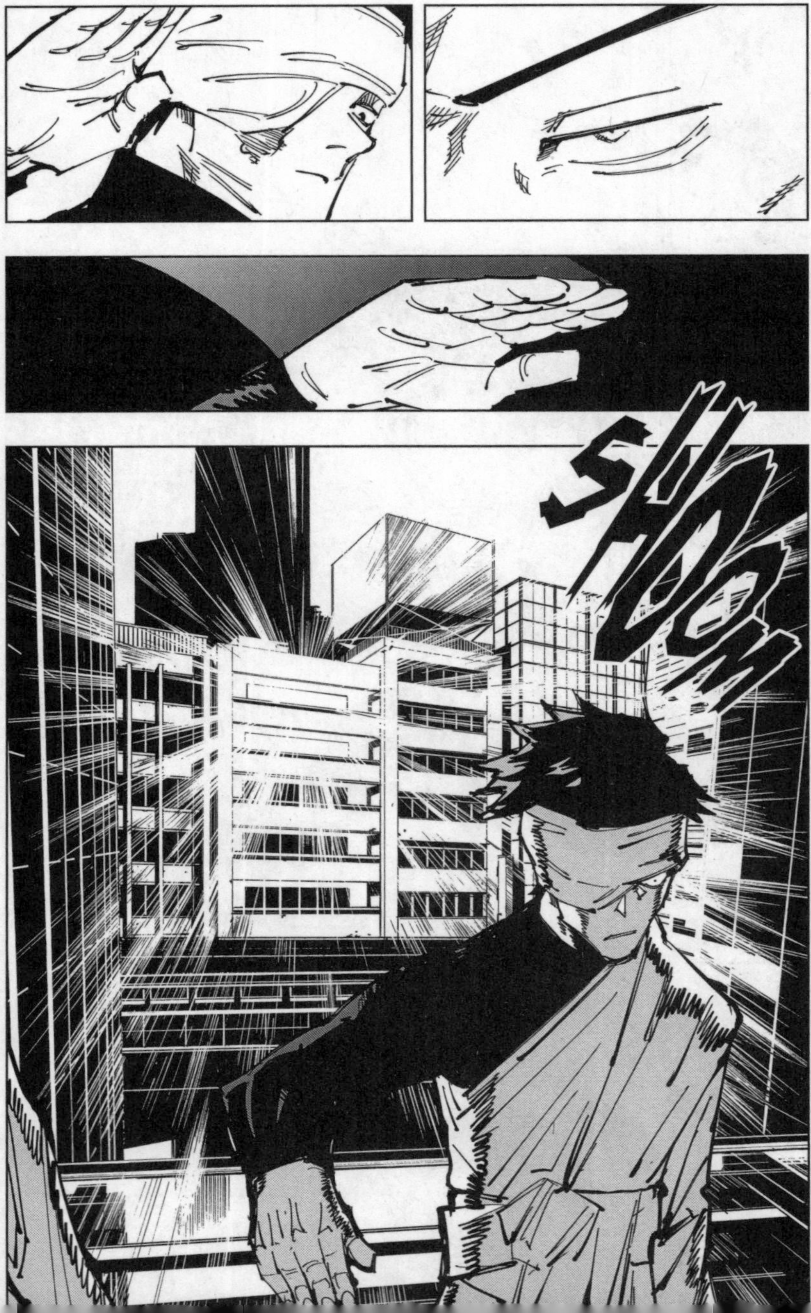
SHOOM

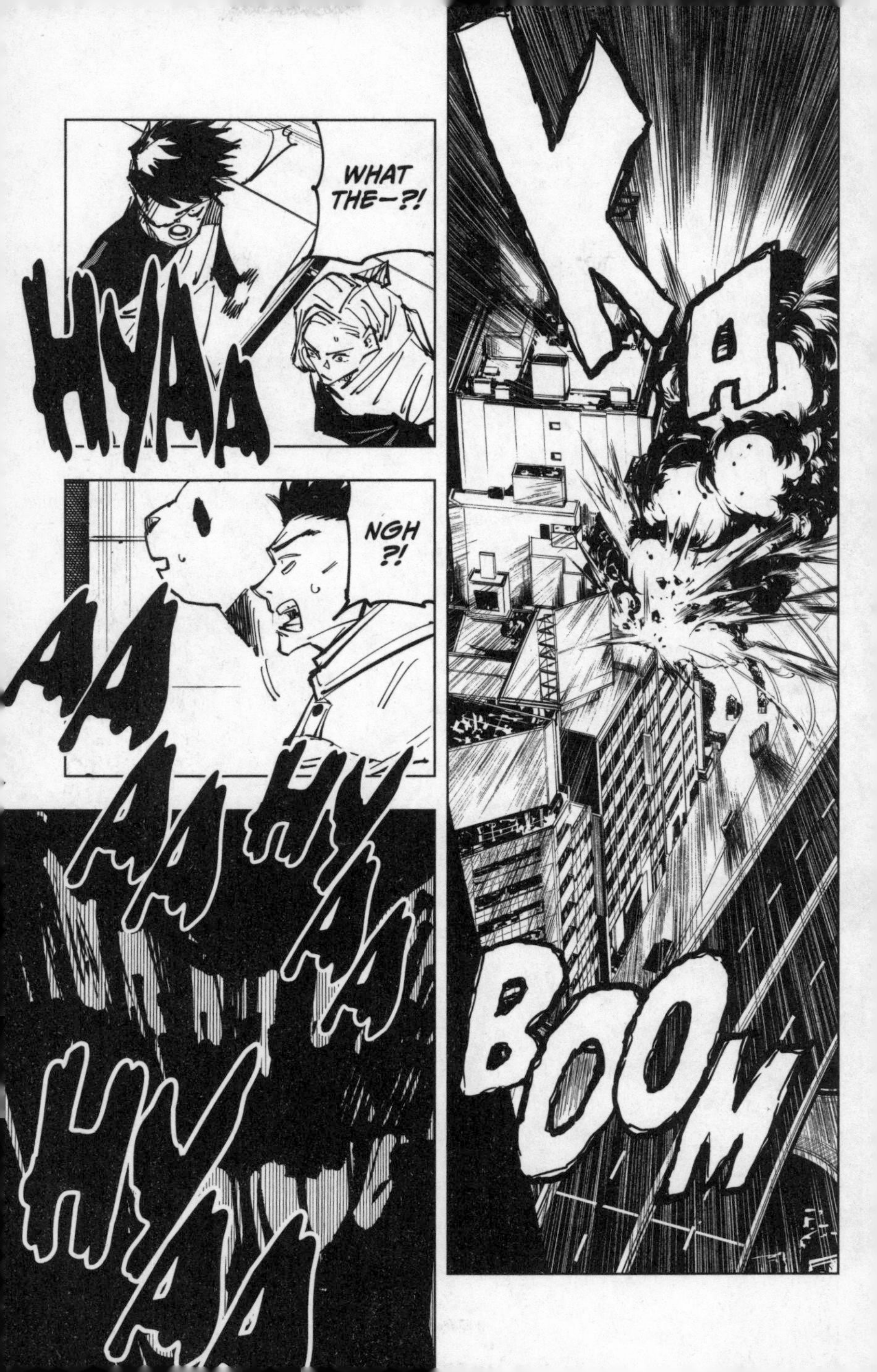
YA
BOOM
WHAT THE—?!
HYAA
NGH ?!
AA

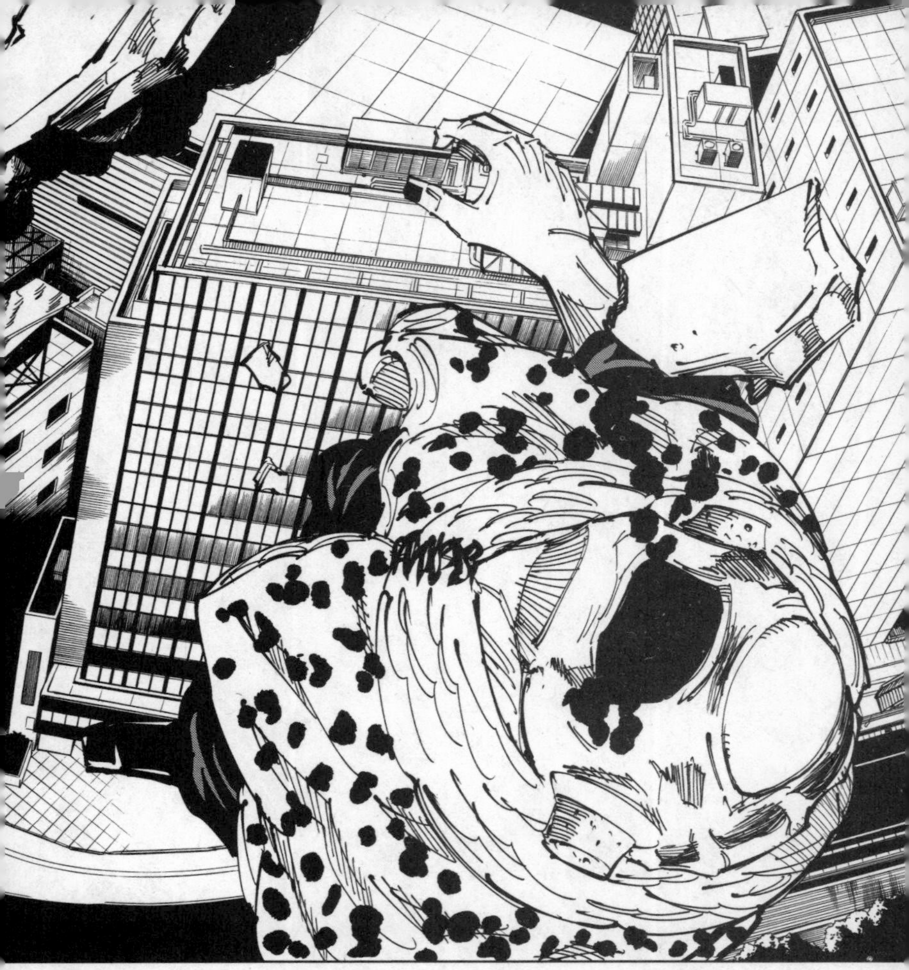

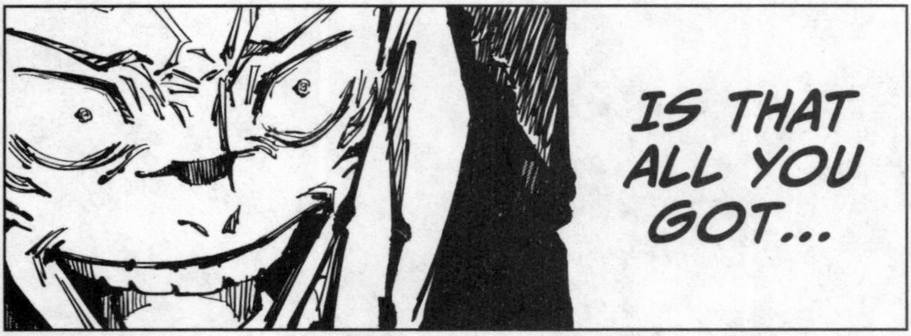
IS THAT ALL YOU GOT...

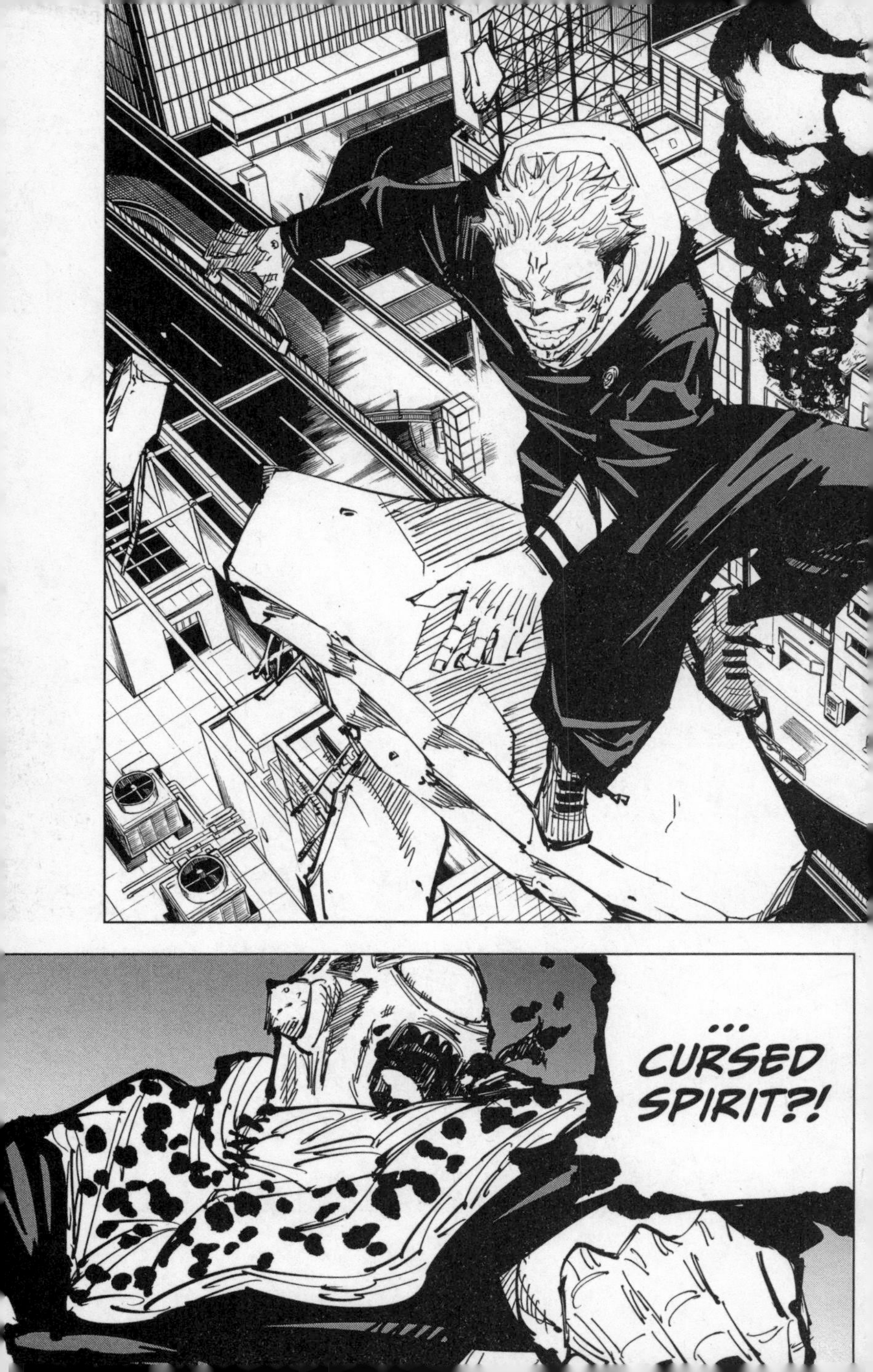
... CURSED SPIRIT?!

My opponents
are always
like this...

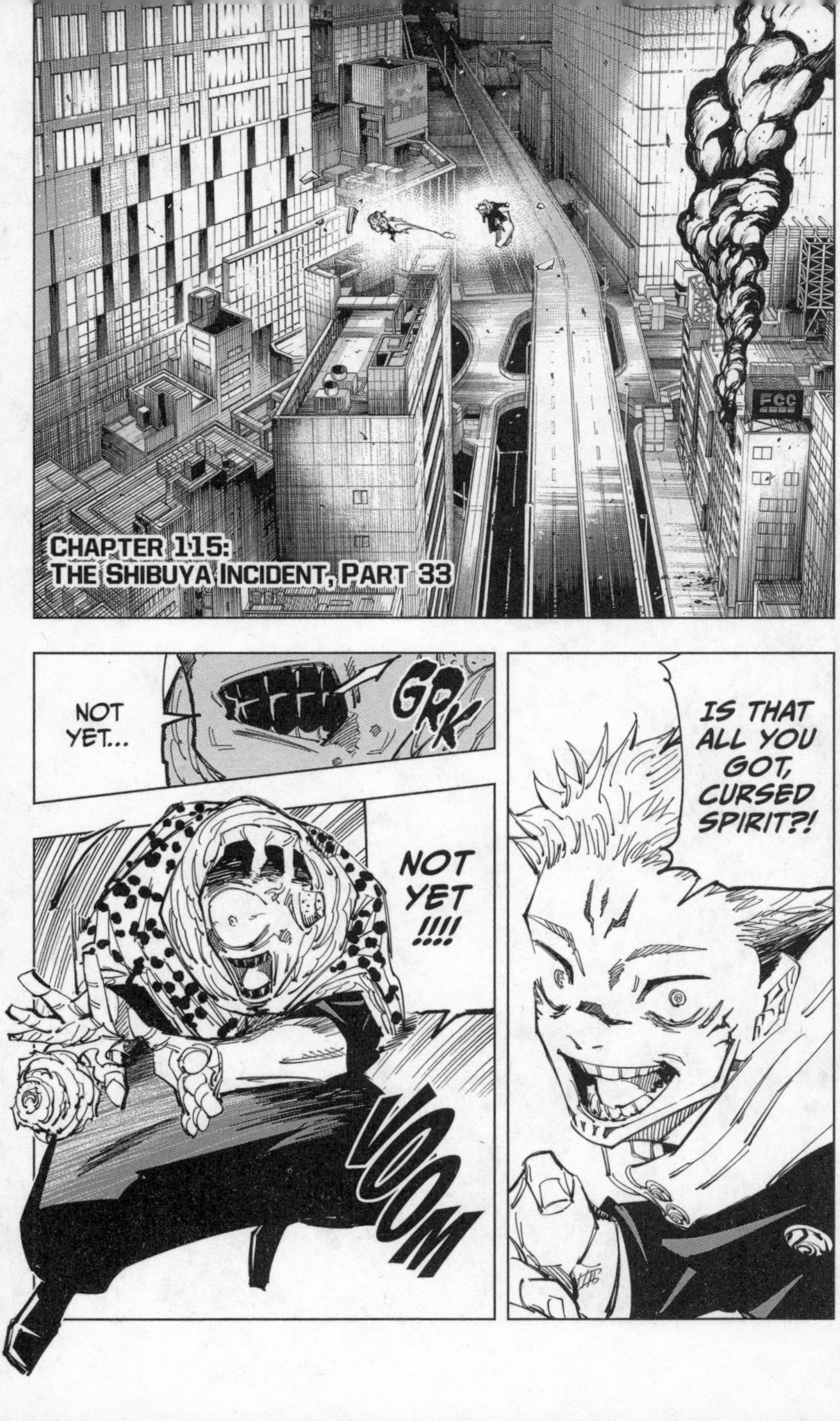
CHAPTER 115:
THE SHIBUYA INCIDENT, PART 33
FCC
IS THAT ALL YOU GOT, CURSED SPIRIT?!
NOT YET...
GRK
NOT YET!!!!
VOOM

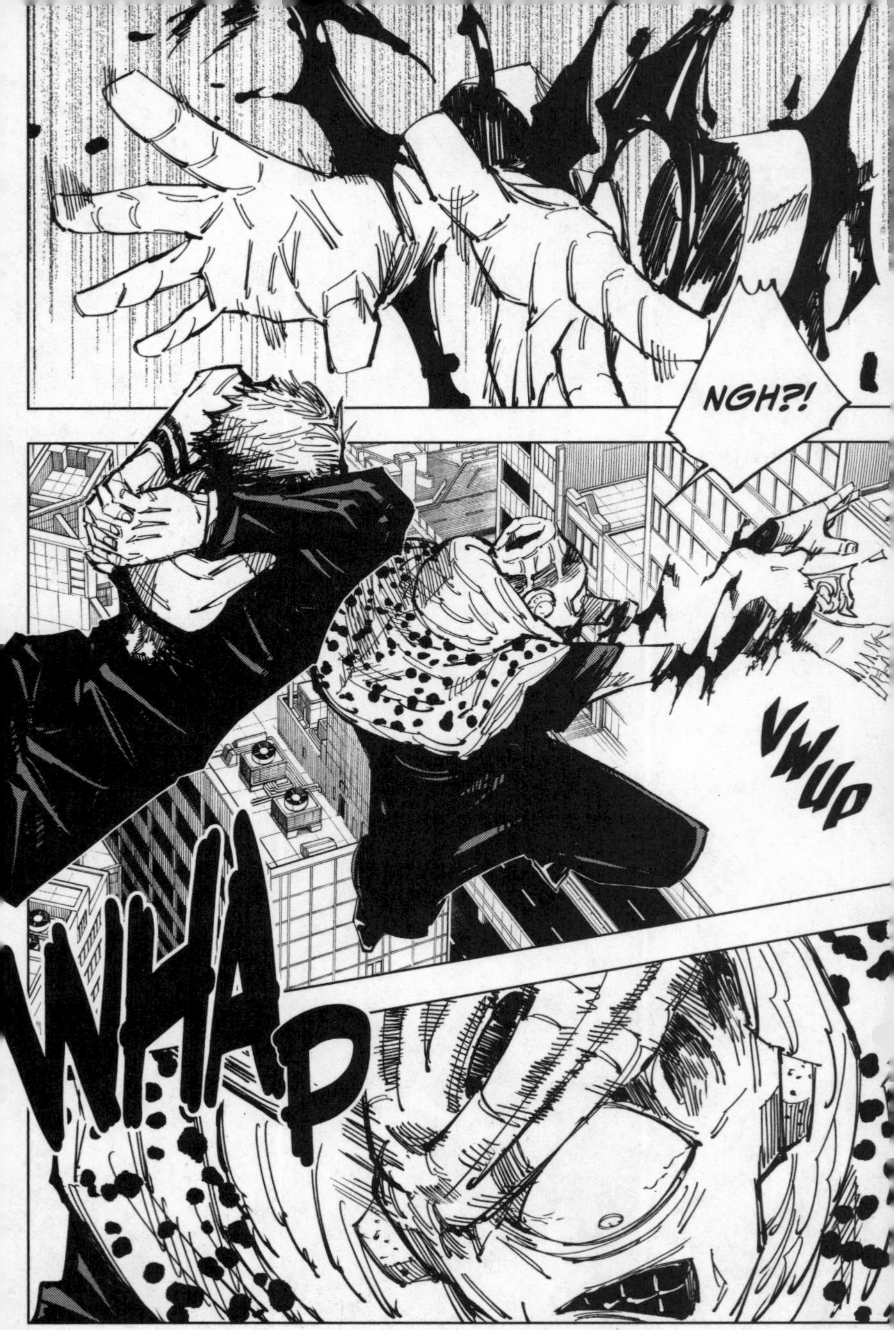
NGH?!
VWUP
WHAP

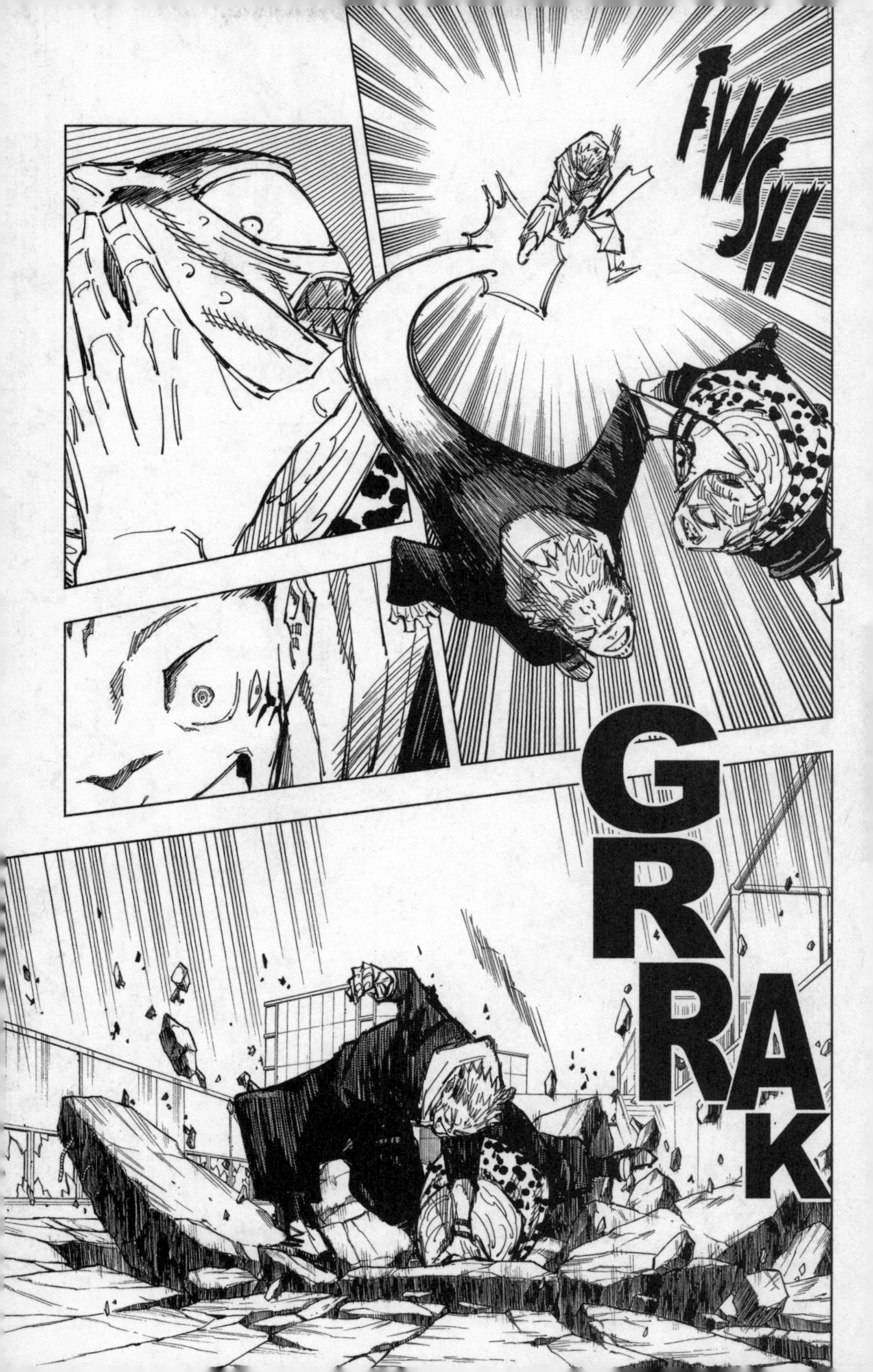
FWSH
GRRAK

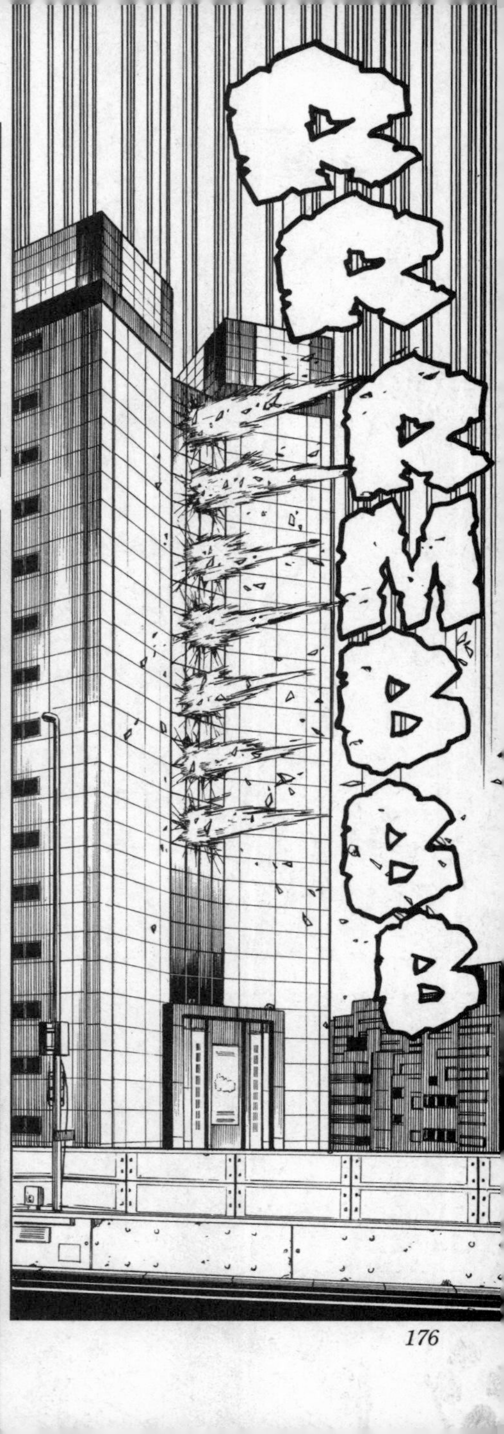
RRRMBBB

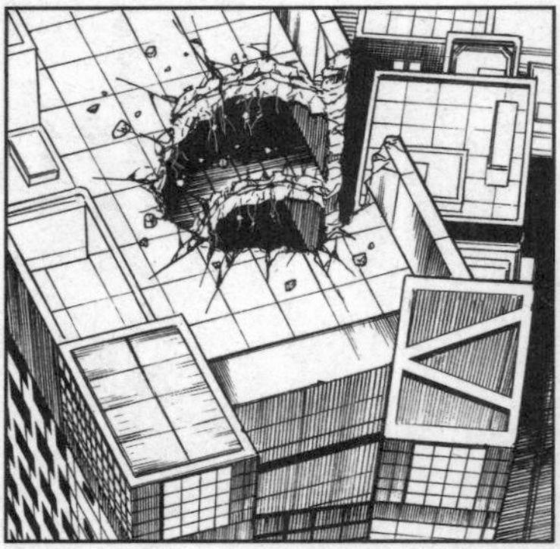

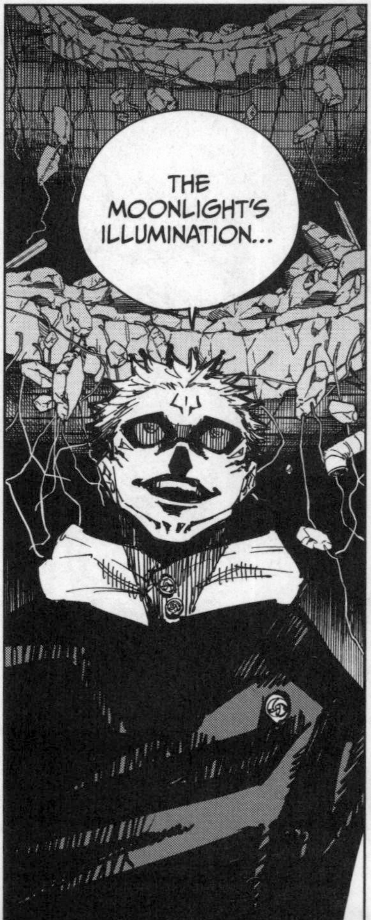
THE MOONLIGHT'S ILLUMINATION...

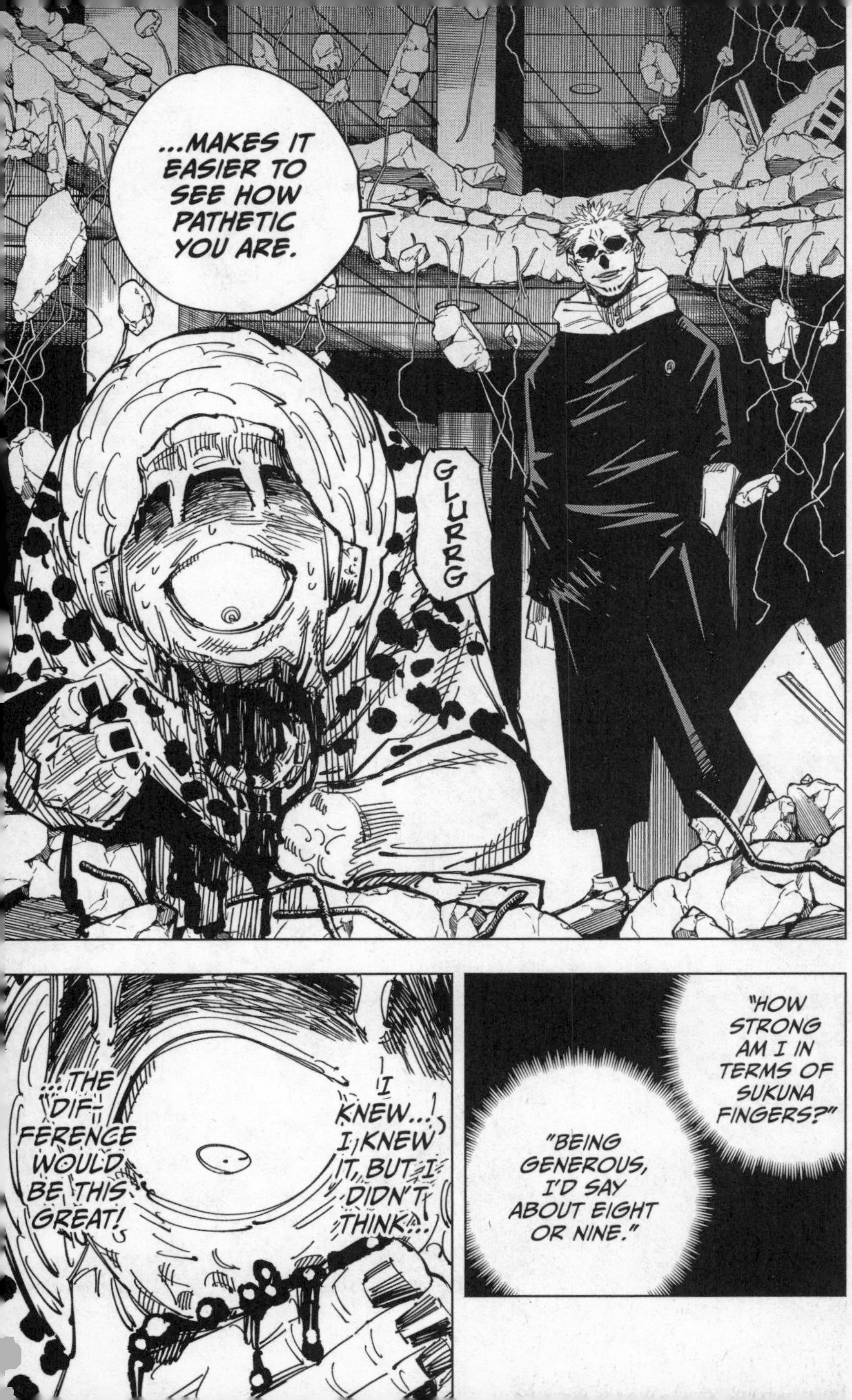
...MAKES IT EASIER TO SEE HOW PATHETIC YOU ARE.
GLURRG
"HOW STRONG AM I IN TERMS OF SUKUNA FINGERS?"
"BEING GENEROUS, I'D SAY ABOUT EIGHT OR NINE."
I KNEW... I KNEW IT, BUT I DIDN'T THINK...
...THE DIF-FERENCE WOULD BE THIS GREAT!

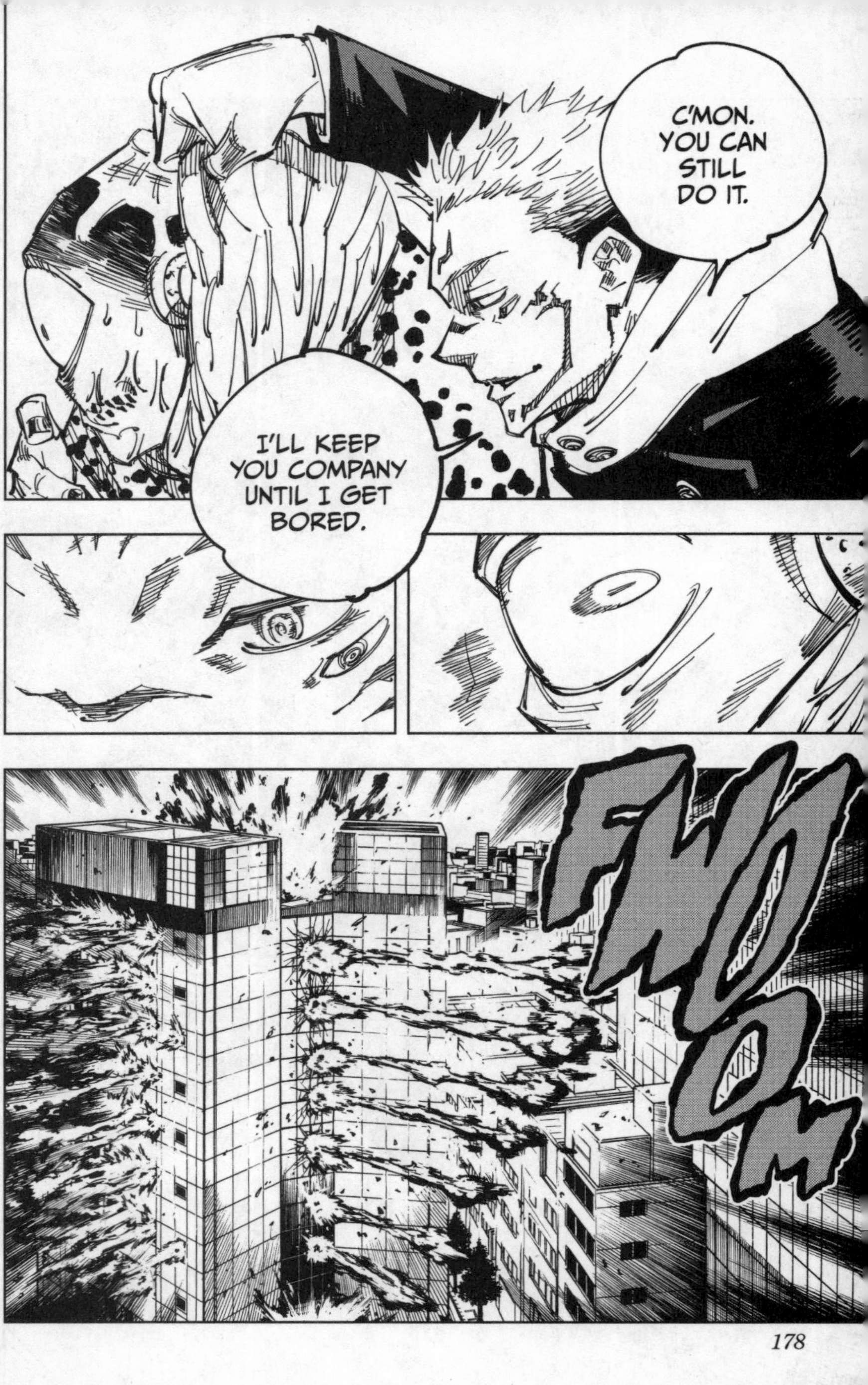
C'MON. YOU CAN STILL DO IT.
I'LL KEEP YOU COMPANY UNTIL I GET BORED.
FWOOM

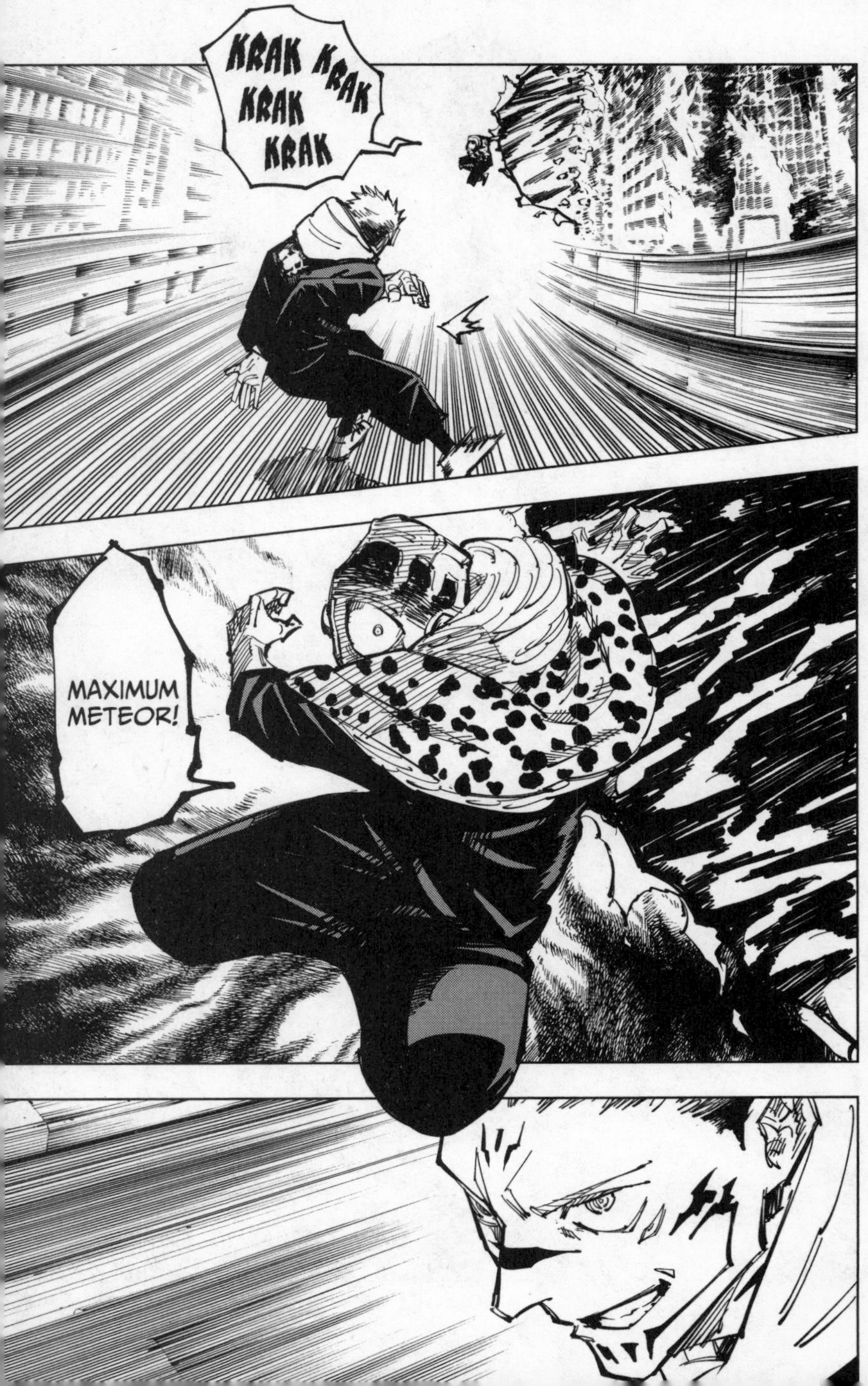
KRAK KRAK KRAK KRAK
MAXIMUM METEOR!

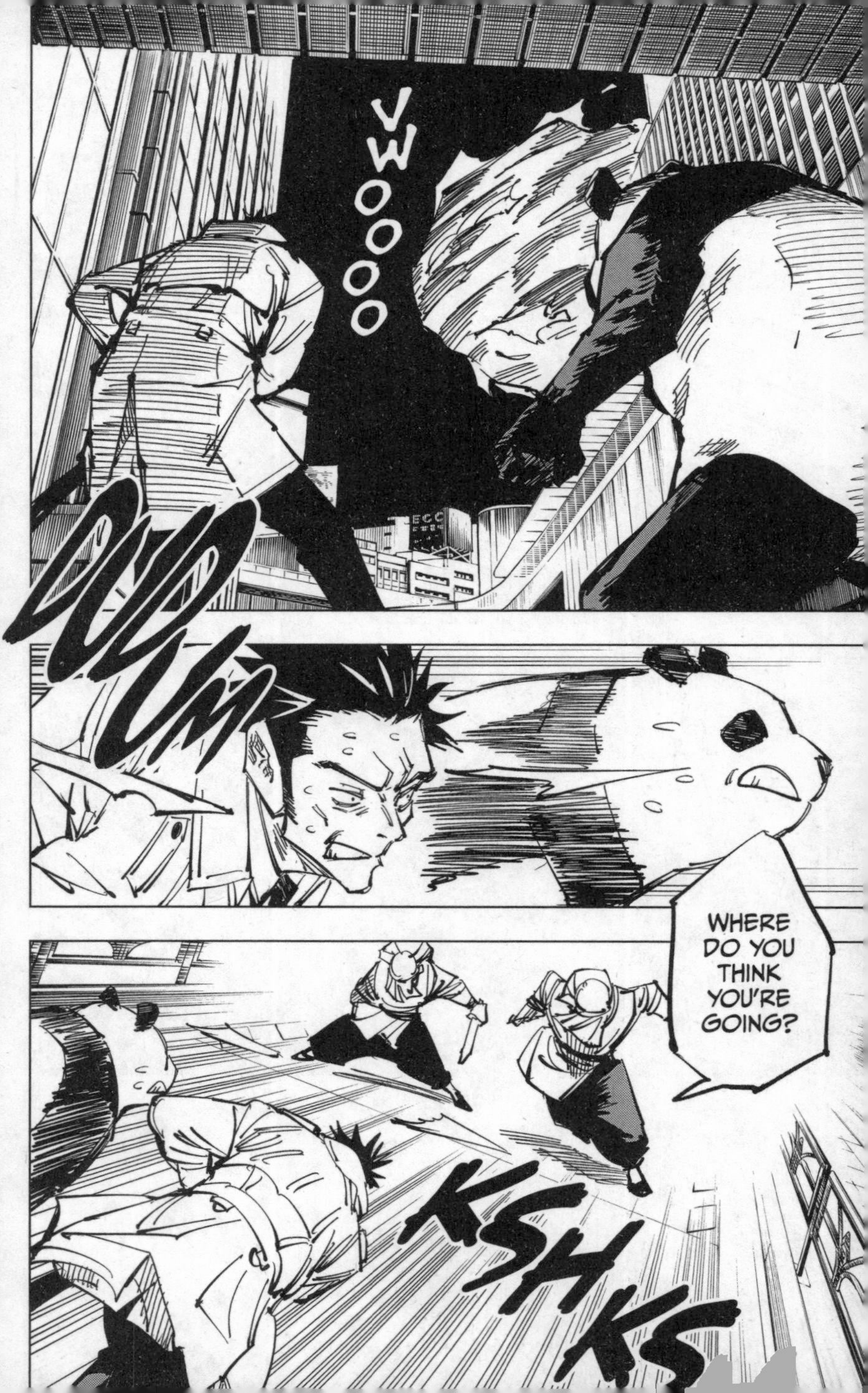
VWOOOOO
DOOM
WHERE DO YOU THINK YOU'RE GOING?
KSHKS

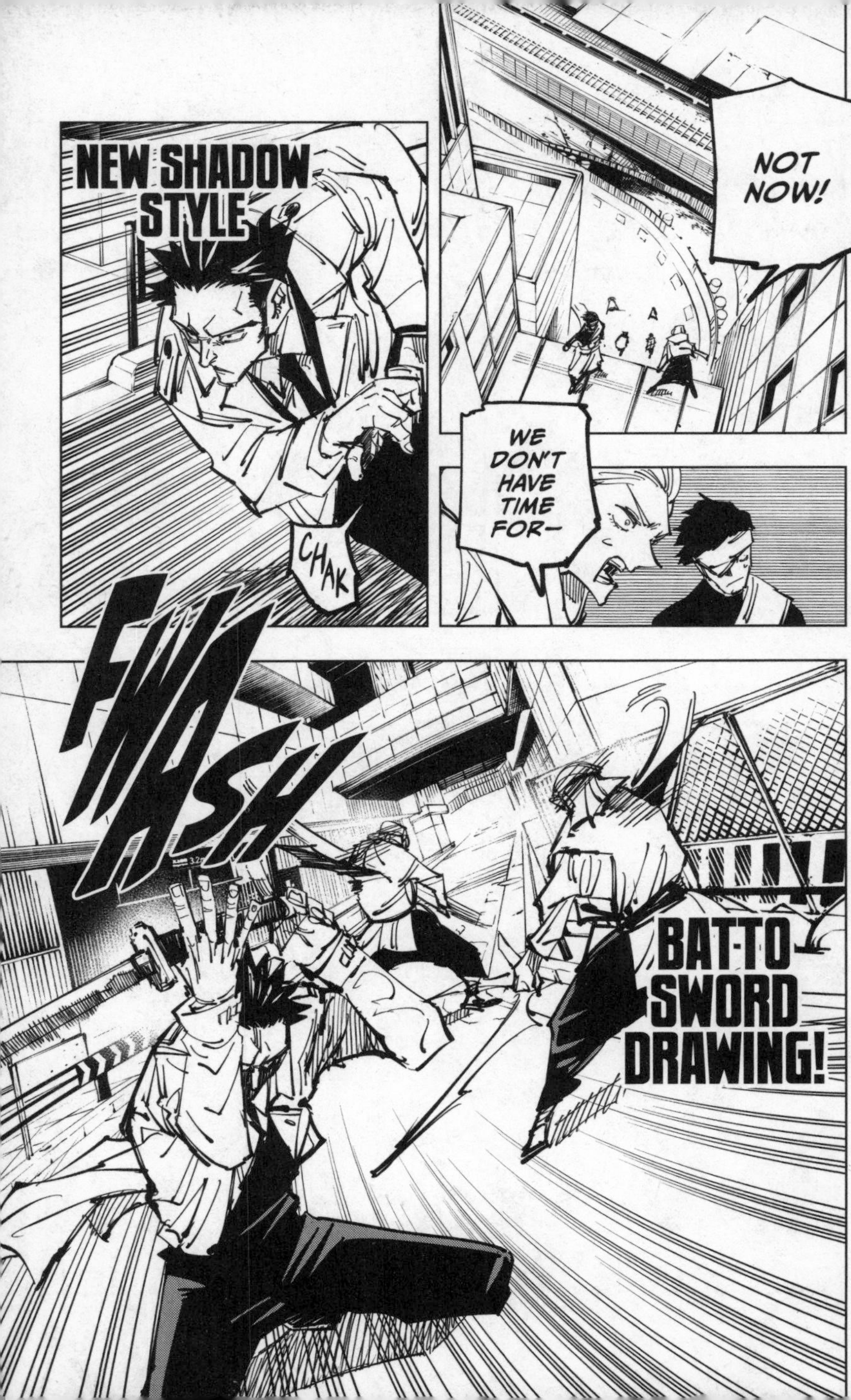
NOT NOW!
WE DON'T HAVE TIME FOR—
NEW SHADOW STYLE
CHAK
BATTO SWORD DRAWING!
FWSH

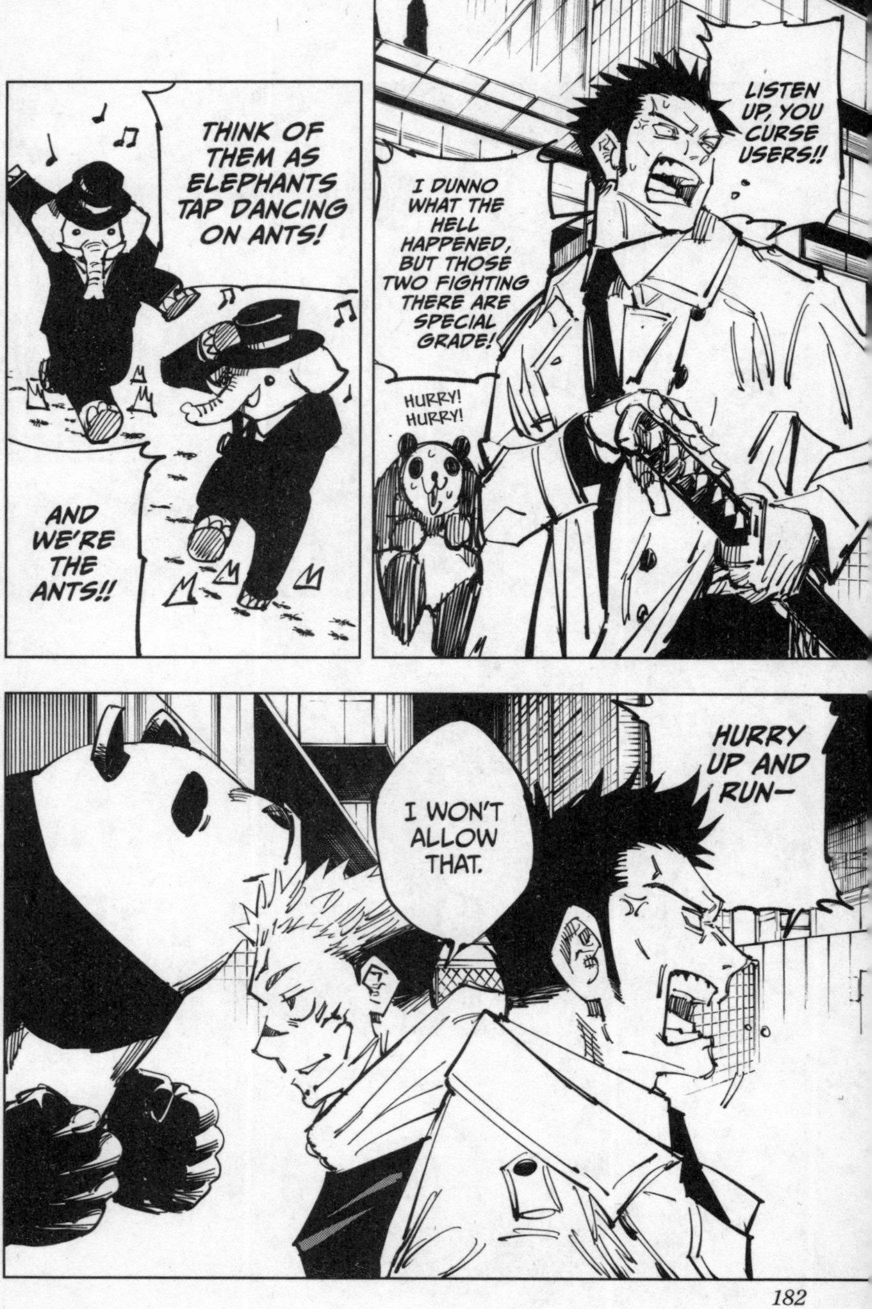
LISTEN UP, YOU CURSE USERS!!
I DUNNO WHAT THE HELL HAPPENED, BUT THOSE TWO FIGHTING THERE ARE SPECIAL GRADE!
HURRY! HURRY!
THINK OF THEM AS ELEPHANTS TAP DANCING ON ANTS!
AND WE'RE THE ANTS!!
HURRY UP AND RUN—
I WON'T ALLOW THAT.

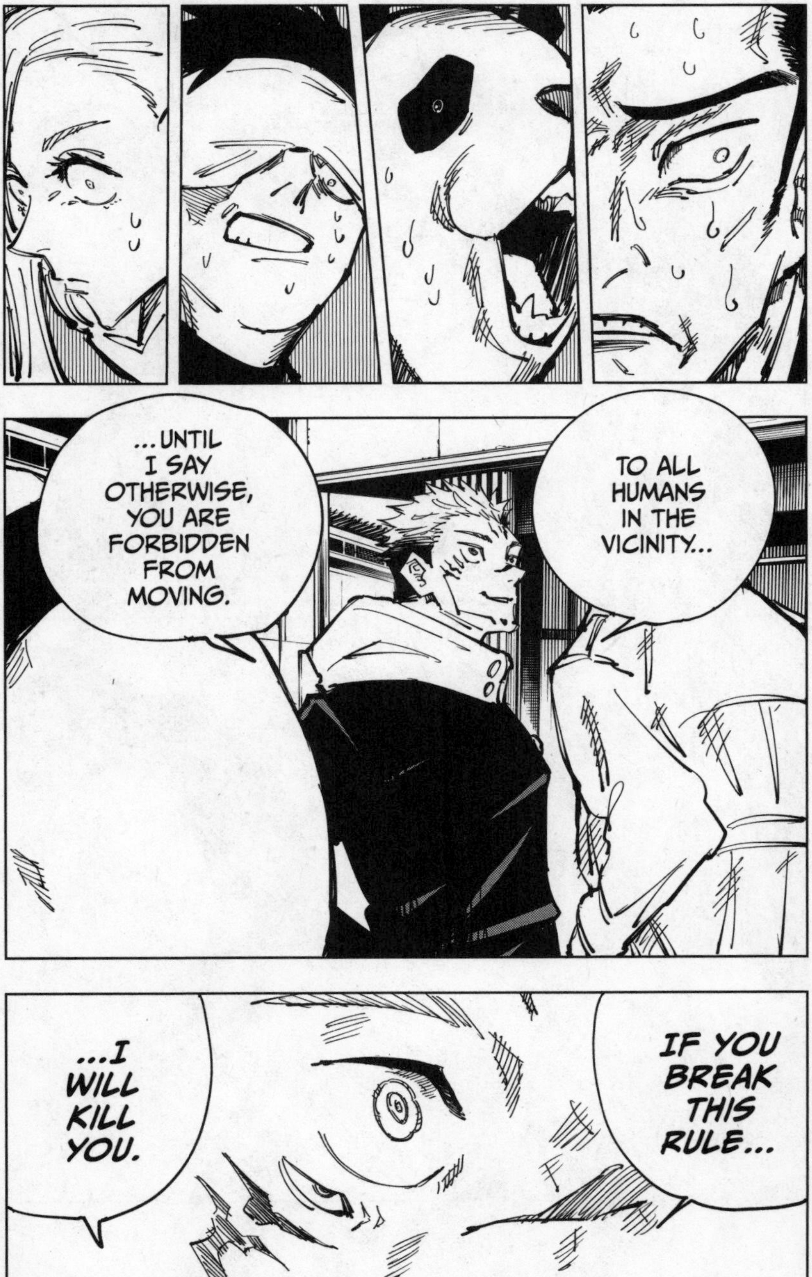
TO ALL HUMANS IN THE VICINITY...
...UNTIL I SAY OTHERWISE, YOU ARE FORBIDDEN FROM MOVING.
IF YOU BREAK THIS RULE...
...I WILL KILL YOU.

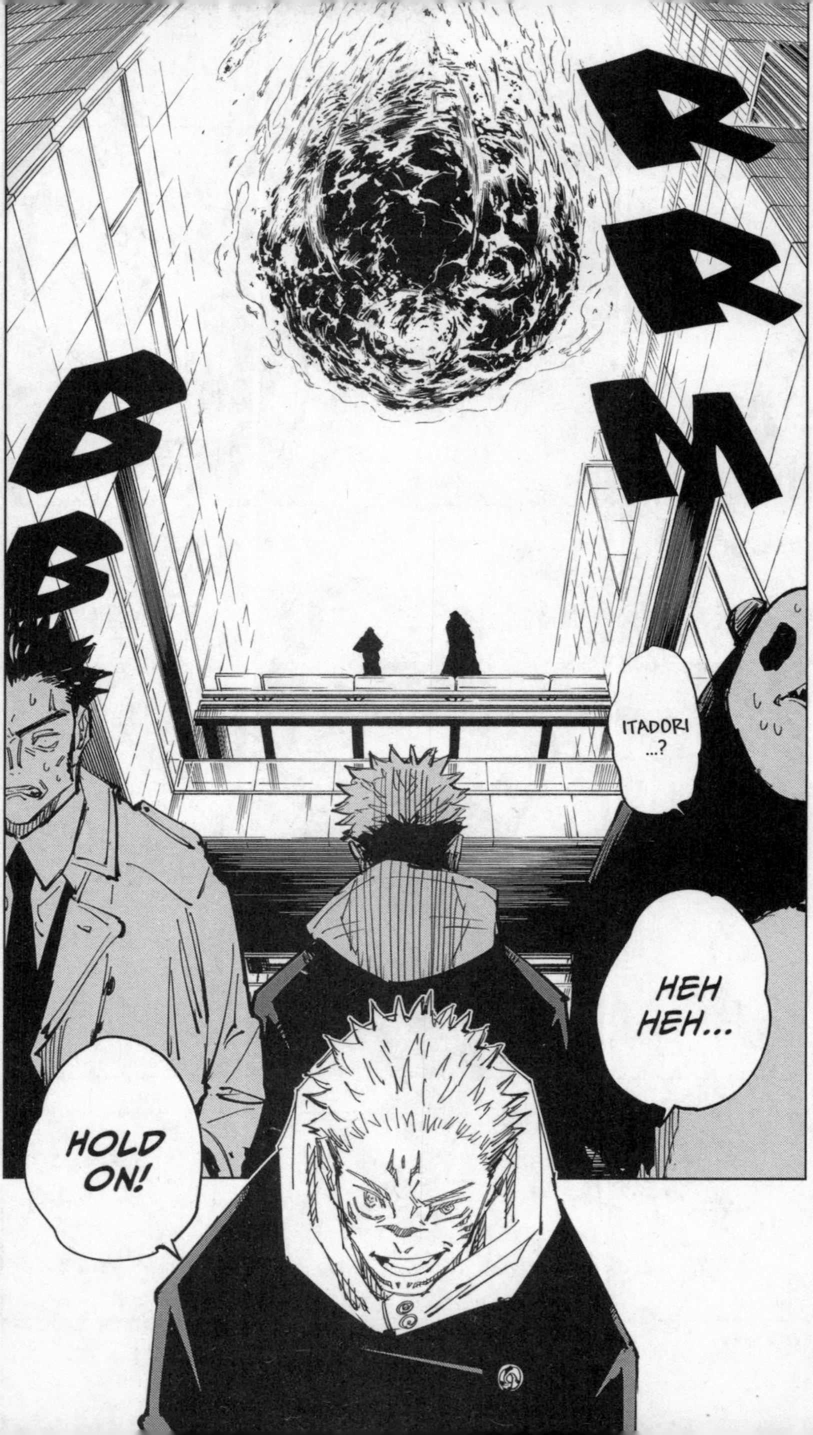
RRMBB
ITADORI ...?
HEH HEH...
HOLD ON!

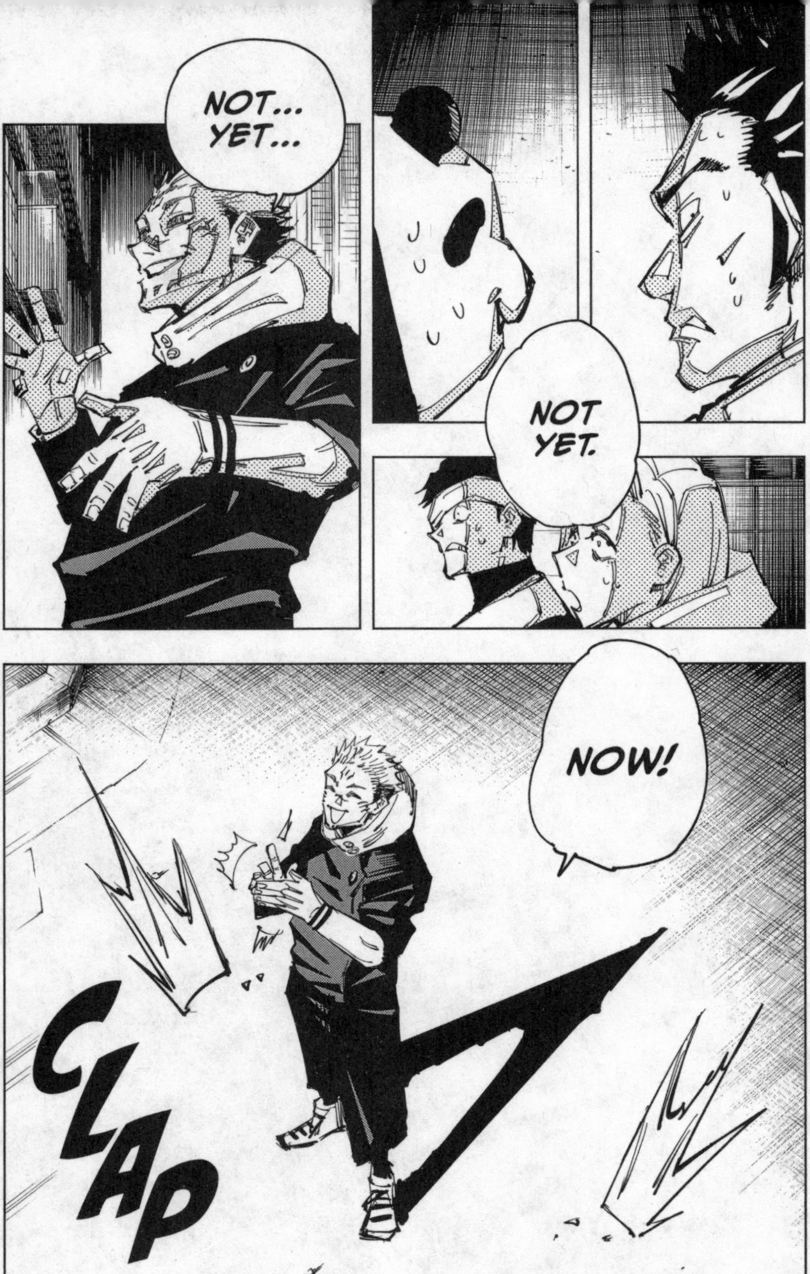
NOT YET.
NOT... YET...
NOW!
CLAP

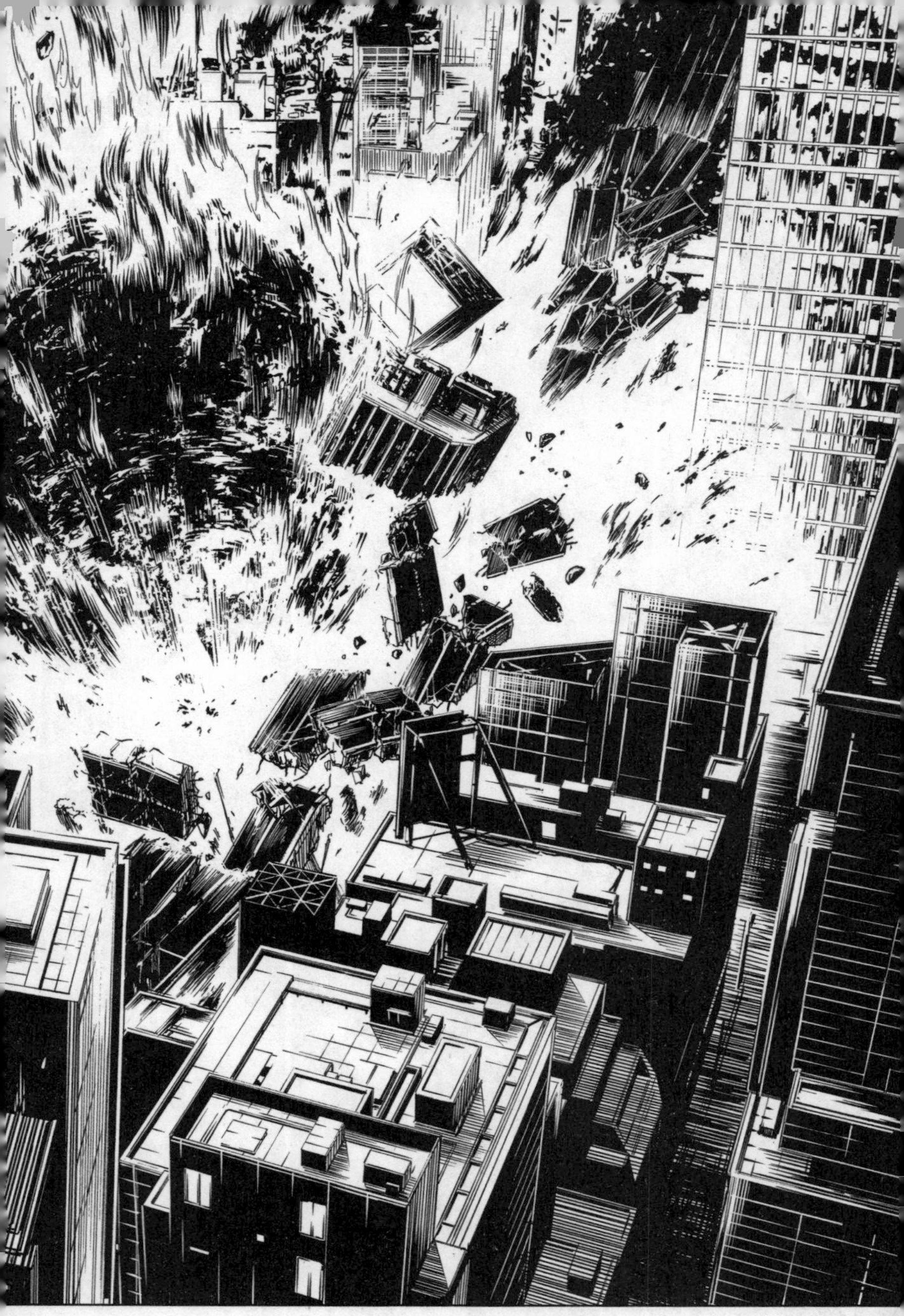

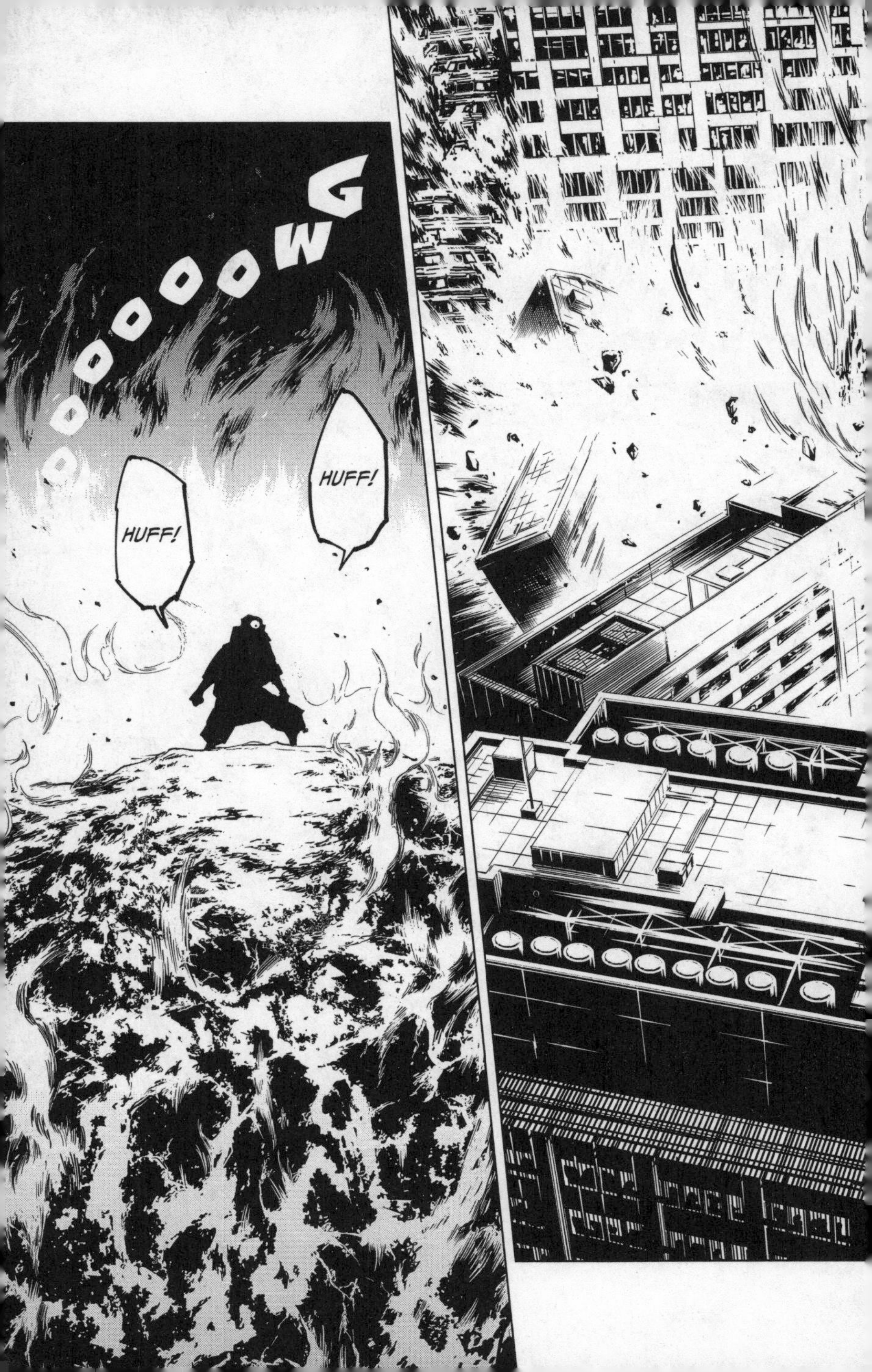
OOOOOOWG
HUFF!
HUFF!

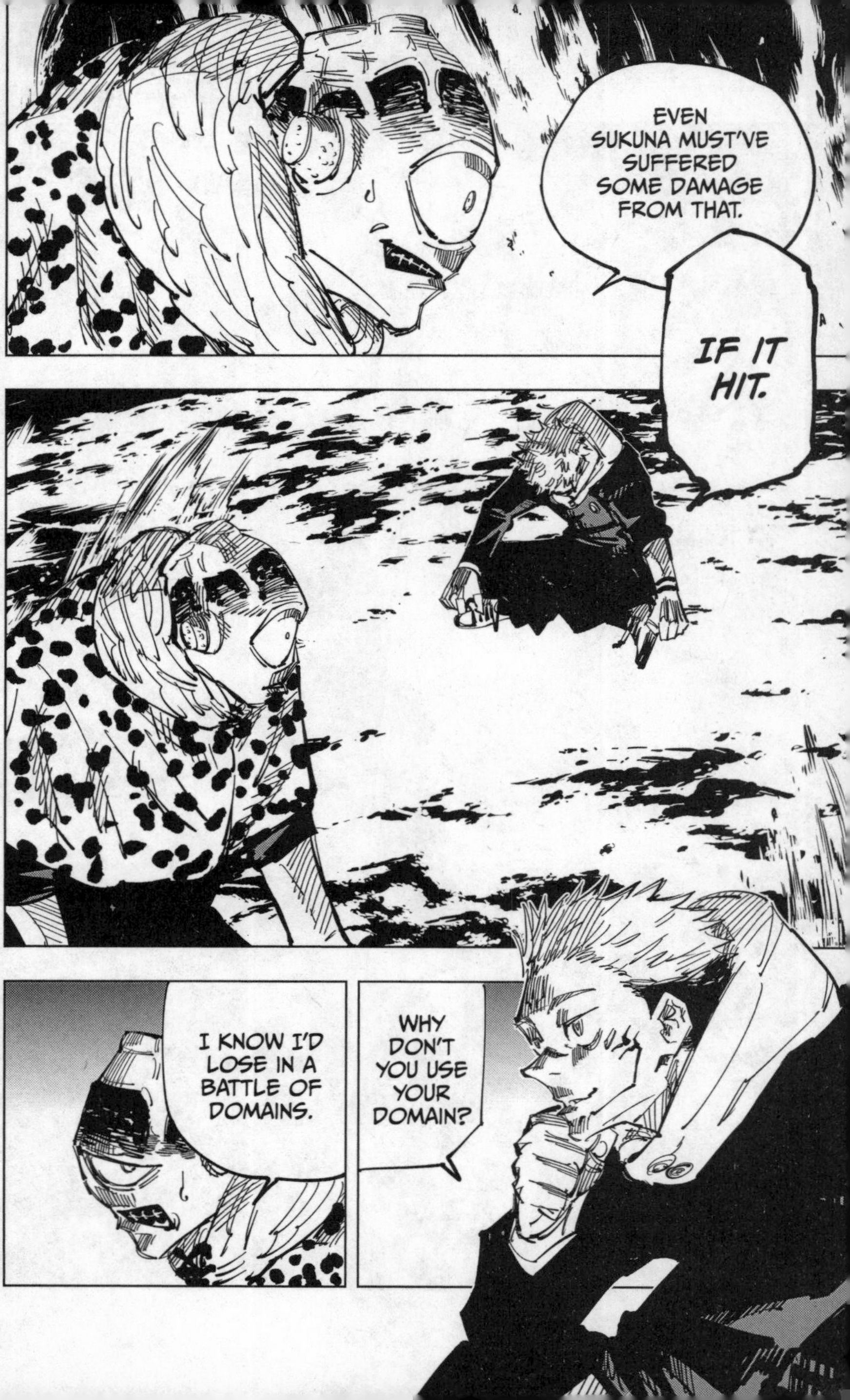
EVEN SUKUNA MUST'VE SUFFERED SOME DAMAGE FROM THAT.
IF IT HIT.
WHY DON'T YOU USE YOUR DOMAIN?
I KNOW I'D LOSE IN A BATTLE OF DOMAINS.

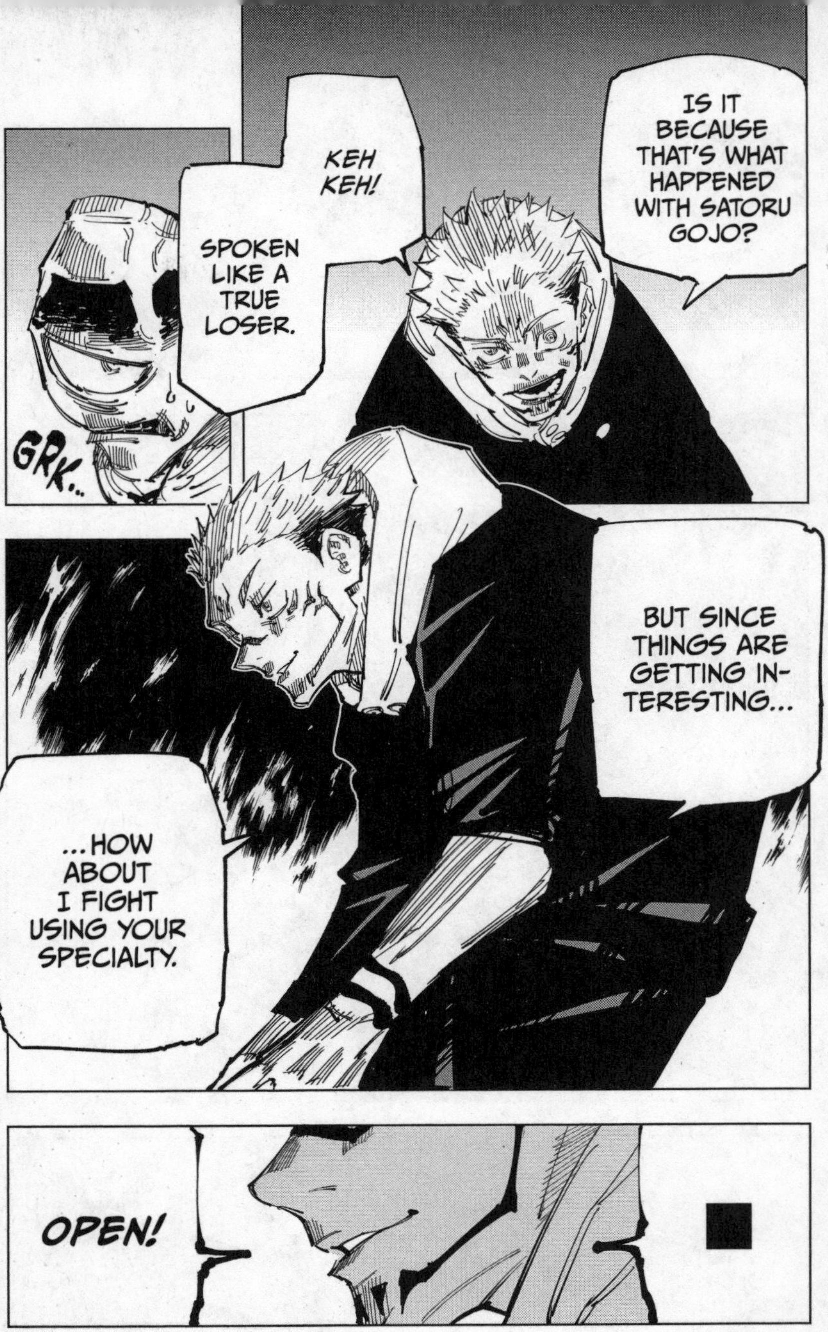
IS IT BECAUSE THAT'S WHAT HAPPENED WITH SATORU GOJO?
KEH KEH!
SPOKEN LIKE A TRUE LOSER.
GRK...
BUT SINCE THINGS ARE GETTING IN-TERESTING...
...HOW ABOUT I FIGHT USING YOUR SPECIALTY.
OPEN!

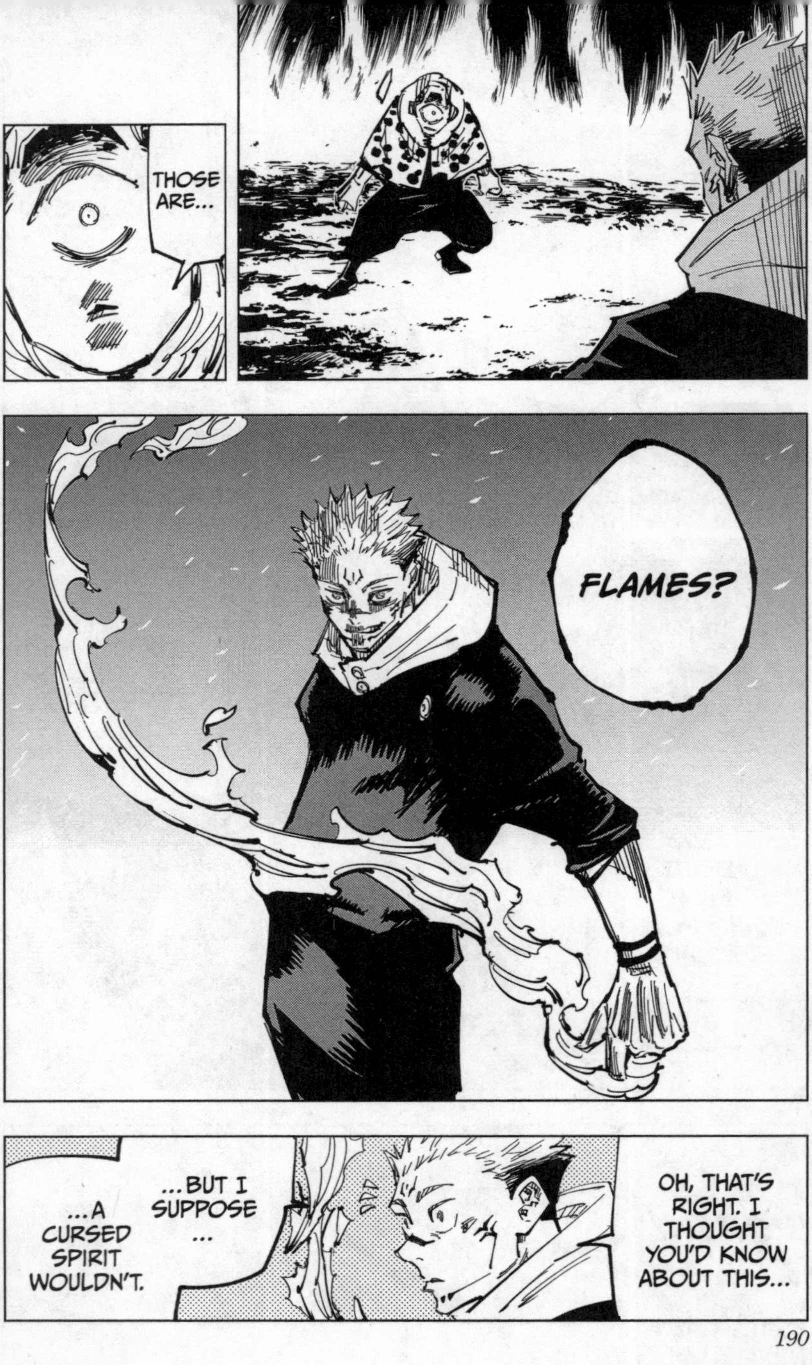
THOSE ARE...
FLAMES?
OH, THAT'S RIGHT. I THOUGHT YOU'D KNOW ABOUT THIS...
...BUT I SUPPOSE ...
...A CURSED SPIRIT WOULDN'T.

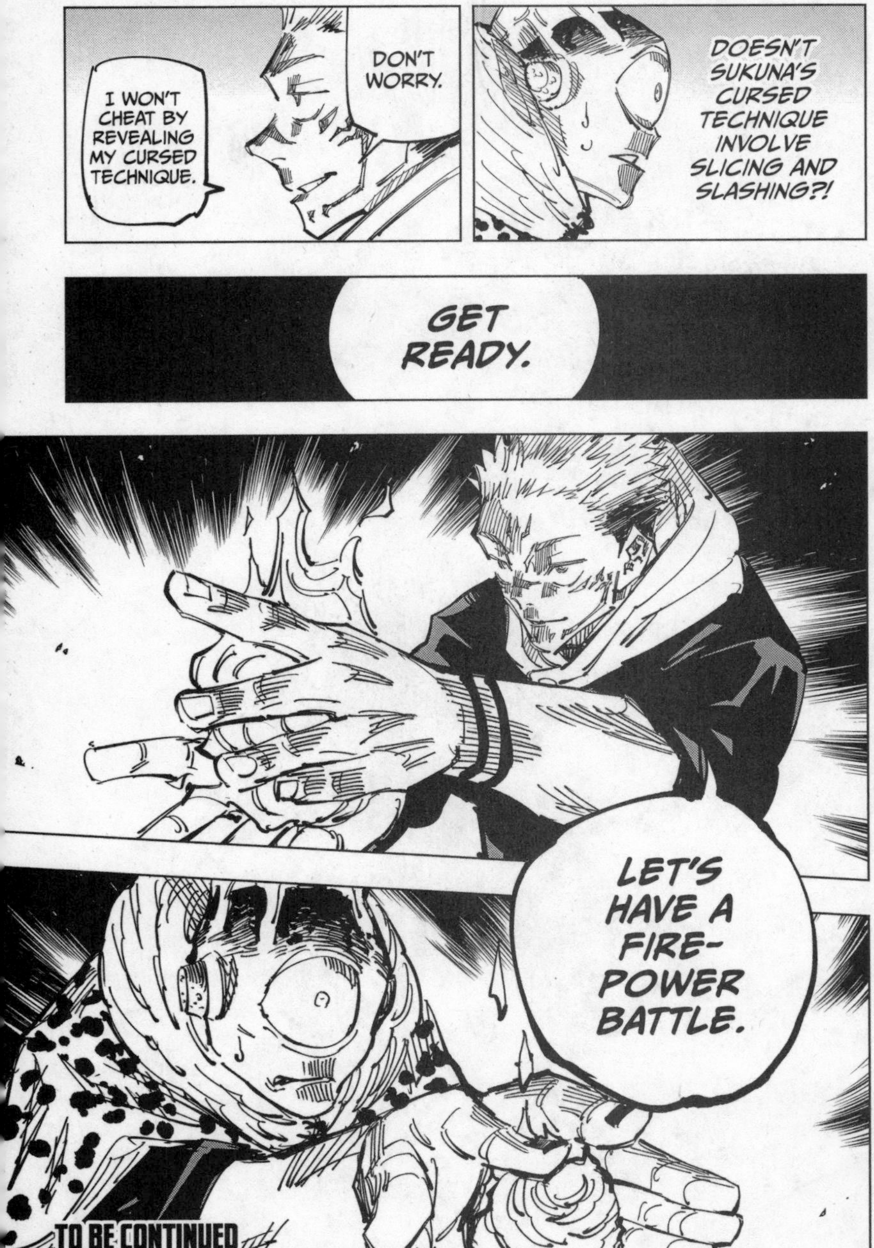
DOESN'T SUKUNA'S CURSED TECHNIQUE INVOLVE SLICING AND SLASHING?!
DON'T WORRY.
I WON'T CHEAT BY REVEALING MY CURSED TECHNIQUE.
GET READY.
LET'S HAVE A FIRE-POWER BATTLE.
TO BE CONTINUED

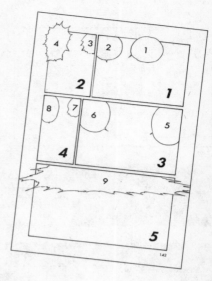

JUJUTSU KAISEN reads from right to left, starting in the upper-right corner. Japanese is read from right to left, meaning that action, sound effects, and word-balloon order are completely reversed from English order.